PASS THE 65 ™

A COMPREHENSIVE STUDY GUIDE DESIGNED TO HELP YOU PASS THE SERIES 65
WITHOUT COMPLETELY LOSING YOUR SANITY

ROBERT WALKER

PASS THE TEST, INC.

FOR MORE HELP AND TO DOWNLOAD UPDATES, VISIT WWW.PASSTHE65.COM
OR SEND EMAIL TO: WALKER@PASSTHE65.COM

FIRST BOOKS

www.firstbooks.com

©2006 Robert Walker

Edited by Linda Weinerman

Cover and Interior designed by Masha Shubin.

NASAA Statements of Policy and Model Rules reprinted with permission.

ISBN-13 978-0912301-65-5
ISBN-10 0-912301-65-1

Publisher: First Books®

www.firstbooks.com

Printed in the United States of America

Table of Contents

The Big Picture 1

THE MAIN STUFF 9
    Lesson 1: What the Heck Is an Investment Adviser? 11
    Lesson 2: What Does an Adviser Do for a Living? 57
    Lesson 3: Types of Clients and Taxation Issues 109
    Lesson 4: Rules and Regulations 140

SECURITIES PRODUCTS 211
    Equity Securities 213
    Debt Securities 225
    Mutual Funds Made Easy 243
    Annuities, Insurance, Retirement Plans 266
    Options Made "Easy" 294
    Trading Securities 305

PRACTICE FINALS 317
    Practice Final 1—Series 65 319
    Practice Final 1—Series 65: Answers 338
    Practice Final 2—Series 65 359
    Practice Final 2—Series 65: Answers 379
    Practice Final 3—Series 65 399
    Practice Final 3—Series 65: Answers 419

Acronyms 439
Glossary 441
Index 451

THE BIG PICTURE

Just down the street a company has been making and selling fruit pies for over 50 years. Frank & Emma's Fruit Pies the company is called. It's been a good business, but now that Frank & Emma have passed on, their three children have decided that the market for their fruit pies is much bigger than either Frank or Emma ever imagined. After talking to several advisers, Jeremy, Jason, and Jennifer decide it's time to raise some serious cash and invest it back into the business.

The local banks, however, aren't interested in lending the company the $100 million it needs to build a new factory, hire 100 more employees, and set up distribution centers throughout the Midwest. Luckily, there are investors who might be willing to provide the capital in exchange for owning a little slice of Frank & Emma's Fruit Pies. That's why they call it the capital market, because investors provide capital ($) to corporations in exchange for ownership positions, called "equity securities." Just as homeowners have equity/ownership in their homes, stockholders have equity/ownership in the corporations whose stock they hold.

Frank & Emma's Fruit Pies would use the stockholders' capital to make the business a whole lot sweeter, and would serve up slices of the bigger, sweeter pie to the investors who bought the stock. The investors' capital/money would allow the business to pay for equipment, wages, computers, and all the basic ingredients businesses need in order to grow from small companies to bigger, sweeter corporations.

So Jeremy, Jason, and Jennifer decide to go ahead and offer 30% of the company for sale to public investors. They don't plan to do the offering themselves, of course. The process of issuing stock to public investors is very complex, with little room for error. So, they hire a firm called an underwriting or investment-banking firm. Like a bank, the firm could raise money for Frank & Emma's Fruit Pies, but this wasn't a loan. The underwriting firm would promise to buy all the stock the company was issuing and immediately re-sell it to investors, keeping a piece of the proceeds for their efforts. It was a firm commitment of capital on the part of the underwriters, but if everything went according to plan, they would walk away with a nice profit, and Frank & Emma's Fruit Pies would have the $100 million it needed to expand the business. Since the brothers and sister would still own the majority of the company, their own wealth would most likely grow, too, right along with the company's increased profits and common stock price. And if everything went as planned, the investors who bought the slices of the big pie would also see their equity/ownership stakes in the company grow, too.

The underwriters register the stock with the Securities and Exchange Commission (SEC), which under the Securities Act of 1933 requires companies issuing securities to provide disclosure to investors in the form of a prospectus. The registration statement with the SEC and the prospectus delivered to investors must reveal not just the promises of success but all the chances for failure, as well. Only if an investor has been provided with essential or "material" facts, can he/she make an informed decision about buying or not buying a particular security.

So the company and the underwriters perform due diligence in providing information on the company's story to investors: its history, plans for the future, purpose for raising the money, as well as information on the management and board of directors. Also, a section on the risks involved in buying stock in this particular company is prepared and placed toward the front of the document. Some of the risks included were:

1. The fluctuating price of oil can unpredictably raise delivery costs and compromise profit margins.
2. Unionized laborers can unpredictably raise labor costs and force slowdowns in production and delivery.
3. Product liability, should contaminated ingredients enter the production line, would have a material negative effect on the stock.

It ends up taking a long time to get the SEC to finally give the green light, but, finally, the underwriters are permitted to sell the shares to pension funds, mutual funds, and individual investors, who all like Frank & Emma's Fruit Pies' chances for future success, weighed carefully against their possibility for failure.

The underwriting is completed in a few days, and after keeping the "spread" or profit margin from the proceeds, the underwriters give the company $100 million, which is quickly invested in new equipment, employee salaries, computer systems, and an aggressive TV and radio marketing campaign.

Frank & Emma's Fruit Pies is suddenly looking a whole lot sweeter with the fresh infusion of capital.

Now that it is a public company, Frank & Emma's has to file quarterly and annual reports with the SEC, which is actually kind of a pain in the neck. So, they hire an in-house attorney and accountant primarily to work on the 10-Q (quarterly) and 10-K (annual) reports. In the reports, the company discloses financial information to investors, as required by the Securities Exchange Act of 1934. This Act, sometimes called the "People Act," requires issuers of securities to file reports so public investors have enough information to decide whether to invest in the company, or stay invested, as the case may be.

Public investors apparently like what they read in the reports because the shares keep trading among investors at higher and higher prices. Sold at a public offering price of $10, the stock is now trading over NASDAQ as high as $25. NASDAQ, the main stocks traded "over the counter," and the NYSE are part of the secondary market. When the stock was first issued, it was issued in the primary market, where the issuer received the proceeds. When those shares trade back and forth among investors, we call that process the secondary market, where the issuer does not get the proceeds. Underwriters work in the primary market. Broker-dealers work in the secondary market, facilitating trades between investors and making commissions or markups for their services. Some broker-dealers maintain an inventory of over-the-counter stock, acting as market makers. A market maker allows investors to sell their securities when the time comes to sell and, hopefully, receive a decent price from an interested buyer. The market maker buys stock from one investor at the lower "bid" price and sells the stock to another investor at the higher "ask" price. Maybe the bid for 10,000 shares of FREM (Frank & Emma's common stock) is $25.00 and the ask is $25.25. If the market maker can buy 10,000 shares at the bid and immediately re-sell them at the ask, he/they will keep the 25 cent "spread" per share, which is a quick $2,500 profit. What if they buy the 10,000 shares and then no buyers show up to take them off their hands?

That's the risk they take by making a market in the stock. Market makers act as principals, which means they have money at risk. When a firm sells a customer a stock from its inventory, it is said to be acting as a "dealer." When it simply arranges the trade for a customer, it is said to be acting as a "broker." That's why the firm is called a "broker-dealer," since it can act either as a broker, earning a commission, or as a dealer, earning a profit or markup on a particular trade. It can't do both on the same trade; it either acts as a broker or a dealer/principal on any particular trade.

And, they also get involved in the primary market taking companies public. When they do that, they call themselves underwriters/investment bankers. When they help investors unload and purchase securities in the secondary market, they call themselves broker-dealers.

If you are studying for the Series 65 or 66 it is because you work for an *investment adviser*, which is a different business model than "broker-dealer," even though many firms perform both activities. See, broker-dealers make money on transactions. They need investors to buy shares from them in initial public offerings (IPOs), and they need investors to buy and sell (trade) securities in the secondary market. Otherwise, how do they get paid? They don't. I mean, they can trade their own account, but *anybody* can trade their own account, right? That's not acting as a broker-dealer, that's acting as a trader.

Investment advisers get paid differently. Rather than getting paid for transactions, they get paid for their advice or portfolio management services. Maybe they charge hourly rates, flat fees, or—most commonly—they charge a percentage of the assets under management. If you've taken the Series 6 or 7 you know that mutual funds charge management fees to cover the investment adviser's compensation. That investment adviser is charging the fund a percentage of assets. Not only does that investment adviser need to be registered—it needs to be registered with the SEC, as we'll see later. So, investment advisers recommend securities to clients, but they get paid for the advice, not a commission or markup *when* or *because* the customer is buying. And, I, myself, like the way it aligns the adviser's interests with the clients. For example, I know a 35-year-old who was set to retire with about $3 million a few years ago. Unfortunately, he hooked up with a smarmy agent who only wanted a big, fat commission and got it. Turned the guy's account into $40,000 in short order. See, this aggressive agent had already made all he was going to make off the client—why bother watching the account after that? Had he been paid 1% of the assets, something tells me he would have noticed and done something a whole lot sooner, right? 1% of $3 million is nice, but 1% of $1 million is nowhere near as nice, and wouldn't you intervene before it dropped anymore, taking your 1% down with every drop. Right? Because 1% of zero is, well, zero.

Anyway, you'll be working for an investment adviser or actually becoming an investment adviser yourself with your Series 65 (and maybe the 63 too). This exam wants to make sure you understand all the basics of securities, which means suitability, risk/reward, basic features, taxation…lots of stuff. The exam will expect you to know pretty much everything you learned for the Series 6 and 7 and maybe a little more. The test covers a lot of ground, so, please, cover a lot of ground yourself as you prepare for what is, without doubt, one of the most difficult exams you will ever take and pass.

In some fashion you will be helping clients choose investments in stocks, bonds, options, mutual funds, annuities, and other products. Some investors will need the income provided by bonds. Others will need the growth offered by stocks. Still others will choose to risk their money on options. So, when a new customer decides to establish an investment account with you, you will need to get basic information on the customer's financial situation and investment goals. The younger the investor, the more likely you will recommend stocks, such as the stock in Frank & Emma's Fruit Pies. Or, maybe some day Frank & Emma will decide to offer bonds to investors, whereby the company simply borrows money from the public investors and pays a rate of interest on the loan/bonds until the loan is paid off in full. Instead of offering equity, then, the company would be offering debt securities. And that would make the bondholders creditors, who have to be paid on time. If not, the company goes into bankruptcy, and all the pie makers and other equipment could be sold at auction, the proceeds returned to the bondholders.

But bankruptcy seems like a remote possibility since Frank & Emma's is now a better-established company, with manufacturing facilities in Chicago, Cleveland, Milwaukee, and Indianapolis. Their fleet of delivery vans now stocks the shelves of regional grocers like Jewel and Dominick's, as well as serving up pies to school, hospital, and large corporate cafeterias. Their cash flow is strong, their sales are growing 20% a year, and their profits are increasing, too.

So, let's let Frank & Emma's run their business a while, while we talk about serving your own customers, the investors kind enough to supply growing companies like Frank & Emma's with capital.

Tomorrow morning you get a phone call from a Ms. Nicole Ramirez. Nicole has been referred to you through a friend, who spoke highly of your recommendations and attention to detail. First thing you do is pull out a new account form for Ms. Ramirez, filling it in with her contact information, employment situation, financial information, and investment goals. If Nicole is showing a high net worth and high tax bracket, you might interest her in tax-free municipal bonds issued by cities and states to fund roads, schools, and other necessary infrastructure improvements. Since the interest is generally not taxed by the IRS, these bonds offer lower nominal interest rates (coupon rates), but high tax-bracket people still come out ahead. If you're in the 30% bracket and receive a 10% nominal yield on a corporate bond, you only keep 70% of that, since the other 30% goes to the IRS. Therefore a 10% corporate bond would be equivalent to a 7% municipal bond, since either way the investor keeps $70 a year. They might receive $100 on the corporate, but $30 is "shared" with Uncle Sam. The munibond pays $70 and the investor keeps all of it.

Equivalent.

Nicole likes the idea of some tax-free income, so you and she agree to put 25% of her money into general obligation munibonds issued by Chicago, Cleveland, and New York City as well as those same issuers' revenue bonds, backed only by the revenues on sports stadiums, convention centers, and toll roads. General obligation bonds are a legal obligation of the issuer to pay bondholders with tax money. Revenue bonds are backed by the revenues generated from the facility built with the proceeds of the bonds. If the revenue bond builds a toll road, the bonds are backed by the tolls, for example. The state or city doesn't have to step in to pay back the bondholders, so revenue bonds are riskier than general obligation (GO) bonds. Therefore, they have a higher yield.

So 25% of Nicole's money is now invested in tax-free municipals.

Nicole is 41 years old and plans to work at least another 20 years. With such a long time horizon, you suggest she invest 50% of her capital in common stock like FREM. Nicole has never considered investing in FREM, but she has seen the pies at the supermarket and was quite taken by a recent French Silk with Pecan creation that she picked up on a whim at Wal-Mart.

You and Nicole decide to invest in common stock for the growth she'll need between here and retirement. Some of the companies have relatively few shares outstanding, making them "small cap" stocks, like FREM. These "small cap stocks" have less established histories but also potentially brighter futures than "large cap" stocks, in general. Their PE ratios are high, since much of the perceived value is built on speculation of future profits. But, if the future is as bright as investors hope, millionaires are created, just as they were when investors took a chance on companies such as Microsoft®, IBM®, Oracle®, and Starbucks®, to name just a few former growth stocks that eventually matured into large cash-generating machines. These days, Microsoft®, IBM®, and Oracle® would be considered "large cap" stocks, since the value of their stock is relatively large. Huge, in fact.

So, you and Nicole put together a diversified portfolio of common stock, investing in FREM, as well as Wal-Mart®, General Electric®, Starbucks®, and Oracle®.

So, Nicole now has 25% in tax-free municipals and 50% in common stocks of companies as small as Frank & Emma's and as large as General Electric. That's diversification, or the "don't put all your eggs in one basket" principle of equity investment.

What about the other 25%?

Nicole puts 20% in the money market, which is a very boring holding place for cash. Money market securities are short-term debt obligations that will be paid back within 1 year (usually 270 days maximum) by high-quality issuers. Commercial paper, banker's acceptances, and jumbo certificates of deposit (CDs) are the most common of these safe, short-term debt securities that will end up paying Nicole some interest without subjecting her principal to any significant risk.

And the final 5% Nicole decides to use speculating in equity options. Calls and puts, in other words. Although not your strong suit, you decide that 5% is not a lot to risk on these high-risk securities that derive their value from an underlying stock. Which is why options are called "derivatives."

Ever heard that you shouldn't try to time the market?

Well, options are all about trying to time the market.

If you think a stock is going up in a hurry, buy a call. If the stock goes up in a hurry, the value of the call skyrockets.

What if the stock drops in a hurry, instead?

The call expires worthless and you lose.

Magically, you can make just as much money when stocks do belly flops by buying puts. If you have a Worldcomm August 70 put when Worldcomm drops to $10 a share, your put would be worth at least that $60 difference. And you might have bought the thing for just $5.

Or not.

It's all speculation, this world of options, but since Nicole has plenty of financial means and is only risking 5% of her capital on options, you decide not to talk her out of it. Instead, you send her the Options Clearing Corporation (OCC) disclosure document that lays out all the risks and characteristics of options trading and get her to sign an options agreement. As soon as your firm's registered options principal (ROP) approves the account, Nicole can start trading.

Now that you have met your suitability requirements with Nicole by carefully recommending securities that make sense given her time horizon, risk tolerance, and financial means, you must continue to deal fairly and ethically with her. State regulators don't like it when investment advisers and their representatives mislead investors or mishandle their money in any way, shape or form. We'll be talking about the state regulators later on, and let's hope you never have to talk to them personally. Just pay your fees, fill out your paperwork, and treat your customers the way you'd treat your grandmother or your own child—with only their best interests in mind. As we'll see, investment advisers and their investment adviser representatives are "fiduciaries," which means their advice and actions have to put the clients first. If an adviser's advice could also end up helping out the adviser, that's a potential conflict of interest, because only the client's interests should enter in. We'll get into that in much more detail later, and I'm sure you can't wait for that.

So, whether you're getting paid as a percentage of assets or getting paid commissions, you're in the securities business. And, here's the big picture: in order for a company to expand, it needs capital. It accesses this capital in the "primary market," where investment bankers sell the company's securities to investors, keeping a "spread" for their trouble. The issuing corporations take the capital and buy equipment, technology, or whatever they need for expansion. Investors can now trade their stocks and bonds with other investors on the secondary market. Securities firms like yours might work both the primary market as underwriters, and the secondary market as broker-dealers or market makers. And, they very likely have an investment advisory business going, too, where they charge a percentage of assets for clients who prefer that billing/compensation model. Whether offering new stock to a customer in the primary market or helping her trade in the secondary market, the actions of a broker-dealer are regulated by their self-regulatory organization (SRO)—the NASD or NYSE—as well as the government body called the SEC. The SEC also regulates investment advisers, and the representatives of the advisers—you, for example—are regulated by the states where you do business.

Regulators like truthfulness and full disclosure. That's why companies who access the public markets have to disclose all kinds of stuff before issuing their securities and then have to disclose all kinds of stuff through quarterly and annual reports filed with the SEC. This way investors have a fair shot at discerning a good investment opportunity from a poor one. There is always risk, but through full disclosure, truthfulness, and fair dealings, investors can manage this risk, using a highly regulated professional such as yourself to help choose suitable investments. We're talking about people's retirement nest eggs in most cases here, so, if you're feeling abused for having to take this big, scary test called the Series 65, try to remember how upset you'd be if somebody took your $3 million nest egg and promptly turned it into $40,000, enriching himself at your expense.

Now that you have a grasp of the big picture, let's start looking at some serious details, but no matter how detailed the material may get, please remember one thing:

This is not rocket science. It isn't even close.

Some of the terminology and math concepts will sound highly sophisticated, but most of them are very simple. There are a few formulae to know, but this is not a calculation exam. It's about concepts, big ideas, creative problem-solving.

Let's go get you a passing score on the Series 65.

Oh, by the way, we didn't tell you anything about the test itself. That's because it isn't our test. The test belongs to NASAA, and everyone taking the test needs to visit www.nasaa.org to read every word they have to say about the Series 65 exam. Print out the exam specs. Find out how long the exam is, how to sign up, what the passing score is, what the cost is, yada, yada.

Our job is to explain the concepts and give you test-taking tips to help you pass, but we have nothing to do with scheduling, sponsoring, administering the exam, or helping you determine if you need to take the test or get licensed in the state of Florida to sell viatical settlements.

The NASAA website is where you go for *all* of that stuff. They're the organization of state regulators, the folks who regulate individuals like you who are studying to become investment adviser representatives. We'll be referring to NASAA all throughout this book, so you might as well introduce yourself to their website right now.

Then, you can come back and jump into Lesson 1, which is so full of intense information that...well, you'll see.

Ready?
Let's get started, anyway.

Online Updates

DO YOU HAVE THE MOST CURRENT UPDATED INFORMATION? VISIT WWW.PASSTHE65.COM TO MAKE SURE!

THE MAIN STUFF

LESSON 1

WHAT THE HECK IS AN INVESTMENT ADVISER?

(Covering definitions, registration, exclusions/exemptions, business practices, and a whole bunch of other exciting stuff)

INVESTMENT ADVISERS AND INVESTMENT ADVISER REPRESENTATIVES

For whatever reason, I'm really good at picking stocks. I've been known to make 50, 60, even 70% returns in a year. Pretty soon everybody's asking me my advice all the time. It gets to where I can't eat lunch in peace without somebody wanting to know my latest stock tips.

So, finally, I decide if I'm going to be bombarded with requests for my expert opinion, I might as well get paid for it. I print up business cards, and I start making investment recommendations to people, charging them a fee for my advice. I could charge them an hourly rate, like a consultant. Or, I could charge, say, 1% of whatever my clients' assets are worth, based on my recommendations.

What the heck am I doing? I'm <u>advising</u> people on <u>investing</u> in securities. Which is why they call the folks who get paid to do this sort of thing investment advisers. The folks who represent investment advisers are called investment adviser *representatives*.

Yes, as you can see, they get real creative with the terminology in the securities business. Remember that one entity is the firm (investment adviser). The other is the individual who works for the firm (investment adviser representative). Sort of like saying that Michael Jordan played for the Chicago Bulls. Michael Jordan was not the Chicago Bulls; the Chicago Bulls was not Michael Jordan.

Huh?

Yep, the law is usually written in stiff, stodgy legalese very similar to the Michael Jordan–Chicago Bulls analogy. For example, the Securities Act of 1933 defines an *underwriter* like so:

> The term "underwriter" means any person who has purchased from an issuer with a view to, or offers or sells for an issuer in connection with, the distribution of any security, or

participates or has a direct or indirect participation in any such undertaking, or participates
or has a participation in the direct or indirect underwriting of any such undertaking

When all it really means, apparently, is:

An "underwriter" means any individual or legal entity who has purchased securities from an issuer with intent to distribute the securities, working either on their own
or as part of a group of other "underwriters."

Well, a lot of books out there are written more like the former stiff legalese, when
they should really be trying to help you simplify things. As you may have noticed from
our side-splitting prose up to now, *Pass the 65*™ is going to simplify things as much as
possible.

Notice how we didn't say this stuff is going to be *simple*. Read every word very
carefully from here on out. Remember when we had a President who said it all depends on what your definition of "is" is?

He was a lawyer, and so are the folks who draft securities industry regulations.
Every word they write must be examined carefully, often from many different angles.
Take apart every word you read carefully and do not assume things that are not pre-
sented in the exam question.

Anyway, when securities law says something stiff like, "The term *investment adviser* does not include an investment adviser representative," we'll have to translate it
into something more readable. What the law is struggling to communicate in its tor-
tured writing style is that somebody gets her Series 65 license, allowing her to do "fee-
based money management." Well, she probably isn't ready to fly solo, so she goes to
work for a firm called an investment adviser. In other words, she represents an investment adviser, which is why they call folks like her *investment adviser representatives*.

If she helps to make recommendations to clients or sells the services of the firm,
she has to register as an investment adviser representative. Or, if she supervises people
who do that kind of stuff, she has to be a registered investment adviser representative.
The employees performing clerical work are not defined as "investment adviser representatives." But, if the employee is managing accounts, determining recommendations, making recommendations, selling the services of the firm, or supervising those
who do that stuff—now that person is an investment adviser representative and must
register.

Investment Adviser Representatives (IARs) are employees who:
 - manage accounts
 - make recommendations
 - help determine recommendations
 - sell services of firm
 - supervise those who do any of the above

So, the investment adviser is the business. The individuals who <u>represent</u> investment advisers are very cleverly called "investment adviser representatives." If you're
taking the Series 65 it could be that you plan to set up your own shop. More likely,
you're going to work for an investment advisory firm. Either way, you need to pass
this exam to get your license.

TYPES OF INVESTMENT ADVISORY BUSINESSES

The term "investment adviser" is a legal definition that actually encompasses many different types of activities. Let's take a quick look at the different types of investment advisers:

PORTFOLIO MANAGERS

In general, portfolio managers manage portfolios, rather than managing clients. In other words, they don't have to smile and dial all day long like a mere stock broker. In fact, the new model is usually that the stock broker bags the client and then finds the right portfolio manager for the client's portfolio. In other words, the investment adviser (portfolio manager) is really good at investing, while the stock broker is really good at golf. And shmoozing. And screaming at the portfolio manager whenever the client isn't happy.

Anyway, the portfolio manager might be the firm managing a mutual fund. In fact, they're often affiliated with a family of funds. For example, let's say that ABC is a family of mutual funds. They market and distribute the funds, while their subsidiary, ABC Capital Management, is the portfolio manager for the funds, getting paid a percentage of the fund's assets. Or, sometimes, a mutual fund family will outsource the portfolio management to an entirely separate investment adviser.

Portfolio managers also might take on individual clients with large amounts of assets to manage. This service is usually called "private money management" or "private account management," two terms that sound rather impressive to me. Jeremy, Jason and Jennifer, owners of the recently public Frank & Emma's Fruit Pies, are probably ideal prospects for this service. Do they really want to spend their time following economic trends and reading annual reports of 15 different companies, on top of the quarterly and annual reports they themselves have to sign off on at Frank & Emma's? Probably not. It would make more sense to find an expert portfolio manager who, in exchange for 1% of assets, will deal with all the hassles and challenges of investing. Of course, I haven't sold enough *Pass the 65*™ books yet to qualify for this service, but if I did, I'd probably have to sign up for a "wrap program." A "wrap program" is usually for clients with a mere six figures to invest. Here, the adviser charges "wrap fees" that, literally, wrap a bunch of services together: portfolio management, execution of trades, asset allocation, and administrative services. Since you really can't make money managing one six-figure portfolio, wrap-based advisers usually have one portfolio model that they use for all their clients. That's what I meant when I was ribbing the stock brokers, who bag the clients. Once they bag the client, they do a client profile and then assign the client to the portfolio manager whose model matches up the best.

FINANCIAL PLANNERS

Some advisers perform financial planning services, which is exactly what it sounds like. They help people put together financial plans. Maybe they charge an hourly rate. Maybe they charge a flat fee. Maybe they charge a fee plus commissions when the clients are kind enough to buy all the stuff recommended in the financial plan, stuff that—quite coincidentally—happens to be annuities, insurance, and mutual funds that pay a commission to the financial planner. If the client's financial situation is highly complex, the planner might even charge a retainer, like an attorney. Or maybe the planner *is* an attorney, since, these days, *everybody* wants to be in the financial services business. Instead of managing Jeremy, Jason, and Jennifer's investment portfolio only, the financial planner would do that as well as help with the whole picture of insurance, annuities, estate planning, buy-sell agreements with business partners, retirement planning…the whole nine yards. Many planners earn their professional credential called a "CFP," which stands for "Certified Financial Planner." Just remember that these folks are certified by a professional organization; they are not certified by state or federal regulators. We register with regulators; we never get approved/certified by them.

BIG-BRAIN ADVISERS

And then there are also what I like to think of as "big-brain advisers," a term that most likely will *not* be on the exam. As we'll soon see, the definition of *investment adviser* under the Investment Advisers Act of 1940 and the Uniform Securities Act includes persons who issue reports/analyses on securities for compensation. Maybe you sell reports to broker-dealers or pension funds that help them determine which stocks to buy or when to buy them. If so, you're an investment adviser.

But, really, when we use the term "investment adviser," we mean a portfolio manager. Except when we don't.

Anyway, a major chunk of the exam will focus on what Investment Advisers and their representatives are prohibited from doing. Makes sense that the test wants you to prove you understand the kinds of things that could end up getting your license suspended or revoked, right? That way if you get caught mistreating clients, they can take away your license and say, "See? Told you so."

If you recently took your Series 63 exam, you remember that the "USA" is an acronym for "Uniform Securities Act," which is the model for state securities laws. There will be a few cases where federal law differs from state law, but not too much. Just remember that when I say "SEC," I'm talking federal. When I say "USA," I'm talking state. Which is counter-intuitive, really. Usually when you see "USA," you think about the nation—don't do that. Not until you pass the test. "USA" means state law, sometimes referred to as "blue sky law," since every concept needs at least three names in this industry. For example, is that guy in the funny-looking yellow blazer long the call, does he own the call, did he buy the call, or did he purchase the call?

Yes.

Wait—the other party to the contract: Is he short the call, did he write the call, or did he sell the call?

Yes.

Anyway, the securities laws are very similar between federal and state, so I'll be slipping in and out of both quite frequently, and where the two differ, I'll point it out.

BUSINESS PRACTICES FOR INVESTMENT ADVISERS, IARS

As the Uniform Securities Act states:

> Section 102. [Advisory Activities]
> It is unlawful for any person who receives any consideration from another person primarily for advising the other person as to the value of securities or their purchase or sale, whether through the issuance of analyses or reports or otherwise,
> to employ any device, scheme, or artifice to *defraud* the other person, or
> to engage in any act, practice, or course of business which operates or would operate as a *fraud* or *deceit* upon the other person.

FRAUD

So, if you get compensation for providing advice as to the value of securities or the advisability of their purchase or sale, you had better not say or do anything that operates as a <u>fraud</u> or <u>deceit</u>.

Unless you want to face 3 years in jail and/or a $5,000 penalty.

Remember that—three years, five grand.

That's the penalty for fraud at the state level.

Don't go there.

Also remember that at the federal level, the maximum penalties are 5 years and $10,000.

Three years, five grand at state level.

Five years, ten grand at the federal level.

Not too surprising that the state securities Administrator gets just as uptight about people selling investment advice as he/she does when people are selling securities in the state. Any deceit or fraud takes place, and the Administrator is going to come down hard. Even if it's a big or "federal covered" firm, the Administrator can make life real difficult for that firm. Remember, the Administrator might not have jurisdiction over a federal covered security or federal covered adviser in terms of filing and inspection requirements. But, anybody who commits fraud in the state—absolutely anybody—is subject to the Administrator's jurisdiction. I'm not saying the Administrator would always claim that jurisdiction, but he/they could if he/they wanted. NSMIA (National Securities Markets Improvement Act, 1996) made it real clear that certain securities and firms would register at the federal level and sort of get a hall pass at the state level. But it still reminded everyone that the Administrator is the appropriate person to enforce anti-fraud rules in the state. If you don't think state regulators can wreak havoc on big firms, you must not have heard of Eliot Spitzer of the state of New York, who has forced big federal covered Wall Street firms to pay out fines (so far) in the billions of dollars. He's the Attorney General of a *state*, and that's usually who the Securities Administrator of a state would refer any really bad stuff to, anyway. The Administrator is usually more concerned with granting, suspending, or revoking licenses. When the activities go beyond prohibited practices into the land of fraud or criminal offenses, he/they usually turn it over to a District Attorney or State-level prosecutor, the way I would turn over the guy who keyed my Land Rover to my Rottweiler.

So, as always, fraud is bad, no matter how big you are or think you are.

COMPENSATION BASED ON CAPITAL GAINS, APPRECIATION

As the USA states:

> (b) It is unlawful for any investment adviser to enter into, extend, or renew any investment advisory contract unless it provides in writing
> (1) that the investment adviser <u>shall not be compensated on the basis of a share of capital gains</u> upon or capital appreciation of the funds or any portion of the funds of the client;

It actually goes on a ways from there, but let's take a second to translate that back to English. Investment advisers get paid a flat fee. They either charge hourly for their advice, or they manage a client's money, taking a flat percentage of the assets over time. Maybe they charge 1% of the assets. That's a great incentive for the adviser, right? One percent of $150,000 is nice, but one percent of $200,000 is even nicer. So, the percentage stays flat and the adviser's compensation only grows if the customer's assets grow.

Sounds like a great way to compensate an investment adviser, right?

Well, some folks would rather just give the adviser a share of the gains. Every time the adviser buys at 10 and sells at 18, the adviser gets a piece of that capital gain. What about the rest of the stocks, which all might be heading down the drain?

Who cares, right? We had one big gain, and I, as your adviser, demand my cut. Them other stocks simply didn't work out the way we figgered—sorry about that.

Does that sound like a good way to compensate your adviser?

Probably not. If a client were to pay an adviser with a share of capital gains, the adviser could just focus on a few winners and let the rest of the stocks wither on the vine to the customer's great detriment. Or, in the old days, some advisers would tell half their clients to buy a volatile stock and the other half to sell it short.

See the problem?

This volatile stock is almost certainly going to go way up or way down. Which means that one-half of the clientele is almost certainly going to have a gain, and the other half is not...but the adviser will make money one way or the other.

What are you, an investment adviser or a bookie, right?

That's why advisers shall NOT be compensated as a share of capital gains, and the contract with the client must state that very fact. Advisers, as a rule, should be compensated as a percentage of assets over a specified time period, or they should just bill their clients a flat or hourly rate.

But investment advisers can not be compensated as a share of capital gains.

Except when they can.

As the federal regulators point out so clearly in their page-turning document called "The Investment Advisers Act of 1940," there are exceptions to this ban on performance-based compensation:

> (b) Compensation prohibition inapplicable to certain compensation computations
> Paragraph (1) of subsection (a) of this section shall not—
> (1) be construed to prohibit an investment advisory contract which provides for compensation based upon the total value of a fund averaged over a definite period, or as of definite dates, or taken as of a definite date;

(2) apply to an investment advisory contract with—

(A) an investment company registered under subchapter I of this chapter, or

(B) any other person (except a trust, governmental plan, collective trust fund, or separate account referred to in section 80a–3 (c)(11) of this title), provided that the contract relates to the investment of assets in excess of $1 million, if the contract provides for compensation based on the asset value of the company or fund under management averaged over a specified period and increasing and decreasing proportionately with the investment performance of the company or fund over a specified period in relation to the investment record of an appropriate index of securities prices or such other measure of investment performance as the Commission by rule, regulation, or order may specify;

(3) apply with respect to any investment advisory contract between an investment adviser and a business development company, as defined in this subchapter, if

(A) the compensation provided for in such contract does not exceed 20 per centum of the realized capital gains upon the funds of the business development company over a specified period or as of definite dates, computed net of all realized capital losses and unrealized capital depreciation, and the condition of section 80a–60 (a)(3)(B)(iii) of this title is satisfied, and

(B) the business development company does not have outstanding any option, warrant, or right issued pursuant to section 80a–60 (a)(3)(B) of this title and does not have a profit-sharing plan described in section 80a–56 (n) of this title;

(4) apply to an investment advisory contract with a company excepted from the definition of an investment company under section 80a–3 (c)(7) of this title; or

(5) apply to an investment advisory contract with a person who is not a resident of the United States.

There, did you get all that?

Of course, if we were like certain other vendors, we would just leave it at that, call it a day, and wish you the best of luck figuring out that horrible legalese on your own. But, we figure since you paid good money for this material, maybe we should do some of the heavy lifting for you.

A radical concept, for sure, but we're sticking to it.

So, let's see if that above chunk of verbiage can be simplified a little.

First, let's start with the concept. The basic rule against performance-based compensation is designed to protect the average investor from getting pulled into an arrangement that is too inherently risky. In fact, most rules are designed to protect the average investor and do not provide as much protection to large, sophisticated, and/or institutional investors. If you have kids, your job is to protect them, so if anybody messes with your kids, you'll come after them with everything you have. But, you put up more protection for a 2-year-old as opposed to a 12-year-old. You don't let your 2-year-old out of your sight for more than a few seconds, while you can—theoretically—leave the 12-year-old at home for an hour while you go shopping. Securities regulators will come after anyone who defrauds investors, but they generally provide more protection to the little guy (non-institutional investor) than to the sophisticated and/or institutional investors.

So, if Joseph L. Schmoe wants to start an advisory account with your firm and have you manage $100,000, he's nowhere near being big and sophisticated enough to pay your firm for performance. But, when we start talking about big institutional investors or rich individuals, maybe it's okay to let them pay their advisers for performance.

So, what that fascinating legalistic ramble is saying (in English this time) is as follows. Point (b)(1) is just saying that the value of the client assets not only can, but usually is, used to figure compensation. But, we simply calculate the value of the assets, say, at the end of each quarter and bill the client a percentage of that total. If we charge 1% of assets (100 basis points) per year, maybe we take the value of the account at the end of each quarter and charge .25% (25 basis points). This way, when the adviser does a good job, that will be reflected in the value of the client account, and when the stock picks stink, that will also be reflected in both the client's account value and the amount of money that the .25% works out to be for the adviser.

See? There's already sort of an inherent "performance" component of the typical adviser fee. We simply don't want little, unsophisticated investors having their IAs go for huge gains on risky stocks and ignoring boring, steady blue chip stocks, which would probably be the *opposite* of what's good for the client. It would be good for the adviser going for the performance-based bonuses, but bad for the client. We could call it an "inherent conflict of interest," a concept that is coming up very soon.

Point (2)(A) says that registered investment companies can pay a performance-based fee to the portfolio managers. Read a prospectus for a mutual fund, and you'll see disclosure that this is a typical arrangement. Mutual funds aren't going to let some portfolio manager jerk them around, any more than a 12-year-old is going to get into a stranger's car if he offers her some candy. A 2-year-old, sure, but not a pre-teenager. So, let's ease up a bit. These are big boys and girls.

In point (2)(B) they're extending it to any other entity ("person" means legal entity, not necessarily an individual) with at least $1 million in assets under management. The fee being discussed is called a "fulcrum fee," by the way. Notice how it takes the portfolio's performance and measures it against the appropriate index, such as the S&P 500, Russell 2000, or the Dow Jones Industrial Average. And, notice how the fee must be *reduced* by the same amount for under-performance that it would be increased for superior performance. This is how performance-based compensation must work—the IA has to throw in the bad stuff with the good stuff. They can't get rich off one lucky stock pick if the other picks have been trampled.

Point (3) is talking about a "business development company," which only takes money from wealthy and institutional investors. The maximum of 20%, by the way, is exactly what most hedge funds charge their clients, which are usually limited partnerships open to just the high-net-worth/institutional clients. I'd be shocked if you saw "hedge fund" on this exam, but you never know. The SEC is starting to watch hedge funds really closely these days. In any case, if the IA wants to charge 20% of the gains, the losses and drops in market value have to be subtracted from the gains.

For point (4) just memorize the "3(c)(7)" and remember that they only take money from "qualified purchasers." But my favorite is point (5), which lets the IA mess with foreigners. You're out to protect *your* kids, not the kids who live five streets over or in another town, right? So, foreign investors aren't even the SEC's kids, and the SEC already has enough kids to protect.

Right?

By the way, if this "kid" analogy is leaving you baffled, give us a call or email us at walker@passthe65.com.

So, there seems to be no reason to prevent IAs from charging performance-based compensation when managing portfolios for the above institutional clients. The SEC has also ruled that IAs may charge performance-based compensation for certain individuals (and businesses) defined as "qualified clients," which include:

- A natural person (that's an individual) or a company that has at least $750,000 under the management of the investment adviser
- A natural person or a company that the investment reasonably believes has a net worth of more than $1,500,000 at the time the contract is entered into (if it's a married couple, that number applies to assets held jointly)
- A qualified purchaser as defined in section 2(a)(51)(A) of the Investment Company Act of 1940 (basically, this is a family-owned corporation with $5 million, a natural person with $5 million, or a corporation with $25 million of assets to invest)
- A natural person who immediately prior to entering into the contract is an executive officer, director, trustee, general partner, or person serving in a similar capacity, of the investment adviser; or
- An employee of the investment adviser who, in connection with his or her regular functions or duties, participates in the investment activities of such investment adviser (not the secretarial/clerical employees, though)

So, unless the exam question points out that the client is special, assume that advisers can not be compensated as a share of capital gains.

Except when they can. The three owners of Frank & Emma's each offered 1 million shares in the IPO, which was priced at $10. You think Jeremy, Jason, and Jennifer might meet the net worth requirements for the performance-based compensation?

Hint: they're still *holding* one million shares each, with FREM closing at $26.75 yesterday.

ASSIGNMENT OF CONTRACT

Wouldn't you be ticked if you called up your advisory firm and found out that since your account balance fell below a certain minimum, they just sold it to a money manager in El Paso, Texas? That's why the account can only be passed off or "assigned" to another party with the written consent of the client, and the contract must state that fact. The USA states:

(2)   that no assignment of the contract may be made by the investment adviser without the consent of the other party to the contract; and
(3)   that the investment adviser, if a partnership, shall notify the other party to the contract of any change in the membership of the partnership within a reasonable time after the change

NOTIFICATION OF CHANGE IN PARTNERSHIP STRUCTURE

The (3) above means that if the advisory firm is organized as a partnership (nobody said nothin' about no corporations, did they?), whenever one of the partners withdraws or dies, or a new member is admitted, the firm must inform all clients in a reasonable time frame that the partnership structure has changed. Doesn't matter in this case if the change was due to a partner with a majority or minority interest. And— not that you thought otherwise—but if a minority partner is admitted, withdraws, or dies, that is not considered "assignment of contract." In other words, your investment adviser has not changed so drastically that the account is now being handled by another party. The contract didn't get assigned by ABC to XYZ. It's just that ABC has a slightly different partnership structure.

Whew! Good thing you know that, huh?

And, just in case you feel cheated by not seeing the original, the USA clearly states:

> …but, if the investment adviser is a partnership, no assignment of an investment advisory contract is considered to result from the death or withdrawal of a minority of the members of the investment adviser having only a minority interest in the business of the investment adviser, or from the admission to the investment adviser of one or more members who, after admission, will be only a minority of the members and will have only a minority interest in the business.

Perhaps I should spare you the original legalese from now on?

Before we move on to even more fascinating topics, recall that the advisory contract must provide in writing three things:

- The IA shall not be compensated for performance (except in certain cases)
- No assignment of contract is allowed without client consent
- If the IA is a partnership, clients will be notified of any change in the partnership structure

CONFLICTS OF INTEREST

Investment advisers are defined as "fiduciaries," which means they have to put the needs of the client first at all times. If a recommendation or transaction could pit the adviser's interests against the interests of the client, or if the adviser's interests suddenly get placed into the mix when, really, it should all be about the client, we have a potential "conflict of interest." So, all potential conflicts of interest must be disclosed to the client ahead of time. For example:

Acting as principal

Investment advisers and investment adviser representatives are often trying to convince their clients that they should buy a particular security. What if it turned out they were trying to sell you one of *their* securities? As a seller they want to get the highest price possible for their security, but as a buyer, you want to get the lowest price possible. Since they're supposed to put your needs first, we now have a conflict of interest, right? Well, that's why the adviser would have to disclose the fact that he/they will act as a principal in the transaction and get your written consent before doing the deal. To act as a principal just means the adviser will either buy the security for inventory from the customer or sell it out of inventory to the customer. It's okay to do it, as long as the potential conflict of interest is disclosed and the customer's written consent is given before the deal.

Acting contrary to recommendations

How would you feel if you found out that an adviser was recommending that you buy a risky tech stock while he is actually selling it short, profiting if it goes down? Sort of like having a personal trainer show up at the gym chowing down on a grilled corned-beef and Swiss cheese sandwich smoking a cigarette and polishing off the third beer of the morning, right? So, if the IA is acting opposite/contrary to his recommendations, that needs to be disclosed.

Benefiting from recommendations acted upon

When a stock trades on the OTC market, it is called a NASDAQ stock if it's big and important enough to quote regularly over NASDAQ. The ones that aren't worth quoting all the time trade on the "OTC Bulletin Board" or "Pink Sheets." These are often illiquid markets, which means that any large buy or sell order tends to shoot the stock price way up or way down. Therefore, if the investment adviser happens to own, say, 10,000 shares of some thinly traded Bulletin Board stock, he/they would benefit if he/they could get about 100 clients to put in buy orders. In fact, that might be the main reason he recommends the stock, which is in direct conflict to his "fiduciary duty" to the client—put the client's needs first. The stock recommended should be recommended only because it benefits the client. If the purchase of the stock would also benefit the adviser, that potential conflict of interest needs to be disclosed ahead of time. Similarly, if the investment adviser is affiliated with the broker-dealer that client trades are placed/cleared through, that needs to be disclosed, since compensation may be paid to the adviser when the clients place orders for securities. Again, did the IA advise you to buy because it's a good stock, or because he/they receive compensation from the broker-dealer?

Agency cross transaction

Another example where the IA will benefit from the customer's acceptance of the advice given is called an "agency cross transaction." Here, the most important thing to remember is that the IA can only be *advising* one side of the transaction. He/they can be advising you to buy 1,000 shares of ABC, and, as it turns out, he/they will also act as the broker between you and the seller.

Excuse me? So, should you buy these 1,000 shares because they're a good investment, or because the IA likes to act as a broker, too, in order to pocket commissions in addition to your advisory fee?

Again with the conflict of interest thing.

So, as usual, the IA would need to disclose the potential conflict of interest, get the advisory client's written consent, and at least once per year send a statement itemizing all the "agency cross transactions" effected on behalf of the client.

Disclose or abstain

Usually, disclosing potential conflicts of interest ahead of time and obtaining the client's consent will take care of the problem; however, sometimes the conflict is so great that the IA must simply abstain. What would be so bad that mere disclosure would not take care of the problem? How about if the portfolio manager manages the investment account of the investment advisory business he works for? In this account there are 1 million shares of XYZ common stock. XYZ common stock has also been placed in many client accounts, based on the portfolio manager's discretion. Well, one morning the portfolio manager reads in the *Wall Street Journal* that XYZ's CEO is about to be indicted for fraud and the company is also going to re-state earnings for the past five years, so he unloads the 1 million shares the firm is holding before starting to sell the shares he's put in client portfolios.

Nope. Advisers are fiduciaries, who must put the needs of their clients first. This obvious conflict of interest is a no-no, and no amount of prior disclosure would make it okay. The adviser should have simply abstained from this self-serving activity.

CUSTODY OF CLIENT FUNDS/SECURITIES

Some advisers just give advice and leave it up to the client to act upon it. Other advisers actually take custody of the customer's money and securities and/or take discretion over the account. Well, if they're going to take that much control of the client's account, they need to be very careful about handling this awesome and potentially dangerous responsibility.

First, what the heck does it mean to have "custody" of client funds and securities? Basically, it means that the adviser is either holding the funds/securities or has the ability to appropriate them. In other words, if the IA has the ability to automatically deduct money from the client's account or write checks out of the account, that would be considered having custody. Let's see how that fun-lovin' bunch of folks at the Securities and Exchange Commission define custody:

An adviser has custody if it:

- Has a general power of attorney over a client's account;
- Has signatory power over a client's checking account;
- Maintains an omnibus-type account in its own name at a broker or bank in which client securities are maintained after trades settle;
- Obtains its advisory fees by directly billing client custodians without effective oversight by the client or an independent party;
- Serves as a trustee of client trusts; or
- Acts as the general partner of a limited partnership client.

The Investment Advisers Act of 1940 (federal law) requires that advisers with custody do the following:

- Segregate each client's securities and keep good records as to who is who and what is what
- Deposit client funds into a bank account holding only client funds…not mixed in with the IA's daytradin' or horse-bettin' account. The accounts

must be maintained in the name of the adviser as agent or trustee. Records must be kept for each account showing where it is maintained, all deposits and withdrawals, and the amount of each client's ownership in the account

- Notify each client, in writing, of the place and manner in which the funds and securities will be maintained
- Send statements at least quarterly to each client that are itemized showing all the client's funds and securities and transactions
- Arrange to have an UNANNOUNCED annual inspection by an independent accountant to verify that everything's on the up-and-up. The accountant must then promptly file a report with the SEC following the examination.

The Uniform Securities Act (state law) says that before taking custody the adviser first has to check with the state securities Administrator to see if there is a rule prohibiting custody of client funds. If there's no rule against it, the adviser can take custody so long as they notify the Administrator in writing. So, what if there's no rule against taking custody, and the adviser, in fact, takes custody but fails to inform the Administrator?

They screwed up. Read each word and each phrase *very* carefully on the Series 65/66 exam. Sort of like negotiating a contract with Slick Willy—what did he actually mean when he said the word "is"?

Also note that if the state-registered adviser has discretion *or* custody, he/they will probably have to post a surety bond, depending on their net capital. For that matter, so will broker-dealers who have custody or discretion over client accounts. In other words, if the IA is taking custody of a client's money and/or securities, the firm had better be on solid financial footing and not using the client's money/securities as collateral to secure emergency loans designed to keep the firm afloat another week, right?

Many advisers prefer to use qualified custodians for their clients' funds and securities. If the exam asks which of the following are considered "qualified custodians," remember this bullet-point list:

- Banks and Savings Associations
- Registered Broker-Dealers
- Registered Futures Commission Merchants
- Foreign Financial Institutions
- And, if we're talking about *mutual fund* shares, the IA can simply use the <u>transfer agent</u>, which is the normal party holding custody of investor's mutual fund shares.

NOTE: Because the qualified custodian needs to be independent, there should not be any affiliation between the investment adviser and the qualified custodian through any direct or indirect common control relationship.

When the investment adviser uses a qualified custodian, the IA must notify the client immediately in writing of the qualified custodian's name, address, and manner in which the funds or securities are maintained when the account is opened. If the IA opens accounts for a client with more than one custodian, the client must be notified of all qualified custodian locations. Prompt notification to the client in writing following any changes to the client's account information also is required.

If the exam asks about account statements, those can be sent from the custodian to the client and must be sent at least quarterly; however, it is still up to the investment adviser to do *billing* statements. The IA has a fiduciary duty to the client to make sure that those account statements are being sent by the custodian, so it's a good idea to ask the custodian to send a duplicate to the IA.

For more information on custody, visit www.nasaa.org and read the FAQs.

DISCLOSING IDENTITY, AFFAIRS OF CLIENTS

If an advisory firm is trying to land new clients, it would probably be really tempting to show prospects what the firm has done for existing clients, disclosing the identity, affairs, or investments of their clients, especially the rich and famous ones.

Yeah, well the existing clients—as well as the Administrator—would probably have a problem with that. The only way the firm can disclose the affairs of its clients is if the clients give permission, or if the firm is forced to turn over the information by court order/subpoena, that sort of thing.

DISCLOSING EMBARRASSING STUFF TO PROSPECTS, CLIENTS

When trying to land new accounts, firms would probably rather not have to disclose the fact that their liabilities are starting to exceed their assets; unfortunately, they have to disclose that fact in many situations. If the IA is going to take custody or have discretion over the account, he/they have to disclose their own financially precarious condition. Why? Well, the regulators want clients to understand that they're about to give possession of their money/securities to an IA who is starting to duck phone calls from creditors. Why would discretion over the account trigger this disclosure? Wouldn't the IA be tempted to go for some huge, very risky short-term gains with your portfolio if Tony Soprano, LLC, were starting to commence with collections activities? Also, check this out: if the adviser accepts prepayment from clients of more than $500 six or more months in advance, he/they would also have to disclose their precarious financial condition. In other words, are they running a Ponzi scheme here, where they use your prepayment to keep the creditors off their back until next Friday? This disclosure isn't just given to prospects—it must be given to existing customers, too, if the adviser has custody/discretion.

If the adviser has been hit with a legal or regulatory action material to the evaluation of the integrity/ability of the firm to do a good job for the potential customer, that has to be disclosed. Such disclosure would include the fact that the adviser has been convicted of a securities-related violation in the past 10 years. The firm has to disclose these annoying facts within 48 hours of entering into the contract, or at the time of signing if the customer has 5 days to cancel. Not sure how the heck the firm will get the customer to sign on the dotted line after making such disclosures, but that's their problem. Shouldn't have gotten in trouble in the first place, right?

And if they sort of "forget" to provide such disclosure, wait until the regulators find out. This, of course, usually happens only after a client has lost, say, $30,000 implementing the IA's lousy stock picks. Failure to disclose such embarrassing realities will lead to the IA's license being denied, suspended, or revoked, or a court might even have to slap an injunction on them.

Hate it when that happens.

The above disclosures of regulatory or financial problems would be made, surprisingly enough, through the IA's "disclosure brochure," which will be discussed later.

ADVERTISEMENTS

Advertisements for Investment Advisers must be fair and accurate. An IA may not use testimonials from satisfied clients. I guess they can't use testimonials from *dissatisfied* clients, either, though, of course, they wouldn't want to pay somebody big money to go on television and rip the heck out of the firm. The IA can list past stock picks provided that they don't imply that future results are somehow guaranteed because of past successes, and if the IA lists past stock picks, they have to include ALL recommendations—winners and losers—over the same period, which must be at least one year. Because it would be real misleading to talk about your 100% winners over the past week, right? Especially if you conveniently failed to bring up the 100% losers. If the actual picks aren't provided, it needs to be clear that a list will be provided upon written request. Also, if the IA's stock picks are up 50%, how does that compare to the market in general? If the S & P gained 52% and this guy's stock picks gained 50%, I'd want to know the *whole* story, right? If the recommendations listed pertain only to a select group of the IA's clients, that needs to be made clear. It also needs to be clear whether the performance figures are including the IA's management fees (deducted from the returns, right?). If the advertisement claims that any graph, chart, formula or other device being offered will assist any person in making his own decisions, the advertisement must prominently disclose the limitations thereof and the difficulties with respect to its use. If the IA offers "free services with no obligation" those services had better actually be free, with no obligation. In general, IA advertisements need to go to great lengths to avoid misleading prospects and clients.

USE OF SOLICITORS

Many IAs are brainy portfolio-manager types with about as much personal charm as Al Gore or my Uncle Phil before the third beer kicks in. Therefore, they stick to money management or analysis and contract with an outside firm to solicit new business. We call the folks who solicit business *solicitors* because we just never get real creative with language in this business. To use a solicitor the IA must be registered; there can be no outstanding SEC order suspending, limiting, or barring the solicitor's activities; and there must be a written agreement between the solicitor and the IA. Also, the following conditions must be met:

- The agreement between the adviser and the solicitor must describe the solicitation activities and the compensation arrangement.
- The solicitor must provide the client with the adviser's disclosure

brochure and a separate solicitor disclosure document.
- The adviser must receive a signed acknowledgment from the client that he/she received both the IA's and the solicitor's disclosure documents.

As we'll see throughout this fascinating book, for every rule there are exceptions. Here, if the advice is considered "impersonal," which means it doesn't even purport to meet the individual needs of each client, no disclosure is required. An example of impersonal advice would be if I charged 1,000 people $199 a year to subscribe to a newsletter addressing, say, retired teachers or firefighters. This would be considered impersonal as well as the easiest 200 grand a feller ever made.

REBATING FEES

A lot of IAs turn out to be real wimps. If they don't "beat the market" or "make at least 10% for the client," they want to put their tail between their legs and offer to give the client their money back.

Not.

You charge clients for the best advice you can give. If the stock market doesn't cooperate with your stock picks, too bad. If the client thinks he/she can do better, fine. Transfer the account but keep your professional compensation. Rebating fees when the portfolio doesn't perform well is really just the flip side of being compensated for the gains/appreciation of the stock picks.

And, in general, only rich folks/institutions can get into that scene.

USE OF REPORTS

If an adviser sells you a recommendation or portfolio analysis, you'd probably assume he/they created the thing, right? So, if somebody else actually put together the recommendation or the report being sold to you, that would have to be disclosed.

Again, with the disclosure thing.

However, if an adviser subscribes to a newsletter or buys reports that help him/ them make recommendations to you, that's just fine. In fact, it makes perfect sense. So, there's a big difference between passing off some other professional's recommended portfolio as the adviser's and using other professionals' work to *help* the IA make/ render his/their own investment advice for the customer.

IMPLYING THAT THE IA IS "CERTIFIED" BY A REGULATOR

Regulators like the SEC (federal) and the Administrator (state) can allow or disallow an adviser from going into or staying in the business. But, they never certify or approve them. A securities professional might earn credentials such as "CFP" or "CFA," but the regulators don't certify or approve the professionals. To indicate that you have been "certified" or "approved" by the regulators will get you into all kinds of trouble.

MISLEADING NAMES

On that same note, the IA firm or sole practitioner may not put the initials "RIA" on their business cards or other communications. It stands for "registered investment adviser," which just means the firm is properly registered. It looks like a "CFP," "CFA," or "MBA" credential, which is misleading. It's not a credential; it's just a statement of fact.

Also, the name of the firm may not imply that the firm is inherently better than everyone else. For example, Pete Best was the drummer for the Beatles right up to the point where they got rich and famous. Assuming he wasn't driven into a bitter bout with the bottle, Mr. Best could have set up an investment advisory business. But, he would not have been allowed to name it "Best Advisers."

That's misleading, right?

The name "Peter Best & Associates" or "Peter Best Investment Advisers" would be okay. But it has to be clear in the name that "Best" is simply someone's last name—it can't imply that this is the best IA you'll ever find.

The phrase "investment counsel" may only be used by those IAs deemed to be performing "supervisory services." In other words, some firms provide "impersonal advisory services" and others just sell reports/analyses. To call yourself an "investment counsel," your firm has to be actively managing money/affairs for particular clients, not just writing newsletters to a group of subscribers.

There, now, wasn't that fun? Since you enjoyed that so much, let's see what NASAA has spelled out in their usual punchy prose, just to make sure everybody knows exactly the kind of nonsense that could end up getting their licenses denied, suspended, or revoked. The Uniform Securities Act has been amended since the '50s, and NASAA periodically updates regulations by publishing model rules and policy statements at www.nasaa.org.

The following is the actual model rule telling Investment Advisers what's what. It is followed by my own Plain-English explanation of the Legalese. If you're not an attorney, chances are, you'll be glad I provided it.

UNETHICAL BUSINESS PRACTICES OF INVESTMENT ADVISERS

Amended 4/27/1997, Adopted in 1985

A person who is an investment adviser or a federal covered adviser is a fiduciary and has a duty to act primarily for the benefit of its clients. The provisions of this subsection apply to federal covered advisers to the extent that the conduct alleged is fraudulent, deceptive, or as otherwise permitted by the National Securities Markets Improvement Act of 1996 Pub. L. No. 104-290). While the extent and nature of this duty varies according to the nature of the relationship between an investment adviser and its clients and the circumstances of each case, an investment adviser or a federal covered adviser shall not engage in unethical business practices, including the following:

1. Recommending to a client to whom supervisory, management or consulting services are provided the purchase, sale or exchange of any security without reasonable grounds to believe that the recommendation is suitable for the client on the basis of information furnished by the client after reasonable inquiry concerning the client's investment objectives, financial situation and needs, and any other information known by the investment adviser.

2. Exercising any discretionary power in placing an order for the purchase or sale of securities for a client without obtaining written discretionary authority from the client within ten (10) business days after the date of the first transaction placed pursuant to oral discretionary authority, unless the discretionary power relates solely to the price at which, or the time when, an order involving a definite amount of a specified security shall be executed, or both.

3. Inducing trading in a client's account that is excessive in size or frequency in view of the financial resources, investment objectives and character of the account in light of the fact that an adviser in such situations can directly benefit from the number of securities transactions effected in a client's account. The rule appropriately forbids an excessive number of transaction orders to be induced by an adviser for a "customer's account."

4. Placing an order to purchase or sell a security for the account of a client without authority to do so.

5. Placing an order to purchase or sell a security for the account of a client upon instruction of a third party without first having obtained a written third-party trading authorization from the client.

6. Borrowing money or securities from a client unless the client is a broker-dealer, an affiliate of the investment adviser, or a financial institution engaged in the business of loaning funds.

7. Loaning money to a client unless the investment adviser is a financial institution engaged in the business of loaning funds or the client is an affiliate of the investment adviser.

8. To misrepresent to any advisory client, or prospective advisory client, the qualifications of the investment adviser or any employee of the investment adviser, or to misrepresent the nature of the advisory services being offered or fees to be charged for such service, or to omit to state a material fact necessary to make the statements made regarding qualifications, services or fees, in light of the circumstances under which they are made, not misleading.

9. Providing a report or recommendation to any advisory client prepared by someone other than the adviser without disclosing that fact. (This prohibition does not apply to a

situation where the adviser uses published research reports or statistical analyses to render advice or where an adviser orders such a report in the normal course of providing service.)

10. Charging a client an unreasonable advisory fee.

11. Failing to disclose to clients in writing before any advice is rendered any material conflict of interest relating to the adviser or any of its employees which could reasonably be expected to impair the rendering of unbiased and objective advice including:

(a) Compensation arrangements connected with advisory services to clients which are in addition to compensation from such clients for such services; and

(b) Charging a client an advisory fee for rendering advice when a commission for executing securities transactions pursuant to such advice will be received by the adviser or its employees.

12. Guaranteeing a client that a specific result will be achieved (gain or no loss) with advice which will be rendered.

13. Publishing, circulating or distributing any advertisement which does not comply with Rule 206 (4)-1 under the Investment Advisers Act of 1940.

14. Disclose the identity, affairs, or investments of any client unless required by law to do so, or unless consented to by the client.

15. Taking any action, directly or indirectly, with respect to those securities or funds in which any client has any beneficial interest, where the investment adviser has custody or possession of such securities or funds when the advisor's action is subject to and does not comply with the requirements of Reg. 206 (4)-2 under the Investment Advisers Act of 1940.

16. Entering into, extending or renewing any investment advisory contract unless such contract is in writing and discloses, in substance, the services to be provided, the term of the contract, the advisory fee, the formula for computing the fee, the amount of prepaid fee to be returned in the event of contract termination or nonperformance, whether the contract grants discretionary power to the adviser and that no assignment of such contract shall be made by the investment adviser without the consent of the other party to the contract.

17. Failing to establish, maintain, and enforce written policies and procedures reasonably designed to prevent the misuse of material nonpublic information contrary to the provisions of Section 204A of the Investment Advisers Act of 1940.

18. Entering into, extending, or renewing any advisory contract contrary to the provisions of section 205 of the Investment Advisers Act of 1940. This provision shall apply to all advisers registered or required to be registered under this Act, notwithstanding whether such adviser would be exempt from federal registration pursuant to section 203 (b) of the Investment Advisers Act of 1940.

19. To indicate, in an advisory contract, any condition, stipulation, or provisions binding any person to waive compliance with any provision of this act or of the Investment Advisers Act of 1940, or any other practice contrary to the provisions of section 215 of the Investment Advisers Act of 1940.

20. Engaging in any act, practice, or course of business which is fraudulent, deceptive, or manipulative in contrary to the provisions of section 206 (4) of the Investment Advisers Act of 1940, notwithstanding the fact that such investment adviser is not registered or required to be registered under section 203 of the Investment Advisers Act of 1940.

21. Engaging in conduct or any act, indirectly or through or by any other person, which would be unlawful for such person to do directly under the provisions of this act or any rule or regulation thereunder. The conduct set forth above is not inclusive. Engaging in other conduct such as nondisclosure, incomplete disclosure, or deceptive practices shall be deemed an unethical business practice. The federal statutory and regulatory provisions referenced herein shall apply to investment advisers and federal covered advisers, to the extent permitted by the National Securities Markets Improvement Act of 1996 (Pub. L. No. 104-290).

ONCE MORE, IN *ENGLISH*. . .

The first point this adopted model rule makes is that <u>an investment adviser is a fiduciary and has a duty to act primarily for the benefit of its clients</u>. Of course, that's basically the definition of the word *fiduciary*: someone who has a duty to act primarily for the benefit of someone else. Remember that a custodian is a fiduciary for the minor in an UGMA account. Same way a trustee is a fiduciary for the beneficial owner of the trust account, or a pension fund manager is a fiduciary for all the pensioners in the plan. If we break down the word *fiduciary*, we see the same root used in the word "<u>fid</u>elity," or "in<u>fid</u>elity," which represent the difference between marital bliss and a quick trip to divorce court. A husband must be <u>faithful</u> to his wife, as a trustee must be <u>faithful</u> to the beneficial owner of the trust account. Fiduciaries must be faithful, show *fidelity*.

At the risk of digressing into an English class, other words that have "fid" in them all have something to do with faithful or true:

- Fido (name of a pet dog, faithful and true to its owner)
- Semper Fidelis (always faithful/true, US Marine Corps)
- Bona Fide (good, authentic, true, as in "bona fide contract")

Why are they telling you that an adviser is a fiduciary? First, it reminds advisers to put their clients' interests ahead of their own. Second, it implies that a registered representative of a broker-dealer is NOT a fiduciary. That's right, as a registered rep/agent/broker, you represent the firm. You owe your clients ethical, equitable behavior, but you represent the firm, bottom line.

But an adviser is a fiduciary who always has to put the client's interests first, avoiding any conflicts of interest.

Let's look at the specifics of this adopted model rule. Not sure why they had to spell out the first point to advisers, but they are simply reminding them not to recommend the purchase or sale of any security unless they have reasonable grounds to believe it's a suitable recommendation.

File that one under the DUH column and keep moving.

The second item is a little surprising to me. I would have figured the adviser needs written discretionary authority from the client *before* using discretionary power, but it turns out the client can give oral authorization to get the discretionary nature of the account going. The adviser then has 10 business days after the first discretionary order is placed to obtain written authorization. And, as always, time/price do NOT equal discretion.

Actually, this makes perfect sense. Broker-dealers need written discretionary authority before making any discretionary trades because they get compensated per transaction and the temptation to just start buying stuff on their client's behalf would be overwhelming, like asking my two cats to babysit your pet hamster for a couple of days. I mean, after a while, what are you gonna do? It's a hamster—we're hungry predators with sharp claws. But an Investment Adviser really gets compensated by charging a percentage of the assets, so if he makes some dumb purchases he'll not only not gain from it, but also his fee will start going down with the assets. One percent of $100,000 is better than 1% of $80,000, right? Or, if he's more of a consultant than a money manager, why would he be tempted to buy anything in a hurry? You owe him $150 an hour for the portfolio analysis. Use it or don't use it, but the bill is due.

The next item simply says that advisers should not try to induce their clients to become frantic traders, especially if the adviser is getting compensated for those transactions. So, churning is always a bad idea, and an even worse idea if the adviser is getting paid to broker the trades. Remember, plenty of IAs get legal kickbacks from the broker-dealers used to place all the trades their clients make. Sometimes it's cold, hard cash. Sometimes it comes in the form of "soft dollars." So-called "soft dollar compensation" includes services such as research reports or analytical software that might be given in exchange for placing trades with the broker-dealer. Remember that vacations or travel are not allowable "soft dollar" compensation. The allowable soft dollar compensation benefits clients—the stuff that isn't allowed would only benefit the adviser. Either way, if the IA gets compensated when their clients trade through a particular broker-dealer, that needs to be disclosed. Also, "wrap fees" could be structured as to give the IA incentive to trade more frequently, so the IA needs to remember that he/she/they are a fiduciary to the client, not Bill Gates reaming every man, woman, and child on the planet for a buggy upgrade of an unstable software product.

Item #4 reminds IAs not to purchase or sell securities when they have no authorization from the client to do so.

Item #5 is basically saying that if your client's husband calls up and says his wife wants you to sell 1,000 shares of MSFT, you can only do so if the client has given her husband written trading authorization and you have that on file. Otherwise, you have to talk to your customer, the wife. Don't take orders from anybody but your client, unless the third party has been granted written third-party trading authorization.

Sometimes it's shocking that they have to spell out such obvious rules. But spell them out they do. In great, oppressive detail.

Borrowing money from clients is a practice that makes regulators real nervous. An investment adviser can only borrow money from a client if the client is a broker-dealer, an affiliate of the adviser, or a financial institution in the business of making loans (Bank, Savings & Loan, Thrift, etc.). Shocking that advisory firms would have the nerve to ask any other client to, like, spot 'em a couple bucks until payday, but, apparently, it's happened in the past and isn't supposed to happen again in the future.

Neither a borrower nor a lender be, except as prescribed by law or properly exempted/excluded statutorily, as the great Benjamin Franklin might have said if he had no interest in being remembered as the great Benjamin Franklin. So, don't borrow from customers unless the customer is in the business of loaning money. And, don't lend money to a customer unless your advisory firm is in the business of making loans, or the customer is an affiliate of your advisory firm.

Item #8 really takes the fun out of being an adviser. These heavy handed regulators insist that I not lie about my qualifications, the qualifications of my employees, or the services we will provide through our contract with the client and the fees we will charge for performing those services. So, I guess now I can't tell my clients I have an MBA from the University of Chicago when, in fact, I have a BA in philosophy from the University of Illinois *at* Chicago.

Geeze, it's gettin' to where a feller can't even sneeze without violating some regulation.

Item #9 is a little tricky and, therefore, fertile ground for harvesting exam questions. If I provide a report or a recommendation to a client when, in fact, that report or recommendation was actually prepared by someone else, I have to disclose the fact and tell you who provided it. However, if I order prepared reports or use published research/statistical analyses to come up with my recommendations, that's different. No disclosure there. I'm just doing my homework to come up with a better plan for my customer.

See the difference?

Item #10 also takes all the fun out of the business by prohibiting advisers from gouging their clients.

The next item would probably produce a test question. Basically, it's just saying that if the advice being given will also lead to the advisory firm or any of its employees receiving a commission or any other compensation should the client act on the advice, that potential conflict of interest must be disclosed in writing in advance of giving/rendering the advice. In other words, wouldn't you feel better about paying for investment advice knowing that the advice is being given by a totally objective professional, rather than someone who will make a big commission check if you take the advice? So, if the person rendering the advice stands to benefit from the transaction being recommended, that needs to be disclosed in writing ahead of time.

Item #12 is the very familiar prohibition against guarantees. Don't guarantee a specific result. Don't guarantee a profit. Don't guarantee against a loss.

Item #13 is what it is.

Item #14 is a likely testable point: don't divulge the identity, affairs, or investments of your client to anyone else without the client's permission or some sort of legal order to turn the information over to a court or the police. Might be tempting to show prospects what you've done for, say, Oprah Winfrey's account, but both Ms. Winfrey and the state securities Administrator would probably have a real problem with that.

Item #15 basically boils down to, "Be real careful what you do with client funds/securities under custody."

Item #16 looks like a test question waiting to be written. It reminds us that all advisory contracts must be in writing and must stipulate all the terms of the contract: services provided, term of the contract, advisory fees, formula for computing the fees, the amount of prepaid fees that are refundable, whether the adviser has discretion, and that no assignment of contract can occur without client consent.

Items #17 and #18 are pretty clear. Item #19 reminds us that no waivers of any provision are allowed. In other words, let's say that you and I don't like the fact that you can't compensate me as a share of capital gains, so we get an attorney to draw up a waiver that says it's okay, since we both agree that it's okay.

Nope. It's not okay.

No waivers allowed. Everybody lives by the same rules, even the ones who don't like the rules. Any such "waiver of non-compliance" would be considered null and void.

Item #20 seems important to me. In its legalistic, circuitous route, it points out that whether an adviser is subject to state registration, federal-only, or exempted from registration at the federal level, the firm can still get busted for fraudulent, deceptive practices by the state Administrator. Remember that. Your firm or your security might not have to be registered at the state (or even the federal) level. Big deal. The Administrator ALWAYS has the power to enforce anti-fraud rules, no matter how big you are or think you are.

Yes?

And item #21 is very typical of these detailed lists. It reminds us that this list is "not inclusive," meaning this is just *some* of the stuff we felt like talking about in THIS particular publication. It does not represent ALL of the stuff that can get you in trouble.

So be on your best behavior.

PRACTICE QUESTIONS

1. **All of the following represent prohibited activities of investment advisers except**
   A. exercising any discretionary power in placing an order to purchase or sell securities for a client after receiving verbal authorization
   B. placing all client transactions through a broker-dealer that compensates the adviser with commissions without disclosing this arrangement to clients
   C. trading opposite of recommendations given to clients without disclosure
   D. revealing client affairs, transactions, account balances, etc., in the absence of a court order

2. **Investment advisers are expressly prohibited from engaging in all the following activities except**
   A. inducing clients to trade frequently
   B. inducing clients to engage in transactions that are excessive in size given the client's financial resources and risk tolerance
   C. recommending agency cross transactions to both sides of the transaction
   D. recommending tax-exempt revenue bonds to high-net-worth clients

3. **Maria Hernandez is a sole practitioner set up as an investment adviser. Maria studies financial statements, focusing primarily on target companies' cash flow, earnings acceleration, and revenue generation metrics. Which of the following is the most accurate way for Maria to describe her approach to rendering investment advice?**
   A. I use the technicals of a company from a technical analysis approach
   B. I use the technicals of a company from a fundamentalist approach
   C. I use fundamental analysis to determine which companies represent strong investment opportunities
   D. I am certified by the state securities Administrator to perform fundamental analysis in rendering advice/recommendations

4. **Which of the following is a true statement concerning reports and recommendations in the investment advisory business?**
   A. An adviser may not use published reports and/or statistical analyses provided by other sources when rendering investment advice
   B. An adviser may not use published reports and/or statistical analyses provided by other sources when rendering investment advice without disclosing the source to clients
   C. An adviser may not present a client with an investment recommendation prepared by someone else without disclosing the source to the client
   D. An adviser may provide clients with reports prepared by outside sources without disclosure for discretionary clients

5. **John Jacobs is an investment adviser who happens to hold 1,000,000 warrants on XYZ common stock. Whenever large numbers of purchase orders on XYZ hit the market, John notices that the stock tends to rise sharply. Therefore, John**
   A. must refrain from recommending XYZ
   B. must refrain from recommending XYZ to non-institutional clients
   C. must provide disclosure to clients on the potential conflict of interest
   D. may recommend XYZ freely, provided he rebates a reasonable percentage of the commissions to his clients

6. In order to improve sales and customer satisfaction, QRZ Advisers have implemented a policy whereby clients are rebated 85% of their advisory fees whenever their accounts lose to the S & P 500 by more than 2 percentage points. What is true of this arrangement?
    A. it is fraudulent
    B. it is prohibited
    C. it is allowable for clients with more than $25,000 under management
    D. it is permissible with prior approval from a principal

7. All of the following statements are true of investment advisory contracts except
    A. they must be in writing
    B. they must state that no assignment of contract can occur without client consent
    C. they must explain the basis for compensation
    D. they must disclose the results of the most recent inspection performed by the state

8. Noting that advisory clients are increasingly demanding results, XYZ Advisers has drafted an agreement that allows clients to compensate the firm as a basis of capital appreciation above the rate of quarterly S&P 500 index appreciation. This type of waiver
    A. is fraudulent
    B. is prohibited
    C. is permissible for clients with $10,000 or more under management
    D. is a prohibited practice known as "selling away"

9. Which of the following persons must register as an investment adviser representative?
    A. a lawyer who sells reports on small cap stocks to pension funds
    B. a firm that receives compensation for advising clients as to the value of their securities portfolios and makes recommendations for a fee
    C. a person who sells the services of an investment advisory firm
    D. a person who works as a receptionist and performs general office work for an investment adviser

Answers

1. ANSWER: A

WHY: Investment Advisers are in a slightly different business from broker-dealers. Broker-dealers and their agents can never use discretion until that discretion has been granted in writing. That's because they make money every time the client trades, and the temptation to start buying stuff is too great to overcome. But an IA typically just gets a % of assets, so there isn't much incentive to make a bunch of trades that might turn south—remember, if you get 1% of your client's assets, you'll, literally, feel their pain when the assets decline. 1% of $1 million is a lot better than 1% of whatever you're left with after making a bunch of bad trades, right?

The other three things are clearly prohibited. If you get kick-backs from the broker-dealer you use as an IA, you might want to let customers know. Well, you might not want to, but you have to. Unless you want to risk losing your license.

2. ANSWER: D

WHY: tax-exempt bonds should definitely be recommended to high-net-worth/high-tax-bracket clients. Choices A and B are both considered "churning." And, although IAs can do "agency cross transactions," they have to be the IA to one side and the broker for both sides—can't recommend the deal to both sides, any more than a divorce attorney can represent the husband and the wife.

3. ANSWER: C

WHY: as you take your exam, remember to just go through the choices eliminating the weakest ones. The choice that is toughest to eliminate has to be your answer choice, whether you like it or not. Perfectionists fail miserably on these exams—if you don't like to move on until you're 100% sure, you'll probably finish about 17 questions on the test. And then they'll see you again at the testing center in no sooner than 30 days.

Choice A is a hideous way to talk to a client: technical analysis and fundamental analysis are two distinct approaches. Don't try to merge them or treat them as interchangeable, any more than you use words like "yield" and "total return" or "sales charge" and "12b-1 fee" interchangeably.

The Big A never certifies or approves.

So, the choice that is toughest to eliminate is C.

4. ANSWER: C

WHY: don't pass off somebody else's research or recommendation as your own. If you sell a client a report produced by someone else, disclose that. If you use reports and analyses to make better recommendations, good for you. Keep doing your homework.

5. ANSWER: C

WHY: so, are you telling me to buy the stock because it's good for me, or because it's good for you, Mr. Adviser Dude?

6. ANSWER: B

WHY: no performance-based compensation except for rich folks and institutions with lots of money under management. Nothing fraudulent going on here, and—as usual—the principal's pen is not a magic wand making bad stuff okay.

7. ANSWER: D

WHY: the other three are the requirements. Note that I'm not trying to point out that D *isn't* required. I'm using that weird choice to remind you that the other three *are* required. That's how most of these "all of the following except" questions work—they allow me to teach you three things that are true. They aren't necessarily trying to teach you that the fourth choice is false, except when the point of the question is to teach you that the fourth choice is false.

8. ANSWER: B

WHY: no waivers of non-compliance are allowed. Also, they are "null and void" in the eyes of any court. In other words, they aren't worth the paper they're printed on.

9. ANSWER: C

WHY: the first two choices are investment advisers, not investment adviser representatives. Choice "D" would be neither an IA nor an IAR.

IA REGISTRATION PROCESS

Some IAs register at the state level (those with under $25 million in assets). Advisers with $25 million - $30 million of assets under management *usually* register with the SEC, although, technically, they have their choice between state and federal registration. The big guys (> $30 million under management) register with the SEC, period.

FEDERAL (SEC) REGISTRATION

When an investment adviser registers with the SEC, he/she/they file a Form ADV and pay a fee for the privilege of being regulated and regularly hassled by said SEC. Within 45 days the SEC will either grant the registration or start proceedings to determine whether registration should or should not be granted. If the registration is granted, the firm can start advising clients for a fee.

Within 90 days of the end of each fiscal year (that's within 90 days *after*, in case they want to be weasels on the exam), the IA must file what the SEC calls an "annual updating amendment" or "Schedule 1" in order to renew the registration. They must update their responses to all items on Form ADV Part I when they do this. Also, if something major changes at the firm—they move to a different state, their business structure changes, or management changes hands—they must file a new Form ADV to inform the SEC of the change promptly (within 30 days of the change). See the difference? You update your ADV part I every year, period. And, if something major changes at your firm, you go ahead and update promptly, whenever this change occurs.

All advisers now register with the SEC *electronically* through IARD, a secure Internet based data system administered by your pals and mine at the NASD. Yes, it's alphabet soup time. The IARD is administered by the NASD on behalf of IAs registering with the SEC.

You're sure you want to get your license, right?

Just checking.

Setting up an IARD Account is the first step in the registration process. Once an adviser establishes an IARD account, the adviser can access Form ADV (Part 1) on IARD, complete this part of Form ADV, and submit it electronically to the SEC. Part II of Form ADV is completed in paper form. As mentioned, the SEC generally has 45 days after receipt of the Form ADV to declare an applicant's registration effective. The SEC will mail an Effective Order to an adviser once an adviser's registration is declared effective. An adviser can also check on IARD under the heading "Registration Status" to see if its registration has been declared effective by the SEC.

What is this Form ADV? Well, the "ADV" part should be obvious. This form contains two parts, cleverly titled "Part I" and "Part II." Part I contains the following information, copied directly from those creative writing types at the SEC:

- the name and form of organization under which the investment adviser engages or intends to engage in business; the name of the State or other sovereign power under which such investment adviser is organized; the location of his or its principal business office and branch offices, if any; the names and addresses of his or its partners, officers, directors, and persons performing similar functions or, if such an investment adviser be an individual, of such individual; and the number of his or its employees;

- the education, the business affiliations for the past ten years, and the present business affiliations of such investment adviser and of his or its partners, officers, directors, and persons performing similar functions and of any controlling person thereof;
- the nature of the business of such investment adviser, including the manner of giving advice and rendering analyses or reports;
- a balance sheet certified by an independent public accountant and other financial statements (which shall, as the Commission specifies, be certified);
- the nature and scope of the authority of such investment adviser with respect to clients' funds and accounts;
- the basis or bases upon which such investment adviser is compensated;
- whether such investment adviser, or any person associated with such investment adviser, is subject to any disqualification which would be a basis for denial, suspension, or revocation of registration of such investment adviser under the provisions of subsection (e) of this section; and
- a statement as to whether the principal business of such investment adviser consists or is to consist of acting as investment adviser and a statement as to whether a substantial part of the business of such investment adviser, consists or is to consist of rendering investment supervisory services.

Note: I have to let you read some of the original legalese, since your exam will be chock full of such dense, awkward prose. If any of this stuff is too hard to decipher, send us an email at walker@passthe65.com

Okay, so which advisers must register with the SEC? Here we go with more bullet points for your studying pleasure:

- Adviser with > $30 million of assets under management (advisers with $25 million + *may* register with the SEC)
- Adviser to a registered investment company
- NRSROs (Nationally Recognized Statistical Rating Organizations, i.e. Moody's and S & P)
- Pension consultants providing advice to employee benefit plans with assets of at least $50 million
- Affiliates of federally registered IAs if the principal office and place of business of the affiliate is the same as that of the SEC-registered adviser
- Newly formed advisers that reasonably believe that they will become eligible for federal registration within 120 days

If the adviser wants to withdraw their registration, they file a Form ADV-W. They don't just stop showing up at the office, in other words. I suppose the IA might just be getting out of the business. More likely, they're switching from federal to state-level registration. Why? Maybe they're lousy stock pickers and they just turned $32 million of assets into $20 million. Hate it when that happens. Or, maybe they're just a bunch of rude, arrogant jerks and all of their big customers have left. In any case, the IA would file their annual updating amendment reporting that they are no longer Mr. Big-Guy-SEC-Registered-Type-Dude because of the level of assets under management. They would then file ADV-W ("w" for "withdrawal") within 180 days after the close of their fiscal year. During this period while they are registered with both the Commission and one or more State securities authorities, the Investment Advisers Act of 1940 and applicable State law will apply to their advisory activities.

Although this next scenario is not a withdrawal, it makes sense to talk about the opposite case here, where the IA is moving up from state-level registration to federal (SEC) registration. Why? Maybe their assets under management have grown to over $30 million, or they now advise registered investment companies. In this case, the IA must apply for SEC registration within 90 days of filing an annual updating amendment to Form ADV that showed why they're suddenly Mr. Big-Guy-SEC-Registered-Type-Dude.

Also know that if a firm has withdrawn its registration with the SEC, they could still end up getting in trouble. In fact, although the ADV-W is considered effective when it's filed, the registration actually continues for 60 days just in case the SEC finds out they need to take regulatory action against the firm that is suddenly in a big hurry to flee the watchful eye of the SEC. A suspension is a definite strike against the firm, and the SEC can suspend a firm for as long as 12 months, which is bad. Why would they cop such an attitude against an investment adviser? Perhaps the person (individual or firm):

- Willfully made or caused to be made any false or misleading report or application regarding a material fact, or omitted a material fact
- Has been convicted within the previous 10 years of any felony or any securities-related misdemeanor
- Is enjoined by court order
- Has willfully violated any provision of federal securities law
- Has willfully aided another person's violation of federal securities law or has failed to supervise a person who commits a violation
- Is subject to an order of the SEC barring or suspending the person from being associated with an investment adviser

The above bullet points would also be a good reason to deny a license to an investment adviser trying to get registered or renew registration.

Disclosure brochure

Most prospects and customers must also be given a disclosure brochure. The test might ask you when the brochure must be delivered to a prospect. The answer is within 48 hours of signing the contract, or at the time of signing the contract if the client has five days to cancel without penalty. If the disclosure brochure is amended, it must be sent to all clients, and any client can also request the disclosure brochure whenever she feels like it. Form ADV has part I, which is filed with the initial registration and filed whenever it needs to be amended. Form ADV has a part II, and the disclosure brochure must either contain substantially the same information or be an actual copy of ADV part II. This part of the form tells customers the essential information on their investment adviser, such as:

- Types of securities about which advice is rendered and the types of analyses used to make such recommendations
- Services provided, fees charged
- Education and business background of all officers of the firm and any employee that determines advice

- Any compensation incentives to the adviser for placing trades through particular broker-dealers/affiliations with other securities professionals
- A balance sheet if the adviser has custody or requires prepayment of fees of >$500 six or more months in advance
- Regulatory action against the firm material to evaluation

But, of course, not ALL Investment Advisers have to deliver this brochure. If the client is an investment company, we don't need to deliver a brochure. Investment companies are big boys and girls. If the advice is considered "impersonal," meaning it isn't tailored to specific client situations and costs less than $200 per year, we don't need a brochure. The opposite of "impersonal" advice would be "supervisory services," where the IA purports to tailor advice to each client, rather than directing advice to a whole group of clients—retirees, teachers, day traders, etc. Or, we could think of the difference between "supervisory" services and "impersonal" services as the difference between my mother, who used to supervise every move I made around the house, and my dad, who occasionally looked up over his *Wall Street Journal* and told me to listen to my mother.

Also, should they *really* want to split hairs, SEC-registered advisers no longer have to file Part II of Form ADV. They just need to keep a copy of it, in case the SEC inspectors would like to have a look-see some day. And, let's face it, if you didn't know that, how in the world could the regulators let you move forward with your career? You could, like, accidentally file something you didn't have to, and then all hell would break loose.

WRAP FEE PROGRAMS

A "wrap fee" includes one fee where all the services provided (advice, execution of trades, asset allocation, administration) are "wrapped" together. If the adviser charges wrap fees, prospects and clients must receive a written disclosure statement of how these wrap fees work, pointing out that the client may pay more this way than if the services were purchased separately. Generally, clients who trade frequently do better under wrap fee programs, while those who trade infrequently would probably save money paying for each transaction if/when it occurs.

Also note that if one adviser refers the client to another adviser who will provide the client with a wrap fee brochure, the first adviser does not need to do so.

STATE REGISTRATION

In general, the large firms register with the SEC (federal), while the smaller firms register with the states. If the firm has not been excluded from the definition of *investment adviser* and not granted an exemption (excuse) from registration, they'll have to register in the states where they have an office, or where their registration is required. The investment adviser would file an application with the State Securities Administrator, and this is usually the same Form ADV used for SEC-registration. On the ADV, the firm would just indicate that they're going to be state-registered. This application would include:

- Applicant's form and place of business organization

- Applicant's proposed method of doing business
- Applicant's qualification and business history and the qualifications and history of any partner, officer, director, or person in similar position of control
- Applicant's financial condition and history
- Any injunction or administrative order, any conviction of a securities-related misdemeanor or *any* felony
- Any information to be provided to any client or prospect

The state securities Administrator might also require the applicant to publish an announcement in one or more specified newspapers published in the state.

In addition to the above bullet points, remember that the initial application is accompanied by a "consent to service of process," which you can see at www.nasaa.org under "uniform forms." This authorizes the Administrator to receive court papers (service of *process*) on the applicant's behalf in any non-criminal legal complaint, meaning that I wouldn't have to chase down the suddenly hard-to-locate adviser; instead, I'd just serve process on the Administrator, which would have the same validity of serving them on the party that doesn't seem to be returning voice mails all of a sudden. Remember this consent to service of process thing—it is filed with the initial application for advisers, adviser reps, broker-dealers, agents, and securities subject to state registration. In fact, it is also included in a *notice filing* with a state for a federal covered adviser or an investment company security. The consent to service of process is filed only initially; it does not have to be filed with every renewal application. Finally, fees must also be paid to the state when the applicant registers. No big surprise there, I assume.

RECORD KEEPING

IAs have to do all kinds of paperwork, which, again, is why so many are so glad to be excluded from the definition or excused from the requirement of registration as an "investment adviser." But, those who couldn't figure out how to get out of the definition or registration requirement have to maintain all kinds of records, such as:

- Receipts and Disbursements Journals
- General Ledger
- Order Memoranda
- Bank Records
- Bills and Statements
- Financial Statements
- Written Communications and Agreements (including electronic transmissions)
- List of Discretionary Accounts
- Advertising
- Personal Transactions of Representatives and Principals
- Client Records:
- Powers Granted by Clients
- Disclosure Statements

- Solicitors' Disclosure Statements
- Performance Claims
- Customer Information Forms and Suitability Information
- Written Supervisory Procedures

If the adviser has custody of client funds or securities, the IA must keep the following records:

- Journals of Securities Transactions and Movements
- Separate Client Ledgers
- Copies of Confirmations
- Record by Security Showing Each Client's Interest and Location Thereof

If the IA actively manages client assets, the firm must maintain the following records:

- Client Purchases and Sales History
- Current Client Securities Position

These records (the two above bullet points) are required to be maintained in an easily accessible place for a period of five years from the end of the fiscal year during which the last entry was made and, for the first two years, the records must be maintained in the adviser's principal office.

Finally, if a firm is deemed to have custody of client funds and securities, what sort of questions would the state regulators be trying to answer? Luckily, NASAA saw fit to tell us. As NAASA states on their website (www.nasaa.org):

If an adviser has direct or indirect access to client funds or securities, it is considered to have custody of client funds and is subject to additional scrutiny. State regulators will want to see how you handle those assets by asking the following:

- Has the adviser complied with the rules relating to safeguarding client assets in the adviser's custody?
- Does the Form ADV reflect that the adviser has custody?
- Are these assets maintained in segregated accounts?
- Does the adviser maintain the required records of client assets in its custody?
- Does the client get an itemized statement at least every three months showing the assets in the adviser's custody and the activity in the account?
- Has a surprise audit of client assets has been conducted at least annually by an independent accountant?
- If the adviser has discretionary authority over the client's account, is there any evidence of excessive trading, self-dealing, preferential treatment, unsuitable recommendations, unauthorized transactions or incomplete disclosure?

BUT I DON'T *WANNA* BE AN INVESTMENT ADVISER!

Here is the verbatim, legalistic definition of "Investment Adviser" under the Investment Advisers Act of 1940:

> "Investment adviser" means any person who, for compensation, engages in the business of advising others, either directly or through publications or writings, as to the value of securities or as to the advisability of investing in, purchasing, or selling securities, or who, for compensation and as part of a regular business, issues or promulgates analyses or reports concerning securities; but does not include (A) a bank, or any bank holding company as defined in the Bank Holding Company Act of 1956, which is not an investment company, except that the term "investment adviser" includes any bank or bank holding company to the extent that such bank or bank holding company serves or acts as an investment adviser to a registered investment company, but if, in the case of a bank, such services or actions are performed through a separately identifiable department or division, the department or division, and not the bank itself, shall be deemed to be the investment adviser; (B) any lawyer, accountant, engineer, or teacher whose performance of such services is solely incidental to the practice of his profession; (C) any broker or dealer whose performance of such services is solely incidental to the conduct of his business as a broker or dealer and who receives no special compensation therefor; (D) the publisher of any bona fide newspaper, news magazine or business or financial publication of general and regular circulation; (E) any person whose advice, analyses, or reports relate to no securities other than securities which are direct obligations of or obligations guaranteed as to principal or interest by the United States, or securities issued or guaranteed by corporations in which the United States has a direct or indirect interest which shall have been designated by the Secretary of the Treasury, pursuant to section 3(a) (12) of the Securities Exchange Act of 1934, as exempted securities for the purposes of that Act; or (F) such other persons not within the intent of this paragraph, as the Commission may designate by rules and regulations or order.

Aren't you glad I'm not communicating to you solely in legalese, as many other vendors like to do? See, that makes *their* job a lot easier. All they have to do is cut and paste sections of the law and throw it in your face, leaving you with all the hard work and frustration. I figure you pay good money for this material, so I'll go ahead and do some of the hard work for you.

A radical concept.

EXCLUSIONS/DO NOT MEET DEFINITION OF "INVESTMENT ADVISER"

Anyway, plenty of folks who look like investment advisers actually turn out *not* to be by definition, which saves them all kinds of time, money, and aggravation. First of all, everybody has an opinion about securities. Not everybody is an investment adviser. I can stand on a street corner shouting for folks to buy convertible debentures in countercyclical issues whenever the yield curve inverts, but that wouldn't make me an investment adviser. Just one of the least understood street preachers in America. Unless I started charging for my advice, nobody would hassle me or try to define me as an investment adviser. If you receive no compensation of any kind, you're not an adviser.

What are you?

A chump.

Broker-dealers and agents have all kinds of opinions about securities. As long as they don't charge for the *opinion*, they aren't defined as investment advisers. At the federal level, banks and bank holding companies (like Citigroup or J.P. Morgan-Chase) are excluded from the definition of "investment adviser." If they want to get into the managed funds business, they set up a separate entity and register it as an investment adviser, just as they have to do if they want to set up a broker-dealership. And, of course, both Citigroup and J.P. Morgan-Chase are in the broker-dealer and investment advisory business, but they have subsidiaries set up to perform those functions—the bank or bank holding company itself is not the adviser. And, I'm not implying anything about either company except that I am certainly available for training on the Series 65, 63, 7, or 6 should either firm care to give me a call and break out their massive, industrial-sized checkbook.

The *Wall Street Journal* passes out all kinds of advice in exchange for the subscription or newsstand price. That doesn't make them an investment adviser. You'd have to be rendering specific advice based on a specific situation and getting compensation for it before anyone would accuse you of being an investment adviser. This point could lead to confusion, unfortunately. Remember, we're talking about general subscription publications, the kind anyone can buy at the newsstand. If we're talking about a newsletter, that's different. An IA could be offering those "impersonal advisory services" mentioned earlier, providing advice to a well-defined audience: teachers, day traders, people desperate and gullible enough to pay $199 for Internet newsletters. As the definition of IA points out, advice can be delivered in person, over the phone, or through publications. So, the folks selling newsletters that give advice ARE investment advisers. But the *Wall Street Journal* or *Forbes* would not be IAs.

Lawyers, accountants, teachers, and engineers could all, theoretically, end up giving advice about a particular security to a particular client. Lawyers could be doing estate planning. An accountant could be advising somebody to do some tax-loss selling. A teacher could be teaching about the value of IBM stock. And a structural engineer could be rendering his opinion that a bridge built from the proceeds of a revenue bond is structurally sound. In none of those cases is the professional acting as an investment adviser. For example, making your maximum 401K contribution could help your tax situation; as long as the accountant isn't charging you to help you select investments to make with the money you contribute, she's just acting as an accountant. Remember the acronym LATE. Lawyers, accountants, teachers, and engineers who give incidental advice without charging a separate fee are not investment advisers.

Doesn't mean they're *never* investment advisers. If they hold themselves out to the public as being in the business of providing specific advice on securities, and get compensated for providing the advice, then they *are* an adviser and would have to register. But if the advice is solely incidental to their practice, and they don't charge a fee for the advice, they're excluded from the definition. Also note that geologists and geophysicists can also be granted the same exclusion given to engineers.

And, as you may (or may not) have read in the above legalistic ramble under point (E), if the advice only pertains to direct US Gov't obligations (Treasuries, GNMA, STRIPS, etc.), then the IA is excluded from the definition of IA and would not have to register.

So those folks are excluded from the definition of "investment adviser." Whatever an investment adviser may or may not be able to do—doesn't apply to them. They are NOT investment advisers. A new rule for investment advisers would affect them as much as a new rule for PGA golfers or NFL draftees would affect me.

I'm not a golfer, and I somehow—just barely—missed being drafted into the NFL, too.

So a bank isn't an investment adviser, just like I'm not an NFL lineman.

Hmm. That means the rules for investment advisers don't apply to banks.

Why not?

Banks are not investment advisers.

Unless they start *acting* like investment advisers. Then, we'll have to define them as such and start regulating them. But, for now, they are NOT advisers.

There's a subtle difference between being "excluded from the definition of" *investment adviser* and being granted an "exemption." Being excluded from the definition gives you an "exception," rather than an "exemption." To be excluded means that you don't fall under the definition of "investment adviser" any more than I fall under the definition of "Heisman Trophy-winning fullback from a major Big 10 school."

If you are granted an "exemption," that basically means that you ARE an adviser, but you get an exemption (you're *excused*) from having to go through the pain-in-the-neck process of registration, fees, et cetera. I don't think the test will split hairs with you there, but they might. Bottom line is, whether you're excluded or exempted, it means you don't have to register.

EXEMPTIONS

So, let's look at some folks who are granted exemptions from registration. First, let's do the business-like bullet-point list, followed by our more creative-type explanations that are currently keeping you up *way* past your bedtime. The SEC says to the following folks, "Yo, yooz guys—get outa' here!" And notice how they say it with such elegance and grace:

> Investment advisers who need not be registered. The provisions of subsection (a) shall not apply to—
> - any investment adviser all of whose clients are residents of the State within which such investment adviser maintains his or its principal office and place of business, and who does not furnish advice or issue analyses or reports with respect to securities listed or admitted to unlisted trading privileges on any national securities exchange;
> - any investment adviser whose only clients are insurance companies;
> - any investment adviser who during the course of the preceding twelve months has had fewer than fifteen clients and who neither holds himself out generally to the public as an investment adviser nor acts as an investment adviser to any investment company registered under title I of this Act, or a company which has elected to be a business development company pursuant to section 54 of title I of this Act and has not withdrawn its election. For purposes of determining the number of clients of an investment adviser under this paragraph, no shareholder, partner, or beneficial owner of a business development company, as defined in this title, shall be deemed to be a client of such investment adviser unless such person is a client of such investment adviser separate and apart from his status as a shareholder, partner, or beneficial owner;
> - any investment adviser that is a charitable organization, as defined in section 3(c)(10)(D) of the Investment Company Act of 1940, or is a trustee, director, officer, employee, or volunteer of such a charitable organization acting within the scope of such person's employment or duties with such organization, whose advice, analyses, or reports are provided only to one or more of the following:

- any such charitable organization;
- a fund that is excluded from the definition of an investment company under section 3(c)(10)(B) of the Investment Company Act of 1940; or
- a trust or other donative instrument described in section 3(c)(10)(B) of the Investment Company Act of 1940, or the trustees, administrators, settlors (or potential settlors), or beneficiaries of any such trust or other instrument;
- any plan described in section 414(e) of the Internal Revenue Code of 1986 [26 USCS § 414(e)], any person or entity eligible to establish and maintain such a plan under the Internal Revenue Code of 1986 [26 USCS §§ 1 et seq.], or any trustee, director, officer, or employee of or volunteer for any such plan or person, if such person or entity, acting in such capacity, provides investment advice exclusively to, or with respect to, any plan, person, or entity or any company, account, or fund that is excluded from the definition of an investment company under section 3(c)(14) of the Investment Company Act of 1940; or
- any investment adviser that is registered with the Commodity Futures Trading Commission as a commodity trading advisor whose business does not consist primarily of acting as an investment adviser, as defined in section 202(a)(11), and that does not act as an investment adviser to—
- an investment company registered under title I of this Act; or
- a company which has elected to be a business development company pursuant to section 54 of title I of this Act and has not withdrawn its election.

And there you have it—go take your Series 65.

Well, okay, perhaps I can help explain all of that stuff, except the stuff I'm not going to explain. Here goes. At the federal level, the SEC says that if you are a local area adviser they could, like, care less about you, so you get an excuse/exemption from having to register. They named that one, very cleverly, the "local area adviser exemption." Remember, the SEC is federal, so if this adviser is dealing with clients who are all residents of his state, and the IA does not give advice about listed or NASDAQ stocks (which trade *nationally*), they don't make him register. He'll probably end up registering with his state in that case, unless he doesn't.

Another excuse/exemption is available to an IA who does not hold himself out generally to the public as being in the business of providing investment advice AND had fewer than 15 clients during the preceding 12 months. Too small to get the SEC's attention, basically. Just like I'm too small to get the Green Bay Packers' defensive coordinator's attention. The SEC cares about those little advisers about as much as the Packers' defensive coordinator cares if I violate this summer's conditioning schedule.

The states might make the IA register, but the SEC could sort of care less.

And, if your only clients are insurance companies, you don't have to register with the SEC. Why not?

Because they said so.

But—other than the folks listed in the SEC's "get-outa'-here" list—all investment advisers have to register. So, if you are in the business of providing advice as to the value of securities or the advisability of investing in securities and that advice is specific in nature, and you receive compensation for this advice, you ARE AN INVESTMENT ADVISER.

But a bank, bank holding company, or broker-dealer who doesn't charge a fee, et cetera—they are NOT Investment Advisers.

And then there are a few advisers that the SEC decided not to regulate, just like in high school certain kids are excused from gym class. They aren't excluded from the definition of "high school student." They're just excused (exempted) from having to follow the requirement that high school students take gym class. *Excused* and *exempt* really mean the same thing. If you keep it all local and limited, we'll let you be excused. If you have very few clients or only advise insurance companies, we'll let you be excused there, too.

But if you haven't been excluded or granted an excuse, you'll have to register as an investment adviser with the SEC. Even if you don't want to.

Especially if you don't want to.

So that's the SEC or federal level.

STATE-LEVEL EXCLUSIONS

At the state level, we have to subtract the term "bank holding company" from our list of exclusions and add "savings institutions and trust companies." So, a little memorization may be in order. At the federal level, the exclusions are for "bank and bank holding company." At the state level, the exclusions are for "banks, savings institutions, and trust companies."

STATE-LEVEL EXEMPTIONS

Many IAs are granted exemptions from having to register. The IA is registered in Wisconsin, for example, and can do some business in, say, Illinois, without having to register in Illinois. Which saves the IA all kinds of time, expense, and heartburn.

Just like with broker-dealers, if the adviser has an office in the state, they have to register, unless granted some exemption. But if they *don't* have an office in the state, they usually don't have to register—they're granted an excuse, an exemption. The Administrator checks to see whom the out-of-state adviser is doing business with. If it's those big, multimillion-dollar institutions (insurance, bank, pension, mutual fund), then, we won't make them register as an investment adviser in our state. They can deal with as many of the big guys as they want. We'll even let them deal with exactly 5 little guys in the state without getting all bent out of shape about it. But if the adviser has more than 5 non-institutional clients in a 12-month period, that adviser will have to register in our state. The "under 6 little guys" rule is known as the *de minimus exemption*, which means, "so few it really don't matter" in the original Latin.

Fascinating stuff, isn't it?

Federal covered advisers

If the term "investment adviser" applies to a firm, that means the firm is defined as such at the state level, giving the state jurisdiction/authority over that firm. But many firms are covered at the federal level, and guess what we call them?

Federal covered.

Just means the SEC is watching them, the lucky devils. If the firm manages over $30 million in assets, it has to register with the SEC and is, therefore, a federal covered adviser. If the firm manages less than $25 million, the firm registers at the state level. What if it's between $25 million and $30 million?

Then, they have their choice between state and federal registration. Unless the firm advises registered investment companies. If so, they are federal covered. So, the

IA is federal covered if it manages over $30 million in assets or if it advises registered investment companies. Also, refer to our previous rant about which advisers must register with the SEC, assuming you can actually stand that much more excitement at this point.

Let's review that confusing ramble. If the IA is in another state, they only have to register in *this* state if they have more than 5 non-institutional clients residing in *this* state. If the IA is in *this* state, they have to register, unless they're so big that they're "federal covered."

Whew! Good thing you know that!

Federal covered advisers are <u>covered</u> at the <u>federal</u> level. They still provide the state with a so-called "notice filing." Believe it or not, this is basically a filing of notice, so we say it backwards to make ourselves sound smarter than we really are. NASAA says on their website:

A notice filing for a federal covered adviser is usually made by:

- Filing a complete copy of its Form ADV as filed with the US SEC.
- Filing a Form U-4 application for each investment adviser representative who will provide services on behalf of the investment adviser.
- Payment of any required notice filing fees.

But really they're on the SEC's turf, whereas a mere "investment adviser" is on the turf of the state securities Administrator. Still, if a federal covered adviser is committing fraud in a particular state, the state regulators can come after them. Remember, it is a state regulator—Eliot Spitzer—who has been making life real difficult for some of the big federal covered firms on Wall Street.

Investment advisers—firms—can be federal covered. Investment adviser representatives are NOT federal covered. If they have an office in the state, they have to register in the state, end of story. Make note of that, please—investment adviser representatives *do not* register with the SEC. Their firm does, but the reps are subject to state registration in the states where they maintain an office/do business.

So, to review all that fascinating material on exemptions/exclusions:

Exclusions at federal level:
- Bank
- Bank holding company
- Person whose advice only pertains to direct or indirect U.S. Government obligations (T-bonds, GNMA, FNMA, etc.)

Federal exemptions (the most likely to show up on the exam):
- Local area adviser: clients are all residents of his state, and the IA does not give advice about listed or NASDAQ stocks. (Registers with his state in that case.)
- IA who does not hold himself out generally to the public as being in the business of providing investment advice AND had less than 15 clients during the preceding 12 months. Too small to get the SEC's attention, basically.
- Adviser to insurance companies only: they're big boys and girls.

Federal Covered (*covered* EXCLUSIVELY at *federal* level):
- Adviser to investment companies
- Adviser with > $30 million under management

Exclusions at state level:
- Bank
- Savings institution
- Trust company
- Person whose advice only pertains to U.S. Government or municipal bonds

Exclusions common to **both** state and federal level:
- Excluded from the definition of Investment Adviser:
- Broker-dealer or agent whose advice is incidental and is getting no specific compensation for "advice"
- LATE if advice is solely incidental to the practice
- Publishers of periodicals of general circulation
- Advice only pertains to direct US Gov't obligations (Treasuries, GNMA, STRIPS, etc.)

Exemptions from registration at state level:
- Out-of-state adviser with institutional clients
- Out-of-state adviser with minimal non-institutional clients
- Federal Covered Adviser (registers with SEC)

PRACTICE QUESTIONS

10. Which of the following investment advisers would not have to register in the state?
   A. adviser with no office in the state who advises 7 high-net-worth individuals who are residents of the state
   B. adviser with an office in the state who advises 5 non-institutional clients who are residents of the state
   C. adviser with an office in the state who advises 11 pension funds located in the state
   D. adviser with no office in the state who advises 11 pension funds located in the state

11. Which of the following persons are excluded from the definition of "investment adviser"?
   A. certified financial planners
   B. sports agents
   C. banks
   D. broker-dealers

12. All of the following are investment adviser representatives except
   A. individual hired by an IA to help determine recommendations to clients
   B. individual hired by an IA to sell the advisory services
   C. individual hired by an IA to do filing and clerical work
   D. individual who supervises a staff of solicitors for the firm

13. All of the following professionals qualify for an exemption to registration as an IA provided their advice is not an integral component of their practice except
   A. lawyer
   B. accountant
   C. teacher
   D. economist

14. All of the following are excluded from the definition of "investment adviser" except
   A. bank
   B. bank holding company
   C. financial planner
   D. broker-dealer who provides advice on securities without compensation

Answers

10. ANSWER: D

WHY: we're looking for IAs who do not have to register in the state, so you can't choose B or C. Whenever you see they have an office in the state, you can safely assume they have to register. It's the out-of-state firms who get exemptions. So, who gets the exemption between choice A and choice D? Only choice D, since the number of institutional investors is irrelevant. In choice A, the IA is going over the "5" allowed in the "de minimus exemption."

11. ANSWER: C

WHY: many broker-dealers are also IAs, and many CFPs and sports agents got pulled reluctantly into the fold via SEC Release IA-1092.

12. ANSWER: C

WHY: they're not out to regulate the temp workers doing filing, typing, and other "clerical work." They want to regulate the money managers, the folks (like you) selling the services of the firm, and the supervisors of those individuals. Those are the folks who directly impact the clients, whom the regulators are out to protect.

13. ANSWER: D

WHY: the "e" stands for engineer, not economist. Economist would have made WAY too much sense.

14. ANSWER: C

WHY: as we're about to see, not only are financial planners not ex-cluded from the definition, but also, SEC Release IA-1092 went out of its way to in-clude them.

SEC RELEASE IA-1092 GOTCHA!

As mentioned, many folks really prefer NOT being called "investment advisers" and NOT having to register. But the SEC doesn't necessarily care whether these folks like being defined and regulated or not. Many sports agents, financial planners, and pension consultants would probably prefer not being included in the definition of "investment adviser," but the SEC and NASAA decided to include them anyway by issuing in 1987 Release IA-1092. This release made clear that the "three-pronged" test to determine if someone is an investment adviser involves the following:

- Does the professional provide investment advice?
- Is he/she in the business of providing advice?
- Do they receive compensation for this advice?

If the answer to all three questions is "yes," then the person is an adviser and must register. The advice in this case doesn't have to be on a specific security. If a financial planner or sports agent is helping clients pick investments in securities as an alternative to an investment in real estate or other assets, then he/she IS an investment adviser.

Harsh.

Pension consultants who help pension plans decide on either *which* securities to invest in or *whether* to invest in securities over some other asset are advisers. The consultants who help the funds determine which investment advisers to hire or retain are also.

Sorry about that. Gotta register.

So what does it mean to "be in the business of providing advice"? The SEC and NASAA determined that the person is in the business of providing advice if he or she gives advice on a regular basis and that advice "constitutes a business activity conducted with some regularity." The frequency is a factor, but it's not the only factor in determining if the person is "in the business" or not. Providing advice doesn't have to be the main activity of the person, either. If the person "holds himself out to the public" as one who provides investment advice—business cards, Yellow Page® ads, etc.—then he/she is in the business and is an adviser.

Lots of financial planners represent broker-dealers or insurance companies and make commissions selling variable annuities, variable life insurance, mutual funds, or specific issues of stocks, bonds, etc. Many of these planners are clever enough to figure that they can just issue the advice for free and get paid off the commissions to avoid being defined as IAs. Unfortunately, Release IA-1092 says they're still advisers, because they receive an economic benefit for providing advice.

Some folks would like to think they're not advisers because they don't receive money for their advice. But regulators wouldn't leave a loophole that big—they use the broader term "compensation" to determine who is and isn't an IA. Compensation is any economic benefit, not necessarily money. Compensation can come in the form of "soft dollars," such as receiving goodies from broker-dealers when you direct clients to put trades through the firm. Goodies such as research reports, custodial and clearing (trade processing) services, and special software aiding in research represent compensation, so if you receive it, you're probably an adviser. These soft dollar compensations are allowable, and they must be disclosed to clients. But the regulators won't let anybody receive the following soft dollar compensation arrangements: furniture and office equipment, salaries or overhead, vacations, cell phones… you know, the stuff you might actually want.

Allowable:

- Research reports
- Custodial and clearing (trade processing) services
- Special software aiding in research

Non-allowable:

- Furniture and office equipment
- Salaries or overhead
- Vacations
- Cell phones

Surprisingly, even if the compensation is paid by someone other than the client, you're still an investment adviser. For example, if you advise Coca-Cola's employees on how to allocate their 401K investment dollars, and you bill the company, you're still an adviser. And if you'd like to share some of that account with me…

Anyway, because of Release IA-1092 advisers must take great care to disclose conflicts of interest. If the IA advises, say, technology stocks, he/she/they will have to disclose the fact that his spouse just happens to be on the boards of many technology companies that will be recommended for purchase. If an agent of a broker-dealer also does some financial planning/advising business on the side, she must inform clients that these services are performed outside the scope of her employment at the broker-dealer. Wouldn't be fair for a brand new rep of some major Wall Street firm to set up shop as an adviser on the side and imply that the advice is being given under the umbrella of, say, Goldman Sachs or Merrill Lynch, right? Many IAs and planners make commissions from broker-dealers when they place or tell customers to place trades through them. That needs to be disclosed to clients. And the IA needs to tell clients they don't have to use the particular broker-dealer in cahoots with the adviser—they might be able to get lower commissions using somebody else. If the planner only recommends products offered by his/her employer, that needs to be disclosed. Wouldn't you feel better getting a recommendation for a mutual fund based on its performance rather than on the fact it's the only one the planner can recommend or the one that pays the best commission?

Study Sheet Lesson 1
"What the Heck Is an Investment Adviser?"

Investment Adviser = the business, a "legal person."
- usually a corporation or partnership, but could be an individual set up as sole proprietor.
- charges a fee/receives compensation for providing advice as to the value of or advisability of investing in particular securities.

Investment Adviser Representatives (IARs) are employees who:
- manage accounts
- make recommendations
- help determine recommendations
- sell services of firm
- supervise those who do any of the above
- secretarial/clerical employees are NOT IARs

So, the investment adviser is the business. The individuals who <u>represent</u> investment advisers are called "investment adviser representatives."

Criminal penalties for fraud:
> Three years, five grand at state level.
> Five years, ten grand at the federal level.

Investment advisers are fiduciaries who must put the needs of the client first
- Disclose all potential conflicts of interest
- If disclosure isn't enough, abstain from the activity

Registration:

<$25 million under management	State-level Registration
>$30 million under management	Federal Registration (federal covered)
between $25 million - $30 million	IA has choice between state and federal
Advises registered investment co.	Federal registration (federal covered)

3-pronged test:
If the answer to the following questions is "yes," you're an IA
- Does the professional provide investment advice?
- Is he/she in the business of providing advice?
- Do they receive compensation for this advice?

Advisory contracts must provide in writing that:
- Compensation shall not be a share of capital gains/appreciation
- No assignment of contract without client consent
- Advisory partnerships will notify all clients if partnership structure changes

Performance-based compensation allowed if:
- Losses/capital depreciation are subtracted from gains/appreciation
- Client is a certain institutional investor
- Client has >$1.5 million net worth or $750,000+ in assets under management
- Client is a "qualified purchaser"

Disclosure brochure:
- If IA uses solicitor, must verify that customer received IA's disclosure brochure
- Disclosure brochure can be copy of ADV Part II or a document containing same info
- Provide disclosure 48 hours before client signs up, or at time of signing if client has 5 days to cancel
- Provide financial impairment disclosure if IA has custody, discretion or accepts prepayment of > $500 six or more months in advance
- No brochure required for registered investment companies or impersonal advice

Online Updates

LESSON 2

WHAT DOES AN ADVISER DO FOR A LIVING?

(Covering Economics and Portfolio Analysis)

MACROECONOMICS

<u>G</u>ross <u>D</u>omestic <u>P</u>roduct (GDP) measures the total output of the American economy. It's the total value of all goods and services, measured as the price paid by the consumer for, say, all the gallons of milk or haircuts purchased over a 3-month period. If GDP is increasing, the economy is growing. If GDP is declining, so is the economy. The American economy rides a continuous roller coaster known as the business cycle. All this means is that the economy goes up (expands), hits a peak, declines, hits bottom, and then comes back up again...just like a roller coaster. Although we refer to the period following the "trough" as a "recovery," it's really just the next expansion, so I would say there are four phases to the business cycle if I got that question on the exam.

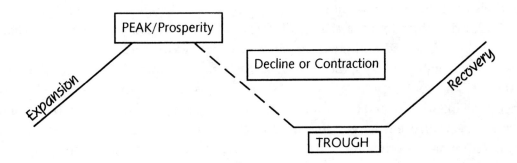

Also remember that rising prices (known as inflation) are factored into this GDP calculation to arrive at "real GDP." In other words, we don't want to kid ourselves that rising prices is the same thing as rising economic output. We use the CPI (consumer price index) to factor in the effects of inflation, which we'll discuss shortly. Note that the word "real" generally means to subtract the rate of inflation from something.

The period of contraction/decline can be referred to as either a recession or a depression. A recession is defined as 6 months (2 consecutive quarters) of GDP decline. A depression is defined as 18 months (6 quarters) of GDP decline. Technically, a recession is when your neighbor loses his job. A depression is when you lose *your* job.

INFLATION, DEFLATION

Ever noticed how the "Fed" often seems obsessed with the price of stuff? If the economy grows/expands too fast, prices can go higher and higher until they're out of control. That's called inflation. Inflation is indicated/measured by the CPI, or "consumer price index." The CPI surveys the prices consumers are paying for the basic things consumers buy (movie tickets, milk, blue jeans, gasoline) and tracks the increases in those prices. They actually give more weighting to the stuff people buy more of (milk over lame Adam Sandler movies) and sometimes they exclude certain items which are volatile (food and energy) because how many people actually buy food or gasoline in any given month? When we exclude food and energy, we're measuring "core inflation," which will not be on the exam, unless it is. The exam might say that inflation occurs when the demand for goods and services is growing faster than the supply of these items. Or, it could say something like, "too many dollars chasing too few goods." I like to think of inflation in terms of what would happen if they ran out of beer during the third inning at Wrigley Field and then somebody stood up and said he'd be happy to sell a cold six-pack he somehow managed to smuggle past security. How high would the price of cold beer rise on a hot August afternoon with 40,000 thirsty fans vying for six cold, sweaty cans of beer?

Then again, I think too much. You might just want to memorize some of this stuff and move on with your life.   .

No, actually, you'd better start thinking like a geek long enough to pass the exam. Speaking of which, the exam might mention two different types/causes of inflation. Cost-push inflation is when raw material prices rise and producers pass on the cost to consumers. The exam might want you to know that the "PPI" stands for the "producer price index," which measures cost-push inflation. The exam might want you to know all kinds of stuff. Demand-pull inflation, on the other hand, is when the demand for stuff outstrips the supply of that stuff. Back to Wrigley Field on a hot day: what I described was demand-pull inflation, since the demand for cold beer far outstripped the limited supply and you know some well-moneyed commodities trader wouldn't rest unless he could say he paid "10 g's" for the last cold six-pack in the ball park. Cost-push inflation would result if the cost of hops, barley, and malt used to manufacture the beer, or even the gasoline used to transport the beer, went up. Just like at Frank & Emma's—if the cost of wheat, sugar, flour, cherries, apples, corn syrup, etc., goes up, the company will have to both spend more on ingredients and charge more for their products.

Anyway, that's IN-flation. Not so long ago we started hearing the Fed worry about the opposite scenario, *de*flation. A beach ball can be inflated or deflated, and so can the economy. If you over-inflate a beach ball it will pop; if you under-inflate it, it's just as useless. Same for the economy. While inflation can make things too expensive for consumers to buy, deflation can make things ever cheaper. Cheaper goods sounds good until you consider that profit margins at businesses will be ever shrinking, as they pay last month's prices for raw materials and then struggle to sell them at next month's cheaper prices. Assuming they can sell anything to anyone—would you rush out to buy something today if you knew it would be cheaper tomorrow? Wouldn't you be tempted to put off your purchases indefinitely, waiting for the price of DVD players, clothing, and automobiles to drop in your favor?

That's an economic slowdown, right? Everybody sitting around waiting to see who'll be the first one to open up his or her wallet. Which is why deflation—while rare—is just as detrimental to the economy as inflation. And that's why the Fed is forever manipulating interest rates in an attempt to find the right economic temperature—not too hot, not too cold. Like Goldilocks, they hope to find the economic porridge just right. Which is another way of saying that demand for stuff and the supply of that stuff are in the right balance. If we have strong demand and tight supply, prices will rise, just as the demand for a sold-out Dave Matthews Band concert will send the ticket price into the stratosphere. If demand for stuff is weak and the supply of that stuff is high, prices will fall, like the price of a ticket to see the Spin Doctors at the Bureau County Fair.

To review, if the economy grows too fast, we can end up with inflation. And, as we'll soon see, the Federal Reserve Board (or FOMC) will raise interest rates to let some of the air out of the over-expanding economy. If the economy starts to sputter and stall, we can end up with deflation. And, as we'll soon see, the Fed will have to pump some air back into the economy by lowering interest rates.

ECONOMIC INDICATORS

The Fed monitors many economic indicators to get an *indication* as to whether inflation is trying to rear its ugly head. The exam tends to focus on employment indicators. As you might guess, employment indicators are based on employment. The following indicators tell us how many people are working and how much compensation they're receiving. The CPI tells us how far that compensation will go at Wal-Mart, and the GDP tells us how well the overall economy is doing. If people aren't working, that signals an economic slowdown. If employment compensation is rising too fast, that signals inflation, and the Fed might have to step in by raising interest rates.

- Average <u>Weekly</u> New Claims for Unemployment Insurance: if people are showing up for unemployment insurance at a higher rate, that's a bad sign, right? It means their employers don't have enough work for them. If the number of new claims drops, that means economic activity is picking up.
- Unemployment Rate (Nonfarm Payroll): since everything needs two or three names, this is also called "payroll employment." It's a figure released by the Bureau of Labor Statistics and includes full-time and part-time workers, whether they're permanent or temporary employees. In other words, if they're on the payroll, we count them as workers, just like they do at City Hall here in Chicago. As the "nonfarm" thing may have tipped you off, we don't count farm workers, since that stuff is very

seasonal, and we also don't count employment at tiny businesses or at government agencies. So, this figure tracks how many people are working in the private sector, basically. It is released <u>monthly</u>.

- Employment Cost Index (ECI): this measures the growth of wages and benefits (compensation) because if wages are rising really fast, inflation can't be far behind. It's a <u>quarterly</u> figure, so it's not the most timely of statistics. Still, it tracks trends in compensation. While the monthly employment rate is useful, the ECI gives us more detail, since it tracks the change in benefits paid to workers, rather than just the number of workers.
- CPI (Consumer Price Index): the most important measure of inflation.
- GDP (Gross Domestic Product): the aggregate/overall output of the domestic economy. The components of the calculation are consumer spending, investments, government spending and net exports (Exports – Imports).

FISCAL AND MONETARY POLICY

Once we have these indicators, what can we do with them? Depends on whom you talk to. As George Bernard Shaw said, if you laid every economist in the world end to end, they still wouldn't reach a conclusion. But, of course, economics is a tough science. Kind of hard to put an economy under a microscope, and you sure can't recreate one in the laboratory. So, we will probably always have economists with sharply different viewpoints. The Keynesians feel that fiscal policy is the best way to control the economy. Fiscal policy is what the president and congress do: tax and spend. Keynesians recommend that fiscal policy be used to increase aggregate (overall) demand. To stimulate the economy, just cut taxes and increase government spending. Lower taxes leaves more money for Americans to spend and invest, fueling the economy. If the government is spending more on interstate highway construction, that means a lot more folks are going to be hired for construction crews. Or maybe the federal government orders 10 million pies from Frank & Emma's for cafeterias at various Department of Defense, Treasury, Commerce, etc., buildings. Frank & Emma's would suddenly buy more equipment and raw materials and hire more workers, which is how to push the economy forward.

On the other hand, if we need to cool things down, the Keynesians suggest that the federal government increase taxes and cut spending. Higher taxes leave less money for Americans to spend and invest, and decreased spending puts less government money into projects that would otherwise be hiring subcontractors, laborers, etc.

Monetarists feel that controlling the money supply is the key to managing the economy. What is the money supply?

It's the supply of money. Money, like any commodity, has a cost. The cost of money equals its "interest rate." If there's too much demand and too little supply, the cost of money (interest rate) goes up. That slows down the economy and fights inflation. If there's too little demand and too much supply, the cost of money (interest rate) goes down. That helps to stimulate the economy and pump some air back into a deflated economy.

Wait, money has a cost? I thought I paid the cost of things *with* money. Sure, but if I want to start a business, I need money. How much do I have to pay to borrow this money?

That's the interest rate—the cost of borrowing money.

So, how can the money supply be influenced? Through monetary policy, enacted by the Federal Reserve Board. Because of that embarrassing little fiasco known as the 1930s, the Fed likes to make sure that banks don't lend out and invest every last dollar they have on deposit. So, the Fed requires that banks keep a certain percentage of their customer deposits in <u>reserve</u>. This is called, surprisingly enough, the reserve requirement. If the Fed raises the reserve requirement, banks have less money to lend out to folks trying to buy homes and start businesses. So if the economy is overheating, the Fed could raise the reserve requirement in order to cool things down, and if the economy is sluggish, they could lower the requirement in order to make more money available to fuel the economy. However, this is a drastic measure because of the multiplier effect, which means that $1 more or less in reserve has more than just $1's effect on the economy. So it's the least used Fed tool.

The most used tool is open market operations. The Fed can either buy or sell T-bills to banks. If they want to cool things down/raise interest rates, they can take money out of banks by selling them T-bills. If they want to fuel a sluggish economy/lower interest rates, they can buy T-bills from banks, thereby pumping money into the system.

Again, interest rates can be thought of as the price of a commodity known as money. Whenever a commodity—corn, sugar, concert tickets—is scarce, its price rises. Whenever something is widely available, its price drops. When money is tight, its cost (interest rate) rises. When money is widely available, its cost (interest rate) falls. So, if the Fed wants to drop rates, they make money more available by buying T-bills from banks. If they want to raise rates, they make money scarce by selling T-bills to banks (who pay for them with...money). Just follow the flow of money.

Then there's the tool that gets talked about the most in the news, the discount rate. When people talk about the Fed raising interest rates by 25 basis points, they're talking about the discount rate. The discount rate is the rate the Fed charges banks that borrow directly from the Fed. If banks have to pay more to borrow, you can imagine that they will in turn charge their customers more to borrow from them. So, if the Fed wants to raise interest rates, they just raise the discount rate and let the banking system take it from there. The Fed doesn't directly set the prime rate or the Fed funds rate. They do have influence over the rates through the discount rate, but they don't actually set the other rates. And, of course, they never, ever have anything to do with taxes.

So, think of the Fed as the driver of the economy. If the economy starts going too fast, they tap the brakes (raise interest rates) by raising the reserve requirement, raising the discount rate, and selling T-bills. If the economy starts to stall out, the Fed gives it gas by lowering the reserve requirement, lowering the discount rate, and buying T-bills.

INTEREST RATES

Let's take a look at this concept of "interest rates." Interest rates represent the cost of money. If you want $50,000 to start a beauty salon chances are you have to borrow it. How much you pay for that "capital" is what we call interest rates. When there's a ton of money to be lent out, lenders will drop their rates in order to get you to borrow. When money is tight, however, borrowers have to compete with each other to get a share of the limited capital and pay higher and higher rates. Again, if the concert is a sell-out, fans bid the price of the tickets ever upward; and when the performer is a has-been, the price of the tickets plummets.

Okay, so one way to borrow money is by selling bonds to investors. How much should you pay the buyers of your bonds?

How about zero? Zero percent financing sure sounds tempting to a borrower; unfortunately, the buyers of debt securities demand compensation. They're the lenders of the money, and they demand current interest rates in return for lending their hard-earned cash. So, debt securities pay investors exactly what they have to pay them in order to entice them to lend money through the purchase of these debt securities (bonds, notes, bills, certificates, etc.). If a corporation could get by with paying zero percent in order to borrow money through a bond issuance, you know they would. Since they can't do that, they offer investors only as much as they have to in order to obtain the loan. Sort of like you would do when applying for a mortgage. Would you give anyone even one extra basis point for a mortgage? Probably not. When you borrow money through a mortgage you have to pay the current rate of interest, just as the issuer of a bond must pay.

The exam may ask you to work with the following interest rates. They don't really warrant an in-depth discussion, so here's a quick list that should suffice:

1. Discount rate: the rate banks have to pay when borrowing from the FRB
2. Fed funds rate: the rate banks charge each other for overnight loans in excess of $1 million. Considered the most volatile rate, subject to daily change
3. Call money rate or "broker call loan rate": the rate broker-dealers pay when borrowing on behalf of their margin customers
4. Prime rate: the rate that the most creditworthy corporate customers pay when borrowing

That list presents the rates from lowest to highest, what the exam might call "ascending order." Whether we use fiscal or monetary policy, our efforts will influence interest rates. And interest rates can either make it easier or harder for companies to do business and for consumers to consume.

YIELD CURVES

City, county, and state governments borrow money by issuing municipal bonds. Municipal bonds are usually issued under a "serial maturity," which means that a little bit of the principal will be returned every year, until the whole issue is paid off. Investors who buy bonds maturing in 2025 will generally demand a higher yield than those getting their principal back in 2007. The longer your money is at risk, the more of a reward you demand, right? If a friend wanted to borrow $1,000 for one month, you'd probably do it interest-free. What if they wanted to take three years to pay you back? You could get some interest on a thousand dollars by buying a bank CD, which carries no risk, right? So, if somebody's going to put your money at risk for an extended period of time, you demand a reward in the form of an interest payment.

Same with bonds. If your bond matures in 2025 when mine matures in 2007, isn't your money at risk for 18 more years? That's why your bond would be offered at a higher yield (interest rate) than mine. If I buy a bond yielding 5.35%, yours might be offered at more like 5.89%. The extra 54 basis points is your extra reward for taking on extra risk.

This is how it works under a normal yield curve, where long-term bonds yield more than short-term bonds.

Guess what, sometimes that <u>yield curve gets inverted</u>. Suddenly, the rule flies out the window, and folks are getting higher yields on short-term bonds than on long-term bonds. The cause of this is generally a peak in interest rates. When bond investors feel that interest rates have gone as high as they're going to go, they all clamor to lock in the high interest rates for the longest period of time. In a rush of activity, they sell off their short-term bonds in order to hurry up and buy long-term bonds at the best interest rate they're likely to see for a long time. Well, if everybody's selling off short-term bonds, the price drops [and the yield *increases*]. And if they're all buying up long-term bonds, the price increases [and the yield *drops*]. That causes the yield curve to invert, a situation that usually corrects itself very quickly. There are also "humped yield curves," where the intermediate maturities have the highest yield, and a "flat yield curve," which has to be the best example of an oxymoron you're likely to see. A flat curve?

Whatever, dude.

A "flat yield curve" would imply that short-, intermediate-, and long-term bonds are all yielding about the same, meaning that demand and supply for all maturities is similar. Believe it or not, as I write these words, the yield curve is close to flattening out, as if I didn't already have enough excitement in my life. Basically, the Fed keeps raising short-term rates, but the bond traders are driving down the yield on the long-term bonds so that the difference between short-term, intermediate-term, and long-term yields is not very great...it's all flattening out.

To figure your way out of any yield curve jam, just remember that yields and prices are inverse. So, if the short-term debt has a higher yield (inverted or "negatively sloped yield curve), its price has gone down due to low demand/high supply. In a normal yield curve, short-term debt would have a lower yield/higher price due to a high demand for the short-term debt relative to supply...why are the long-term bonds yielding more on the right side of this yield curve? Long-term commitments scare investors, so their demand for these long-term commitments is lower than the supply, pushing price *down* and *yield* up.

Another yield concept the test might throw at you considers the difference in yields between high-rated and low-rated bonds, known as a yield spread. Remember that coupon rates don't change—they're simply printed on the bond. So, how could the yield of a bond that's already been issued go up? Only if its price starts to fall. If you get 5% a year, that's $50. If you get that $50 by paying $400, your yield is higher than for someone who bought that same bond paying $50 a year for $800. In fact, it's twice as high, right? Then again, why the heck is your $1,000 face value bond worth only $400 in the open market? Because it's a poor credit risk, a junk bond, a high-yield bond—whatever the heck we decide to call it. So, if folks are only willing to pay cheap prices for these higher-risk bonds, that makes the yield spread widen, and that's a negative indicator for the economy. Basically, it means folks are nervous about issuers' ability to repay. If investors don't demand a significantly higher yield on the low-rated bonds (they're willing to pay higher market prices for junk bonds), that means in general they are confident about issuers' ability to repay, which is a positive indicator.

Aren't you glad they signed you up for this test?

BALANCE OF TRADE, BALANCE OF PAYMENTS

Balance of trade tracks money in and money out of the economy specifically for goods. If we export more than we import, we have a trade surplus. If we import more than we export, we have a trade deficit. Imports and exports are directly affected by the value of the American dollar relative to foreign currencies.

As our dollar strengthens, our exports became less attractive to consumers in other countries, whose weak currency can't buy our expensive stuff. When our dollar weakens, our exports are more attractive because suddenly their strong currencies can buy lots of our relatively cheap stuff. Likewise, a strong dollar makes foreign travel less expensive for Americans, whereas a weak dollar makes foreign travel *more* expensive. It's just a way of asking how much of their stuff does our dollar buy?

Balance of payments tracks all money coming in versus going out of the economy. So, it counts both imports vs. exports and also investments. If more money is coming in than going out, we have a surplus. That could happen if the Japanese are suddenly buying lots of American securities. If more money is going out than coming in, we have a deficit, which could happen if Americans start buying Japanese securities.

So if we had a trade deficit with France, would a strong dollar or a weak dollar help to bring us back to a surplus?

Well, if we were already importing more from France than we're exporting, we would want to make our exports more attractive to the French and our imports from France less attractive to Americans, which would happen as the dollar…weakens.

The value of the dollar compared to another currency also comes into play when an investor buys an ADR. In a later chapter we'll look more at ADRs; for now, just know that you can buy shares of Toyota or Nokia, for example, as American Depository Receipts, priced in American dollars. This way, you don't have to figure out how much you just paid for a stock priced as 1,176.453 Yen. However, the relative values of the dollar to the Yen will come into play, especially when it comes time to paying dividends. If the US Dollar increases in value, when the underlying stock pays a dividend in the foreign currency, the foreign currency received by the bank will need to be converted to US Dollars for distribution to the holder of the ADR. As a result of the rise in the value of the dollar relative to the foreign currency received by the bank, the foreign currency will purchase fewer US Dollars for distribution to the holder of the

ADR. As a result of the rise in the value of the US Dollar the dividend payment received by the holder of the ADR is lower.

As if you didn't already have enough shhh—I mean, important information—to learn for this exam.

TYPES OF INDUSTRIES

That ends the big view of the overall economy. Now let's look at industries within the economy: defensive, cyclical, and growth. Remember the business cycle and GDP? Well, defensive industries do okay regardless of where we are in the business cycle. These industries produce products that consumers buy no matter what, like food, cigarettes, and alcohol. You know, the important stuff. Prescription drugs and bandages also represent defensive industries. Or the exam might lump such things under the more general heading of "healthcare." Certainly utilities also qualify. When you come home at night do you check the current economic figures before turning on the heat or air conditioning? Heck no.

But if we're in a recession, you might put off the purchase of a new car, which is why automobiles represent a cyclical industry. In good times, people load up, but in bad times they hold off. If you think of steel and products made from steel, like cars, heavy equipment, and big industrial machinery, you're thinking of cyclical industries. Raw materials would be a likely example of a cyclical industry on the exam. During expansions, these industries do well. During contractions, they don't. All depends on the business *cycle*.

Then there are growth industries, like technology. Growth industry stocks tend not to pay dividends because they're reinvesting their earnings into—you guessed it—*growth*. Remember that, to date, the amazing cash cow known officially as Oracle® has paid exactly zero dividends to the holders of common stock.

Zero. Which means the Oracle dividend plus a couple of bucks might buy you a cup of coffee at Starbucks®, a company also still finding better things to do with their earnings than just sending it out to the shareholders.

So, if the test tells you that one company pays a lot of dividends (high dividend pay-out) and another pays low dividends, the former is a utility or at least a defensive company, while the latter is a growth or maybe a technology company. While Frank & Emma's is in an old, mature boring business—manufacturing—they are a growth *company*. A company whose earnings are growing fast and which appears to have a lot more room to grow…guess what we call stock in that growth company?

Growth stock.

Again with the lack of creativity.

FUNDAMENTAL ANALYSIS

There are two ways to analyze investments: fundamental analysis and technical analysis. Technical analysts don't really analyze companies; they analyze stocks. Fundamental analysts analyze companies to see if their stocks and bonds are priced attractively.

Fundamental analysts, believe it or not, look at the company's fundamentals. Of primary importance are the balance sheet and the income statement.

BALANCE SHEET

The basic formula for the balance sheet or "statement of financial condition" states that Assets have to equal Liabilities plus Net Worth.

$$Assets = Liabilities + Net\ Worth.$$
$$Or:$$
$$Assets - Liabilities = Net\ Worth$$

Assets represent what a company owns. Liabilities represent what a company owes. You take what a company owns, subtract what it owes, and that's the net worth of the company. Just like if you took your assets and subtracted all your liabilities, you'd come up with your personal financial "net worth."

Assets

Assets are divided into three types. The first type is current assets. Current assets represent cash and anything that could easily be converted into cash: cash & equivalents, accounts receivable, inventory. Cash is cash, and it's a good thing. "Equivalents" are money market instruments—cash earning little tiny rates of interest, which is also a good thing. Commercial paper, banker's acceptances, repurchase agreements, T-bills…those are all "cash equivalents" listed here on the balance sheet. Accounts receivable is what customers owe the company. Frank & Emma's has already sold and shipped pies to supermarkets and big retail outlets, for which they fully anticipate getting paid over the next few months. So, they list that payment as an asset (money coming IN). Inventory is the stuff the company makes and plans to sell (convert to cash) just as soon as possible. Frank & Emma's doesn't let their pies sit in a warehouse very long, but on any given day there could be well over $5 million worth of pies waiting to be shipped out to customers. That stuff has value, and the company fully intends to sell that inventory for cash very soon, making the inventory a current asset.

Fixed assets include machinery, furniture and fixtures. This stuff is being used by the business every day. It could all be converted into cash, but it would take a while, and we wouldn't get anywhere near what we paid for the stuff if we liquidated it. Frank & Emma's would list the value of the land and buildings, as well as the value of the assembly line equipment, as well as the furniture and cheesy artwork hanging on the walls of the visitor lobby. Those are all fixed assets. They get depreciated over time, so the company usually reflects the original cost of the equipment and then shows how much value has been depreciated (written down) at this point. I don't think the 65 is going to turn this into an accounting exam, though. In fact, I'm betting that we're going a little overboard here, although if that's the worst thing we do in preparing for the exam, we're in pretty good shape, just like Frank & Emma's.

Then there are intangible assets. What is the value of the brand name Oreo®?

Who knows, but it must be worth millions. Whatever the company says it's worth is the value of this intangible asset. How would you like to own the patents protecting all Microsoft operating systems? Or, heck, just the ones protecting Internet Explorer®? Whatever those are worth is listed under "intangible assets." Intangible assets would include: patents, trademarks, and goodwill. What is goodwill? Some day Frank & Emma's may discover that as they try to break into the Pacific Northwest, some regional pie maker sort of has the market sewn up. So, FREM could either choose to compete with the smaller competitor or use the Bill Gates method of competition, known technically as "crush them or buy them, whichever is cheaper." Since Jeremy, Jason, and Jennifer like to avoid nasty legal battles, maybe they decide to buy the competitor for $30 million, when all the assets are really worth only $25 million. FREM would carry that $5 million excess as "goodwill" on the balance sheet and periodically re-asses the value of the goodwill. The brand name is so strong and the customer base so loyal that FREM feels the extra $5 million was well worth it. It brings them, literally, goodwill.

Add all three types of assets (what the company owns), and you have Total Assets.

Liabilities

On the other side of the equation we find liabilities, which represent what a company owes. Anything that has to be paid within 12 months is a current liability. Accounts payable, accrued wages, and accrued taxes all represent bills the company has to pay in the short-term, which is why they're called current liabilities. Bond interest, paid twice a year, is also a current liability, since it has to be paid in the current year.

The principal amount of the bond that has to be paid more than a year out is simply a long-term liability. Add the two together and you have Total Liabilities.

Net worth

Net worth (AKA "shareholder equity" or "owners' equity") has to do with stock and any earnings that haven't been paid out since the company's inception. We know that the par value of preferred stock is $100. So a company places the total par value of its preferred stock under Net Worth. Common stock is assigned a par value of, say, $1, so if a company has 1,000,000 shares of common, they would list the par value of their common stock as $1,000,000 and place it under Net Worth. If investors bought the IPO at $11, that represents a surplus of $10 above the par value, so the company would list "paid-in surplus" of $10,000,000 under Net Worth as well. And then any earnings that have been retained are listed as—you guessed it—retained earnings.

When looking at a balance sheet, you will find that Total Assets = Total Liabilities + Net Worth. In other words, everything balances.

Ratios and other measures

Current Assets represent what a company owns. Current Liabilities represent what a company owes. Hopefully, the company owns more than it owes, right? Fundamental analysts take Current Assets and subtract Current Liabilities in order to measure working capital (sometimes called "net working capital"). This is a measure of how able a company is to finance current operations. We're talking about short-term liquidity. Same thing you think about for your home budget. How many bills do we have to pay this month, versus how much income we'll be receiving? When a company's liabilities (bills) exceed its assets (stuff used to pay bills), that company is in great danger of becoming insolvent. Likewise, if a company's assets exceed its liabilities, that company is in a strong position to fund current operations, just as you would be if you had $1,000 in total bills and $4,000 in gross income.

Working Capital = Current Assets – Current Liabilities

If a company has $6 million in Current Assets and $1 million in Current Liabilities, it has $5 million in working capital.

Analysts also express current assets and current liabilities as a ratio, known as the current ratio. If a company has $6,000,000 in current assets and $1,000,000 in current liabilities, that's a current ratio of 6:1.

They could also apply a more stringent test, known as either the AcId Test or QuIck Ratio. The "I" has been accented to remind you that "Inventory" is subtracted from current assets before we compare them to current liabilities. So if $3,000,000 of the company's current assets were made up of inventory, we would subtract that out, leaving us with $3,000,000 in current assets to divide by $1,000,000 in current liabilities for a quick ratio of 3:1.

The bond ratio just shows us how much of a company's capitalization comes from debt. The formula is:

Long-Term Debt DIVIDED BY (Long-Term Debt + Net Worth)

So, if a company has $50,000,000 in long-term debt and $40,000,000 in Net Worth, we would take 50 and divide it by 50 (again) plus 40 to get 50/90 or a bond ratio of 5/9. Just means that more than half of the company's total capitalization comes from borrowing. If too much of a company's capitalization comes from borrowing, fundamental analysts could start to worry that future profits will be eroded by future interest payments on the debt. Utility companies are the most highly leveraged, which means they do most of their capitalization through borrowing. So, if interest rates are up, that affects utility companies more than most other companies, since interest rates represent the cost of borrowing. Working capital and current ratio measure short-term liquidity. The bond ratio measures long-term solvency.

Let's take a few minutes and see if you're ready to apply the preceding concepts. Using the balance sheet below, come up with the following measures:

1. Working capital
2. Current ratio
3. Quick ratio
4. Bond ratio

Current Assets			
Cash & Equivs	$9,000,000		
Accts Receivable	$1,000,000		
Inventory	$10,000,000		
Total Current Assets		$20,000,000	
Fixed Assets	$6,000,000		
Other Assets Intangible, goodwill	$4,000,000		
TOTAL ASSETS			$30,000,000
Current Liabilities			
Accts Payable	$3,000,000		
Accrued Wages	$3,000,000		
Accrued Taxes	$4,000,000		
Total Current Liabs		$10,000,000	
Long-Term Liabs 7% 10-year bonds		$10,000,000	
TOTAL LIABILITIES			$20,000,000
Net Worth			
Preferred Stock @par 10,000 shares	$1,000,000		
Common stock @par 1,000,000 shares		$1,000,000	
Paid-In Surplus		$4,000,000	
Retained Earnings		$4,000,000	
TOTAL NET WORTH			$10,000,000

ANSWERS:
- Working capital is $10 million.
- Current ratio is 2:1.
- Quick ratio/Acid test is 1:1 (subtract $10 million inventory first!)

And the bond ratio is 50%. We raised $10 million through long-term bonds out of $10 million (again) plus the $10 million net worth. In other words our "total capitalization" is the long-term bonds we sold plus the net worth. What % was the bonds? That's the debt or "leverage" ratio.

INCOME OR EARNINGS STATEMENT

The income statement starts with revenue and ends up with earnings available to common, assuming there *are* any earnings, which can sometimes be a dangerous assumption. And, since everything needs at least three names in this business, the income statement is sometimes called the "earnings statement," or the "profit & loss" statement, or the "statement of earnings," or "that hilarious piece of fiction we finally got the auditors to sign off on."

One of the most basic questions you can ask a corporation is, "Are you guys making more than you're spending?" To see the answer for yourself, read the income statement. On the income statement, a company takes sales (revenue) and subtracts the cost of goods sold. If Frank & Emma's sells $50 million of pies and has a cost of goods sold (what they paid to buy flour, sugar, butter, corn syrup, fruit, etc.) of $25 million, we could say they have "gross margins" of 50%. In other words, after subtracting the cost of the stuff they bought to make the pies, the company is left with $25 million out a' $50 million. Remember that in math, "out a'" means *divide*. 25 out a' 50 = 50%.

The company then subtracts all the costs for selling products and running the office: sales commissions, advertising, salaries, etc. The exam might also call them "SG&A" expenses, which stands for "Selling, General, and Administrative" expenses. Some companies list SG&A expenses separately from depreciation and amortization, but it all gets subtracted before figuring "operating earnings." If the company buys a piece of equipment with a useful life of five years, they subtract 1/5 of its value every year to represent the portion they use that year. So, depreciation expense is not a cash outlay that year, but it's a more accurate way to reflect the cost of the equipment than pretending it was purchased and consumed in one year. We depreciate tangible stuff and we "amortize" intangible stuff. An intangible asset—as we saw on the balance sheet—would include the value of patents, copyrights, and goodwill. These days accountants have to estimate the loss of value each year on these intangibles and put it down as a number on the income statement (and balance sheet). So, we were left with $25 million after subtracting the cost of the pie ingredients (cost of goods sold). If the SG&A, depreciation of the assembly line, and amortization all totaled $5 million, we'd be left with $20 million of "operating earnings." To figure the operating profit margin, we would just divide this $20 million out a' $50 million to get a 40% operating profit margin. Another name (because everything needs at least two or three names!) would be EBIT, which stands for "Earnings Before Interest and Taxes."

If EBIT stands for "Earnings *Before* Interest and Taxes," we would then, naturally, subtract the interest the company has to pay *before* figuring their taxable income. Yes, the IRS rewards companies for borrowing money, just like they reward you for the interest you pay on your mortgage. It's all tax deductible.

To review, the company takes their revenue then deducts cost of goods sold, SG&A expenses, depreciation, and amortization. We're at the "operating earnings" point now. Then, they subtract the interest they have to pay to borrow money and arrive at pre-tax income or taxable income. Yes, that's one problem with making a profit—the IRS expects a piece in the form of corporate taxes. So, to answer a question about a company's "pre-tax margins," just divide what they have before (pre-) paying tax by revenues.

The company pays their taxes on their taxable income and subtracts that amount to get "net income <u>after</u> tax." Some folks like to call it "the bottom line," which is exactly what it is—the bottom line of the income statement. The "put your cards on the table" line that shows whether the company made a profit or not. If, after all the above subtractions, we're left with, say, $5 million, we'd have a "net margin" of 10%, right? $5 million out a' $50 million means we're left with 10% of what we started with. A 10% net margin. A profit.

Cool.

Measurements such as EPS, PE, etc.

But the company has to get all the way down to this line of the income statement before they even think about paying dividends. Who gets dividends first? Preferred stockholders. So, they subtract the preferred dividends from net income after tax and end up with earnings available to common. Then they divide the earnings available to common by the number of outstanding common shares to get Earnings per Share or EPS. If the company has $5,000,000 in earnings with 1,000,000 shares outstanding, that represents $5 of earnings per share. EPS = $5.

Think of earnings available to common as the big pie the corporation bakes for common stockholders every year. The question stockholders ask is how big is this year's pie, and how many slices do we have to cut it into?

That's earnings per share.

We could apply a more stringent test that assumes all convertibles (bonds, preferred, warrants) are actually turned into common stock. This means that our $5,000,000 in earnings could end up being divided among more shares, sort of like sharing a cherry pie big enough for eight friends among 75 friends. We'd all get a piece, but it probably wouldn't be worth eating. If the above company ended up with 1,250,000 shares outstanding after conversion, their fully diluted EPS would be only $4. Same old earnings pie cut up into more slices.

Now that we have our earnings per share, we can also find out how much gets paid out in dividends. Guess what we call this?

The dividend payout ratio. This just takes the annual dividends paid and divides it by the EPS. Our above company has an EPS of $5. If they paid out $1 in common dividends, they'd have a 1:5 or 20% dividend payout ratio. If they paid $2.50 in dividends, that would be a 50% payout ratio, which means they must be a utility company. Utility companies pay more dividends than most other companies. So, they can do more borrowing than other companies and also pay more dividends…must be a defensive industry, right? An industry that can depend on people using their product regardless of economic figures. Growth companies reinvest their earnings into growing their business, so their dividend payout ratio would be among the lowest. Frank & Emma's, as indicated in their annual report, has no intention of paying dividends at this time or in the near future. For now, this growth company is better off reinvesting profits into expansion. Those radio and TV ads aren't cheap. Neither are the factory and distribution facilities. Maybe some day, when they're more mature and don't have any real need for the next $10 million of profits, they'll start passing it out to shareholders as dividends. Until then, the shareholders will simply have to be satisfied with the growth they receive through an increased share price. If they're an income investor, they'll want to buy some FREM common stock later on, when the company starts paying, you know, *income.*

By the way, guess what we call the earnings that *don't* get paid out?

Retained earnings, which are on the balance sheet under "net worth," AKA "shareholder equity."

With EPS figured, we can also express the PE ratio. This just compares the market price of a stock to its earnings per share. Sort of like asking how much do I have to put down in order to get how much in earnings per share? If I pay $30 for a stock with an EPS of $5, I'm paying "six times earnings," or a PE ratio of 6. The exam could get real tricky and tell you that a stock has an EPS of 5 and a PE of 20...what's the price of the stock?

Twenty times five = $100.

PE of 20 means that the stock's price is 20 times greater than its EPS.

Just basic algebra and a basic understanding of the terminology.

For practice, use an income or "Profit & Loss" Statement to come up with gross margin, operating margin, pre-tax margin, and net margin.

REVENUE	$100,000,000
Cost of Goods Sold	-$50,000,000
SG&A Expenses	-$6,000,000
Depreciation, Amortization	-$4,000,000
OPERATING INCOME	$40,000,000
(Interest Expense)	-$10,000,000
PRE-TAX INCOME	$30,000,000
Taxes	-$10,000,000
NET INCOME after tax	$20,000,000
Preferred dividend	-$1,000,000
EARNINGS AVAILABLE TO COMMON	$19,000,000

ANSWERS:
- Gross margin = 50%
- Operating margin = 40%
- Pre-tax margin = 30%
- Net margin = 20%

And, to figure EPS just take the $19 million of earnings divided by the number of outstanding shares, which would be found on the company's balance sheet.

FOOTNOTES

In a company's quarterly and annual reports, the financial statements are accompanied by footnotes that help to clarify the numbers. For example, is the inventory valued as LIFO or FIFO? What does the company mean by "equivalents" in its "cash and equivalents" line item—debt securities with 1 year to maturity? Six months? Three months? How/when does a company recognize "revenue"? Is it when the company ships pies to a distributor, or only when somebody has actually paid for the product? They might even list the high and low closing prices of the stock over each quarter in the footnotes.

In general, reading the footnotes is an integral component to analyzing the financial picture of a company and almost as interesting as watching paint dry.

TECHNICAL ANALYSIS

Okay, so that's what a fundamental analyst looks at. Technical analysts don't care about that stuff. They don't care about EPS, PE ratio, current ratio, debt ratio, etc. Technical analysts primarily look at charts of stock prices. They study past trends and price patterns in order to predict future trends and price patterns. If you tried to give a technical analyst a hot stock tip concerning Frank & Emma's, he'd cut you off as soon as he had the stock symbol FREM. See, he couldn't care less if they make pies, computers, cars, or loans. All he wants to see is what the stock has been doing and, based on that, try to figure out what it's going to do next.

CHARTS AND PATTERNS

If a technical analyst sees that a stock has been trading between 20 and 25 for the past three months, he'll call the low number—20—support and the high number—25—resistance, like this:

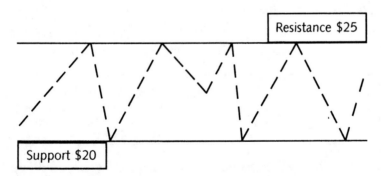

This just means that whenever the stock goes up, it meets resistance at $25, and whenever it falls, it finds support at $20. Resistance is often referred to as the market being "overbought" and support is called an "oversold" market, since everything needs at least two names in this business. So, maybe the technical trader consistently tries to buy close to $20 and sell as soon as it nears $25. Or, maybe he waits until the stock breaks through resistance before buying it, reasoning that if it hits a breakout it will keep running up. He could enter a buy-stop order slightly above the resistance point, based on the idea that if the stock price breaks through resistance it will keep going up a while. Or, maybe he hangs onto a stock until it loses support before selling, known as a breakdown/breakout. The technical trader could place a sell-stop order to sell the stock short below the support line, figuring if the stock lost support it would go into a free fall from there. That way, even if 5,000 factory workers lose their jobs and the company's bondholders get stiffed, at least this guy will make a quick profit on a well-timed short sale.

No, short-sellers are not the most popular folks on Wall Street, especially the ones who brag about their recent profits at, say, an Enron or Worldcomm employee Christmas party.

There are head and shoulders patterns for those with clearly too much time on their hands. A head and shoulders pattern signals the reversal of a trend. So, a head and shoulders "top" indicates the bull trend is about to end—a bearish signal. A head and shoulders bottom indicates the bear trend is about to end—a bullish signal.

And it would look something like this:

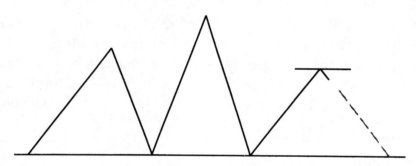

So, when you see that right shoulder beginning to form, you're supposed to conclude that the stock price is headed for a big drop. And, if this pattern were flipped upside down, just flip what I said upside down.

But, please, don't try this at home. Especially when you should be studying for a difficult test called the Series 65.

If a stock is trading in a narrow range between support and resistance, it is consolidating. A chart of a stock in consolidation appears to be moving sideways, like this:

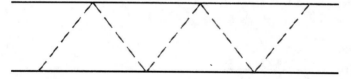

The exam might talk about consolidation as the place where sophisticated investors (mutual funds, pension funds, big Wall Street traders, etc.) are getting into or out of the stock. Since these geniuses are so incredibly savvy, when we see them buying, it must mean the stock is going up, and when we see them selling, it must mean the stock is heading down. At this accumulation or distribution point, the price moves "sideways," which is also known as "consolidation."

Technical analysts look to see how many stocks advance versus how many stocks decline. Guess what we call this? The advance/decline line. If advancers outpace decliners by 2:1, that means that twice as many stocks went up that day. And if decliners outpace advancers 2:1, that means that twice as many stocks went down that day. This tells the technical analyst something about buying/selling opportunities, based on pure supply and demand of shares in the marketplace.

Volume is also of interest to the technical analyst. Volume just indicates the total number of shares traded on, say, the NYSE, AMEX, NASDAQ, or the regional exchanges in Chicago, Philadelphia, Boston, etc. Analysts expect stock prices to rise on increasing volume. They would tend to place more significance on the fact that stock prices increased minutely on decreasing volume. Often, that situation is considered a reversal of a bullish trend, which is, of course, a bearish signal.

THEORIES

The technical analyst knows how incredibly smart he is. So much smarter than the small time investor, in fact, that all he has to do is track what odd lot investors are doing and bet the other way. If odd-lotters are buying, he sells. If odd-lotters are selling, he buys. Why? Because folks who can only afford an odd lot (<100 shares) of stock at a time always buy too high and sell too low. This is known as the **odd-lot theory**, and please do not try this at home.

The **short interest theory** has to do with how many open short sales are out there. Now, we know that short sellers profit when a stock's price drops, but this theory also recognizes that short sellers eventually have to cover or buy back their shorts. So, if there are a lot of uncovered or "open" shorts out there, they might all suddenly be forced to buy the stock in a hurry. That would create buying pressure that would drive up the stock's price, which is why a large number of open short positions is a *bullish* indicator.

Technical analysts also use indexes such as the Dow, the S&P 500, the NASDAQ 100, the Russell 2000, the Dow Jones Wilshire 5000, and others to confirm trends. If the Dow is making new highs or new lows, a technical analyst might conclude that we are in either a bull or a bear market. Remember that the number included in the index's name usually refers to how many stocks make up the index. So, the Dow Jones Wilshire 5000 covers many more stocks than the S&P 500. The Dow Jones Industrial Average (DJIA) is comprised of only 30 industrial stocks; the Dow Jones Composite is made up of only 65 stocks. The theory is that however these indexes move is how the overall market will move.

Or not.

The so-called **Dow Theory** places major importance on the movement in the DJIA and the DJ Transportation Index. Believers of the Dow Theory preach that a major trend is confirmed only when both of the aforementioned indices reach a new high or low.

INVESTMENT RISKS

Investors have to deal with many different types of risk. **Business risk** is specific to a particular company or industry. The computer manufacturing industry carries different risks than the financial services industry, right? Business risk would be exemplified by the risk of competition or the risk that the company is getting into VHS right as DVDs are taking off. That sort of thing. **Market risk** is the risk that an investment will lose its value due to an overall market decline. It is measured by the beta coefficient. All this shows is how volatile a particular stock is compared to the S&P 500. A beta of .6 means that when the market goes up or down by 1 point, this stock only moves .6 in either direction. A beta of 1.5 means that when the market moves 1 point, this stock jumps 1.5 points in either direction. So, a beta of less than 1 is less volatile than the market, while a beta of more than 1 is more volatile than the overall market.

Marketability or **liquidity risk** has to do with the ability to sell an investment quickly and at a fair price. Money market securities are easy to buy and sell at a fair price; municipal bonds, DPPs (limited partnerships), and thinly traded stocks are not. How much money could you make on your house if you had to sell it today?

Might have to drop your asking price pretty severely, unless there were, like, 10 buyers pounding on your door for an opportunity to put in a bid, right?

Legislative or **regulatory risk** means that if laws change, certain companies could be greatly affected. Suddenly, Microsoft® has to give away its operating systems for free.

Ouch. That would certainly impact the stock price, right?

Or, what if an investor bought a bunch of dividend-paying stocks in order to reap the rewards of a Republican-inspired lower tax rate on dividends, only to see a Democrat take office and rescind the kinder, gentler tax rate?

Hate it when that happens.

Non-systematic risk hits any particular stock individually. Diversifying a portfolio reduces this risk, by spreading it out among more holdings. **Systematic risk**, however, hits the whole market, so diversifying won't help to avoid that. **Systematic** and **market risk** are, again, two names for the same darned thing.

Opportunity cost is just the shoulda'/coulda' principle. If you pass up an investment opportunity to make 5%, your opportunity cost is 5%, and you need to do better than 5% with the opportunity you choose instead. If you coulda' made 5% and you end up making 7% with another investment, you made 2% better than your opportunity cost.

Political risk is part of the package if you want to invest in emerging market funds. An emerging market by definition is in a country where the markets are still, you know, emerging. They're not fully developed, a little awkward, a little bit volatile, basically like teenagers—bright future, but some days you really aren't sure if they're going to make it. You could buy 1 million shares of a networking startup company headquartered in Baghdad. That would certainly be a growth opportunity where everybody's talking about "getting in on the ground floor." Trouble is, the political insurgents in Iraq may turn that ground floor into a pile of rubble, and if the rebels sort of take over the country and nationalize all industry, well those 1 million shares might not be worth the paper they're printed on. Also, since most countries use a different currency from the American dollar, **foreign exchange risk** is also part of the package. The value of the American dollar relative to foreign currencies, in other words, is a risk to international and emerging markets investors. So, even if it's a developed market, such as Japan, if you're investing internationally into Japanese stocks, the value of the yen versus the dollar presents **foreign exchange** or **currency risk**.

RISKS TO BONDHOLDERS

Credit risk is the risk of default, which is what Moody's and Standard & Poor's measure when they rate bonds. Treasury debt has no real **default risk**, while many corporate bonds carry major default risk. Remember that "high-yield" is just a polite way of saying "junk," which means "serious default risk." **Event risk** for a bondholder entails the chance that the corporation whose bonds they own is acquired by another company that is highly leveraged. What if S&P and Moody's decide to downgrade the bond ratings once they become the obligation of the highly leveraged acquiring company?

Hate it when that happens.

Interest rate risk is the risk that rates will suddenly shoot up, sending the market price of your bond down. The longer the term on the bond, the more volatile its price. When rates go up, all bond prices fall, but the long-term bonds suffer the most. And, when rates go down, all bond prices rise, but the long-term bonds go up the most. So, a 30-year government bond has no default risk, but carries more interest rate risk than a 10-year corporate bond. As we'll mention later, "duration" is how we measure a bond's price volatility given a small change in interest rates, while "convexity" (I'm not making this up) is how we measure a bond's price volatility given a large change in interest rates.

Bet you can't wait.

Inflation or **purchasing power risk** has to do with the time value of money. If inflation erodes the value of money, an investor's return simply ain't worth what it used to be. Fixed-income investments carry purchasing power risk, which is why investors often try to beat inflation by investing in common stock. The ride might be a wild one, but the reward for investing in common stock is that we should be able to grow faster than the rate of inflation, whereas a fixed-income payment is, well, fixed, even when inflation rises. Note that high inflation does not *help* stocks. It's just that in a period of high inflation, stock will probably perform better than fixed-income securities. So, during an expansion, where inflation tends to rise, you're better off in equities/stock. During a period of decline/contraction, bonds are the place to be, since their price will rise as interest rates fall due to the cooling demand for money/capital.

Call risk is the risk that interest rates will drop and bondholders will have their bonds called. If this happens, they reinvest at lower rates and lose the full appreciation in price that would have resulted as interest rates kept falling. **Reinvestment risk** is somewhat related to call risk. When you receive the principal, you go ahead and reinvest it into new bonds—what kind of rates/yields are bonds offering now?

Low ones.

Another way to look at reinvestment risk is to remember that bonds paying regular interest checks force investors to reinvest into new bonds every few months or so. What kind of rates/yields will debt securities be offering when they go to reinvest the coupon payments?

Nobody knows, which is why it's a risk.

To avoid reinvestment risk buy a debt security that gives you nothing to reinvest along the way—zero coupons, i.e., Treasury STRIPS.

Notice how bondholders can get hit comin' or goin'. If it's a corporate bond—and even some munibonds—you could end up getting stiffed (default risk). If rates go up, the price of your bond gets knocked down (interest rate risk). If rates go down, callable bonds are called (call risk), and the party's over, plus you have to re-invest the proceeds at a lower rate than you were getting (reinvestment risk). And, even if none of the above calamities strikes, inflation could inch its way up, making those coupon payments less and less valuable (purchasing power risk.)

Oh well. If you want fixed-income, you take on these risks to varying degrees, depending on which bond you buy and when you buy it.

So, nobody ever wins by purchasing bonds?

No.

Except when they do.

Can you think of a situation where buying bonds could turn out extremely profitable? What if you purchased a bunch of 30-year, non-callable bonds right when interest rates were sky high and getting ready to plummet? Wouldn't that make your purchase price extremely cheap (rates high/price low) and, then, suddenly the market price would shoot sky high as interest rates started to fall, the faster the better?

How often is that going to happen, and how are you going to know when rates have peaked?

Beats me. But if you figure it out, please contact me at your earliest convenience.

PRACTICE QUESTIONS

1. Which of the following would be of least interest to a technical analyst?
    A. Advance/decline line
    B. Historical prices
    C. Daily trading volumes
    D. PE ratio

2. A fundamental analyst would be concerned with all of the following except
    A. Current ratio
    B. Working capital
    C. Income statements
    D. Open short positions

3. XXR common stock has a dividend payout ratio of 40%, EPS of $3.00 and a PE ratio of 12. What is the market price of XXR common stock?
    A. $12
    B. $20
    C. $36
    D. $15

4. RRT Corp. had Net Income of $10,000,000 last year. After the company pays $1,000,000 in preferred dividends, an owner of one of the company's 1,000,000 common shares would notice an EPS of
    A. $10
    B. $9
    C. $3.33
    D. $5

5. If the American dollar weakens relative to the Japanese Yen, which of the following statements is true?
    A. American exports to Japan become more competitive with Japanese goods
    B. American exports to Japan become less competitive with Japanese goods
    C. Americans vacation dollars go farther in Japan
    D. None of the above

6. Which of the following is a leading indicator?
    A. Housing starts
    B. GDP
    C. Savings
    D. Personal income

7. In order to stimulate a sluggish American economy the Federal Reserve Board might take which of the following actions?
    A. Cut taxes
    B. Raise taxes
    C. Cut the discount rate
    D. Raise the reserve requirement

8. **In order to stimulate a sluggish economy, the administrators of fiscal policy have which of the following tools available?**
   A. reserve requirement
   B. discount rate
   C. tax rates
   D. LIBOR

9. **Which of the following is the least defensive industry?**
   A. aerospace
   B. tobacco
   C. alcohol
   D. prescription drugs

10. **When a company issues long-term convertible debentures, all of the following are affected except**
    A. current assets
    B. accounts payable
    C. total assets
    D. working capital

11. **Where would an investor go to determine if a change in accounting methods has had a material effect on a company's reported earnings?**
    A. Statement of cash flows
    B. Footnotes
    C. Corporate Charter
    D. CNBC

12. **A shareholder vote to determine control of a public corporation is called a**
    A. control vote
    B. fiduciary revocation proceeding
    C. proxy contest
    D. anti-predatory proceeding

13. **A company's net profit margin is**
    A. higher than its gross margin
    B. always the same as its gross margin
    C. net income divided by revenues
    D. net income divided by interest expense

14. **A company's gross margin would include revenue and**
    A. bond interest
    B. federal taxes
    C. cost of goods sold
    D. paid-in surplus

15. **The theoretical liquidation value of a share of common stock is known as the**
    A. liquidation ratio
    B. book value
    C. par value
    D. market value

Answers

1. **ANSWER: D**

   WHY: if it has to do with the company in any way, it's not a concern for technical analysts. They only care about stock prices and what other traders are doing: volume, advance/decline, support/resistance.

2. **ANSWER: D**

   WHY: the fundamental analyst doesn't care whose shorts are open. He/ she cares about companies and industries—not traders.

3. **ANSWER: C**

   WHY: PE just means "price to earnings." If the price is 12 times the earnings, the price of the stock must be 12 x $3, or $36.

4. **ANSWER: B**

   WHY: EPS is simply "earnings available to common" divided by the number of outstanding shares. After paying the preferred dividend, the pie would be worth $9,000,000 cut into 1,000,000 slices. Each slice of equity is worth $9 in earnings.

5. **ANSWER: A**

   WHY: a "weak dollar" is equated with "cheap American goods" and "expensive foreign goods" from our perspective.
      Does that help?
      Our exports are cheap from the foreign buyer's perspective, and the foreign goods are expensive, since our weak dollars don't go very far when compared to the other stronger, inflated currency.

6. **ANSWER: A**

   WHY: memorize it; not worth delving into.

7. **ANSWER: C**

   WHY: they can't do anything with taxes. Raising reserve requirements (along with raising the discount rate and selling Treasuries) would slow down the economy, not stimulate it.

8. **ANSWER: C**

   WHY: fiscal policy is tax and spend, period.

9. ANSWER: A

WHY: which purchase could be postponed the longest, a purchase of medicine, alcohol, tobacco, or a new airplane? When you need a smoke, you need a smoke. We can always forgo something as unimportant as an airplane.

10. ANSWER: B

WHY: if you issue securities, you sell them for cash, which affects current assets, total assets, and working capital right there. How would that affect "accounts payable"? It wouldn't. Those are the bills the company owes their suppliers.

11. ANSWER: B

WHY: was there a more tempting answer given?

12. ANSWER: C

WHY: who knows—just about anything could be tested on this exam.

13. ANSWER: C

WHY: like most fancy-sounding terms, net margin is simpler than it sounds. It just means, "how much are you left with on the bottom line compared to what you started with on the top line?"

14. ANSWER: C

WHY: revenue – cost of goods sold = gross "profit." Divide that by the revenue to get "gross margin." And, if your company can't make an actual profit, just keep talking about this one long enough to exercise your stock options.

15. ANSWER: B

WHY: sure hope all those assets are listed accurately on the balance sheet.

PORTFOLIO ANALYSIS

We've now introduced many important economic concepts: GDP, economic indicators, economic policy, interest rates, investment risks, and financial statements.

In this section, we'll try to apply those concepts (and many new ones, too) toward the important goal of helping to recommend investment strategy to clients, and how to measure the success of that strategy.

YIELD

One of the easiest concepts in investing is "yield." Think of the word "yield" as "get." What do I "get" for <u>holding</u> an investment? The interest rate that a bond pays is called the "nominal yield" because "nom" means *named*, and this rate of return (what you "get") is named right on the bond. If you buy a bond from another investor, who knows the price you pay? Whatever it is affects your "current yield," but if the bond has a nominal yield of 5%, it pays $50 a year, end of story.

Well, that's the end of the story for the issuer who has to pay the $50 per year, usually in two semi-annual installments of $25.

But for investors buying the bonds at various prices on the secondary market, the story goes on in the form of "current yield." That $50 per year the issuer pays would sure be a lot sweeter if you could get it for $500 rather than for, say, $1,000, right? In fact, it would be exactly twice as sweet. Getting (yielding) $50 from an investment of $1,000 represents a 5% current yield, but getting that same $50 from a $500 investment is a 10% current yield.

Twice as sweet.

And, when the bond matures, it pays out $1,000. So if you bought it for $1,000 and you get $1,000 at maturity, big deal. However, if you bought it for $500 and receive $1,000 at maturity, you gained $500, on top of all the nice interest/coupon payments you received. Now we're talking about yield to maturity. The yield an investor would receive in the form of all the interest payments plus (or minus) the difference between what they paid for the bond, and the par value the bond pays out at maturity. If you buy a bond for less than par, your yield to maturity is higher than the coupon rate, because you get back more than you paid. If you buy a bond for more than par, your yield to maturity is lower than the coupon rate, because you get back less than you paid.

For yield to call, just remember that a call can happen a whole lot sooner than the maturity date. So, for people who bought the bond at a discount from par, their yield to call is even better, since they make their gain sooner. And, for people who bought the bond at a premium to par, their yield to call is even worse, since they realize their loss a lot sooner. I don't know about you, but if I'm making money, I like to make it fast. And, if I'm going to lose money on a bond, let's make it a slow loss and give me lots of years to collect all those interest payments that would otherwise be lost to a call.

Right?

So, the yields go in this order: nominal yield, current yield, yield to maturity, and yield to call. For a discount bond, they go UP in that order; for a premium bond, they go DOWN in that order. That is the bond see-saw covered in the chapter on debt securities, and it's also a way of measuring returns on bonds.

But, of course, the Series 65/66 is going to take these concepts a little further. For example, our discussion of bond yields so far has been very academic. We've been acting as if inflation and taxes don't exist.

After-tax, tax-free equivalent yield

Let's start with taxes. It's not what you make; it's what you keep that counts, right? If you just finished your Series 7 or 6 you remember that stuff about "tax-free equivalent yield," right? You took the corporate (taxable) bond yield and multiplied it by the percentage the investor actually keeps. Your book might have said "100% minus the tax bracket," which is just another way of saying "the percentage you actually keep." Why talk about the yield you receive, when the government takes a percentage of it every year? Let's talk about *after*-tax yield. Take the rate of return a bond pays and multiply it by the percentage you keep. If you're in the 28% federal tax bracket, you give up 28% of your return and keep 72%. So, if a bond pays you $100 a year, you keep 72% of that, or $72 per year.

Your after-tax yield on a bond paying 10% is 7.2%. Not as impressive when you factor in the taxes.

If the test gives you the yield that a municipal bond pays, just take that yield and <u>divide</u> it by 100% minus the tax bracket. For a person in the 28% bracket, take the muni yield and DIVIDE by 72%. If the muni pays a yield of 8%, that's really a tax-equivalent yield of 11.11%. That just means that given this tax bracket, a bond paying 11.11% taxable would LEAVE you with exactly $80 or an 8% after-tax yield. This investor would find that a municipal bond yielding 8% is exactly equal (equivalent) to a corporate/taxable bond paying 11.11%. So if a munibond offered 8% and a corporate offered anything less than 11.11%, he'd buy the municipal bond. If a munibond offered 8% and a comparable corporate bond offered more than 11.11%, he'd buy the corporate bond.

What if the exam is in an especially foul mood the day you take it and includes the fact that the munibond investor is in a 3% state tax bracket and a 30% federal tax bracket? Use the number 33% (67%) in your calculations. So, if a corporate bond pays 9%, I'd multiply that by .67 to get a tax-free equivalent yield of 6.0%. If they gave me a muni yielding 7%, this investor's tax-equivalent yield would be .07 divided by .67 or 10.45%.

As if the exam weren't hard enough already.

Oh yeah, and if they give you the nominal yield and the YTM, use the YTM. YTM (yield to maturity) is generally the most important yield to an investor.

Yield vs. total return

NASAA has adopted a statement of policy on the sale of investment company shares that makes a very big deal out of the difference between "yield" and "total return" for a mutual fund. If you pay $10 for a mutual fund share and receive $1 in an income or dividend distribution, your yield (your "get") is 10%. What if the fund share dropped $2 in the meantime? That's bad! That's a drop of 20% in value. Suddenly, who cares about the 10% "yield," when you are, in fact, down by more than that. Your "total return" is actually negative. If you go down 20% and the dividend is only "up 10%," your "total return is –10%.

Yowza.

Of course, if you get a $1 dividend on this $10 mutual fund share and the share price goes up—appreciates—that's a good thing. Let's say you get the dividend of $1 and the share price appreciates $2. Now you're up in total (total return) $3. Three bucks on top of $10 is a 30% total return. Doesn't have to be a mutual fund, either. Any stock or bond would have a "total return" because there are exactly TWO ways an investment can help you. Number one, it pays you some income and, number two, it goes UP in value (don't be a smart aleck and ask about short sales, please). A stock pays a dividend and goes up in price. Cool! A bond makes a bunch of interest payments and is then cool enough to go UP in value. Way cool!

That's total return. It can be positive or negative depending on how things turn out for you. If the question gives you dividends, capital gains distributions (mutual funds), and share appreciation, factor in all three.

Are you starting to notice that most of this fancy-sounding stuff really isn't?

Good.

INFLATION-ADJUSTED OR "REAL" RETURN

Of course, inflation is also a factor. If you receive a 4% after-tax return from a bond, is that enough to help you pay bills when you're retired?

Not if the price of everything you need to buy is rising by more than 4%, right? What if you're receiving 4%, but the price of everything (inflation) is up, say, 8%?

You're falling behind.

So, if inflation (the price of stuff) is rising, you need a return on your investment that is rising even higher and faster than the rate of inflation.

This, of course, is called inflation-adjusted return, because we never get real creative with the language of investing. But, since everything needs at least two names, we can also refer to this as "real return." Just subtract the rate of inflation from a portfolio's return to get inflation-adjusted/real return. If your investment returns 8% when inflation is 3%, you have an inflation-adjusted return of 5%. If your investment returns 3% when inflation is 8%, you have a nasty inflation-adjusted return of –5%.

Which means you won't be eating filet mignon or drinking Dom Perignon that year. Unless you're already rich.

Remember that language is often used to intimidate. Like any other type of bully, though, when you challenge it, it quickly backs down. Inflation-adjusted return—ooh, I'm scared. After-tax return...stop, I'm all a' quiver.

HOLDING PERIOD AND ANNUALIZED RETURN

Two very easy and related measuring sticks are called "holding period return" and "annualized return." If it takes you three years to achieve a 9% return, your holding period return is 9%. In other words, who cares how long it took to get 9%—you got 9% over your holding period. But, if you like to measure everything in one-year increments, you annualize everything. You would take the 9% holding period return and divide it by the three years it took to get it. This way you'd have only a 3% annualized rate of return. It's more fun to take the return you get in one month and then multiply it by 12 (12 months in a year) to get your annualized rate of return from that direction.

Get a 10% return in one month and suddenly you're thinking of it as a 120% annualized rate of return, even if the bank is still counting it the same either way at the teller window. In fact, many daytraders probably became drunk with annualized return calculations. Make 100% in one day and then multiply that by 365 for an annualized rate of return of...and before you can finish your calculation the stock has already crashed and burned and there's nothing left to count at the teller window.

So, if it took more than one year to get a return, divide the percent return by the number of years: 9% over 3 years is a 3% yearly (annualized) return. A 5% return over 6 months would give you a 10% annualized return, since there are 12 months per year, right? Two 6-month periods, so double that 5% to get a 10% annualized return if you're obsessed with rates of return.

Personally, I like actual cash, but lots of folks get more excited by rates of return. The bank will count our returns exactly the same way, though. Assuming we have any to count.

POSSIBLE OUTCOMES, DEALING WITH "RISK"

We measure the risk of a stock in terms of its volatility—its tendency to go up and down. We measure how much a particular stock went up and down compared to the overall market and call this "beta." Remember that a beta of "1" means a security moves exactly in step with the overall market (S&P 500). A beta of more than 1 implies that the stock is more volatile than the overall market, while a beta of less than 1 implies that the stock is less volatile than the overall market. The exam might want you to say that a stock with a beta of more than 1 (1.5, for example) will outperform the market when stock prices rise but underperform the market when stock prices fall. Or, we could reverse that if the beta were less than 1, right?

Expected return

We'll be discussing "Modern Portfolio Theory" soon, and I know you can't wait for that. Expected return is a major tenet of that school of thought. See, if we feel an investment will most likely return 8% and has a 75% probability of actually doing so, we can say the investment has an expected return of 6%. In other words 8% times the 75% probability of getting the 8% equals 6% (.75 x .08 = .06). How do we know the investment will achieve 8%, let alone that it has a 75% chance of doing so?

We take historical outcomes and assume those patterns will be repeated. More likely, the exam would express two possible outcomes. That same investment has a 75% chance of returning 8% and a 50% chance of returning 10%. What's the total expected return? Just take 75% of 8% (6%) and add it to 50% of 10% (5%). That's a total expected return of 11%.

What happens if we expect 11% and get –18%?

Hate it when that happens.

Rather than use numbers or calculations, the exam might just want you to define expected return as "possible return on an investment weighted by the likelihood that the return will occur." The exam, remember, has absolutely no social life.

Standard deviation

Since our expected return is simply that—an expectation—we might want to also know how much our actual returns could deviate from our expectations (hint: a *lot*). Standard deviation compares how much an investment is *likely* to deviate from its expected return. So, a stock with an anticipated return of 5% won't look as good through this lens of "standard deviation" if the expected deviation is 10% compared to a 5% anticipated return on an investment expected to deviate only 3%. I think the bank will still count the 5% the same at the teller window, but this is just a way of analyzing portfolio returns for some folks. Standard deviation is expressed as a percent, so a standard deviation of 5.5 means that our actual return could be 5.5 points above or below our expected return. If you get a question on this (bet on it), just add and subtract the number from the expected return. If the expected return is 10% and the standard deviation is 5, the most likely range of outcomes will be from 5% to 15%.

How does somebody make a prediction of a stock's future return and than add another prediction on top of that as to how much he could be wrong?

Pay him $300 an hour and he'll be happy to explain it to you, nice and slow.

Alpha

So, if a portfolio has an expected return of, say, 8%, will it actually get an 8% return?

Yes.

Unless it doesn't. If the expected return is 8%, but we only see a 6% return, we could call that "negative alpha," which sounds so much better than "missed it by two." The portfolio manager apparently didn't do as well as he should have. But, if the portfolio manager took a portfolio with an expected return of 8% and actually got a 10% return, that excess return could be referred to as "positive alpha." Portfolio managers who get excess returns or show positive alpha are said to be adding value with their money management skills.

Sharpe ratio

Basically, the Sharpe ratio tells you if you're being fairly compensated for the risk you're taking. Mathematically, it would be the actual return you get minus the "riskless rate of return," divided by the standard deviation.

In other words, the answer to any question on the Sharpe ratio is "C."

No, you can't throw in the towel on any of these questions, even the goofy ones. At least understand the basics. First, the Sharpe ratio measures volatility, just like alpha, beta, and standard deviation. Second, the higher the number, the better. Third, the "riskless rate of return" is the yield on 3-month T-bills. So, if an investment gets a 10% return when the yield on 3-month T-bills was 5%, we're down to 5%. That actually makes sense—why take risk unless you're doing better than the "riskless rate of return" on 3-month T-bills? Three-month T-bills have no default risk and virtually no interest rate risk, so if I can't get any better than what they pay, I'm staying in T-bills. Anyway, we're down to a return that is 5% better than the "riskless rate of return." If the standard deviation is 5, we'd have 5 divided by 5, or a Sharpe ratio of 1. Notice how if the standard deviation had been, say, 10, that Sharpe ratio would have started with a decimal point.

Which is bad.

The higher the Sharpe ratio, the better the investor is being compensated for the risk he took.

Correlation

Some people like to find pairs of stocks that move together or, perhaps, move in opposite directions. If ABC and XYZ tend to rise and fall together, we say they have a perfect correlation of "1." If ABC gains 5%, so does XYZ. If ABC loses 5%, so does XYZ. What if the correlation is ".5"? Then, if ABC gains 10%, XYZ only gains 5%. What if the correlation is "–.5"? Then, if ABC gains 10%, XYZ will *lose* 5%. What if the correlation is "0"? Then the two securities aren't correlated.

How does correlation relate to risk measurements? The exam might want you to know that stocks which are negatively correlated move in opposite directions. Therefore, if one goes down, the other goes up, balancing out the volatility of the overall portfolio. Eventually, we'll see that Modern Portfolio Theory has influenced fiduciaries' standards of "prudence" by showing that no one investment is too risky to touch. Rather, the risk of one security can be balanced by investing in another, especially if the two are negatively correlated.

Duration

Speaking of risk measurements, the exam might be cranky enough to start talking about "duration." Bond duration has to do with measuring how a change in interest rates would affect a bond's price. The higher a bond's duration, the more sensitive it is to a change in interest rates. So, when interest rates go up, they smack the prices of bonds with high durations much harder than those with lower durations.

Another way of talking about duration is to say that at some point all the coupon payments received by an investor will represent what the investor paid for the bond. If you pay par for a 30-year bond paying $50 a year, it would take you 20 years to get your $1,000 back, right? So the duration could be expressed as 20 years. Since a coupon payment of 5% is pretty low and a 30-year maturity pretty long, the bond's duration is high. A bond with a high duration is more susceptible to a rise in interest rates. To express that mathematically, we could see how much the bond's price would decline if rates rose 1%. Just multiply the 20 (duration) by 1% to get an expected 20% decline in the bond's price should rates rise by just 1 point. And if rates shot up 2%, the price decline would be 40%. That's pretty volatile. If the bond paid a higher coupon, you'd get your original investment back sooner, knocking down the duration and making the bond's price less sensitive to interest rates.

Remember: the lower the coupon and the longer the maturity, the higher/greater the duration. And the greater the duration, the more susceptible the bond's price is to interest rate spikes.

For coupon bonds, the duration is always less than the years to maturity, thankfully. I'd sure hate to be planning to get my original money back several years after they would have already given me my original money back.

But, for zero coupon bonds, the duration IS the maturity.

Convexity

As mentioned earlier, while duration is a good measurement of a bond's price movement given a small change in interest rates, convexity is a better measurement for a bond's price volatility given a *large* change in interest rates.

Monte Carlo Simulation

Finally, there is a computer simulation we could run with our client to show how a portfolio would react to various developments. If interest rates went to this level, your portfolio would look like this. If the average duration went to this number, the portfolio would look like that.

PLANNING FOR THE FUTURE

Future value

Portfolio analysts also like to talk about future value and present value. Just means that we can either start with what you invest and project what it will be worth in the future, or we can start with what you need to achieve in the future and backwards plan how much you need to invest to get there.

Yes, they pay people to perform these amazing calculations.

Future value—often cleverly abbreviated as FV—takes an investment and assigns a given rate of return over a particular time frame. For example, if you invest $10,000 today and achieve a 10% return each year over a 5-year period, the future value of your investment will be:

$$FV = \$1 \times (1 + R)^T$$

R means "rate of return" and T means "time." Remember, our returns are compounded. So if you get 10% the first year, you'll have more money earning 10% the next year, and so on. Even if it's the same 10% rate of return, it's always 10% of a bigger number. Einstein said that compounding interest was at least as fascinating as $E = mc^2$. Just put the old Nobel Prize money into relatively safe debt securities and watch your money grow faster and faster every year.

So, if we expect to get 10% each year over a 5-year period, we would say that the FV (future value) of a dollar invested today will be $1 x (1.10)^5$. 1.10 is just the "1" plus 10%. Why use a 1? It represents "100% of what we have up to now," and that catches the compounding effect. It means that we're taking the money we start with (1 or 100%) and adding the 10% gain, and we do this every year—compounding interest. Each year we start with more and get the same 10% return on a bigger amount of principal.

So what we're doing in our example is multiplying 1.10 by itself 5 times, then multiplying that answer (1.61) by the dollar invested. The dollar would be worth $1.61, and you can add as many zeroes as your client is willing to invest. One million bucks now equals 1.61 million.

And then we can get all depressed by factoring in taxes (after-tax return), inflation (inflation-adjusted return), and risk (risk-adjusted return), rather than enjoying an easy gain of about 600K.

No wonder they call economics "the dismal science."

The formula I just used is the most simplified version; unfortunately, I've also seen a more egghead version that looks like this:

$$P_n = P_o (1 + r)^n$$

All that's doing is putting a big "P" where I put the "FV," which means that "P" is the future value. The little "n" is just the number of years the portfolio will be compounding. Instead of just using "$1" the egghead who wrote the formula this way uses "Po," which means "the principal you put in."

So, it's really the same idea and formula expressed differently. See? You can't even get these folks to agree on the same *formula*, let alone draw the same conclusions from these formulas.

We just looked at a magical portfolio that compounds conveniently once per year, right on schedule. Well, if we had an investment that compounded more frequently—every six months, quarter, or month—that would be known technically as a "really cool thing." So tell the exam that the more frequently an investment return compounds, the better that is for the investor, should it care to ask such an obvious and silly question.

Present value

We can also amuse ourselves by working backward in the form of present value. Present value starts with a need in the future. You need a certain amount of money to put your kid through college. Given a particular rate of return, how much do you need to invest today to get there? That's present value. Personally, I'd rename it something like the "put-in ratio," as it tells me how much I must "put in" to get where I need to go. But present value makes the insiders feel smarter, so we'll humor them, at least long enough to pass this exam.

The formula for present value is:

$$PV = FV / (1 + R)^T$$

So, we're just working backwards. For future value, we said that $1 invested today at 10% interest would be worth $1.61 in five years. Well, what if your client said she needed exactly $161,000 in five years—how much must she invest at 10% to get there?

Start with the future value of $161,000 and DIVIDE by 1.61 to arrive at the amazing conclusion that she needs to put in $100,000 today. Where did we get 1.61? We took our assumption of a 10% compounded return and added it to the 1 or "100% of what we have up to now (1.10). Then we multiplied 1.10 by itself 5 times (which is how compound interest works over a five-year period).

How do we know she'll get a 10% compounded return?

Beats me. In fact, if you can give me a guaranteed 10% compounded return, please email me at your earliest convenience. I'll liquidate everything I own and stick it in that magic hopper.

But this is all academic, right? Just an exam.

Internal rate of return

The exam might want you to say that the internal rate of return is what makes an investment's future value equal to its present value because the exam has all the personality of a lug nut. Basically, that 10% number we were using in our future value and present value calculations is our "internal rate of return."

And, it relates to expected return and standard deviation in the sense that if a client wants to go for a 10% return, we have to show her how far a particular portfolio could deviate from that expectation. Can she handle putting in $100,000 and watching it turn into $70,000?

If not, we need a portfolio that presents less risk.

Net present value

Another concept the test might spring on you is called net present value. To calculate net present value we need an investment that produces a stream of income. Then, we see if that future stream of income is worth the cost of getting it. If we're a corporation, we try to see if building a new call center will generate enough income to make it worth our investment of capital. Technically, we discount the anticipated income to its present value, using our required rate of return as the discount rate. If we require a 5% return, we use that as our "discount rate" and then basically run the calculation we discussed under "present value," where we started with our goal and then worked backward to see where we'd need to start. When a company does this, they're looking to see if this discounted present value would be greater than the cost of the investment. If so, the net present value is positive and represents an opportunity. If the discounted present value is less than the cost of the project, net present value is negative, and they'll skip it.

An investment adviser could calculate net present value for any investment with an income stream associated with it. One form of income stream would be the expected dividends provided by common stock. So, many analysts use a "dividend discount model" to determine if a stock is worth more or less than what it's currently selling for in the open market. The analysts take the expected cash flow from dividends in the future and use a certain discount rate (rate of return) to see if the stock is trading above or below its net present value. This is, basically, what Warren Buffett has made a fortune doing. He knows how to calculate the true value of a business using this type of valuation, and he's only looking to buy stocks below their calculated present value. What happens if an analyst assumes a certain stream of dividends that doesn't materialize?

Ouch. Hate it when that happens.

If your luck is running dangerously low on exam day, the test might also want you to know that if interest rates rise, we'd have to use a higher discount rate when running this calculation, lowering the present value of the stock, and vice versa for falling interest rates.

BENCHMARKS

How well should any portfolio perform? Portfolio managers often compare their portfolios to some benchmark, like the S&P 500 index. The best comparisons compare a portfolio to a benchmark that most accurately reflects the make-up of the portfolio. In other words, if your client owns only technology stocks, why compare it to the overall market (S&P 500 or the Dow Jones Wilshire 5000)? More accurately, we would compare it to a technology index that more closely matches up with the make-up of the portfolio. The NASDAQ 100, for example, would be a common benchmark for a technology portfolio manager. If my client is into biotech and pharmaceutical stocks only, I need benchmark portfolios that reflect that make-up. And, if they invest in blue-chip companies in various industries, maybe I use a blue chip index or the Dow Jones Industrial Average as my benchmark. If I manage a small-cap portfolio, I'm trying to beat the Russell 2000. If I'm the manager of a mid-cap portfolio, I'm hoping to beat the S&P MidCap 400. If I'm a bond fund manager, I'm being matched up with various bond indexes, such as those compiled by Lehman Brothers.

And, I hope I can beat these indexes I'm using as benchmarks; otherwise, the client could just stick all her money in low-cost, no-brainer index mutual funds or ETFs (closed-end index funds).

INVESTMENT STYLES

How do I decide which stocks to put in my client's portfolio? Well, there are lots of ways of valuing stocks. In the economics discussion we talked about earnings per share (EPS) and dividend payout ratios. I'd certainly pay more for a stock that keeps reporting higher earnings and keeps paying out more to me in the form of dividends. But how much should I pay for earnings?

That, as you may recall, is expressed as the Price to Earnings ratio or PE ratio. And it's exactly what it sounds like: market price compared to (divided by) the earnings. If a company has Earnings per Share (EPS) of $3, that's great. The question is, how much are you willing to pay for those earnings? If you pay $30 for the stock, you just paid 10 times the earnings, or a PE ratio of 10. What if the stock costs $90? If it's still earning $3, you paid a PE ratio of 30 (30 times as much as the EPS). What if the stock has no earnings and you're willing to pay $100 a share, anyway?

You're crazy and I think I remember you from that daytraders convention in Atlanta back in '99.

GROWTH INVESTING

Growth stocks have high PE ratios, assuming they have an "E" at all. During the tech bubble YHOO was trading for 1,000 times earnings.

And then the drugs wore off.

More established "blue chip companies" usually trade at lower PEs, because there isn't so much speculation/expectation built into the price. We know that GE is a great company, but we also know they won't triple their earnings next year. So the PE should be lower than some dot-com stock that might implode tomorrow or grow earnings by a factor of 100. The higher the PE ratio, the more speculative the stock.

What's a "good" or "bad" Price-to-Earnings ratio?

Nobody knows, and if the exam ever asked you to determine a good from a bad PE ratio, sue somebody.

It's the American way.

So, what is a "growth investor"?

Would you believe an investor looking for growth?

Yep. If you invest in a stock because you think it will grow faster than other stocks or the market overall, you call this thing a growth stock and consider yourself a growth investor. You usually pay dearly for any earnings the company might or might not have at this point. But you're convinced this is the next Coca-Cola or Microsoft, so you're willing to pay a premium for the bright future that inconveniently hasn't shown up yet. Maybe you think Frank & Emma's will someday be the powerful brand that Dunkin' Donuts® or Starbucks® has become. Well, that future hasn't shown up yet, so much of the price you pay for FREM common stock is propped up by the crutch of speculation. If Frank & Emma's reports disappointing earnings one quarter to Wall Street and then the SEC, the stock price could easily drop quicker than you can eat a slice of lemon meringue.

That's growth investing. Lots of ups and downs. But a growth investor will deal with the frequent strikeouts in order to enjoy a few home runs along the way.

VALUE INVESTING

What's a "value investor"?

Would you believe an investor looking for value?

Who does this sort of thing?

Well, it's not for the faint of heart. You take a stock that has been trounced lately, trashed in the media, and maybe even mentioned in headlines along with the phrase "Fully Cooperating with the SEC."

The market panics and dumps this stock just as irrationally as they bought it on the way up.

Take a deep breath. Look at the financials. What are the sales figures? What's the balance sheet look like—are they strong or vulnerable? Is there any more bad news buried in these numbers?

If not, maybe we see that this suddenly out-of-favor stock is worth $10, even though the herd of spooked investors is selling it for $2.50.

Now there's a value opportunity!

What happens if you load up at $2.50 and the stock goes to zero?

Hate it when that happens.

Again, it's not for the faint of heart.

Speaking of "value investors," the price-to-book ratio often signals buying opportunities as well. The "book value" of a stock is a worst-case scenario. Take all the tangible assets of a company and subtract all the liabilities. In other words, if we held a fire sale tomorrow and sold all the tangible assets (the securities, the building, the equipment, the $15,000 umbrella stands), used the proceeds to pay the creditors, then the preferred stock holders, what would be left per share for the common stock holder?

That's the book value per share.

If the book value per share of a stock is $5, and you see it trading for just $3, wouldn't you be tempted to buy it? Worst case, the company goes out of business and gives you $5 per share in proceeds, when you only paid $3. Sounds like a margin of safety, right? Benjamin Graham (almost certainly not on the test) was Warren Buffett's teacher at Columbia University, and he was forever looking to buy stocks below their book value. That way if the company stumbled, there was room for this type of bad news in the stock's price. He called this a "margin of safety," which, also, will not be on the exam, unless it is.

Likewise, if the book value is $3 and you pay $30 for the stock, you bought it at a price-to-book ratio of 10. So, just as with the PE ratio, the exam could simplify things and want you to know that growth investors are likely to buy stocks trading at high PE and price-to-book ratios, while value investors prefer stocks trading at lower ratios/ multiples. Companies that put together growth and value indexes would explain the mathematical criteria for determining which stocks go into the growth index and which go into the value index. Wherever they set the cutoff point, the growth index will have stocks trading at high multiples, while the value index will have stocks trading at lower multiples. Krispy Kreme® used to be a growth stock. Now that it's run into some serious snags (like any great company), it's a value stock. Why? The price has plummeted. Should I be bummed out? If I were a growth investor, I probably bought it high and am freaking out that it's now trading low and doesn't show any immediate signs of earnings acceleration. If I'm a value investor, I'm salivating right now like a crowd watching the hot, glazed donuts coming down the assembly line at 7:00 a.m. as I contemplate how cheaply I can buy this stock. Value investors like to buy great companies on the cheap. We just hope they don't get a whole lot cheaper after we buy them.

Another way to think about the difference between "growth" and "value" investing is to think in terms of two different properties that a potential home buyer might be considering. One is a brand-new townhouse going up in a hot, new area of town, near the best schools, the best restaurants, shopping, and entertainment outlets, etc. The price tag is very high, but since it's in such a hot market, the market price will only go up from here, and, clearly, no price could be too high for this hot property. That's a "growth" investment. You pay a lot, but you expect to get a lot, too, given the inevitable increase in price that inconveniently hasn't materialized yet. Another property on the other side of the tracks is a run-down two-bedroom bungalow. As-is, this thing is a dog, but, still, the market seems to be giving too much weight to the ugly aluminum siding and dilapidated windows—both of which can easily be fixed up. After all, doesn't anybody else notice that this "ugly" house is sitting on a double lot, has a three-car garage, and is just two blocks away from public transportation? That's a "value" investment. Buy it low, wait for the major improvements, and, some day, this thing will be worth a lot more than the low price it's going for now.

ACTIVE VS. PASSIVE

So, who buys growth and value stocks: active portfolio managers, or passive portfolio managers?

Yes.

If you seek out particular stocks (or bonds), you are an *active* manager. If you simply buy "growth" or "value" index funds, you are a *passive* manager. Let the words talk to you: Is the investor actively determining that one investment is more attractive than another? If so, that's "active portfolio management," because even the simplest of concepts have to be dressed up to look fancier than they really are. Now, who uses active management styles—fundamental or technical analysts?

Yes. You could determine that ORCL is a better investment right now than MSFT by looking at the fundamentals (balance sheet, income statement), or you could just look at the price patterns revealed in charts (technical analysis). Either way, if you're coming down on the side of one stock versus another, you're using active stock selection or active portfolio management.

A passive management style usually involves the use of indexes rather than trying to pick one investment over another. You could buy a "growth index fund" or a "value index fund," but you would never try to pick one growth or value stock over another. You've probably heard of the closed-end funds known as "ETFs." These "exchange-traded funds" are index funds that you can trade throughout the day, just like any other share of stock. Maybe you want to do as well as the Wilshire 5000—if so, buy the ETF that represents that index. I suppose if you were trying to pick the NASDAQ 100 opportunity over the Dow Jones Wilshire 5000 opportunity, you'd be "actively" selecting investments, but, usually, you want to equate the exclusive use of indexing as a *passive* investment style. Your decision to pick one index over another probably has more to do with your perceived risk tolerance than your opinion as to which index will perform better this coming year. Using this passive indexing strategy, you will pay lower expenses, because these funds aren't doing a lot of trading and, therefore, don't have to extract big management fees. Also, if you never want to be beaten by an index, you can join it, right? Have you ever paid big management fees and sales charges for an actively managed "small cap" fund that can't even beat a "small cap index" like the Russell 2000? Doesn't that kind of tick you off? If so, just buy the index fund that will neither beat nor lose to the index, and will cost you less in any event.

No, I do not have a referral relationship with any of these index fund companies. Except Vanguard®.

BUY AND HOLD

The phrase "buy and hold" might pop up. Whether I'm a growth, value, passive, or active manager, I could use "buy and hold" as a strategy.

Surprisingly, what this approach involves is buying and then holding.

There are lower transaction costs, because you aren't trading and generating commissions/markups, not to mention short-term capital gains. So there's some potentially confusing overlap there with passive management. Both can lead to lower transaction costs and fewer short-term capital gains. The subtle difference would be illustrated by this analogy. One investor buys index funds because of the low management fees; however, he's constantly trading his ETFs and generating his own transaction costs (commissions, markups) and, possibly, short-term capital gains. He's "passive" in the sense that he doesn't pick one stock over another, but he's sort of missing the point by trading these indexes like any other share of stock. A "buy and hold" investor using index funds would—get this—buy them and then...*hold* them.

Wow. Maybe this stuff really *is* rocket science.

Right. And Paris Hilton is talented, Adam Sandler is a comic genius, and I have a glass house I'd like to sell you in Florida right before the next hurricane season.

But, as always, I'll refrain from expressing any opinions on this subject matter.

MODERN PORTFOLIO THEORY, EFFICIENT MARKET THEORY, RANDOM WALK

Speaking of which, let's talk about efficient market theorists, modern portfolio people, random walkers, and various other cynics. First, what's the best way to choose investments?

What, you thought all this stuff we're talking about could actually answer such an important question? Boy, are you naïve!

Actually, this is the big question nobody's really been able to answer yet. Warren Buffett has made billions actively picking stocks. Efficient market theorists, who collectively haven't made as much money investing as Mr. Buffett, think stock picking is useless. You may be shocked to discover that efficient market theorists feel that the market is—get this—efficient. Sure, that's why YHOO traded for 1,000 times earnings and why a web site selling pet food could be just as valuable as Exxon-Mobil, a company that makes, like, a profit and will probably be in business at least through next Friday.

Sorry, no more opinions.

The exam might want you to know that the efficient market theory assumes that all information is absorbed instantly and immediately acted upon. In other words, all known information about an investment is already "priced in," so why try to pick one investment opportunity over another? The market is so efficient that everything is worth exactly what it's trading for. Mr. Buffett has simply been getting lucky the past four or five decades.

If you see any reference to "CAPM" on the test, this is in the same neighborhood. To do a CAPM (capital asset pricing model) presentation, just take out a cocktail napkin and draw a little grid. Then figure out how much "risk" the client can stand, and place this as a point on the graph and put him into a portfolio that lies precisely there on the little graph in order to get precisely *this* amount of return. CAPM is attributed with the following revelation: There are two types of risk, one which can be diversified away, and one which can't. *Diversifiable risk* is the risk connected with owning the securities of specific companies. To remember this concept, please say the following words aloud: Enron, WorldComm, Pets-dot-com.

With me?

See, if those three wonderful investment opportunities had represented only, say, 3% of your portfolio, none of the impending implosions would have really hurt you that much. You, effectively, diversified away this so-called "non-systematic risk." Since this risk can be avoided, investors should not expect to be compensated for taking this risk. Well, if the first type of risk is "diversifiable," you can probably guess what we call the other type of risk—non-diversifiable. That's right, I don't care how many different companies or industries are represented in your portfolio, if the overall market crashes, they're all going down with the ship.

Right?

Well, this is the risk that investors should expect to be compensated for taking. We measure this risk in terms of beta, which is the volatility of one investment compared to the volatility of the overall market. Once we know the beta of an investment or of the overall portfolio, we'd be hoping to achieve excess returns, which are—believe it or not—returns in excess of our expectations based on the beta.

Dang, no wonder college professors make so much money!

And, this concept could also be expressed in a graph as the "Security Market Line." The book that really threw the spotlight on the efficient market theory movement is called *A Random Walk Down Wall Street* by Burton Malkiel. One of the best books I've read on investing, actually, so after you pass your exam, you might pick up a copy for yourself. It purports that actively picking stocks is about as effective as throwing darts at the stock page. Actually, it doesn't say that, but that's what people took it to mean, so even the exam will be inclined to oversimplify the book in those terms. According to the exam, random selection is just as good as active stock picking to proponents of the random walk/efficient market theories.

The random walk theory/efficient market theory are related to what the exam might call "Modern Portfolio Theory." In the old days investors would consider the risk of any one security. Modern Portfolio Theory looks at how a particular investment affects the risk/reward ratio of the entire portfolio. It also assumes that investors are risk-averse, no matter what they tell you when you sit down to do a needs analysis. Since investors don't like risk, we could say that they would prefer to make, say, 10% through the least risky path or that, given a particular level of risk, they want to get the highest possible return. So, what these folks try to do is construct "optimal portfolios," which means that the investor is likely to get the highest possible return given the amount of risk he/she is willing to bear. If we reverse the words, we get "portfolio optimization," which sure sounds impressive, don't it? I mean, who wouldn't want some of that in their investing lives? An optimal portfolio has the greatest return for a certain amount of risk taken. A graph of optimal portfolios produces a diagram called an *efficient frontier*. Any point on this graph that is behind the frontier is a portfolio that is not optimal. There are different portfolios that fall along this efficient frontier, so which one is better? It depends on the amount of risk the investor is willing to take. All of these optimal portfolios are most likely constructed of a percentage mix of equity, bonds, and cash (money market), so these various mixes can, theoretically, determine the amount of risk involved. Whichever portfolio the investor chooses, we just want to make sure it lies along (not behind) the efficient frontier.

We discussed expected return, standard deviation, and correlation, all of which are major tenets of Modern Portfolio Theory (MPT). MPT is also highly interested in asset allocation. Rather than selecting one stock over another, or one bond over another, we, instead, try to come up with the perfect mix of assets. Maybe it's 60% stock, 30% bonds, and 10% cash. Or, maybe it's 30% stock, 60% bonds, and 10% cash. Either way, what we're doing, obviously, is allocating our investment capital into various asset classes. Asset allocation. Ideally, we'd like to see negative correlation between these asset classes so that if it's a lousy year for bonds, maybe it will be a great year for equities. We could certainly go a lot deeper than just stock-bonds-cash. Inside a 50% stock allocation, we could put 10% on large-cap, 10% on mid-cap, 20% on small-cap, 5% on international, and 5% on emerging markets, just as we could divide our bond allocation into percentages for long-term, intermediate-term, or short-term, or divide the bond allocation among taxable, non-taxable, high-yield, investment grade, etc. Of course, no matter what we decide, given a nice PowerPoint® presentation with a full-color pie chart, this stuff is almost guaranteed to impress the heck out of a potential customer.

Rather than selecting investments, MPT would have us merely "rebalance" our portfolio in terms of the percentages devoted to the various classes of investments. You could actively rebalance your portfolio if you weren't a true believer in efficient markets—if you thought you could spot an opportunity in, say, bonds before the rest of the market gets hip. That's called "tactical asset allocation." But, more likely, you do believe in efficient markets and, therefore, you keep your clients in a certain rigid mix of equity, debt, and money market securities based on age and risk tolerance. That's called "strategic asset allocation," and to date it has been just as effective at helping people lose money as any other investment style out there, so don't knock it. Also, we could do systematic rebalancing on, say, a monthly, quarterly, or annual basis. We might be trying to keep the portfolio in balance with our intended goals, or maybe we're so rigid that if our 10% in small caps has now grown to represent 20% of our portfolio, for God sakes dump those lousy equities that are increasing in value and screwing up our nice, neat little full-color pie chart.

I'm sorry. I promised to keep the opinions out of this, didn't I?

DIVERSIFICATION

We talked about "asset allocation," which is a kissin' cousin of "diversification." Where they differ is that asset allocation puts percentages of capital into stocks, bonds, and cash. Diversification might actually be part of an active stock selector's plan. I select 10 stocks, but most of them aren't in the same industry and tend not to move in the same direction at the same time. The exam might even talk about "negative correlation" among these stocks, meaning, basically, that as one goes down, another goes up. Many people think of this as the ultimate form of diversification. Probably the ones who check their account balance every day, I'm guessing. So, a diversified portfolio of stocks would not contain all technology or pharmaceutical companies, in other words. But they could all be stocks, or all bonds, while an asset allocator would always have a percentage in equities, bonds, and "cash," and might further divide the equity percentage among large-cap, mid-cap, small-cap, etc.

MARKET CAP

The smaller the company, the more volatile the stock price usually, so you need to know that small cap stocks are riskier than mid cap stocks, which, in turn, are riskier than large cap stocks. "Cap" is like a hip way of abbreviating "capitalization" or "market capitalization." All "market capitalization" involves is taking the total number of outstanding shares a company has and multiplying that by today's closing price on the stock. The total value of all the outstanding shares. If that's a "small" number, we call it a "small cap" stock. A stock with a market capitalization under $1 billion is usually considered small cap. If Frank & Emma's has 10 million shares outstanding, and the shares close @$25 today, the market capitalization is simply $250 million, which makes it a small cap stock. Mid cap would be up to $5 billion, and above that is the "large cap" world of IBM, Microsoft, GE, etc.

I would not expect the test to ask that, because those numbers are hardly gospel and subject to constant revision. In fact, if you checked three other sources right now, you'd end up with three new sets of numbers. Know the concept of "market cap" and remember that small cap = higher risk/reward, while large cap = lower risk/reward. Also, the stocks that are smaller than small cap, guess what we call them?

Micro cap.

PRACTICE QUESTIONS

16. **For every 1% change in interest rates, a bond rises or falls by 10%. Therefore, the duration is**
    A. 20%
    B. –10
    C. 10
    D. 15

17. **An investor needs to have $90,000 available to fund her daughter's education in 7 years. Which of the following should the investment representative discuss with the client?**
    A. Future value
    B. Present value
    C. Sharpe ratio
    D. Convexity

18. **All of the following measure volatility except**
    A. Sharpe ratio
    B. Standard deviation
    C. Net present value
    D. Beta

19. **Which of the following investment selection approaches would most likely involve an analysis of a company's net margin?**
    A. Efficient Market Theory (EMT)
    B. Value Investing
    C. Modern Portfolio Theory
    D. Technical Analysis

20. **Which of the following Sharpe ratios indicates that the investor has been fairly compensated for the risk taken?**
    A. 1
    B. 2
    C. .35
    D. .50

21. **In 2001, an investor purchased common stock at $10 per share. Three years later, the stock trades at $13 per share. What is the investor's holding period return?**
    A. 15%
    B. 30%
    C. 10%
    D. –5%

22. **If common stock appreciates 3% over a 3-month period, the annualized rate of return is**
    A. 3%
    B. 12%
    C. 43.75%
    D. 0.5%

23. **A corporation is discounting future cash flows from a proposed call center to determine the attractiveness of the project. The corporation is calculating**
    A. Future Value
    B. Present Value
    C. Net Present Value
    D. Beta

24. **When calculating the "Sharpe ratio," an investment's return is compared to the riskless rate of return before dividing by the standard deviation. The riskless rate of return is**
    A. theoretical
    B. the return on 6-month T-bills
    C. the return on 3-month T-bills
    D. the return on large cap stock with low volatility

25. **An aggressive growth investor is least likely affected by**
    A. market risk
    B. business risk
    C. purchasing power risk
    D. regulatory risk

Answers

16. ANSWER: C

WHY: I would expect the exam to make sure you know that duration measures a bond's price volatility rather than making you calculate it. Still, if you can calculate it, you must know the concept. And, nobody can predict exactly what the test will do, which is what makes it so darned much fun. If the question had said the bond would rise/fall 20% for every 1% change in rates, the duration would be 20.

17. ANSWER: B

WHY: present value (PV) will tell us how much we need to put in based on a likely rate of return in order to have $90,000 for college. Note that if the question asked how much $90,000 invested would be worth in the future...that's future value.

18. ANSWER: C

WHY: net present value is all about "discounting future cash flows" back to their present value using an internal rate of return. Beta measures the up and down movement of a stock compared to the "overall market." And the Sharpe ratio measures the return above the "riskless rate of return" divided by or "compared to" standard deviation (the amount above and below the expected return).

19. ANSWER: B

WHY: you can get this one through process of elimination. Technical analysts don't analyze companies—they analyze stocks. EMT and Modern Portfolio Theory never try to pick particular stocks. So, you're left with value investing, which involves doing homework to uncover...value.

20. ANSWER: B

WHY: the higher the number, the better the Sharpe ratio. Anything that starts with a decimal is probably not a good Sharpe ratio.

21. ANSWER: B

WHY: the stock is up 30% over the holding period.

22. ANSWER: B

WHY: how many 3-month periods are in 1 year? Four. So, multiply the return by 4, but I wouldn't take out any loans on the street based on your expectation of getting 12% this year. The year isn't even up yet.

23. ANSWER: C

WHY: memorize and keep moving.

24. ANSWER: C

WHY: a T-bill has no default risk. A 3-month T-bill would have, essentially, no interest rate risk, either. How much can rates move in three months? Even if they did move, big deal? Buy a new T-bill in a few weeks reflecting the higher rates.

25. ANSWER: C

WHY: remember that common stock is the best hedge against inflation or purchasing power risk, but it certainly exposes the investor to many other risks.

Study Sheet Lesson 2
"What Does an Adviser Do for a Living?"

ECONOMICS

GDP = Gross Domestic Product
Inflation-Adjusted GDP = "Real" GDP

2 consecutive quarters of GDP increase = Expansion
2 consecutive quarters of GDP decline = Recession
6 consecutive quarters of GDP decline = Depression

Business Cycle:
Expansion - Peak - Contraction - Trough

Non-Cyclical/Defensive industries are more resistant to business cycle
　　e.g., food, pharmaceuticals, energy
Cyclical industries react to business cycle
　　e.g., automobiles, steel, durable goods

Inflation
  • usually occurs during expansion
  • interest rates usually rise due to high demand for capital
  • FRB/FOMC raises interest rates further to fight inflation
  • bond prices fall
  • demand-pull = demand for goods outstrips supply
  • cost-push = rising raw material prices (measured by PPI)

Deflation
  • usually occurs during recession/contraction
  • interest rates usually drop due to cooling demand for capital
  • FRB/FOMC lowers interest rates further to stimulate economy
  • bond prices rise

Employment Indicators
  • Avg Weekly Claims for Unemployment Insurance
  • Unemployment Rate (Nonfarm Payroll) - released monthly
  • Employment Cost Index - released quarterly

ECONOMIC INDICATORS

Leading – show up before reflected in the economy
  • the average weekly hours worked by manufacturing workers
  • the average number of initial applications for unemployment insurance

- the amount of manufacturers' new orders for consumer goods and materials
- the speed of delivery of new merchandise to vendors from suppliers
- the amount of new orders for capital goods unrelated to defense
- the amount of new building permits for residential buildings
- the S&P 500 stock index
- the inflation-adjusted monetary supply (M2)
- the spread between long and short interest rates
- consumer sentiment

Coincident – show up at about the same time as reflected in the economy
- the number of employees on non-agricultural payrolls
- the Index of Industrial Production
- the level of manufacturing and trade sales
- the aggregate amount of personal income excluding transfer payments

Lagging – show up after the fact
- the value of outstanding commercial and industrial loans
- the change in the consumer price index for services from the previous month
- the change in labor cost per unit of labor output
- the ratio of manufacturing and trade inventories to sales made
- the ratio of consumer credit outstanding to personal income
- the average prime rate charged by banks
- the inverted average length of employment

Fiscal Policy
- Congress & President
- Cut Taxes/Increase Spending to stimulate economy
- Raise Taxes/Decrease Spending to fight inflation

Monetary Policy
- FRB/FOMC
- Cut Discount Rate/Lower Reserve Requirement/Buy Treasuries to STIMULATE
- Raise Discount Rate/Raise Reserve Requirement/Sell Treasuries to FIGHT INFLATION
- can't do ANYTHING about tax rates

Interest Rates
- Rise during Expansions
- Fall during Contractions/Recession
- Discount Rate = rate FRB charges banks
- Fed Funds = rate banks charge each other
- Broker Call = rate banks charge broker-dealers
- Prime = rate banks charge best corporate customers for unsecured loans

Yield Curves
- Normal/Positive = long maturities have higher yields
- Humped = intermediate maturities have higher yields
- Flat = all yields are similar
- Inverted/Negative = short maturities have higher yields, usually happens when rates have peaked

Balance of Trade
- If we import more, we have a deficit
- If we export more, we have a surplus
- Weak dollar helps exports
- Strong dollar hurts exports

Fundamental Analyst
- Looks at balance sheet, income statement
- Concerned with:
  - EPS
  - PE
  - Book Value
  - Working Capital
  - Profit Margins
  - Revenue
- Balance Sheet, Assets - Liabilities = Net Worth
  Assets = Liabilities + Net Worth

Technical Analyst
- Analyzes Stock Prices, Volume
- Concerned with:
  - Charts
  - Support, Resistance
  - Head & Shoulders
  - Short Interest
  - Odd Lot Theory

Investment Risks
- To Bondholders
  - Default - measured by S&P, Moody's
  - Purchasing Power - inflation erodes value of interest payments
  - Event - corporation with shaky credit could acquire the company
  - Call - rates down, company could call your bond
  - Interest Rate - rates up, price down. Greatest on long-term bonds.
  - Reinvestment Risk - avoided with zero coupons, e.g., STRIPS
- Business Risk - company has competitors, its industry can hit snags, etc.
- Market/systematic - overall market could collapse. Protect with index options.

- Nonsystematic - one investment could plummet. Protect with diversification.
- Liquidity - thinly-traded securities can't be sold for good prices quickly.
- Legislative - changes in law/policy can hurt stock and bond prices
- Political Risk - international/emerging markets can have unstable political climates

PORTFOLIO ANALYSIS

- Yield (think "get")
  - Current Yield - annual income divided by price of security
  - YTM - income plus gain/loss at maturity
  - YTC - income plus gain/loss at first call date
  - After-tax - take yield times (100% minus tax bracket)
  - Tax-equivalent - take muni yield divided by (100% minus tax bracket)

- Total Return - capital appreciation plus any income distributed divided by price paid.
- Inflation-Adjusted (real) Return - return minus rate of inflation
- Holding Period Return - return over investor's holding period, regardless of time
- Annualized Return - return measured in yearly increments
- Expected Return - possible return weighted by likelihood
- Standard Deviation - degree that expected return could be "off"
- Alpha - difference between actual and expected return. Positive Alpha = excess returns
- Sharpe ratio - return minus riskless rate (3-month T-bills) divided by Standard Deviation
      "Is investor fairly compensated for risk taken?"
      Higher the number, the better investor is compensated
- Correlation - the degree to which two investments move together or in opposite directions
      1 - perfect correlation
      .5 - one goes up 10%, the other 5%
      -.5 - one goes up 10%, the other DOWN 5%
      negatively correlated investments = diversified portfolio
- Duration - measures a bond's price sensitivity to a small change in interest rates
      Zero coupon duration = maturity
      "Coupon Bonds" have durations SHORTER/LESS THAN maturity
      low coupons/long maturities = high duration
      high coupons/short maturities = low duration
- Convexity - measures a bond's price sensitivity to a LARGE change in rates

- Monte Carlo Simulation - computer program that shows range of outcomes given different economic climates
- Future Value - what an investment will be worth given a rate of return and a time frame
- Present Value - what an investor must put in to have a certain future value
- Internal Rate of Return - the return used to calculate FV and PV
- Net Present Value - discounted cash flows of an investment
- Benchmarks - indexes used to compare a portfolio's results
- Growth Investing - buys stocks in companies whose earnings have or should grow faster than others. High PE and Price-to-Book ratios
- Value Investing - buys stocks in companies currently out-of-favor. Lower PE and price-to-book ratios
- Active Management - what it sounds like
- Passive Management - exclusive use of index funds, never picks one investment over another
- Buy and Hold - buy, and then hold. Lower transaction costs, few short-term cap gains.
- Modern Portfolio Theory - uses expected return, alpha, standard deviation. Tries to optimize portfolios along efficient frontier. Uses asset allocation to get highest return for amount of risk taken.
- Efficient Market Theory - assumes stocks are priced efficiently because information is disseminated and acted upon immediately. Never picks one investment over another, uses index funds (passive management).
- Random Walk Theory - because markets are efficient, there is no value in active management. A randomly selected portfolio is no worse than an actively managed portfolio, especially over a long time-frame.
- Diversification - the "don't put all your eggs in one basket" approach to fight non-systematic risk. A stock portfolio could be diversified among various industries and/or market caps.
- Asset Allocation - allocation %'s of capital to equity/debt/money market.
- Strategic Allocation - based on age/risk tolerance, doesn't alter allocation for market movement.
- Tactical Allocation - changes %'s based on market conditions
- Rebalancing - selling off positions to maintain the allocation percentages
- Market Cap - share price times shares outstanding. Micro cap highest risk/reward, large cap lowest risk/reward.

Online Updates

Lesson 3

Types of Clients and Taxation Issues

Types of Clients

So, are all investors the same? Only in the sense that they all have money we'd like to share with them. Other than that, we have to pay attention to suitability issues and remember that some investors need growth, while others need income. Still others need a little of both, so we go way out on a limb and offer them "growth and income" mutual funds.

No, this isn't rocket science.

An investment adviser will usually end up servicing many different types of clients. The first type of client is an individual, and the exam wants you to understand that you may only take orders from this individual. Not the individual's husband or wife, secretary, or attorney. The only way to take an order from anyone other than the individual is if the individual has granted the other person trading authorization. Otherwise, only communicate with the individual on the account. Limited trading authorization (power of attorney) means the other party may place buy and sell orders; full trading authorization (power of attorney) means the other party can do that as well as request a distribution of securities and/or cash, payable to the name on the account.

Sometimes husbands and wives, or even college buddies, decide to set up accounts jointly. We call these accounts, very cleverly, joint accounts. In a joint account we have a joint account agreement that must be signed by all owners on the account. We can take orders from any of the parties, and we can send mail to any of the parties. But, when we cut a check, it has to be payable to all names on the account. A Joint Tenants with Rights of Survivorship (JTWROS or JTROS) account gives the survivor rights to all the assets, meaning that if one account owner dies, the other owner (the survivor) owns all the assets, regardless of how much he/she put in. But, if the account is a Joint Tenants In Common (JTIC), when one party dies, the assets go to that person's estate. For JTIC accounts, we'd have to indicate what % each party owns, so we know what % goes to the estate. For JTWROS, that wouldn't matter, as all assets go to the survivor, bypassing probate court, should the exam decide to go there.

A trust account is run, surprisingly enough, by a trustee. The trustee manages the account for somebody else but might also be interested in receiving advice from an investment adviser. The investment adviser must have a copy of the trust agreement on file, and if the agreement says that no options may be traded, the adviser needs to make sure the trustee doesn't suddenly develop a penchant for put spreads. Establishing trusts is a key part of estate planning that can maximize the amount of money that passes from the deceased to his/her heirs, minimizing the amount that passes to Uncle Sam in the form of estate taxes.

An estate account is a custodial account, like a trust account, overseen by an executor of the estate. The executor makes the decisions but might also like some pointers from the investment adviser. The exam would consider an estate account temporary and therefore would want you to recommend short-term debt securities, specifically money market securities. Just let the money earn some interest until it all gets distributed to the heirs or to various trusts that have been established. No "growth stocks" or speculative options. Dad just passed away, do you really want to face your bereaved siblings and announce that you, the executor, accidentally lost the $5 million estate writing naked calls? That's not exactly living up to the ol' fiduciary duty thing, is it?

Speaking of which, trustees and executors are both fiduciaries. We'll be looking at the "Uniform Prudent Investor Act" later in this section. Part of that model act points out that both trustees and executors are fiduciaries, but that there is a higher standard for a professional fiduciary, like a trust company, than for an "amateur," which describes many executors of estates named in wills. Often the executor named in the will is just the oldest child, or the one who was always "good with numbers." So, we'd expect a higher standard of prudence from a bank's trust department managing a $10 million trust fund than Joe, the eldest of nine children, who got suckered into buying an index fund with a 5% load attached. Joe probably didn't do as much due diligence overseeing the estate account as we'd like, but we're not going to come down on him as hard as we might come down on a bank's trust department, who should know that index funds don't really need to have big sales loads attached.

A sole proprietor is an individual business owner and, therefore, you would treat the account pretty much the way you would treat an individual account. I could maybe see a question pointing out that a small business owner probably has large liquidity needs. In business, who knows when you'll need a big infusion of cash to replace broken equipment, or repair a leaky roof. Or, just to make a mortgage payment when your business isn't doing particularly well. So, a healthy "cash position" sure sounds prudent to me. In case you need, you know, some cash. If the question is about a musician or a client who runs a restaurant in a resort town, it's probably pointing out that this person has serious liquidity needs at least half the year for the restaurant owner and at least every Friday for the musician. Why the exam wants us to pretend that a local musician would actually open an account at an investment advisory firm I have no idea, but we can humor it long enough to get you a 68.5% or higher.

Why not?

Many businesses are set up as partnerships. If your customer is a partnership, you need the partnership agreement to see who has the authority to trade the account and if, say, options or margin trading is allowed. A partnership is taxed differently from a C Corporation in that, unlike a C Corporation, the business isn't taxed as a business. Rather, each partner takes a share of income and expenses on his/her own tax forms. The partnership could be a group of doctors, lawyers, or accountants, or maybe a real estate or oil and gas partnership. Whenever one of the partners dies, freeze the account, meaning stop trading for a while until you get an amended partnership agreement on file.

A limited liability company (LLC) is a lot like a partnership. Rather than calling the owners partners or shareholders, we call them members. These members are not personally liable for the debts of the business—they can only lose what they put in, which is known technically as "a good thing." Unlike for S Corps, there is no limit to the number of members in an LLC. You would need the articles of incorporation required by state law to set up the account as well as documentation of which members have the authority to trade the account.

An S Corporation is similar to both a partnership and an LLC in that the individual owners take a share of income and expenses. Unlike an LLC, we call the owners shareholders (not members) and we can have a maximum of 75 shareholders. All stock is of the same class, too, meaning it all has the same voting rights. Why form an S-Corp over a C Corp?

To avoid the double taxation of dividends. See, if we set up a C Corp, the business gets taxed on its profit or net income. As you remember from our long-winded discussion of the income statement, net income is the "bottom line," which means the company has to pay tax before paying dividends from these bottom-line profits. So when the C Corp then distributes dividends to the owners, the owners get taxed on that income, too.

Harsh!

Yep, so S Corps avoid the double taxation of dividends, while C Corps subject the owners to that unpleasant reality. Of course, if you have over 10 billion outstanding shares, as does Microsoft, it's kind of tough to be an S-Corp. Although I'm sure if it were possible, Mr. Gates would have done so long ago.

So, why form a corporation or a partnership at all? Because if you're a sole proprietor, you're totally exposed to lawsuits and creditors. That means that if you own your business as a sole proprietor and go belly up, the creditors can come after your house, fishing boat, and 1964 Corvette. If you've incorporated or formed a partnership, they have to stop after liquidating all the business assets. So, you can drive your 1964 Corvette to the bankruptcy court proceedings and sing "Nah-nah-nah-nah-nah—you can't have it" at the creditors' attorneys.

Should you be so inclined.

CLIENT PROFILES

No matter who (or what) your client is, you must gather some information so that you can make suitable recommendations. You must determine the financial status of the client, gathering key information such as:

- Income sources
- Current expenditures (bills, obligations)
- Discretionary income (what's left after paying bills)
- Assets (cash, real estate pension/retirement accounts, life insurance)
- Tax bracket

We looked at the income statement that public companies present in their quarterly and annual reports to the SEC. Individual investors also prepare income statements, which help IAs to determine suitable investment strategies. Probably the most important figure to obtain from a client is known as "discretionary income" or "excess cash flow." This is the money left over after covering all essentials. Because, let's face it, if the client has no money after paying "the bills," he really has no money to invest. A personal income statement might look like this:

Monthly Income

Salary	$7,000
Investment Income	$1,000
Other Income	$ 500
Total Monthly Income	$8,500

Monthly Expenditures

Taxes	$2,000
Mortgage Payment	$2,000
Living Expenses	$2,000
Insurance Premiums	$ 300
Loan Payments	$ 200
Travel/Entertainment	$ 300
Other Expenses	$ 200
Total Monthly Expenses	$7,000
Monthly Capital for Investing	$1,500

So, a client with the above income statement has excess cash flow or discretionary income of $1,500. If you start talking him into investing $3,000 a month in speculative investments...well, you'd never do a thing like that, right? Instead, you'd make recommendations that make sense given the fact that he has $1,500 available for investing in a typical month. Notice how the client above had income from a job and income from investments. That's the way to become affluent or wealthy—let your money make money as you go out and earn a living. Pretty soon, they tell me, you can stop going out to earn a living and just manage your investments from the captain's quarters of your 80-foot yacht.

Of course, taxes always play a part in an investment strategy. If your client is in a high marginal tax bracket, you may want to recommend municipal bonds, which, generally, pay interest that is tax-free at the federal level. This same client probably doesn't want to do a lot of short-term trading, either, since any gain taken within the space of a year will be taxed at the short-term capital gains rate (which equals the ordinary income rate). He also might want to buy stocks that pay qualified dividends rather than REITs or royalty trusts, which will force him to pay his ordinary income rate on the dividends. Tax situations aren't the major driver of an investment strategy, but they definitely need to be taken into account. Of course, one of the best answers you can give a client is, "Please consult with a qualified tax professional."

A business has both an income (earnings) statement and a balance sheet (statement of financial condition). So do your clients. Remember that assets represent what somebody owns, while liabilities represents what he owes. The difference would be his net worth. A client's assets would include the value of his home(s), automobiles, personal possessions (furniture, jewelry, Armani suits), investments, savings, and checking accounts. Liabilities would include mortgages and other loans, credit card balances, and, perhaps, debit balances in margin accounts.

A personal balance sheet might look like this:

Assets

Tangible Property

House	$400,000
Automobiles	$ 30,000
Personal possessions	$ 15,000

Investments

Stocks and Bonds	$100,000
Keogh Plan	$ 80,000
IRA	$ 20,000

Savings

Checking	$ 5,000
Savings Account	$ 5,000
Money Market	$ 5,000

Liabilities

Mortgage	$250,000
Auto Loans	$ 10,000
Credit Card Balances	$ 15,000
Net Worth	$ 385,000

This represents "total net worth." Since some assets are difficult to liquidate, we could exclude those items (house, limited partnerships, rental property) to calculate "liquid net worth." Which is very similar to excluding the hard-to-sell inventory when calculating a company's quick ratio as opposed to their current ratio, right? If a client has high total net worth but low liquid net worth, an IA might try to steer the client toward more liquid investments, like heavily traded stocks and bonds, as opposed to limited partnerships.

I would not be at all surprised if the Series 65/66 exam asked you to calculate a pretend client's discretionary income, net worth, or both. Or neither. You just never know what this test might decide to ask you. They can't ask you everything we touch on in this material, but they could ask you *anything*.

While you're gathering this information on a client's assets, you're also uncovering his current holdings. Many investors have a huge percentage of their portfolio tied up in one company's stock—their employers. Can you say En-ron, boys and girls? I thought you could. If a client has too much money concentrated in just one stock, an IA might advise him to sell some of that holding in order to diversify. Other clients will already be diversified, which is just as important to determine before recommending investments. If they already hold 20 large industrial company stocks, you probably don't want to recommend that they plow the rest of their discretionary income into Dow Jones Index funds, which would be sort of redundant.

But there are also non-financial considerations, and these can actually be just as important if not more so. So, you need a sort of personality profile of the investor:

- Age
- Investment experience
- Marital status
- Attitudes and values (what kind of attitude would he get over losing value?)
- Number and age of children
- Employment stability
- Employment of family members (if we get burned in junk bonds, is anybody willing to start a paper route?)
- Current and future educational needs for the family or individual
- Current and future health care needs

What would you do with such information? Well, if this investor has no investment experience, is 55 years old, and has never put money into anything outside of an FDIC-insured bank product, would you stick her in high-yield bonds, options, and short sales?

Only if you cared to spend some serious time in arbitration.

But if the investor has lots of experience, maybe she won't freak if a stock gains 15% one week and loses 20% the next.

Maybe.

If the family needs money for a child's education, let's not stick all the investment capital in small-cap or aggressive growth funds. Let's put some of the principal into guaranteed obligations of the U.S. Government or one of the agencies like Ginnie Mae. STRIPS are also good for educational savings, as are 529 Plans and the Educational IRA (Coverdell Savings Accounts). Of course, a STRIP is a security, while the other two are savings *plans* within which securities (stocks, bonds, mutual funds) are placed for favorable tax treatment. And, if you recall my friend, whose agent took a $3.2 million account all the way to $40,000, you might be wondering why that agent didn't put say $1 million in U.S. Treasuries. That way, after losing $2 million, his client would still have been a millionaire.

Of course, that would have involved thinking about the client rather than the fact that Treasuries pay lousy commissions, so…

Anyway, if the investor has plenty of income from a good job and no credit card debt, we can afford to be more aggressive, since he isn't likely to need to dip into the account just to keep the lights on, right?

That sort of thing.

Risk tolerance can be referred to in different ways. Risk-averse, conservative, and low risk tolerance all mean the same thing—dude doesn't like to party. High risk tolerance, aggressive, and speculative also go together, more or less. If somebody's risk-averse, keep him out of things like "biotech, small cap, or aggressive growth funds." If somebody has a higher risk tolerance, we can put her into stocks with high betas or "standard deviations" or even high-yield bonds, options, and short sales.

In general the younger the investor the more volatility she can withstand. If you're in for the long haul, who cares what happens this year? It's what happens over a 20- or 30-year period that matters. The S&P 500 has gained 10-11% average over the past 70 years or so, which means your money would double approximately every 7 years. Sure, the index can drop 50% one year and gain 70% the next, but we're not keeping score every year—it's where we go over the long haul that counts.

So when the investor is young the only thing that would keep me from recommending "small cap fund," or "growth stock" would be if the question points out that she has a low risk tolerance or needs to make a large down payment on a house very soon (money market). I'd still stick her in a stock, but the stock would be "large cap" or "blue chip," or if she needed $200 a month for her mother's nursing home expenses or was looking to buy a house in the near future, I'd put the required amount in the money market. But I think it would be a seriously goofy question if it wanted you to recommend a bond or most any debt security to a young investor. Older investors almost always need bonds in a test question, and younger investors almost always need stock.

Except when they don't.

Younger investors have a long "time horizon," so they can withstand more ups and downs along the long road to retirement. Unfortunately, some folks don't have time on their side. When you're 69 years old, you probably need some income and not so much volatility in your investing life. You might not have 10 or 15 years to "get it all back in the next big bull market." So the farther from retirement she is, the more likely she'll be buying stock. The closer she gets to retirement, the less stock she needs and the more bonds/income investments she should be buying.

In the so-called "real world" many advisers pass out little charts that say, "If you're this old and have this much risk tolerance, you should have this % in bonds, stocks, and money market."

Which sounds a lot like asset allocation, which is exactly what it is.

FIDUCIARY RESPONSIBILITY

Now, let's get a little more specific. As we saw in "What the Heck is an Investment Adviser," an IA is a fiduciary. A fiduciary is someone who acts on behalf of and for the benefit of someone else. If you're a fiduciary you have certain obligations to the person on whose behalf you're acting; therefore, you have "fiduciary duties." Not only

must an IA never engage in anything fraudulent, deceptive, misleading, or manipulative, but also, they must act solely in the best interest of the client.

The traditional view on fiduciaries and investments came about through court
cases back in the 1800s. The guideline that developed was called the "Prudent Man
Standard," and—no—nobody back then thought the word "man" might somehow be
chauvinistic. This was the 1800s, remember. Anyway, this "Prudent Man Standard"
was about as uptight as the 1800s—risk control was the main concern for a fiduciary.
Even government bonds have interest rate risk, so that needed to be considered when
recommending government bonds. Even this uptight standard wasn't conservative
enough for some states, who actually put out "legal lists" telling a fiduciary what he
could or couldn't invest in. About the only stuff to make that list boiled down to high-
credit-quality bonds.

Safe and boring. Preserving capital was the main duty for a fiduciary using this
conservative standard.

Well, as you may recall from our fascinating look at different investment approaches, Modern Portfolio Theory has had a major impact on investment approaches.
While the old standard thought of just about every investment as potentially "risky,"
Modern Portfolio Theory tells us to look at the whole portfolio, not just one investment. If you have two stocks that are "negatively correlated," when one goes down,
the other goes up. If you have a few high-yield bonds in the portfolio, the bonds might
be risky, but that risk can be offset by other bonds that are about as likely to default as
a spaceship is to land at Fenway Park this afternoon. So, fiduciaries now need to look
at the whole portfolio in terms of risk, focusing on the trade-off between risk and
reward, rather than just running away from a particular investment that might seem
"risky" in and of itself. We're focusing on IAs, but other fiduciaries include executors,
trustees, custodians in an UGMA, and registered representatives/broker-dealers with
discretion over the account. Now, you might think that somebody managing a pension
fund for tens of thousands of workers would have to be a complete wimp with the
stock picks, but, actually, using this new standard based on Modern Portfolio Theory,
pension funds do all types of "risky" investments and get away with it by trying to
balance the risk of one investment with the safety of another. There is probably nothing riskier than putting money into a "hedge fund," yet pension funds and university
endowments do it all the time. But, they don't put so much into the hedge fund that
the whole portfolio could be wiped out in one fell swoop. They counter the risk with
other, safer investments.

So, fiduciaries still have a fiduciary duty to the folks they're looking out for. They
just manage the risk differently. In the past, you had to stay away from risky investments. Now, you consider the risk-reward ratio and view the risk of the portfolio
rather than the risk of one investment all on its own.

This new standard is codified in a very exciting document called the "Uniform
Prudent Investor Act," which you might want to read, unless you were waiting for the
DVD. The UPIA boils down to these main bullet points:

- Prudence is applied to the whole portfolio, not individual investments
- Fiduciaries don't just avoid risk—they consider the trade-off between
  risk and reward

- There are no categorical restrictions. For example, we don't say "no junk bonds" anymore. Instead, we say, "How does this junk bond add to the risk/reward ratio of the overall portfolio?"
- Diversification is a major part of managing a portfolio

So, what does this exciting new development mean to investment advisers? Basically, it means that IAs should:

- Pay close attention to the goals of the client
- Develop an investment policy and stick to it
- Focus on managing, rather than avoiding, risk
- Determine the risk tolerance of the client
- Diversify

The SEC says that investment advisers have a duty to be loyal to their clients (fiduciary means loyal, but the SEC often likes to state the obvious). IAs have a duty to get the best execution for clients' securities transactions whenever the IA is in a position to direct trades through brokerages. Remember that—it's not okay to direct all your client trades through some expensive broker-dealer just because they compensate your firm for the favor. Get the best execution (best price, best commissions) for your clients. Remember, you're a fiduciary. IAs have to make sure that their advice is suitable for the client's objectives, needs, and circumstances. And, it would be real nice if the IA actually had a reasonable, independent basis for giving advice.

So, if the SEC (not that the states disagree) says you have a duty to your clients to consider risk tolerance and suitability, let's talk about how an IA goes about satisfying that requirement. First, the adviser has a duty to inquire into the client's financial situation, investing experience, and objectives. Different types of advisers would possibly have different levels of inquiry—for example, if I'm doing a comprehensive financial plan I may have a duty to get more detailed information than if I were just recommending an asset allocation fund or a government bond fund.

IAs have the duty to inquire and, just as important, to give advice that is suitable for the client based on the information they've gathered. Always take risk tolerance into consideration, and remember that a client has to be able to bear risk financially but also accept that risk on a personal level. I'm not sure I've ever met such a person, myself, but the point is, just because a client is wealthy with little need for liquidity, don't start putting her into naked calls unless you know she's comfortable with the unlimited loss potential on this speculative, borderline psychotic investment strategy.

As we said when talking about fiduciaries, Modern Portfolio Theory has changed the way the investment world thinks to a large degree, so it's not the risk of just one security that we look at—it's the way it fits into the risk of the whole portfolio. I wouldn't be able to sleep holding an entire portfolio of junk bonds. But, if junk bonds represented just 5% of my portfolio, I could actually withstand the unlikely event that all the issuers would default at the same time.

It's not just the investment advice that has to be reasonable. Since the IA is a fiduciary, the firm can't just stick clients into whatever fee and service structure enriches the adviser firm the most. We're not coming from the Larry Ellison or Bill Gates school of ethics here—this industry is actually regulated and IAs actually have to put the needs of the customer not just into the business plan, but ahead of the needs of the IA.

If a customer isn't going to trade very often, the wrap fee might be more expensive than a fee-plus-commission structure. And if the customer likes to trade often, the wrap fee might make more sense for him, since it's a flat fee that already includes executions/trades. So, don't just base the structure on whatever puts the most money in the firm's pocket; base it on what works for the client. The firm is already going to pocket plenty of the client's money, trust me.

FUNDING & TAXING THE ACCOUNT

There are different ways that an investment account can be funded and taxed, and the exam might go there for a few questions. So let's be ready for terms like dollar cost averaging, dividend reinvestment, cost base, capital gains, and such.

FUNDING

Dollar cost averaging is a great way to avoid the perilous game of trying to time the market. Right at the peak of the tech bubble my buddy bought 1,000 shares of MSFT at $86.50.

Unfortunately, he pretty much called the top on that one. Had he SHORTED Microsoft that day, he could have made about $30,000 in a few months, but, no, he decided it was the day to buy all 1,000 shares at the same price (timing risk).

My own feeling here is that he bought a great company at a really lousy price. Had he, instead, put in $5,000 each month, as the price dropped he would have picked up more and more shares. When the stock was expensive, his $5,000 wouldn't have bought so many shares, but when the stock fell into the 50's and 40's, he would have loaded up like my Aunt Barbara at a back-to-school sale.

That's called dollar cost averaging. You don't buy the same amount of shares, and you don't buy them all on one day. You put in the same amount of *money*, say every month, and when the share price is up, you don't buy so much. When the share price is down, you load up your cart with it.

This also magically leaves you with a lower average cost compared with buying equal numbers of shares. If you put in the same dollar amount—rather than paying a variable dollar amount for the same number of shares—your average cost is lower.

Of course, most of you don't believe that, so now I have to take the time to prove it.

Here goes. Your investor puts in $1,000 each month for three months. In January, the stock trades at $50. In February, the stock trades at $40. And, in March, the stock trades at $20.

What color is the bear?

Oops, wrong riddle.

Find her average cost. Then compare it to the average share price. And if you're groaning about all these numbers and having to run an actual calculation, let me just say with all the sympathy I can muster, "Get over it—you're in a numbers business. It's all based on math, percentages, that kind of thing."

Average share price is the average of three prices: ($50 + $40 + $20) / 3 = $36.67. If she had bought the same *number* of shares each time, her average cost WOULD have been $36.67 per share.

But it isn't.

In January, her $1,000 only picked up 20 shares. In February, she nabbed 25, and in March she loaded up the shopping cart with 50 deeply discounted shares. That's a total of 95 shares. If she puts in $3,000 and buys 95 shares, her average cost is $31.58, which is more than $5 lower per share than if she'd bought equal numbers for an average cost of $36.67.

Pretty spiffy, huh? So, if the investor puts in the same dollar amount and the stock's price fluctuates (gee, what are the odds?), her average cost will be better than the average share price.

Many corporations have **DRIPs (dividend re-investment programs)**, whereby your dividends are automatically reinvested into more shares; parts of shares, sometimes. If you reinvest a $50 dividend check, at the time of this writing you would own exactly .069756 of a share of IBM, assuming the company charged you nothing for the DRIP, and I'm not sure I'd assume that. Might be kind of fun to say you now own .069756 of an IBM common share and are diligently working toward your first full share.

Or not.

Normally, we equate this dividend reinvestment with mutual funds, where the practice is very common, but some companies have decided to let investors do the same thing with their common stock. Usually, it's the large, blue chip companies that are into this, which only makes sense—small cap growth stocks usually provide no dividends to reinvest.

The exam will have a thing or two to say about taxation, so let's be ready for that.

TAXATION

There are only two types of taxes on investments:
- Taxes on income (dividends, interest payments for holding stuff)
- Taxes on capital gains (for selling stuff)

Portfolio income, dividends

Let's say you buy 1,000 shares of GE for $30. Every three months you get a quarterly dividend check for 25 cents per share, or $250 total.

Pretty cool, huh? Sure beats working for a living, even though this income—like the stuff you work for—is also going to be taxed. But, believe it or not, it's only taxed at a maximum rate of 15%. Before the big switcheroo on policy, those dividends were taxed at your ordinary income rate. That means that folks who were recently paying 39% tax on dividends are now paying no more than 15%.

But, of course, nothing is simple when it comes to investments and taxation, not even the simple stuff.

The dividends that get taxed at 15% are called **"qualified dividends."** These would definitely include dividends from GE or any other traditional corporation. Remember, GE and other companies pay dividends *after* they've already paid tax on their bottom line—unlike bond interest, dividends don't get deducted from a company's income pre-tax to reduce their tax burden. That's the idea behind the drastic drop to 15%, by the way. Since GE already paid tax on the earnings before giving you some of their bottom line in the form of a dividend check, why should you get fully taxed?

The dividends that don't qualify include **REITs** and **royalty trusts**, which kick out 90% of their earnings to shareholders already in order to act as a conduit to the shareholders. Since the REIT and/or royalty trust already gets favorable tax treatment, the shareholder doesn't.

But, who cares? I own a royalty trust that pays me earnings on oil and natural gas sales. I bought it at $10—it's now worth $30. And every month it kicks out about a 10% yield to me.

I'll gladly pay my ordinary income rate on income I get for sitting on my lazy duff, although paying 15% would be more fun, but you can't have everything.

So, when GE pays me a dividend, I get taxed at a rate of 15%.

When HGT, the royalty trust, pays me a dividend, I pay my ordinary income rate on that, which could be as high as 35% once I get enough people to buy my Pass the 6, 7, 65, and 63 materials.

So, dividends are definitely taxable, and if you know anyone studying for a license exam…

Portfolio income, bond interest

Anyway, interest paid on corporate or government bonds is also taxable, at my ordinary income rate. Corporate bonds are taxable at the federal, state, and local government level, while U.S. government bonds are taxable "only" at the federal level. The federal level is the one that takes the biggest bite out of my wallet, but I'd still love to have $1 million in U.S. Government bonds yielding, say, 5%. I'd get $50,000 a year in guaranteed interest payments and would pay the same tax on that as if I'd had to get up every morning and, like, work for it.

Rich people complain about paying up to 35% tax on this interest, but it's the same rate they pay on the income they earn at the office. And it's not taxable by the states.

Corporate bond interest *is* taxable in states that have an income tax, but so what? If you're paying taxes, you're making money.

So the income you receive from your portfolio is called, very cleverly, "portfolio income." It's taxable, but it sure beats working for a living. Think of it as the money you make from an investment just for holding it.

Capital gains

On the other hand, think of capital gains as the money you make when you sell a stock or bond for more than you bought it. Now, before you get all ticked off that you have to pay tax, remember what I just said: you SOLD a stock or bond for MORE than you bought it.

That's known in the world of investing, technically, as a *good thing*.

Of course, the IRS knows how to spot a good thing, too, and they'd like to share some of this capital gain with you.

Back to GE. You bought 1,000 shares @$30. Let's say you sell 100 shares for $40 in order to take a vacation. If you held GE for more than 1 year, you'd realize a long-term gain of $1,000. $10 times 100 shares = $1,000 in capital gains. Go ahead and go on your vacation, and at the end of the year, you'll owe Uncle Sam 15% of that $1,000, or $150.

If you sold that stock within the space of a year, it would get taxed at your ordinary income rate since it's a "short-term" capital gain. If your ordinary income rate is 28%, you owe $280.

Sorry about that. Don't eat out as much, maybe, or check out Priceline-dot-com first. But, either way, go on your vacation. It's not like you had to work for this money.

Capital losses

You don't pay the tax on the day you sell the stock—you pay it with your income taxes. But, you definitely keep track of the gain. Then, when you sit down with your accountant at the end of the year, you might decide to sell some other stocks at a loss. You took a $1,000 gain on GE. If you sell another stock at a $1,000 loss, you'd end up at zero capital gains for the year.

Congratulations, you made absolutely no money on your stocks this year.

And, you'd have no capital gains taxes to pay.

You could get real clever and sell, say, *$4,000* of stock at a loss. Now you'd have a net loss of $3,000. You could use that $3,000 to offset (reduce) your adjusted gross income for the year. So, if your AGI was going to be $53,000, now it's only $50,000. That reduces your tax bill.

But you really did lose money.

See the relationship? If you're paying no tax, it's because you're making no money. If you're paying taxes, it's because you're making money.

Personally, I prefer the latter, but that's not the point, and many would argue until they're blue in the face that it's better to reduce your tax burden then have the temerity to actually make money in the stock market. Some will even purposely take a huge net loss for the year and continue to carry the excess over $3,000 forward. I know a few genius part-time investors who have enough capital losses to last the rest of their lives, $3,000 at a time. They took, say, $90,000 in capital losses in 2001, and it's going to take quite some time to use that up at three grand a pop.

I guess that's the silver lining to the dark cloud known as the "tech bubble."

Whatever.

Just know that the income a security kicks out is taxable (dividends, interest). And the profits you take when you sell are taxable, too.

That's for stocks and bonds bought individually.

Mutual fund income distributions

For mutual funds, things get more complicated, but only a little bit.

Remember the owner of all the stocks and bonds inside the mutual fund is the fund. The fund sells pieces of this big portfolio pie to investors in the form of common stock. So, as with any common stock, you will probably receive dividends and capital gains from time to time. A mutual fund earns dividends and interest payments from the vast quantities of stocks and bonds they own. They pay expenses with that money and if there's a profit left over, they distribute it to the shareholders. The shareholders also get convenient 1099-DIV statements that help keep track of this income, which will be taxable, either at the nice 15% level, or the higher ordinary income rate. Usually, at the nice 15%.

That's if it's a stock fund.

If it's a bond fund, your income checks will be taxed just like bond interest, because that's where it came from.

If it's a government bond fund, it's only taxable at the federal level.

If it's a corporate bond fund, it's taxable at all levels.

And, if it's a municipal bond fund, it's tax-free at the federal level; consult with your accountant for the state level (it's a mess).

Capital gains in mutual funds

There are two ways that capital gains come into play for mutual funds. First, you have no control over when the investment adviser for the fund decides to sell a stock. If he/she ends the year taking (realizing) more gains than losses, the fund realizes a net gain. They can either distribute this to the shareholders or not—either way, you'll get taxed on your proportional share of this capital gain that you may or may not actually get a check for.

Sorry about that. That's the trouble with investing in funds that, like, buy low and sell high. It's called a capital gain and is taxed at the capital gains rate.

The fund almost always makes sure it's a long-term capital gain, since, as we saw, the difference to a high-tax-bracket investor could be the difference between 15% and 35%.

The long-term versus short-term determination has nothing to do with how long the investor held the shares. The investor didn't sell anything—she just gets a check for her proportional share of what the fund realized in capital gains. Assume it's a long-term gain on the exam.

Could it be a short-term gain?

Sure, if the fund doesn't mind fielding a few million angry phone calls from high-bracket shareholders. They'd just identify the gains as short-term and get ready for the switchboard to light up.

Shareholder sales

The other type of capital gain is entirely within the investor's control. It's exactly the same as it is on a share of GE. If she sells it within a year, it's a short-term gain, taxed at her ordinary income rate. If she holds it for more than one year, it's a long-term gain, taxed at a maximum of 15%. If she's a really-low-bracket individual it could be taxed as low as 10%. How many folks in the 10% bracket are taking serious capital gains, I have no idea.

So, the only thing that changed between a share of GE and a mutual fund share is that there are two types of capital gains for fund shares: the ones that the fund takes and distributes to the shareholder, and the one the shareholder takes when she sells/redeems her shares. By the way, "taking" and "realizing" a capital gain are synonymous.

Unrealized gains

If the test starts talking about an "unrealized gain," just break down the words. An "unrealized gain" is just an increase in value, a "paper gain," as some folks like to say. If a mutual fund buys a stock at $10, and the stock now trades at $15, there's no tax to pay...not until the portfolio manager takes/realizes the gain. Unrealized gains can make the net asset value (NAV) of the fund go up, but that doesn't affect the investor unless or until A) the fund realizes a gain on the shares or B) the investor does.

Cost basis on reinvestments

Many investors in funds choose not to take the income and capital gains distributions as checks. Rather, they put it towards more shares of the fund, which they buy without a sales load (at the NAV). Since the distributions get taxed either way, the investor simply adds to her cost basis by the amount of the distribution.

Let's say she bought ACE Growth Fund at $10 per share. Last year, she received $1 in dividends and $1 in capital gains distributions. If she reinvests the $2 per share, she pays tax on that amount, and her cost basis rises, too.

Every time you pay tax on a dividend or interest payment and reinvest, you add to your cost basis. That's what "cost basis" means—the money you've already paid tax on. The amount above that is subject to capital gains tax, but not until you take the gain.

See, our culture is obsessed with tax deferral, but we've sort of forgotten that there was already a tax-deferred vehicle available long before IRAs came about. It's called *common stock*. If a common stock pays no dividends, you have absolutely nothing to pay tax on until you finally decide to sell it.

Seriously.

If you bought 100 shares of XYZ for $10, and they're worth $90 fifteen years later, what's your tax bill?

Zero.

What if it's worth $100 five years later?

Still no tax bill.

Not until you sell it.

So common stocks that don't pay dividends are already tax-deferred.

The ones that pay dividends do subject shareholders to taxation, but they also subject them to some very nice checks that nobody had to lift a finger to "earn."

And, there's no capital gain on a regular old share of common stock until the investor decides to sell. As we said, mutual funds are different in that they can pay *out* capital gains to shareholders. But shares of, say, GE, wouldn't have any capital gains associated with them unless and until the investor decided to sell.

And, some investors will *never* sell. On his death bed, Grandpa told the kinfolk to never sell General Electric. He was an old drinking buddy of Tom Edison, and he promised that no one in his family would ever sell their stock in GE.

So, they never do.

They just hang onto it while they're alive, and when they die, they pass it on to their heirs or donate it to a charitable trust that funds ballet and symphonic programs for inner-city youth.

Remember, nobody's forcing you to sell your stock. And—just ask Warren Buffett—holding on to stocks for decades can be a very rewarding experience.

Inherited securities

What if your grandmother bought GE at $10 and passed it to you through her will when she passed away—what's your cost basis?

Whatever GE was worth on the day Grandma passed away. If it's worth $30 on that day, then that's your cost basis, $30. You get to step up your cost basis to the fair market value on the date of death. Same for a mutual fund.

Gifted securities

What if she decided to give you the stock while she's still alive?

Now you take her original cost basis of $10. If it's worth $40 when you sell it, your gain is $30 a share. Not like when you inherited the shares. Then, your gain would have only been $10, which would make April a much more enjoyable month next time it comes around.

Either way, you're making money when you sell some stock you never had to buy, so I hope you're not complaining too loudly.

Tax-deductible charitable donations

What if Grandma had a more worthy cause than, say, you, and decided to donate the stock to a charity? If she does that while she's alive, she gets to deduct the fair market value of the stock on the date of the donation. If it's worth $50,000 when she donates it, she can deduct $50,000 from her taxable income that year. This way she can maybe buy textbooks for underprivileged school children and also stick it to the IRS at the same time.

Other types of taxation

The exam might start talking about *progressive* versus *regressive* taxes. Progressive taxes include income, estate, and gift taxes. The bigger the income, estate, or gift, the higher the rate the IRS charges. If you make a living, you pay 25% for ordinary income taxes. If you make a killing, you pay up to 35%. That's progressive—as the income progresses, so does the rate of taxation.

Estates that are very large get taxed, too. So, when Bill Gates passes away, his heirs will receive a ton of money, but the IRS will take some first in the form of estate taxes. The bigger the estate, the higher the rate of taxation. Progressive.

And, if you should bump into Bill Gates on the red-eye to Seattle some night, maybe you'll impress him so much with your understanding of middleware in a non-Linux environment that he'll just *give you $100,000*. He'll have to keep track of that and pay gift tax on the excess above $12,000, which is another reason I don't think he'll be doing it, but you never know.

How much tax would he pay?

It's progressive. The bigger the gift, the higher the rate.

A regressive tax is flat. It includes sales, gas, payroll, and excise taxes. Everybody pays the same rate there. When you check out your items at Wal-Mart, the cashier doesn't ask you your marginal tax bracket before giving you your total, right?

No, it's a flat tax. Just like gas taxes are applied to gallons of gas, regardless of whether they're being poured into a rusty, 1981 Monte Carlo, or a beautiful, 2006 Lexus.

Equate "flat tax" with "regressive," because it isn't worth digressing into why they call it "regressive."

They just do.

Types of income

One type of income is the income you earn. We call that, very cleverly, earned income. It includes salary, bonuses, tips, and any income derived from actively participating in a business. So, it doesn't include rental income you get from a rental property. But it would include anything you actively worked for.

The rental income from your rental property is called "passive income." Yes, you lose some sleep over the rowdy new tenants, but you don't actively "work" for that rental income. You hold title to the property and you let the property work for you.

Passive income.

Direct participation programs (partnerships) give the limited partners (LPs) passive income. These LPs put in some money and then sit back and take a share of the income and expenses of the partnership, the business. If they have any passive losses, they can only deduct those against passive income from other partnerships or any rental properties they might own. They can't deduct passive losses against earned income or portfolio income, much as they'd like to. While mutual funds send you convenient 1099's for the dividends and capital gains, partnerships send the LPs K-1's, which are more complicated. Not too surprising that if you want favorable tax treatment from a partnership, the IRS just might make getting that treatment a little bit complicated, right?

Portfolio income seems passive, but it's treated and labeled as, well, portfolio income. We already discussed the rather complex tax treatment of dividends and interest, so I'll spare you the details. Lord knows you've suffered enough at this point.

Tax deferral

You probably have money in a retirement account. You aren't necessarily going to avoid taxes this way, although it sure is fun to put them off until retirement. That's called "tax deferral," because we never get real creative with our terminology here. Why defer taxes? If you invest in a regular account, you pay taxes on capital gains, dividends, and interest every year, thereby depleting your "principal." As we saw in our fascinating look at Future Value (FV), compounded returns are all about an ever-growing principal or "base," right? So if you deplete that base every year through tax payments, you lose part of the compounding effect.

So a tax-deferred retirement plan will definitely have you paying taxes, but not until you take the money at retirement. Theoretically, your money should grow faster that way. When you retire, your IRA, 401K, pension plan, etc., will be taxed at your ordinary income rate, but since you didn't have to deplete the principal by paying tax each year the past 20 years, your money grew into a bigger pile.

And that pile grew into an even bigger pile you didn't pay taxes on.

And so on, and so on.

A great dance to be sure, but now it's time to pay the fiddler. But, forget about capital gains in a retirement account—they don't exist. It's taxed as ordinary income upon "constructive receipt," which is a fancy way of saying, "when you get the money."

And, if you want your money too soon, the IRS will slap a penalty on top of the tax. If you're only, say, 48 and you take money out of your traditional IRA, you'll pay 10% against the money coming out PLUS your ordinary income rate on the money.

Hmm, that oughta' get you to re-think *that* strategy, huh?

The magic age for retirement distributions is 59½. If you want your money from your IRA, 401K, 403b, Keogh, etc., you'll pay not just ordinary income tax (which you'd pay anyway) but also 10% of whatever you take. So if you liquidate your IRA worth $100,000 and you're in the 28% tax bracket, you'll pay $10,000 as the 10% penalty, plus $28,000 in ordinary income taxes. That 100K is really only going to give you $62,000.

Might as well keep it in there until you reach 59½.

Further details on retirement plans have been placed cleverly in the chapter called "Retirement, Annuities, Insurance."

That's enough on them for now.

Tax loss selling

If you're getting a Series 65 or 66, that means you work for a money management firm, which means you deal with plenty of rich folks.

Which is great, because rich people are very amusing.

Rich people often hate taxes so much that they will go out of their way to LOSE money just so the IRS can't have any. Sort of like a nearly defeated military dictator blowing up the bridges and oil wells of his country just so the conquerors won't get any of the good stuff. It hurts the enemy but also hurts the one doing the destruction.

Still, every December many rich folks get together with their accountants and try to figure out which stocks to sell at a loss in order to get the tax benefit.

As we saw, the IRS lets you deduct $3,000 of your capital losses against ordinary income. So, if you made $40,000 on the job, you could say you only made $37,000 if you have a $3,000 loss to deduct.

But don't you really have to lose $3,000 to get this so-called "benefit"?

Yes, but rich folks get such a buzz knowing that they just reduced their ordinary income by $3,000 that they feel as if they've won something. Of course, this is only reducing their ordinary income—not a tax credit—which means they save a *percentage* of this actual $3,000 loss. If they're in the 35% tax bracket, they lose $3,000 in order to save $1,050, that way.

Basically, they're losing a dollar in order to save 35 cents.

Darned ingenious, isn't it?

Whatever it is, it's called "tax loss selling," and every year people go out of their way to sell stocks at a loss in order to get this "benefit."

Wash sale rule

The IRS will let you sell a stock at a loss in order to reduce your tax burden, but you have to stay out of that stock for 30 days after taking the loss. You can buy it back on the 31st day, but not until. Otherwise, they disallow the loss because you violated the "wash sale" rule. And, if this is XYZ stock, for example, you can't buy any XYZ for 30 days after the sale—and you better not have bought any XYZ 30 days *before* the sale. So, there's a 60-day window pointing forward and backward here. You can sell your stock at a loss, but you can't jump right back in. They won't give you the tax benefit and then let you jump into a cheap stock. They'll at least make you worry that it will skyrocket over the next 30 days, leaving you cruelly behind. And, for those who figured they could get around it by purchasing convertible preferred, convertible bonds, rights, warrants, or calls, I commend your creativity; unfortunately, the IRS saw that one coming a mile away and said you can't do it.

Nice try, though.

Methods of determining cost basis

So, how does one go about "tax loss selling"?

Well, when you sell a stock, the IRS wants to know what you paid for it. What you sell it for is the "proceeds." What you paid for it is your "cost base." If your cost base is $10, and you sell the stock for $15, that's a five-dollar capital gain. The IRS will tax it at the higher short-term capital gains rate if you did this within the space of a year, and the lower long-term capital gains rate if you held on one year plus one day.

So you enjoy the $5 profit you didn't have to, like, work for, but the IRS will take a percentage of the $5 gain as a capital gains tax.

The investor would match short-term gains with short-term losses and long-term gains with long-term losses, by the way.

So proceeds = sales price minus commissions.

Cost base = price paid for the security plus commissions.

Your cost basis is the money going into an investment that has already been taxed. You buy a stock for $10 out of after-tax money, right? You don't get to deduct the $10 you spent. So you won't be taxed on the first $10 you started with again. You'd only pay tax against the gains above the $10.

If this is a mutual fund share, you'll probably re-invest all your dividends.

Great. But, you'll pay tax on those dividends, just as if you took the cash and went shopping.

So, if you receive a dividend of $2 and reinvest it, your cost base is now $12.

And somebody has to keep track of all the dividend reinvestments so that when you finally sell this share someday, you'll have a cost base to compare the selling price to.

Proceeds minus cost base equals capital gain/capital loss.

That's the formula.

If you sell the share for, say, $20, and all your dividend re-investments plus your original $10 add up to, say, $14.50, you have a capital gain of $5.50. And you'd pay your capital gains tax on that $5.50.

Pretty simple, actually.

Remember that commissions are added to your cost basis when you buy and subtracted from your proceeds when you sell.

How do you determine which shares you sold if you bought them through several purchases over many years?

First of all, you keep track. You save your trade confirmations or maybe use some handy software that downloads them and keeps track of your cost base for you.

Let's say you bought 100 shares of ABC at 30. A few years later you bought 100 shares at 40. And a few years later, you picked up another 100 shares at 50.

If you sell 100 shares of ABC for $90 a few years after that, which 100 shares of ABC did you sell?

There are three methods you could use.

FIFO means first-in-first-out. So whichever ones you sell first are the ones you bought first. That would be the ones you bought for $30, giving you a capital gain of (proceeds minus cost base) $60.

You could use share identification and say you sold the ones you bought for $50. That would be a capital gain of only $40, which would lower your tax bill.

Or, you could keep an average cost, which would be $40. You bought 300 shares at an average cost of $40 per share, so no matter which ones you sell, their average cost is $40.

Any of those three methods is available to an investor.

Corporate taxes

Corporations are taxed at their corporate tax rate. Yep, if they have the misfortune of making a profit they have to pay their corporate tax rate on the profit. What's left of it, anyway, after their accountants scour for tax write-offs and beneficial amortization/depreciation schedules. Some companies use the IRS's Subchapter M to set themselves up as a "conduit" to investors. REITs do this. Many mutual funds do it, too. If a mutual fund has $1,000,000 in net income, they often send at least 90% of it (900K) to shareholders as a dividend or "income" distribution. That way, the mutual fund company only pays tax on the remaining $100,000. The shareholders pay tax on the money the fund sends them. The company has to send at least 90% to qualify for this tax treatment, and they can send more if they want.

When a corporation invests in the stocks of other companies, they receive dividends like any other investor. Unlike ordinary investors, though, the corporation receiving these fat dividend checks from other companies' <u>stock</u> gets to exclude the first 70% from tax. Which means they only get taxed on 30% of what they receive. And, if they're really an owner of the other company, they can exclude 80% of the income from tax. Why the test would get that trivial, I have no idea. I think the Series 65 simply lacks a healthy social life, not to mention the folks who spend their careers coming up with questions for the test bank.

And, as you may recall from our lively discussion of economics, the companies who pay the dividends have already paid tax on that money. So the receiving corporation shouldn't have to pay tax on all of it.

And they don't. Only on 30% (or 20%) of it.

If a corporation holds bonds of another corporation, they do NOT get to deduct any of the interest. That's because the company who paid the interest already deducted it from their taxable income (remember the income statement earlier?). Municipal bond interest is tax-exempt to a corporate owner just as it is to any other owner.

Tax-exempt and tax-deferred

No reason to confuse these two terms. A tax-exempt investment does not subject the investor to tax. Which is a good thing. Municipal bonds and munibond funds pay income distributions that are tax-exempt at the federal level. So, if an investor earns $100,000 worth of interest payments from tax-exempt municipal bonds or bond funds, how much tax does she pay?

Nothing. Not to the federal government, which is why rich folks like muni's so much. What about the states?

The states generally tax the interest on any municipal bond issued from some entity outside the state. If you're an Illinois resident, do you really expect Illinois to give you a break on interest you earned from a Kansas state municipal bond?

No. If you bought a bond issued by the state of Illinois, or the city of Chicago, that would be different. Then, you'd get a break from the federal government because it's a municipal bond, and your state of residence, Illinois, would give you a break since you were kind enough to sponsor yet another convention center or toll road by buying an Illinois municipal bond.

The interest on Treasury securities is taxable only at the federal level, so a wealthy investor could avoid state taxes on her Treasury bills, notes, bonds, and STRIPS, and avoid federal tax on her municipal bonds. For some people, tax avoidance is a favorite aspect of investing, so don't be surprised if the exam wants you to know how folks can stick it to the IRS and/or their state's department of revenue.

A tax-deferred investment is exactly what it sounds like—it's taxable, but not yet. Think of a tax-deferred retirement account as a protective shell that you can place around your stocks, bonds, and mutual funds until you get ready to take out the money at retirement. Instead of having to dip into the account and sell stuff just to pay the tax bill every year, you can leave all the dividends, interest, and capital gains in the account until you're ready for the money at retirement. You'll pay tax on all the money coming out of a traditional IRA, SEP, Keogh, 401K, or 403b plan. But, since you didn't have to dip in there every year depleting the principal, the whole thing snowballed and grew much faster.

Now at retirement, though, it's time to start paying the piper. You pay your ordinary income tax rate on all money coming out of an IRA, SEP, Keogh, 401K, 403b, or defined benefit pension plan. You *wish* you could pay your long-term capital gains rate—which, as we noted—is just 15% at this point.

Well, keep wishing. But know that all distributions you take from your retirement plan will be taxable at your ordinary income rate, not capital gains.

Unless it's a Roth IRA, which will give you tax-free distributions. Yes, all the money coming out of your Roth is tax-free, provided the account is at least 5 years old, and you're at least 59½ years old. The money coming out of 529 plans and ESAs/Coverdell plans is also tax-free...as long as you play by the rules.

For a non-qualified annuity, the earnings above what you put in—your after-tax cost basis—are also fully taxable at your ordinary income rate.

STUDY SHEET LESSON 3
"TYPES OF CLIENTS AND TAXATION ISSUES"

SECURITY	INCOME SOURCE	TAX TREATMENT	TAXABLE AT WHAT LEVEL?	CAP GAINS
Stock (including Equity Mutual Funds)	Dividends	Qualified=15% max	Any	Taxable
REITs, Royalty Trusts	Dividends	Ordinary Income	Any	Taxable
Corporate Bond	Interest	Ordinary Income	Any	Taxable
GNMA, FNMA, etc.	Interest	Ordinary Income	Any	Taxable
Treasury Securities	Interest	Ordinary Income	Federal *only*	Taxable
Municipal Bonds	Interest	Exempt at Federal	State/Local depends on residence	Taxable

Capital gains are fully taxable on *all* debt securities.

Dividends: qualified dividends currently taxed at maximum of 15%. Ordinary dividends taxed at investor's ordinary income rate.

Capital gains: long-term capital gains taxed at maximum of 15%. Short-term capital gains (taken within 1 year) taxed at ordinary income rate. For mutual funds, capital gains distributions most likely treated as long-term. For fund shares sold, investor's holding period determines long- or short-term treatment.

Bond interest: taxable as ordinary income to the investor, unless exempt (see chart above).
Capital gains on bonds: fully taxable, even municipal bonds

Inherited securities: recipient steps up cost basis to fair market value on date of death.
Gifted securities: receiver takes giver's original cost basis.
Donated securities: donor deducts fair market value on date of donation from taxable income.

Progressive taxes: the rate rises with the size of the INCOME, GIFT, or, ESTATE.

Regressive taxes: taxed at a flat rate, i.e., SALES, GASOLINE, EXCISE.

Pre-tax contributions (money going in): SEP-IRA, SIMPLE IRA, Keogh, 401K, 403b (tax-sheltered annuity [TSA]), Traditional IRA, Section 457 plan, defined-benefit pension plan, any qualified annuities.

After-tax contributions: Roth, non-qualified annuity, Coverdell (ESA), 529 plan, insurance policies.

Retirement plan distributions (money coming out): for qualified plans, distributions to the retiree are taxed as ordinary income. For variable annuities, the excess over the cost basis is taxed as ordinary income. For the Roth IRA, all distributions are tax-free as long as the account has been established for 5 years *and* the individual is at least 59½ years old. For both Coverdell (ESA) and 529 plans, tax-free distributions if money is used according to plan rules.

PRACTICE QUESTIONS

1. An investor has contributed $20,000 to a periodic deferred non-qualified variable annuity. The contract is worth $50,000 at retirement. If the investor takes a random withdrawal of $35,000, what are the tax consequences?
    A. $50,000 taxed as ordinary income
    B. $20,000 taxed as ordinary income
    C. $35,000 taxed at long-term capital gains rate
    D. $30,000 taxed as ordinary income

2. An investor in a municipal bond fund receives both income and capital gains distributions. What is true of the tax treatment of these distributions?
    A. both are taxed at ordinary income rates
    B. both are taxed as long-term capital gains
    C. the income distribution is most likely tax-exempt at the federal level, while the capital gains distribution is fully taxable
    D. both distributions are tax-exempt at the federal level

3. If an individual makes qualified contributions to her IRA, her cost basis is
    A. equal to her contributions
    B. equal to her contributions times a cost of living index multiplier
    C. zero
    D. equal to her average income over the preceding five years

4. All of the following plans are funded pre-tax except
    A. IRA
    B. SEP-IRA
    C. 529 Plan
    D. Tax-sheltered annuity

5. All of the following are funded with after-tax contributions except
    A. Coverdell plan
    B. 529 Plan
    C. Roth IRA
    D. 403b/TSA

6. Interest earned on all of the following is taxable at the state level except
    A. GNMA
    B. FNMA
    C. T-bill
    D. Municipal bonds

7. All of the following are subject to taxation at the federal level except
    A. common stock
    B. preferred stock
    C. municipal bond
    D. Treasury note

8. Which of the following allows an individual to make the largest contribution?
   A. Roth
   B. Traditional IRA
   C. Keogh
   D. Variable annuity

9. Which of the following represents a violation for a securities agent?
   A. recommending that an income investor purchase shares of the ABC Equity Income fund simply because it pays regular dividends
   B. providing a mutual fund prospect with a prospectus before beginning the solicitation
   C. recommending that an income investor purchase shares of the ABC Equity Income Fund primarily to receive an upcoming dividend distribution
   D. following up oral recommendations with accompanying statements of risk

10. All of the following offer tax deferral except
    A. insurance policy
    B. non-qualified annuity
    C. qualified annuity
    D. mutual fund

11. An investor originally invested $10,000 in the XYZ Growth & Income Fund. After re-investing a $2,000 income distribution and a $1,000 capital gains distribution, her cost basis is
    A. $10,000
    B. $7,000
    C. $13,000
    D. not determinable without marginal tax bracket provided

12. All of the following statements accurately summarize major thrusts of the Uniform Prudent Investor Act except
    A. Modern Portfolio Theory is referenced and integrated into the Act
    B. Junk bonds may not be purchased by a pension fund
    C. Professional fiduciaries are held to a higher standard than amateur fiduciaries
    D. Risk management has supplanted risk avoidance

13. Which of the following business structures is limited to 75 shareholders?
    A. C Corporation
    B. S Corporation
    C. LLC
    D. LLP

14. All of the following would be listed as assets on a personal balance sheet except
    A. appraised value of a home
    B. checking account balance
    C. mortgage balance
    D. IRA balance

15. Which of the following represents the best reason for persuading a client to enroll in a wrap-fee account?
    A. the client trades frequently
    B. the client trades infrequently
    C. the wrap-fee structure is the easiest for the investment adviser to implement
    D. the wrap-fee structure is the most cost-effective for the client

Answers

1. **ANSWER: D**

   WHY: there is only $30,000 of earnings or "excess over cost basis."
   The extra $5,000 is part of her cost basis—she already paid tax on $20,000, remember. Also, if you take it nice and slow, you can eliminate the other choices. Nobody pays "capital gains" on a retirement account. Why would 20K or 50K be the answer?

2. **ANSWER: C**

   WHY: the only thing tax-exempt about a munibond is the interest/income. Capital gains are fully taxable on all bonds.

3. **ANSWER: C**

   WHY: if the contributions haven't been taxed yet, she has no cost basis. It will all be taxed when it's distributed at retirement.

4. **ANSWER: C**

   WHY: the plans for education (Coverdell, ESA, 529) are all funded with after-tax dollars. The distributions are tax-free as long as everybody plays by the rules. Choice D was a bit of a trick—you have to read closely. It didn't say "non-qualified variable annuity," right? A tax-sheltered annuity (TSA) is funded with pre-tax deductions from the teacher's paycheck. No cost basis.

5. **ANSWER: D**

   WHY: TSA/403b-501c3...all means the same thing. Pre-tax contributions, zero cost basis, all distributions taxed at ordinary income rate.

6. **ANSWER: C**

   WHY: states can't tax Treasury securities, period.

7. **ANSWER:C**

   WHY: munibonds offer tax-exempt interest at the federal level. Treasury securities definitely get taxed at the federal level, but only at the federal level.

8. **ANSWER: D**

   WHY: assume there are NO limits to the amount you can put into an annuity. Which is what makes them so much fun to sell.

9. ANSWER: C

WHY: choice C represents "selling dividends." Choice A is fine—the agent is selling the fund. In choice C he's trying to sell the dividend—the NAV will drop, and the investor will be taxed. So you don't buy a fund for the upcoming dividend. You buy funds because they make regular dividend payments. See the important difference?

10. ANSWER: D

WHY: mutual funds offer no tax advantages per se.

11. ANSWER: C

WHY: she gets taxed on reinvested distributions, just as if she'd taken the check and cashed it. If you get taxed, it adds to your cost basis.

12. ANSWER: B

WHY: remember to view the risk of the portfolio rather than categorically denying a specific type of investment. The pension fund might offset the risk of holding junk bonds by holding a percentage of Treasury bonds.

13. ANSWER: B

WHY: just a point to memorize

14. ANSWER: C

WHY: the stuff you have to pay out is definitely on the balance sheet, but it's a liability.

15. ANSWER: D

WHY: choice "A" isn't a bad answer, but choice "D" is a better answer. Whoah! You mean there is subjectivity involved on this exam?

Big time.

MORE STUFF ON TAXATION
(TYPES OF CLIENTS AND TAXATION ISSUES)

TRUSTS

Trusts are considered taxable entities, just as corporations are. The way that a trust is taxed depends on whether it's a revocable or irrevocable trust. We're talking about the word "revoke" here, so the title of the trust tells us whether the grantor has the right to take any of the assets back. In a revocable trust, the grantor could end up getting ticked at the heirs, terminate the trust, and take back all the property. In an irrevocable trust, once the property goes in, it can't be revoked. So, only in rare cases would the grantor to an irrevocable trust have to worry about paying taxes. I don't see how this exam could get detailed about these concepts, since this isn't the CPA or CFP exam, but the folks responsible for this nightmare of a test are capable of just about anything. I swear they feel they have the right to ask you what the middle name of the 3rd SEC chairman was before he changed it. Although probably not.

Myron, by the way.

Just kidding. It was Milton.

Income distributed to the beneficiaries of a trust is taxable, unless we're talking about municipal bond interest. Or, if 20% of the income distributed to the beneficiaries comes from munibond interest, 20% is tax-exempt.

The income that is not distributed to beneficiaries is taxable to the trust itself.

Since both the federal government and most states tax the transfer of property, you have to know some of the basics of gift taxes and estate taxes. Gifts over $12,000 per person per year are taxable, and the securities bequeathed to the heirs of an estate are also taxable. Since an IAR is not a qualified tax professional, you should recommend that your clients with significant assets who want to minimize estate taxes on the money they leave to their heirs consult a tax professional or estate attorney in order to design the most effective estate plan.

Up to now, I've been driving a certain percentage of readers absolutely crazy each time I say that the excess over $12,000 per person per year is taxable. They've been shouting back at the book about the unified estate and gift tax credit, possibly abbreviating that as simply the "unified credit" and wondering what the heck is wrong with this Walker guy. Okay, you can relax now—we'll bring it up, in case the exam does. Like most things, this whole gift and estate tax thing is more complicated than you'd like it to be. The $12,000 figure is accurate (until it goes up again), but when I said the giver has to "pay tax" on the excess above $12,000, actually what the giver can do is start chiseling away at his/her "unified credit" that the IRS gives them. A "tax credit" is an amount you don't have to pay, remember. So, if you had a "unified credit" of $1.5 million, you could actually get out of paying gift and estate taxes if all the gifts you made while alive plus the estate you left behind totaled no more than $1.5 million. I'm just using that number as a figure—I'd be shocked if the test wanted to keep changing questions every year, as the unified credit is scheduled to rise every year between 2002 and 2009 and, therefore, will rise, unless it doesn't. So, more accurately, should Bill Gates be so impressed with your techno-knowledge on the red eye to Seattle, he wouldn't have to pay tax on the excess above $12,000 that he gave you—he'd just have to subtract the excess from his lifetime unified estate and gift tax credit. Who knows, maybe he has a little Excel spreadsheet fired up for that very purpose...I still don't think he's likely to give you the first $12,000, let alone the $88,000 excess above that, which would start chiseling away at his unified credit. See? That's why I didn't bring it up earlier. If I told "the whole story" about every potentially testable point, this book would be 1,500 pages long.

And nobody wants that.

But we aren't done yet.

GIFTS

A gift is defined as money or property that a taxpayer gives to someone without expecting to receive something of at least equal value in return. Therefore, if a good buddy sells you a home for much less than its full value, the discount he gives you could be considered a gift. Or, if he makes you an interest-free or reduced-interest loan, that might be considered a gift, too.

Remember, it's the giver's responsibility to deal with this tax, not the recipient's.

Also, a married couple could mutually give a third party annual gifts up to $24,000 (at the time of writing), a practice sometimes called "gift splitting." These numbers are indexed for inflation, by the way, so they may have gone up recently, and I'm not going to spend my time changing them every six months or so. If the numbers seem dated, look up the new numbers.

Nontaxable gifts: since Congress and the IRS are such swell guys, they don't tax all gifts. For example, spouses don't get taxed when they give each other gifts. If you pay somebody else's educational or medical expenses, that's generally tax-free, too.

No, I didn't say "tax-deductible." You don't get to deduct the amount of your kid's tuition from your ordinary income, but you also don't have to pay gift tax on it. I mean, even the IRS has limits to their propensity to irritate.

What if the exam was in a really bad mood on test day and gave you a question like this, just to see how much you wanted your little license?:

> Joe Schmoe paid his son's tuition of $20,000 this year, gave his buddy Bill $8,000, gave his daughter Tina $17,000, his daughter Krystal $16,000, and his wife, Barbara, $12,000. How much would he have to declare in gift tax?

Ouch!

Well, just in case you get one like that, remember that the tuition payment for junior doesn't count, nor does the gift to Bill-buddy, since it's under $12,000. The gift to his wife doesn't count, either. So, just take the excess above $12,000 on the gifts to Tina and Krystal. $5,000 excess on the gift to Tina and $4,000 excess on the gift to Krystal. So, he'll just reduce his unified lifetime credit by $12,000 and keep on keeping track of all his generous impulses.

Of course, if he keeps giving so freely, he's going to use up the unified credit, which will trigger estate taxes for his heirs. But, you can't have everything. Or maybe he wants them to have the money now when he can watch them spend it. Or fight over it—no idea why this guy gave one daughter $1,000 more than the other. Pretty sick puppy if you ask me.

ESTATES

When figuring estate tax liability at the federal level, we start with the "gross estate," which includes all the property that a person owned at death. This does not include any assets placed in irrevocable trusts. So, if it does not include assets placed in irrevocable trusts, you'd probably not be surprised to discover that it does cover assets placed in revocable trusts.

According to the IRS, "gross estate" includes:
- Any property the decedent (dead person) transferred within 3 years of dying
- (and this DOES include transfers to irrevocable trusts, because all basic rules simply have to be violated in the world of finance)
- Life insurance proceeds on policies owned by the decedent
- Value of certain annuities payable to the estate or the decedent's heirs

The TAXABLE estate is the portion of the gross estate subject to federal taxes. To get to the taxable part subtract the following from the gross estate:
- Funeral and administrative expenses
- Debts owed at the time of death
- Any charitable gifts made after death
- The marital deduction (mentioned below)

After subtracting that stuff, we have the "tentative estate tax." It's "tentative" because we now see how much of that unified credit is left. With any luck, there will be more left in the credit than this tentative estate tax figure, but, if not, the amount left after subtracting what's left in the unified credit is taxable.

The "marital deduction" mentioned is fairly self-explanatory. It means that a spouse may transfer property to the surviving spouse upon death tax-free. Basically, a husband and wife are considered one "economic unit." During their lifetimes and at death husbands and wives may transfer property to each other without limit. We still need a will or trust document to specify the transfers, or the property needs to be held jointly by the spouses. Also note that life insurance death benefits payable to the surviving spouse are tax-free.

So, if that's the case, why bother with estate planning? Because, eventually, the surviving spouse will pass away, too, and what happens to all the property set to pass to the heirs? That's where it gets tricky, which is why careful estate planning is so important and is such a hot industry.

ALTERNATIVE MINIMUM TAX (AMT)

Because of AMT many taxpayers have to calculate their income taxes twice.

First, they calculate their tax using regular rules. Then, they calculate their tax using a separate set of AMT rules. In typical governmentspeak, the "minimum" means you pay the maximum—the higher of the two numbers. The types of things that get added to tax liability for purposes of AMT would include:

- tax-preference items like the interest on private purpose municipal bonds, or accelerated depreciation taken from a partnership
- adjustments, including personal exemptions, standard deductions, and itemized deductions such as state and local taxes, stock options

If a taxpayer in a test question is concerned about AMT taxes/tax preference items, keep her out of any munibond that is likely considered a "private purpose" bond. So, a parking garage or convention center would likely be deemed "private purpose," while a school or "GO bond" would almost certainly not subject the person to AMT hassles.

TAXATION ON DIVIDENDS RECEIVED BY CORPORATIONS

In this chapter, I wrote that a corporation gets to exclude the first 70% of dividend income it receives for holding common or preferred stock in another corporation.

Of course, nothing could be quite that simple.

First, that's if the corporation owns less than 20% of the other corporation.

If the corporation owns 20% or more then 80% of the dividend income is excluded from taxes.

And remember that if a corporation owns mutual fund shares, REITs, or royalty trusts, those dividends may or may not be "qualified dividends." For example, if it's a mutual fund holding all debt securities, those don't get the favorable treatment—they aren't qualifying dividends; they're really just interest payments. To keep this stuff straight, refer to your understanding of the income statement. Bond interest is tax-deductible, so you don't get a break on bond interest received, except when you do (munibonds). But, dividends are paid after-tax…after the "bottom line" has been figured. So, if the corporation was fully taxed before paying the dividend, why should the receiver be fully taxed?

Therefore, if it's a REIT or a royalty trust acting as a "conduit" to the shareholders, the corporation is getting a tax break. So, why should the shareholders also get a break?

See? Nice and simple. Just the way Congress and the IRS like it.

Online Updates

Do you have the most current updated information? Visit www.passthe65.com to make sure!

Lesson 4

Rules and Regulations

Federal Acts

Securities Act of 1933

The Securities Act of 1933—sometimes referred to as the "Paper Act"—is all about registering the security (the paper) with the SEC, which then gives the company the green light to sell or "issue" their paper to the public. As a customer, before you buy a brand new share of stock, you have to be provided with a prospectus that discloses everything you might want to know about the company issuing the paper. You can read about its history, its board of directors, its products and services, its chances for success, and its chances for failure. You can look at the balance sheet and the income statement. You'll still be taking a risk if you buy—because all securities carry risk—but at least you'll be able to make an informed decision because of this full and fair disclosure. When a corporation wants to raise cash by selling securities, they have to get a group of underwriters together and fill out a bunch of paperwork for the federal government in the form of a registration statement, or "S1." Part of this information will become the prospectus, which is the disclosure brochure that the public will be provided with. An "underwriter" is just a broker-dealer that likes to take companies public, by the way. Another name for an underwriter is "investment banker," but they don't act like a traditional bank. No deposits or checking offered here. They're just salesmen who like to play a high stakes game of poker known as taking companies public.

Anyway, once the underwriters and the issuer file the registration papers, they go into a "cooling off" period, which will last a minimum of 20 days. This process can drag on and on, but no matter how long it takes, the corporation can only do certain things during this "cooling off" period. Number one, they can't sell anything. They can't even advertise. They can announce that a sale is going to take place by publishing a tombstone ad in the financial press. A tombstone ad is just a boring rectangle with some text—looks like a tombstone. It announces that a sale will take place and informs the reader how he/she can obtain a prospectus. But it is neither an offer nor a solicitation. The underwriters can send out a preliminary prospectus/**red herring** to certain clients, then call them up to find out if anyone wants to give an "indication of interest," but those aren't sales. Just names on a list. The red herring, by the way, contains almost everything that the final prospectus will contain except for the effective date and the final offering price or "POP." The registered rep may NOT send a research report along with the red herring and may not highlight or alter it in any way.

The issuer and the underwriters perform due diligence during the cooling off period, which just means they make sure they provided the SEC and the public with accurate and full disclosure.

Nothing gets sold until the SEC "releases" the security on the release or effective date. Starting on that date the prospectus will have to be delivered to all buyers of these new securities for a certain length of time. And, even though the SEC makes issuers jump through all kinds of hoops, once it's all done, the SEC pretty much washes its hands of the whole affair. They don't approve or disapprove of the security. They don't guarantee accuracy or adequacy of the information provided by the issuer and its underwriters. In other words, if this whole thing goes belly up because of inaccurate disclosure, the liability still rests squarely on the shoulders of the issuers and underwriters, not on the SEC. And, there has to be a disclaimer saying basically that on the prospectus. It usually looks like this:

> The Securities and Exchange Commission has not approved or disapproved of these securities. Further, it has not determined that this prospectus is accurate or complete. Any representation to the contrary is a criminal offense.

Hmm, so how does the SEC feel about the investment merits of the security?

No opinion whatsoever. They just want to make sure you receive full and fair disclosure in order to make up your mind.

Exempt issuers/securities

The Act of 1933 is a piece of federal legislation, so it's not surprising that the folks who passed it gave themselves an exemption from the rule. That's right, government securities are exempt from this act. They don't have to be registered in this way. Neither do municipal securities. Charitable organization securities, such as church bonds, are exempt from the act. So are bank securities, which are already plenty regulated by bank regulators (FDIC, FRB, Comptroller of the Currency). These are all exempt securities issued by exempt issuers. Securities that mature in 270 days or less—commercial paper, banker's acceptances—are also exempt from this arduous registration process.

Exempt transactions

And there are also transactions that qualify for exemptions. Believe it or not, you should probably memorize all the nitpicky factoids that follow:

Under Reg A, an issuer can sell up to $5,000,000 worth of securities in a year without having to jump through all the usual hoops. Rather than filing a standard registration statement, the issuer files an offering circular, a much more scaled-down document. If the issuer agrees to sell the stock to residents of only one state, they will qualify for a Rule 147 exemption. The issuer's main business is located in this state, and 80% of its assets are located here. Also, the buyers can't sell the security to a nonresident for 9 months. The issuer registers with the state, rather than the SEC, since it's all taking place in that one state. IntrAstate. All in A state. When we get down to the state (Uniform Securities Act) level, we'll see that the issuer would most likely use "registration by qualification" to do the intra-state IPO. The SEC is federal, in charge of inter-state commerce. So if it's all within a state, it's that state's concern.

Sometimes issuers offer their shares primarily to "accredited investors." These are sophisticated investors, often with millions of dollars at their disposal. If the individual has more than $1 million net worth or makes more than $200,000 grand a year (more than $300,000 for married, filing jointly), he/she is accredited. So, an issuer can place their securities under a Reg D transaction with as many of these folks as they want. This "private placement" is, by definition, not being offered to the general public, so the SEC eases up a bit. As much as the SEC ever eases up, anyway. Beyond wealthy individuals, the issuer can place these securities with as many institutional investors—mutual funds, pension plans, insurance companies—as they want. And they can sell to insiders of the corporation, which includes officers, directors, and large shareholders. So, a Reg D/private placement transaction is exempt from the Act of 1933 because it is offered to an exclusive group of investors. No more than 35 non-accredited investors can buy these securities, and everybody has to hold the stock for the first year before selling it. After that, a non-affiliated investor would have to comply with volume limits during the second year, and an affiliated investor would have to comply with volume limits all the time because they're, well, affiliated and all.

See, if you're an insider or affiliate of the company, you always have to file Form 144 with the SEC, announcing that you intend to sell a certain amount of your stock over the next 90 days. Your volume is limited to 1% of the shares outstanding or the average weekly trading volume over the four most recent weeks, whichever is larger. That's surprising, too, because you might think the SEC would stick you with the smaller number. Go figure.

So you can bet the test will give you at least five weeks—only average the four most recent. And then compare that number to 1% of the outstanding shares. Whichever is larger, that's what an insider/affiliate could sell over the next 90 days.

Oh yeah, and there's also an exemption to the exemption. If the amount being sold is less than or equal to 500 shares OR less than or equal to $10,000, the investor doesn't even have to file form 144.

Aren't you glad you know that?

Rule 144 also covers "control stock." Nothing different about the stock—it's the people who hold the stock that are different. If you're the CEO of a corporation, or the CFO, or the owner of a major chunk of the stock, you could control the success of the company and even the share price by buying and selling huge chunks of your stock at strategic times. Therefore, you tell the SEC what you're planning to do with your stock every time you think about selling some of it. You do this by filing a Form 144, which also covers "restricted" stock.

What is restricted stock, you may be wondering. Well, stock sold through a private placement (Reg D) is unregistered and therefore *restricted*. Restricted means its transfer or sale is restricted—investors have to hold it for a full year before selling it. In the second year, a non-affiliate of the company has to fill out Form 144 and comply with the volume limits just mentioned. In the third year and beyond, though, he/she can sell the shares freely. Control persons (officers, directors, 10% shareholders, immediate family of insiders) always have to comply with volume limits.

Always.

And, those people can never sell the company's stock short. They can't profit from their company's poor stock performance, in other words. And, if they make a profit on their company's stock held less than 6 months, they'll wish they hadn't. This is called a short-swing profit, and it has to be turned back over to the company with the gain still being taxed by the IRS—who, as always, is here to help.

By the way, a private placement at the federal level uses the number 35 for non-accredited investors. If you're subject to state-level registration, the number is 10.

The final exemption is the 144a exemption. This is for unregistered foreign securities being sold to American institutional investors. Why should the SEC lose sleep over protecting mutual funds from buying speculative foreign securities?

SECURITIES EXCHANGE ACT OF 1934

The Securities Exchange Act of 1934 is the second piece of legislation passed, and it is concerned with the secondary market. This is often referred to as the "People Act," which is easy to remember, because it dictates how people may act in the securities markets. It talks about broker-dealers and registered reps having to register with the SEC. As you might already know, "associated persons" such as registered reps have to register with a "member firm" through a U-4 form. So the <u>firm</u> is the member; you, the registered rep, are an associate of the member firm. Member firms need a principal who reviews correspondence, approves every account, initials order tickets, handles written customer complaints, and writes a procedural manual for the office to use. In other words, somebody at the firm is ultimately responsible for the business of the firm—that person is the principal. The principal makes sure that registered reps never **guarantee** customers will make a profit or not lose their money. As professionals, they know that people lose money all the time, which is what makes investing so darned much fun in the first place. Reps can't go "halvsies" with customers, promising to split gains and losses personally. Only time a rep can **share** is if the rep is in an approved joint account with a customer and only shares to the extent of his or her investment in the account. Reps can never borrow money from customers—unless the customer happens to be a lending institution. But no way can you call your best customers and ask them to spot you a hundred bucks until the end of the month. The firm and the rep can never mix and match their assets with their customers, either. That's called **commingling**, and the SEC frowns on that sort of thing. Since this is the securities business, we made sure to use fancy language like "no misrepresentations of fact, no omissions of material facts, no manipulative or deceptive devices..." when all we really mean is: don't lie, cheat, or steal when dealing with your customers.

The word **churning** is always bad. Always. It means the rep is getting the customer to buy and sell frequently just to generate commissions for the rep. Sounds like a great way to make money, but it will get you in trouble faster than just about anything, and the NASD or SEC could fine you thousands if not millions of dollars just to help you remember not to churn in the future. Both organizations are generally very helpful in that way.

The Act of 1934 talked about insider trading, warning investors not to pass around or use non-public information, and also made sure that short sales only take place on an uptick or a repeat of an uptick. In other words, the stock can't already be moving down when you want to sell it short. This Act gave the Federal Reserve Board the power to regulate margin. It also requires public companies to file quarterly and annual reports with the SEC. Finally, proxies have to be sent to customers at the issuer's expense to enable shareholders to vote without having to attend the annual shareholder meeting in Keokuk, Iowa.

TRUST INDENTURE ACT OF 1939

To protect bondholders, Congress passed the Trust Indenture Act of 1939. If a corporation wants to sell $5,000,000 or more worth of bonds in a year, they have to do it under a contract or indenture with a trustee, who will enforce the terms of the indenture <u>to the benefit of the bondholders</u>. In other words, if the issuer stiffs the bondholders, the trustee can get a bankruptcy court to sell off the assets of the company so that bondholders can recover some of their hard-earned money. Sometimes corporations secure the bonds with specific assets like airplanes, securities, or real estate. If so, they pledge title of the assets to the trustee, who just might end up selling them off if the issuer gets behind on its interest payments. So just remember that an indenture is a contract with a trustee, who looks out for the bondholders.

INVESTMENT COMPANY ACT OF 1940

The Investment Company Act of 1940 classified investment companies as face amount certificates, unit investment trusts (UITs), or management companies. Remember that this Act said the board of directors for a mutual fund must contain 40% outsiders or non-affiliated members. That % has been updated to a "majority," and funds will probably soon need 75% of the board (and the chairman) to be independent/noninterested. I could almost see a reason for including this idea on the Series 65 exam. Since folks with the Series 65 license are portfolio managers, they may be advising mutual fund portfolios for a percentage of assets plus performance fees. Okay, so the board of directors is supposed to look out for the shareholders, who are best served by paying low annual expenses, of which management fees are usually the biggest piece. Let's say you're on this board of directors. I'm the portfolio manager, and I pay you $10 million a year to act as my accountant. Now, when it comes time for me to negotiate my contract with the board of directors for the fund, are you going to try to reduce what I'm asking the board to pay for my money management services? Sort of depends on how much you want to keep your little $10 million contract with me, right?

So, you're an interested member of the board, due to your obvious self-interest in keeping the investment adviser happy. If the whole board were interested/affiliated, we could probably just keep sticking it to the shareholders in the form of higher and higher management fees, right?

And that's why most funds need to have a majority of the board made up of independent/non-interested/non-affiliated parties. More important than the percentages, though, would be the concept of what it means to be "independent/non-interested" and why anybody should care.

The Act of '40 also said investment companies have to register and laid out the rules and processes for registration. The reason the federal government gets to regulate investment companies is because their shares are usually sold inter-state. Remember "inter-state" leads to federal authority; intra-state involves state-level authority.

INVESTMENT ADVISERS ACT OF 1940

Obviously, we've already discussed this exciting piece of legislation, but I like to bring up important concepts from more than one angle. Convexity gets a sentence or two, but the Investment Advisers Act of 1940 is hugely important on this exam for Investment Advisers and IARs. As you already know, if you want to give people your expert advice on their specific investment situation and receive compensation, you have to register under the Investment Advisers Act of 1940. The rules are covered in detail in our chapter cleverly entitled "What the Heck Is an Investment Adviser?"

ERISA

ERISA is an acronym standing for "Employee Retirement Income Security Act." Since investment advisers manage pension plans, the act is highly relevant to the Series 65/66. ERISA covers plans in the private sector, not the public or government sector. Remember, whenever the government makes a rule, it's assumed that everybody understands that the rule doesn't apply to *the government.*

Anyway, the first thing to remember is that the manager of a pension fund is a "fiduciary" with huge obligations to the participants and beneficiaries of the plan. The following is copy-and-pasted from the act itself:

- a fiduciary shall discharge his duties with respect to a plan solely in the interest of the participants and beneficiaries
- and for the exclusive purpose of: (i) providing benefits to participants and their beneficiaries; and (ii) defraying reasonable expenses of administering the plan
- with the care, skill, prudence, and diligence under the circumstances then prevailing that a prudent man acting in a like capacity and familiar with such matters would use in the conduct of an enterprise of a like character and with like aims
- by diversifying the investments of the plan so as to minimize the risk of large losses, unless under the circumstances it is clearly prudent not to do so; and
- in accordance with the documents and instruments governing the plan insofar as such documents and instruments are consistent with the provisions of this subchapter and subchapter III of this chapter.

The "documents and instruments governing the plan" might be referred to on the exam as an "investment policy statement." Investment advisers in general, and pension fund managers in specific, generally need to write investment policy statements and stick to them. Or, the trustees write the policy statement, and the portfolio manager sticks to it. Either way, you don't manage a $1 billion pension fund wearing a Grateful Dead T-shirt and cutoffs telling the investment committee you usually just pick stocks the same way Phil Lesh picks out bass notes, "like, by feel, you know?" If the policy statement says that no more than 40% of the plan assets are to be invested in equities, guess what? Don't put more than 40% into equities—even if you ended up having a good year because of your disobedience, you'd still be in trouble. The only time to override the policy statement is if it clearly violates ERISA.

There are also prohibited transactions for pension funds. A plan may not "acquire any employer security or real property, if immediately after such acquisition the aggregate fair market value of employer securities and employer real property held by the plan exceeds 10 percent of the fair market value of the assets of the plan." In other words, we don't want the pension fund for XYZ Corporation to invest more than 10% of the pension fund's assets into XYZ securities. It would be bad enough if XYZ goes down the tubes; no need to drag the pension fund down with it, right? We also don't want the plan to devote an inordinate amount of assets toward buying property that is then leased to the employing corporation. Again, if the plan put 90% of its assets into buying property that the suddenly deadbeat employer can't afford to make payment on, we'd have ourselves a real mess.

Also, this heavy fiduciary duty implies that the plan is managing the assets on behalf of employees/participants/beneficiaries. Basically, we're talking about defined *benefit* plans. If we're talking about a 401K that lets the employee choose among mutual funds or individual securities, now it's the employee's problem what happens in the big, scary stock and bond markets. Which makes sense. Remember, a defined-benefit plan puts the investment risk on the plan; a defined contribution plan forces the participants to shoulder investment risk. Another reason they're all the rage with employers these days. SEP IRAs and SIMPLE IRAs not only provide immediate vesting to the employees, but as soon as the employees start deciding how to invest the funds, the employer is relieved of its fiduciary obligation.

INSIDER TRADING ACT OF 1988

Although the Act of 1934 talked about insider trading, apparently it didn't quite get the message across. So in 1988 Congress raised the penalties for insider trading, making it a criminal offense with stiff civil penalties as well. If your brother-in-law happens to be the Chief Financial Officer of a public company and over a few too many martinis lets it slip that his company is going to miss earnings estimates badly this quarter, just pretend like you didn't hear it. Tell your principal and no one else. If you start passing out that information, or if you—God forbid—buy a bunch of puts on the stock, you could go to federal prison. The SEC could fine you three times the amount of your profit (or even your loss avoided). In other words, if you made (or avoided losing) $800,000, they could fine you 2.4 million bucks in a civil suit...and the U.S. Attorney's Office could prosecute you and convince the judge/jury to stick you in a cage for 10 years in a criminal suit.

Sure, but how the heck would they ever catch me?

Interestingly enough, those words have been carved into many federal prison cell walls since they passed the Insider Trading Act of 1988. Check this out—the SEC offers a bounty to anyone interested in dropping a dime on an inside trader. The bounty is 10% of whatever penalty the SEC extracts out of the person in civil court. Any information the public doesn't have, that's inside information. Don't pass it around, don't use it. Wait until it's disclosed, then do whatever you want with it.

PENNY STOCK COLD CALLING RULE

Ironically, only the very rich can afford very cheap stocks. If you buy a stock priced at 70 cents, that might sound like a bargain. But guess what else it is—a stock trading dangerously close to zero. If it goes down just 10 cents, that represents a sudden drop of 14%. If it fell a quarter, that would be a drop of 36%. In other words, a very dangerous stock to own. Highly speculative, well-funded investors might play with such volatile issues, but they aren't the sort of stocks that you should be pitching to people over the telephone, especially people you've never met. So, if you want to do the smilin' and dialin' routine, you should probably talk about stocks trading above $5 a share. Otherwise, you'll have to send out a penny stock disclosure document and get the customer to sign a suitability statement, due to the massive risks associated with cheap stocks. Once a customer has made three penny stock purchases with you, or has had an account at your firm for one year, you don't have to worry about it. This rule protects new customers. Established customers are a different story. A penny stock is not listed on an exchange, does not trade regularly over NASDAQ, and also trades below $5 a share. It has to have all of those characteristics to be a "penny stock." In other words, SUNW might trade at $2 today (if it's lucky), but it's not a penny stock since it's still trading over NASDAQ'S National Market System. An unlisted/Non-NASDAQ stock would have to be trading above $5; otherwise, it's a penny stock.

CONSUMER PROTECTION ACT

Speaking of smiling and dialing, when you start doing that you'll have to remember to call the victim—I mean, the *prospect*—only between eight in the morning and nine o'clock at night in the prospect's time zone. If the prospect says she's not interested and wants you to never call her again, you have to put her on a Don't-Call list so that nobody at the firm calls her back for at least 10 years. If you send a fax, make sure to include your contact information so the customer can call back and politely request to be placed on the Don't-Call list.

Charitable organizations are exempt from this rule, as is legitimate debt collection. So, if the nice folks at VISA® call you up about your $20,000 balance, you can't say, "Not interested, please put me on your Don't-Call list."

SEC VS. SROS

The SEC is a government body. They have handed off many responsibilities to self-regulatory organizations (SROs) like the NASD, a process which started in 1938 with the passage of the Maloney Act. This Act created the NASD as the SRO for the OTC. In other words, the NASD oversees the over-the-counter market, where securities like MSFT and ORCL trade millions of shares daily over NASDAQ. Boy, that's a lot of acronyms, isn't it? The SRO for the exchanges would be the NYSE. And the MSRB is the SRO for the munibond business. Options? CBOE.

And that's a generous enough helping of alphabet soup for now.

THE UNIFORM SECURITIES ACT

Well, as if you haven't had enough fun at this point, you now get to look at some specifics of the Uniform Securities Act. You might think the only relevant parts of that act are those pertaining to IAs and IARs.

No. That would make too much sense.

You also have to know about agents, broker-dealers, issuers, securities registration, and the Administrator's power to deny, suspend, and revoke licenses. If you recently took the Series 63 exam, you have a major edge there. If not, you'll have to suffer through the following section highlighting the most testable points from the USA.

BACKGROUND

The state regulators get real nervous whenever somebody tries to sell securities in their state, and for good reason. It would be very easy for some fly-by-night operation to set up shop in a state, sell a bunch of worthless stock, then take the proceeds and run away, leaving investors holding the bag. States don't take kindly to that sort of thing. They're out to protect the average investor from fraud and unethical practices in the purchase and sale of securities.

So in the 1950s securities regulators from around the country passed the Uniform Securities Act. This model legislation serves as a template that the state regulators use to draft securities laws within their states, keeping all the laws fairly "uniform." Notice how we don't get real creative with the language here. If the act is designed to keep the <u>securities</u> laws of the states <u>uniform</u>, we simply name it the <u>Uniform</u> <u>Securities</u> Act. When somebody represents an investment adviser, we call that person an <u>investment adviser</u> *representative*. When somebody issues securities, guess what we call them?

An issuer.

We also use some words you might not be familiar with—like *contumacy, adjudication, enjoin,* and *non-exempt*—but we'll get to that later. For now, let's take a look at the story behind the Uniform Securities Act.

The major concern of a state securities regulator is that a group of operators calling themselves a "corporation" will try to dump a bunch of worthless paper on the average investor, take the proceeds, and flee the state. So, whenever somebody even proposes to issue a security, the state defines that person as an "issuer." Now all the rules on "issuers" spelled out in the USA apply to this person. This person is going to have to register the securities before they can be sold in the state. Investors have to receive a disclosure document that doesn't just make big promises but also details the risks involved with purchasing this—or any—security. The state might even force these issuers to establish an escrow account whose proceeds will not be released by the state until the issuer has raised the amount they're attempting to raise. If the issuer is registering the stock at the federal (SEC) level, the state often wants to see the same stuff they're showing the SEC. If the company is in shaky condition, or if they're going to pay the underwriters way too much money, or if the whole thing just doesn't pass the smell test, the issuer might not even get to sell the stock in the state.

See, selling securities isn't a right. It's a privilege. If you want the privilege of using other people's money to finance your business, you have to earn that privilege. Which means you pay your fees and file all the paperwork required by the state. And— above all—you make sure that you do nothing unethical or fraudulent, unless you care to spend a few years in jail.

Remember, the criminal penalty for fraud at the state level can go up to a fine of $5,000, three years in jail, or both.

So, the states expect these issuers to be on their best behavior when they come into the state trying to raise money by selling stock.

In fact, the states expect <u>everybody</u> to be on their best behavior when issuing or selling this stock. The investment advisers, broker-dealers, and agents pushing this stock on residents of the state also need to be registered and also need to watch their P's and Q's. Unless, of course, they want to donate $5,000 to the state coffers and spend three years getting acquainted with a 285-pound, heavily tattooed cell mate serving time for assault with a deadly weapon.

No thanks, right?

So if your firm is an investment adviser or a broker-dealer doing business in that state, or if you're an individual representing those firms, you have to file paperwork, pay your fees, and be on your best behavior.

Again, selling securities and financial advice is a privilege, not a right, and it's a privilege that can be taken away by the Administrator any time it's in the public interest and provides protection to the average investor.

So, the state securities Administrator is first of all going to regulate all the firms and the representatives of the firms that have set up shop within the state. If I'm the Administrator for Illinois, I'm regulating the investment advisers and broker-dealers, as well as the representatives of those firms, doing business in Illinois. I don't give a rip about the firms doing business in Wisconsin, right? They don't even show up on my radar screen until they start selling securities/advice to folks in Illinois. If a firm doing business in Wisconsin wants to sell securities or advice to someone in Illinois, the key question I have is "To whom are they trying to sell?" If they just want to sell to professional or institutional investors (banks, insurance companies, mutual funds, and pension funds), then I won't even make them register as a broker-dealer or investment adviser in Illinois. If this Wisconsin firm pulls any funny stuff, I'll go after them with everything I've got, but I don't have to provide as much protection to the sophisticated, well-funded institutional investors in my state as I have to provide to the average investor. So, if the firm wants to sell to more than 5 "little guys" or non-institutional investors, then the Wisconsin firm WILL have to register as a broker-dealer or investment adviser in the state of Illinois, because I provide more protection to the little guy.

What's the big deal with being defined by and forced to register with the Administrator?

Well, look at your current situation. How has your life been impacted now that you have been defined as an "agent" of a licensed "broker-dealer" or "investment adviser"? Suddenly, there are fees to pay, paperwork to be filed, and several tough exams to be passed with no small effort on your part. Even after you get your license you'll be subject to more fees, paperwork, and continuing education requirements.

Wouldn't it be great if the state you operate in told you that you were excluded from the definition of "registered representative"? Then all this stuff would be somebody else's problem, not yours.

Nobody wants to be defined and regulated under the Uniform Securities Act. But if they haven't been granted an exemption/exclusion, then the USA does, in fact, apply to them, and they do, in fact, have to mind their P's and Q's.

So if the firm or the representative of the firm <u>does not</u> have an office in a particular state, they often do not have to register in that state. If they sell to institutions, they do not have to register in that state. But, if they sell to more than a few non-institutional investors, they will have to register in that state.

Fascinating stuff, isn't it?

Okay, so securities firms (broker-dealers, investment advisers) have to be properly registered or properly excused (exempted/excluded) from registration. The individuals working at such firms (agents, investment adviser representatives) have to be properly registered at the state level, or properly excused from registration. And, securities also have to be properly registered or properly excused from the arduous process of registration.

Some securities have to be registered. Some don't. Those that don't have to be registered have been granted exemptions from registration. Guess what we call them?

Exempt securities. Exempt means *excused*.

Now, see if you can guess what we call those securities that have to be registered because they DON'T have an exemption.

Non-exempt securities. Non-exempt means *not excused*.

The registration requirements apply to all securities, except to all the securities they don't apply to. If the requirements don't apply, that's an exempt security. If the requirements do apply, the security didn't qualify for an exemption and is, therefore, called a non-exempt security.

You're sure you want to get your license, right?

Just checking.

Anyway, lots of securities are exempt from registering with the SEC. Government bonds, municipal bonds, bank securities, small business investment company securities, non-profit securities, and securities that mature in 270 days or less—like commercial paper and bankers acceptances—are all exempt from registering under the Securities Act of 1933. So, if the security is exempt at the federal level, it is almost always exempt at the state level. The SEC (federal) recognizes a class of securities as *federal covered* because of NSMIA (National Securities Markets Improvement Act of 1996). These securities are covered exclusively at the federal level. Since NSMIA is written in such page-turning, punchy prose, let's see the original text on federal covered securities:

COVERED SECURITIES.—For purposes of this section, the following are covered securities:

(1) EXCLUSIVE FEDERAL REGISTRATION OF NATIONALLY TRADED SECURITIES.—A security is a covered security if such security is—

(A) listed, or authorized for listing, on the New York Stock Exchange or the American Stock Exchange, or listed on the National Market System of the Nasdaq Stock Market (or any successor to such entities);

(B) listed, or authorized for listing, on a national securities exchange (or tier or segment thereof) that has listing standards that the Commission determines by rule (on its own initiative or on the basis of a petition) are substantially similar to the listing standards applicable to securities described in subparagraph (A); or

(C) is a security of the same issuer that is equal in seniority or that is a senior security to a security described in subparagraph (A) or (B).

(2) EXCLUSIVE FEDERAL REGISTRATION OF INVESTMENT COMPANIES.—A security is a covered security if such security is a security issued by an investment company that is registered, or that has filed a registration statement, under the Investment Company Act of 1940.

(3) SALES TO QUALIFIED PURCHASERS.—A security is a covered security with respect to the offer or sale of the security to qualified purchasers, as defined by the Commission by rule. In prescribing such rule, the Commission may define the term 'qualified purchaser' differently with respect to different categories of securities, consistent with the public interest and the protection of investors.

We already mentioned qualified purchasers when we talked about IAs who can get performance-based compensation from private investment companies, who only take money from qualified buyers.

So, all the above list is saying is that if the stock trades on a recognized exchange or is called a "NASDAQ" stock, then it is federal covered. Its registration is handled by the SEC (federal), which is actually plenty to deal with, as it turns out. Mutual funds/investment company securities are federal covered, and that includes variable annuities. So, if the security is covered exclusively at the federal level, it does not have to be registered at the state level because it is federal covered—covered by the federal organization known as the SEC. The investment company shares may be asked to file notice with the states, but that is not a registration—just a filing of notice. To make it sound better, we reverse the words and call it a notice filing. To complete a notice filing, the issuer would provide the state with a consent to service of process, a filing fee, and all the documents filed with the SEC that the state would like to have on file. You can actually print out a notice filing and a consent to service of process at www.nasaa.org, unless you've already had enough excitement at this point

So, if the security is federal covered, it registers with the SEC, which means if the security is *not* federal covered (and not exempted by the USA), then it *does* have to be registered at the state level. Companies trading on the OTC Bulletin Board and the Pink Sheets have to register at the state level. There isn't as much information on these companies, so they'll have to register with the states by coordination, filing, or qualification, which will be discussed later.

The U.S. Government is an exempt *issuer*. Commercial paper is an exempt *security*. That's why neither a T-bond nor a piece of GE commercial paper would have to be registered. So, if an agent sold either security and it turned out the security wasn't registered, that's okay.

In fact, that's how it's supposed to go down. Those securities are exempt from registration. If the agent is doing business in Florida, she needs to be registered in the state of Florida. She needs to be registered in every state in which she is doing business. But an Illinois revenue bond would not have to be registered in any state. Therefore, if she is properly registered as an agent in Florida and sells an unregistered IL Revenue Bond, good for her! She made a nice sale of an exempt security as a properly registered agent in Florida.

She has to be registered. The exempt security does not.

If she sells an unregistered non-exempt security, *that's* a problem. Non-exempt securities have to be registered. Why?

They have no excuse, no exemption.

NO   EXEMPTION

Closer, please.

NO   EXEMPTION.

Still closer.

NOnEXEMPT-ion

Non-Exempt.

Hey! That's all they're trying to say.

Ain't got NO EXCUSE.

Non-exempt.

If the agent accidentally sold a non-exempt security that turned out not to be registered in the state, she committed a prohibited act. If she knew the stock was unregistered and sold it anyway, she committed fraud.

Fraud is the willful attempt to deceive someone for financial gain.

Don't do it.

And when you do, please don't get caught.

We'll discuss all the stuff you can't do later, but for now just remember that fraud is willful deception. Prohibited acts are things you just don't want to do.

So, how much power does the state securities Administrator have, anyway?

A lot.

The Administrator can investigate both inside and outside the state. If you commit fraud in Fort Myers, Florida, the Administrator can chase you all the way to Walla Walla, Washington. And, if the official in Florida doesn't feel like flying, he/she can just send the subpoena to the Administrator in Washington, who will be happy to greet you at the local airport with the out-of-state subpoena for everybody's convenience. Just look for the guy in the dark suit holding up the big sign with the word "Busted!" across it in red ink. If you're formally found to have violated provisions of the USA, you can have your license denied, suspended, or revoked, which is bad. And, the Administrator just loves to publish violations in newspapers, websites, or any other embarrassing, far-reaching forum he can think of.

Now that you've been in trouble with the folks in Florida, good luck trying to set up shop in other states. Remember, your license can be denied, suspended, or revoked in a state based on the trouble you got into in any other state. In fact, if you were busted by a foreign banking authority or were convicted of any securities-related misdemeanor or any felony, your license can be denied, suspended, and revoked in any other state.

So, let's talk about what the Administrator can NOT do.

The Administrator can not issue an injunction. Only a court can do that. And, the Administrator can not sentence a person to jail—again, only a court can do that. The Administrator can take you to court—but they have to go to the trouble of proving you guilty before a judge first. And what chance is there that the Administrator helped get the judge elected?

Basically, don't mess with the Administrator, and the Administrator won't mess with you.

So, there IS a story behind all this stuff—it's not just a bunch of details out to make your life miserable. The miserable part is just a byproduct. What's really going on here is that the state securities Administrators are just trying to protect the average investor from fraud and unethical business practices. They regulate everybody they need to regulate, and before they can do that they have to carefully define who does and does not fall under the various definitions spelled out in the Uniform Securities Act. You and your firm, obviously, both fall under some of the definitions of the Act, which is why you have to pass your state-level exam before you can use your license.

So, let's get down to details now and define the players as well as what they can and can't do. Ready?

Let's do it, anyway.

AGENTS DEFINED

Imagine trying to explain the game of baseball to someone who has absolutely no knowledge of the game. Terms that you have taken for granted since childhood would suddenly involve lots of tedious, complicated explanations. You would have to define the "pitcher" and the "catcher" so that the person unfamiliar with baseball would soon understand that the pitcher is not the catcher, and the catcher is not the pitcher. Neither one would be the first baseman, nor the shortstop, nor the left fielder, right? When the *batter* steps up to the *plate*, he gets four *balls* and three *strikes*.

What's a strike?

That's when he swings the *bat* and misses, or when he should have swung the bat and didn't.

Who decides when he should swing the bat?

An official called the *umpire*.

Are those the only two ways to get a strike?

Well, no, he could also swing the bat and hit the ball, but send the ball either behind him or too far to the left or right, which is a *foul ball*, also recorded as a strike.

But after three strikes, the batter is out?

Absolutely.

No matter how the strike occurred?

Well, no, actually, the third strike triggering the official "strike out" could never be effected via a foul ball, unless the batter tried to bunt or somebody on the other team *catches* the foul ball—then he's *out*.

A strike out?

No, that's a *foul out*.

So, after the third strike—unless it's a foul ball—the batter is out?

Yes, except when the catcher drops the ball on the third strike. Then, the batter gets to run toward first base where he might—or might not—make it safely.

Why?

Cause that's a "dropped third strike."

And you thought baseball was simple.

Pretty simple to step on the field and start playing, but not so simple when you step off the field and try to define all the terminology and complex structure of rules. If you defined "short stop" for purposes of a rulebook, you might have to say something weird like, "The short-stop is defined as an infielder other than the third baseman, second basemen, first basemen, pitcher, or catcher."

Huh? The shortstop is the dude standing between second and third base!

What's a base?

It's that white square the other team is trying to occupy.

How come he's the only one that isn't attached to a particular base?

Of course no true sports fan would tolerate such talk, and I could have gotten myself seriously injured talking that way at the White Sox game I went to last weekend. But a committee did in fact write the dry rules of baseball, carefully defining terms and throwing in weird exemptions to the rules.

Well, the securities industry is just as fast-paced and complicated as any sport, so we have to lay down a lot of ground rules before we turn the players loose. And, before we can even begin to lay down all the complex rules and exemptions to the rules, we first have to define all the players and terminology. Only after clearly defining who is and isn't a *broker-dealer, agent,* or *investment adviser,* and what we mean by seemingly simple terms like "person" or "security" can we tell these broker-dealers, agents, advisers and other "persons" what they can and can't do when they're dealing with "securities."

Defining the players and basic terminology of the securities industry is a major focus of the Series 63/65/66 exam and one of the trickier aspects. So let's get started.

An agent is always an individual and always represents someone else. An agent can either represent a firm defined as a *broker-dealer,* or the agent can represent an entity known as an *issuer* of securities. That means that an agent is NOT a broker-dealer, and is NOT an issuer. Just like the pitcher is NOT the catcher, the shortstop, or the right fielder. So, if you get a test question asking, "Which of the following are agents?" you can eliminate any choice that starts off like this:

A broker-dealer who…

An issuer who…

Broker-dealers and issuers are NOT agents. The agent represents one of those two entities, but the agent is not one of those entities him- or herself. Sort of like saying that Sammy Sosa played for the Chicago Cubs. Sammy Sosa, however, was NOT the Chicago Cubs, even if he has been known to carry the team from time to time.

Sounds goofy, but if we don't establish who is and isn't an agent, how are we going to tell these agents what they can and can't do? In baseball you wouldn't be able to tell the shortstop to stay off the pitcher's mound until you first clarify that the shortstop is NOT the pitcher, and the pitcher sure isn't the shortstop.

Anyway, if the individual selling securities represents a broker-dealer, that individual is defined as an agent, end of story. However, an individual can also represent an issuer, and this is where it gets tricky. First of all, an issuer is anyone who actually issues or proposes to issue securities. In other words, as soon as you file paperwork announcing your intention to raise money by selling securities to investors, you're an "issuer" as defined by the Uniform Securities Act. Chances are, you hire a few individuals to help sell your securities. Sometimes these folks have to register as agents; sometimes, they do not have to register as agents.

Exempt Securities

The following securities are exempt (excused) from state-level registration:

- any security issued/guaranteed by U.S. Treasury/U.S. Government
- municipal securities
- any security issued by ANY Canadian government
- any security issued by a foreign government with diplomatic relations (national/federal only...except Canada, ey?)
- bank, savings institution, trust company security (not bank holding company)
- savings & loan, building & loan securities, credit union securities
- debt securities issued by an insurance company
- securities issued by railroad or other common carrier, public utility, or holding company subject to Interstate Commerce Commission, or the Public Utility Holding Co. Act of 1935
- federal covered security
- non-profit securities (i.e., religious, educational, fraternal, charitable, social, or trade/professional associations)
- promissory note maturing in 9 months/270 days or less, issued with denominations of $50,000+, and rated in top 3 credit tiers by a nationally recognized statistical rating agency (Moody's, Fitch, S&P, etc.)
- investment contract issued in connection with pension/employee benefit program

So, if the individual represents the <u>issuers</u> of any of those exempt securities, the individual is NOT defined as an agent. The foreign government issuer requires some explanation, though. First of all, if the U.S. has diplomatic relations with the foreign government, any security issued by that foreign government is exempt. But we're talking about <u>national</u> governments only. The government of France is an exempt issuer; the government of Paris is *not* exempt or "non-exempt." Bonds issued by the federal/national government of Mexico are exempt; bonds issued by Mexico *City* are not.

See the pattern?

Good—now let's throw it out the window for our neighbors to the north, Canada. We're so close to our Canadian counterparts, that any <u>government</u> security issued way up north there is exempt. National, provincial (state), or local—all exempt. So the bonds issued by the city of Montreal are just as exempt as the bonds issued by the province/state of Quebec or the national government of Canada.

But for all the *other* countries, only the securities issued at the national/country-wide level are exempt.

Don't take it too far, though. There is no exemption for Canadian *corporations*. Only governments.

There are exempt <u>issuers</u>, and there are exempt <u>securities</u>. An exempt issuer would be the U.S. Government. An example of an exempt security would be a promissory note that matures in 270 days or less (banker's acceptance, commercial paper) as long as it's at least $50,000 in denomination and in the top three tiers of credit ratings. So, if the individual represents an issuer in a sale of exempt securities, that person is NOT an agent. You sell T-bonds for the U.S. Government? Not an agent. But, if you sell T-bonds for a broker-dealer, you ARE an agent. You sell commercial paper for the issuer of the commercial paper? Not an agent. You sell commercial paper for a broker-dealer? You ARE an agent.

Remember, if the individual represents the broker-dealer, that individual is always an agent. If the individual represents an exempt issuer, or if he/she represents an issuer in selling an exempt security, he/she is not an agent.

So, there are exempt <u>issuers</u>, and there are exempt <u>securities</u>. General Electric, for example, is not an exempt issuer—they do, after all, have to register their stock with the SEC. But GE also sells some securities exempt from registration, like commercial paper. So, GE is a non-exempt issuer. Their common stock is non-exempt, meaning it has to be registered. But, their commercial paper does NOT have to be registered because it is an exempt security.

So, there are exempt issuers and there are exempt securities.

Then, you got your exempt *transactions*. If the transaction qualifies for one of many exemptions, then the individual representing the issuer will NOT be defined as an agent.

Exempt Transactions

The following transactions are exempt under the Uniform Securities Act, and, therefore the stock wouldn't have to be registered due to the manner in which it's been sold (transacted):

- isolated nonissuer transactions (very few per year)
- unsolicited nonissuer transactions effected through a broker-dealer
- transactions between issuers and their underwriters
- transactions by certain fiduciaries: executors, administrators, sheriffs, marshals, receivers/trustees
- pledges
- any sale or offer to a bank, savings institution, trust company, insurance company, investment company, pension or profit-sharing trust, or other financial or institutional buyer, or to a broker-dealer
- private placements
  - Offered to no fewer than 10 non-institutional buyers in the state per 12-month period
  - Seller believes that all non-institutional buyers hold for "investment purposes"

- No commissions paid for soliciting any non-institutional buyer
- any transaction to existing security holders of the issuer, if no commission is paid for soliciting buyers
- offerings of preorganization certificates
  - No more than 10 buyers, period
  - No commissions paid for soliciting any buyer
  - No payment made by any subscriber
- nonissuer transactions in securities subject to reporting requirements of the Exchange Act of 1934, or in securities registered under the Investment Company Act of 1940, or in securities where the issuer has filed with the Administrator information substantially the same as that required for registered issuers by the Securities Exchange Act of 1934 for a period of at least 180 days prior to the transaction
- any offer (but not a sale) of a security for which a registration statement has been filed under the Uniform Securities Act and the Securities Act of 1933 if no stop order is in effect. Sales may only take place after registration is effective
- any transaction in a bond secured by a real mortgage or deed of trust provided that the entire mortgage or deed of trust, together with the bonds, is offered and sold as a unit

So, if the individual represents the *issuer* in those transactions, he/she is excused from registration and is rather happy to know that.

Let's start with unsolicited nonissuer orders. A nonissuer order is just a trade between two investors, where no money is going to an issuer. Remember how the states get real nervous when issuers try to raise capital on the primary market? Well, this is the secondary or "nonissuer" market. Also, nobody tried to talk the customer into buying the stock, so it's an unsolicited, nonissuer order. How does somebody represent an issuer in a nonissuer transaction?

Not worth going there—memorize it. Or, if you're really bored, give us a call and haze us over this point.

If the individual is representing an <u>issuer</u> when selling to a financial institution, that's also an exempt transaction, so the individual would NOT be defined as an agent under the Uniform Securities Act when representing an <u>issuer</u> and selling to banks, savings & loans, thrifts, or credit unions.

Let's say you work for Coca-Cola® selling Coca-Cola® stock to Coca-Cola® employees and you don't charge commissions. If so, you would not be defined as an agent. If you got commissions, you would be, but since you don't get commissions, you're not defined as an agent, just an employee of Coca-Cola® doing his or her job.

There are also individuals working for broker-dealers who are either not defined as agents at all or not required to register as agents. Technically, someone who is not defined as an agent has been granted an exclusion, whereas someone who simply doesn't have to register has been granted an exemption. But, the test will almost certainly not split hairs with you on that point. Whether the individual does not regis-

ter due to an exclusion or due to an exemption is not really what the exam is after—
the exam just wants you to know who does and doesn't have to register.

Partners and officers of the broker-dealer are not agents, unless they start selling
securities. That's one of the few rules that actually make perfect sense, so let's enjoy it
while we can. If they aren't selling, they aren't agents.

The Administrator in Illinois will let an agent registered in Wisconsin do business with an existing client just visiting the state of Illinois without defining that
individual as an agent in Illinois. That customer is not a resident of Illinois since he or
she is only here temporarily (30 days or less), so the sales rep is NOT an agent in
Illinois. If that customer hangs around too long, we've got a different story, but if he/
she is here temporarily (not a resident of the state) the sales rep is not considered an
agent in Illinois.

What's the big deal with being defined as an agent? Well, once the Administrator
has defined you as an agent in the state, now you have to register in the state. And
registration costs time and money, which is why so many people kicked and screamed
to get an exemption from this inconvenience. Wouldn't you like an exemption from
filling out paperwork, paying fees, and passing some test called the Series 65?

But, if you don't have some kind of exemption, you'll have to register as an agent.
Someone without an exemption is called "non-exempt" in the language of the Uniform Securities Act. So if you see the word "non-exempt," remember that that person
or that security has <u>no excuse</u> or exemption to hide behind. The rules apply to non-
exempt people and securities; they don't apply to exempt people and securities.

You'll need to do lots of practice questions before your exam, so let's do some
practice questions right now on who IS and is NOT an agent.

Ready?

Let's do 'em anyway.

PRACTICE QUESTIONS

1. **Which of the following is defined as an agent?**
    A. a broker-dealer with an office in the state who sells exempt securities
    B. a broker-dealer with no office in the state who sells non-exempt securities
    C. an individual who represents the U.S. Government in selling T-bonds to wealthy investors
    D. an individual who represents a broker-dealer selling exempt securities

2. **Which of the following are not agents?**
    A. broker-dealer who sells exempt securities
    B. broker-dealer who sells nonexempt securities
    C. individual with no office in the state who sells to a customer staying 25 days in the state
    D. all of the above

3. **None of the following is an agent except**
    A. individual who sells Montreal revenue bonds on behalf of the issuer
    B. individual who represents XXY Corporation in selling XXY stock to XXY employees and charges no commissions
    C. individual who sells Mexico City revenue bonds on behalf of the issuer
    D. none of the above is an agent

ANSWERS

1. **ANSWER: D**

   WHY: eliminate the first two choices, since B/D's and agents are never the same thing. Now, you have an individual representing an exempt issuer and one representing a broker-dealer.

2. **ANSWER: D**

   WHY: since broker-dealers are NOT agents, you know the answer has to include both A and B...D!

3. **ANSWER: C**

   WHY: the federal government of Mexico is an exempt issuer, but the provincial and city governments are not exempt. So, this individual is an agent. Lo siento.

AGENTS—FRAUD AND OTHER PROHIBITED ACTIVITIES

Okay, now that we've defined what an agent is—and is not—let's talk about what these agents can and can not do. Something you aren't supposed to do is called a prohibited practice, whether you meant to do it or not. Prohibited practices can get your license denied, suspended, or revoked, which is bad. Fraud has to do with deceiving, misleading, or lying to people in order to wrongfully take their money. People get fined and thrown in jail for committing fraud, which is also bad.

Fraud. Here is the legalistic version, pulled right from the USA itself:

Section 101. [Sales and Purchases.] It is unlawful for any person, in connection with the offer, sale, or purchase of any security, directly or indirectly

to employ any device, scheme, or artifice to defraud,

to make any untrue statement of a material fact or to omit to state a material fact necessary in order to make the statements made, in the light of the circumstances under which they are made, not misleading, or

to engage in any act, practice, or course of business which operates or would operate as a fraud or deceit upon any person

Now, let's translate the above back into a language you are probably more familiar with—*English*.

What that legalese is saying is, "Don't lie, cheat, or steal from your customers when offering/selling securities to them." Material facts are the key—if the facts are material/important/relevant to the customer's decision, you can't misrepresent those facts or fail to provide them. If you do, you have probably committed fraud. Let's say you're trying to sell a brand new share of stock to a skeptical customer. You know this customer will hang up on you if you inform her that the company hasn't made a profit in any of the past three years, so you conveniently omit that material fact from your presentation.

Oops! Any time you *omit material information*, you have probably committed fraud, which is bad. If you omit material information or lie about material information, you're going to have the opportunity to donate $5,000 to the state and spend three years explaining your crime to a large cell mate serving 15 years for assault with a deadly weapon. Three years, five grand. Remember that.

What if the information is IM-material?

Then you should definitely omit it from your presentation to the customer. An IM-material fact would be the average height of GE's vice-presidents or the particular model of water cooler selected for the break room. If you omit that kind of irrelevant information, good for you—it should be omitted. And if you told the customer the company was painting their visitor lobby red, when, in fact, the color was mauve, so what? The customer can't come after you for that—it wasn't material information.

So fraud is basically the intentional/willful attempt to deceive someone for financial gain. If you lie about material facts or conceal them from customers, you have probably committed fraud, which is bad.

The law also says that fraud is not limited to judicial or case-law definitions—it can be established by statute, meaning if the governor and/or legislature defines something as fraud, guess what?

It's fraud.

Also remember that the penalties and sanctions for fraud include:
- administrative proceedings
- judicial injunctions
- criminal or civil prosecutions

So, fraud is bad. Really bad. If you deceive someone when selling securities, you could go to jail for three years and pay a fine up to $5,000, which is bad.

The rest of this stuff is all prohibited. That means, DON'T DO IT.

If you commit prohibited acts, you probably won't end up in jail, but you could easily end up having your license denied, suspended, or revoked.

Which is bad.

So these are most of the things to do and not do once you start work as an agent.

Unsuitable recommendations

Investors trust agents to make suitable recommendations. High-rollers can afford to buy junk bonds and penny stocks, so if your customer is a high roller, go ahead and recommend risky investments. Look out, though, if you start recommending high-risk investments to senior citizens living on modest fixed incomes. A senior citizen living on a modest fixed income would probably put some money in a money market account, a high-grade corporate or government bond fund, or maybe a few select blue chip stocks, right? So, recommend what's appropriate to each individual customer; otherwise, you can get in trouble for making *unsuitable recommendations*. They don't all have to be profitable, but all your recommendations to clients must be suitable.

Churning

Of course, if you're an agent, all your customer's transactions generate a commission for you. That's right, whether your customer makes money or loses money, you get a commission when they buy and a commission when they sell.

Sounds like a pretty good deal, huh? So, the best way for you to make money is to get your customers buying and selling all day every day, right?

Yep, except that's a major no-no called *churning*. If you're pressuring customers to trade frequently just so you can pocket commissions, you can get busted for churning, which is bad.

The dreaded A-word

To impress this skeptical customer, you tell her the security has been approved for sale, either by the SEC or the state securities Administrator.

Not! Securities are never "approved." Regulators <u>allow</u>, they don't *approve*.

Accepting orders on behalf of customers from a third party without trading authorization

One of your best customers is too busy to call you, so he has his wife give you a ring. Buy 10,000 shares of ORCL at $15.75, fill or kill, she says.

What do you do?

Not a darned thing. Not until you've talked to your client. If the couple had a joint account with you, that would be different, but if it's an individual account, you can only accept orders from that individual. If that individual gives trading authorization to another individual—e.g., his wife—and you have that on paper, then it's okay. But a third party without authorization can't tell you what to do for your client's account.

Unauthorized borrowing of money or securities from a customer

> Hi, Mrs. Wilson. This is Ryan Reynolds. Look, it's been a tough quarter for me, Ma'am, now that everybody's too chicken to buy stocks and all, and I was wondering if you could, like, spot me a few c-notes until payday?

Well, that conversation isn't going to happen, right?

An agent can not borrow money from a client, nor would he/she want to try. The only customer that an agent can borrow money from is a bank, since banks are in the business of lending people money, as long as they can prove on paper they don't actually need it.

Commingling

Wouldn't it be fun to control one big account with millions of dollars of assets all mixed in together between you and your millionaire customers? Might be fun, but it's actually a big no-no called *commingling*. Assets have to be separate. You can put customer assets in a common trust, just make sure you don't put customer assets in with your own or your firm's assets. Keep it all nice and separated—customer stuff here, agent stuff here—and everybody's happy.

Deliberately failing to follow a customer's instructions

Here's another conversation that isn't going to happen:

> Hi, Mrs. Wilson, this is Ryan again. Remember when you told me to sell E-toys when it hit three bucks a share? Well, it hit three bucks a share, only guess what? I didn't sell it. Where's it trading at? Let me see...uh, looks like it's about to find support at twelve. No, *cents*. Hello? Mrs. Wilson?

Failure to follow your customers' instructions can get you in all kinds of trouble and is a prohibited practice. So, never would you want to not follow your customers' explicit instructions.

Written complaints

If your customer gives you a written complaint should you A, take it to your supervisor or B, take it to the shredder? Always take written complaints to your supervisor, who can always take it to the shredder himself and probably needs the exercise. If it's in writing, you have to take it to your supervisor, who isn't going to be real happy to see it. But if you think he's mad now, see how he reacts when the firm gets fined and/or sanctioned because you "forgot" to tell him that Mrs. Wilson had written a dozen letters to express her displeasure with the firm.

Ouch.

Guaranteeing customers a profit; guaranteeing against a loss

> Oracle is such a great buy at fifteen, Mrs. Wilson, I tell you what I'm gonna do. If you end up losing anything on the deal, I'll personally refund your money. That's right, I guarantee you'll make money on this investment, Ma'am. No, you can't possibly lose. I guarantee it.

Not.

The word *guarantee* can be used in a very limited sense. The U.S. Government guarantees payment on their T-bonds, which are issued by the folks at the Treasury Department with their fingers conveniently on the printing press. Insurance companies guarantee payment on fixed annuities, but you and your broker-dealer guarantee nothing.

Even if you sell a Treasury bond, which is, of course, guaranteed to pay interest and principal, you would still point out that the investor has interest rate risk. Remember, if you buy a T-bond for par and then interest rates shoot up, the market price of your bond will drop. If you had to sell, you could actually lose money on a Treasury bond. Which would put you in the saddest class of American investors, those who can't even make a little money on securities guaranteed by Uncle Sam, but that's another issue.

In the corporate world, sometimes the subsidiary company issues bonds that are "guaranteed" by the parent company. XYZ issues the bonds, but the parent company, GE, is "guaranteeing them."

Does that mean the investor can't lose?

Heck no. It means that GE is basically a co-signer on the loan. If the little kid defaults, Big Daddy is here to try and bail them out.

What if GE also defaults?

Well, whadaya want, a "guarantee" or something?

Sharing profits or losses with customers

Let's say your customer is hesitant about buying a stock you're sure is set to rally. To ease her mind you offer to go halvsies on the deal. You know, if the stock goes up, we split the gain, and if the stock goes down, we split the loss.

Not.

Only way an agent can *share* with a client is to have an approved joint account with that client, and only share in proportion to what the agent has invested. On the exam, make sure the agent has the customer's written authorization and that of the firm.

Misrepresenting status of customer accounts

You finally talked Mrs. Wilson into buying 1,000 shares of XYZ at $15. Luckily, Mrs. Wilson is in the state of Washington visiting her sister Wilma when XYZ gets walloped the next day. Next day Mrs. Wilson gives you a call, with XYZ currently trading at $3 a share.

> How's that stock you sold me doing there, young fella?

> Just fine, Mrs. Wilson. Right about where we bought it.

That's a lie. The law would never call it a "lie," but the law would tell you not to misrepresent the status of a customer's account, no matter how tempting.

Mutual fund projections

> Mrs. Wilson, this mutual fund has returned an average of 22% the past five years. Based on that performance, I expect it to do at least that well next year, probably better.

Oh no. No mutual fund projections, ever. Past performance does not guarantee future results, end of story.

Making recommendations on the basis of material inside information

What if your sister, the CFO of a large public company, tells you that her firm is about to be purchased by an even larger public company? That should boost her company's stock price, so you call all your clients and tell them to hurry up and buy the stock.

Well, that's called *acting on material inside information* and you can get yourself into all kinds of trouble making recommendations based on such information. Wait until the information has become public unless you want to explain your actions to a roomful of ticked-off regulators.

Promising to perform services without intent or ability to perform them

You also shouldn't go around promising to perform services that you aren't likely or even able to perform. For example, if you're trying to land new customers, don't do so by promising to wash their car every Saturday for the next five years or balance their checkbook for them. That isn't your job, and you aren't likely to follow through, anyway.

Soliciting orders for unregistered, non-exempt securities

Break down those words. The security is "non-exempt," which means it has *no excuse* from registration. It must be registered, so if you're soliciting orders for securities that should be registered but are NOT registered, you're going to get yourself into all kinds of trouble. In fact, making sure that securities offered on the primary market are properly registered is one of the main goals of all this regulation. The states just don't like it when fly-by-night companies try to set up shop in some vacant strip mall just long enough to dump unregistered, bogus securities on the public, take the proceeds, and flee the state.

So, if the security has no exemption/excuse from registration (non-exempt), and you solicit orders for it—watch out! If you knew what you were doing and did it anyway, that could be considered fraud. And even if it was an "honest mistake," it's definitely a prohibited activity that can get your license denied, suspended, or revoked.

Which is bad.

All right. Let's look at a few practice questions on what you can and can't do as an agent.

PRACTICE QUESTIONS

4. **All of the following are prohibited practices except**
   A. depositing client funds into the agent's bank account
   B. recommending municipal bonds to a low-income investor with growth as an objective
   C. recommending municipal securities to a high-tax bracket investor within a qualified retirement account
   D. not ignoring a customer's explicit instructions to not sell a security

5. **Minnie Mizerton is a risk-averse investor. An agent recommends that Minnie purchase T-bonds because they are riskless securities. What is true of this recommendation?**
   A. unsuitable, due to the high beta of treasury securities
   B. unsuitable and unlawful
   C. suitable and lawful
   D. suitable but unlawful due to interest rate risk retained by the investor

6. **Which of the following is an example of fraud?**
   A. an agent deliberately omits an immaterial fact when selling a security in order to avoid distracting the customer
   B. a customer claims that an agent sold an unsuitable security
   C. an agent deliberately omits a material fact when selling a security
   D. all of the above

7. **All of the following are prohibited acts except**
   A. an agent informs clients that she has been approved by the Administrator to recommend securities
   B. an agent shares commissions with other agents at the firm
   C. an agent deliberately fails to follow a customer's explicit instructions
   D. an agent promises to clean a client's bathroom every Saturday for the next 11 years if the client will purchase 1,000 shares of XYZ

8. **All of the following activities are prohibited except**
   A. an agent solicits orders for unregistered, non-exempt securities
   B. an agent solicits orders for unregistered, exempt securities
   C. an agent places a client's funds and securities into the agent's account with no intention of replacing them
   D. an agent places a client's funds and securities into the agent's account with every intention of replacing them at his earliest convenience

9. **All of the following are either fraudulent or prohibited except**
   A. telling a client that a security will be exchange-listed when the agent has no knowledge of that fact
   B. marking up a security by $1.00 and telling the client the markup is 25 cents
   C. failing to state all facts about an issuer when selling unregistered exempt securities
   D. offering to give a client her money back if a recommended security does not appreciate in value over the next 90 days

10. Which of the following activities is fraudulent?
   A. unwittingly accepting an order for an unregistered, nonexempt security
   B. marking up a security by $1.00 and telling the client the markup is 25 cents
   C. failing to state all facts about an issuer when selling unregistered, exempt securities
   D. all of the above

11. Which of the following activities is/are considered unethical?
   A. charging commissions that are higher than usual with client's written consent
   B. charging markups that are higher than usual with the client's written consent
   C. indicating to clients that the agent has earned an MBA from the University of Chicago, when, in fact, the agent has only completed a BA
   D. all of the above

12. Which of the following are considered dishonest or unethical practices?
   A. an agent discloses the current yield of a mutual fund without clearly explaining the difference between current yield and total return
   B. an agent states that an investment company's performance is similar to that of a savings account, CD, or other bank deposit account without disclosing that the shares of the investment company are not guaranteed or insured by the FDIC or any other governmental agency
   C. an agent states that a government bond mutual fund portfolio holds securities guaranteed against default by the U.S. Government without also disclosing other risks such as interest rate risk
   D. all of the following

13. Which of the following are true concerning criminal penalties?
   A. there is no statute of limitations for securities fraud
   B. the statute of limitations for securities fraud is 2 years from discovery or 3 years from the alleged event, whichever comes first
   C. ignorance of the law/rule has no bearing in criminal proceedings
   D. the maximum penalty is 3 years in jail, $5,000 fine or both

Answers

4. ANSWER: D

WHY: if you did NOT ignore your client's instructions, that's good. Munibonds are not for low-tax-bracket investors and don't go into qualified plans. Distributions from qualified plans are taxable—munibond interest is not taxable. Why pay taxes when you don't have to?

5. ANSWER: D

WHY: perfectly suitable, but you have to tell Minnie about the interest-rate risk if you're going to bring up the lack of default risk, right?

6. ANSWER: C

WHY: always omit im-material information.

7. ANSWER: B

WHY: you can share commissions, as long as they're agents, registered.

8. ANSWER: B

WHY: exempt securities are always unregistered.

9. ANSWER: C

WHY: what would be "all the facts" about an issuer? We just need the material ones.

10. ANSWER: B

WHY: that's a perfect example of fraud: lying about the amount of money you're charging someone.

11. ANSWER: C

WHY: don't mislead clients about your credentials. Choices A and B are okay—as long as you have the client's consent ahead of time. Some transactions cost more than others. Go figure.

12. ANSWER: D

WHY: this is from a www.nasaa.org model rule.

13. ANSWER: D

WHY: memorize it.

BROKER-DEALERS DEFINED

Always remember—and please never forget:

> AN AGENT IS NEVER A BROKER-DEALER, AND A BROKER-DEALER IS
> NEVER AN AGENT.

Not that you woke up this morning thinking otherwise; it's just that the Series 65 is somewhat obsessive when it comes to making sure you know that, so once again:

> AN AGENT IS NEVER A BROKER-DEALER, AND A BROKER-DEALER IS
> NEVER AN AGENT.

An agent is always an individual. You are about to become an agent, right? You're not about to become a firm. A broker-dealer is a firm. You might be called a "broker" at the firm, but that's just shorthand for "stock broker," a term not used by the exam. The exam talks about agents, or investment representatives, because the exam is all about stodgy, legalistic language nobody ever actually uses.

A broker-dealer is a firm. The registered representatives smiling and dialing for the firm are agents. The exam might refer to the sales reps as *registered representatives, investment representatives,* or *agents.* In any case, the exam is talking about an individual. A broker-dealer is an entity, a business.

So, if the question asks something like, "Which of the following are agents?" you can eliminate any choice that starts out, "A broker-dealer who..."

Eliminate it.

The unskilled test taker will read the rest of the sentence, which might be something as annoying as:

> . . . a broker-dealer properly registered in a neighboring state as well as the state in which the offer either originated or was accepted in the transference of non-exempt, properly registered securities for value.

You don't have time to read all that nonsense. Remember, as soon as you read, "A broker-dealer who..." you can stop right there. Agents are never broker-dealers, and broker-dealers are never agents.

Just like the right fielder isn't the shortstop, and the shortstop isn't the right fielder.

Okay, so what the heck IS a broker-dealer, then?

A broker-dealer is a firm *in the business of effecting transactions in securities for others or for its own account.* See, it's an either-or situation, which is why the term broker-dealer is hyphenated. On a particular transaction, the firm could act as a broker and charge a commission, or act as a dealer and make a markup/markdown. In the business of effecting transactions in securities for others (broker) or for its own account (dealer).

Agents only effect transactions for others. They are not broker-*dealers*. They don't have the authority or capacity to deal securities. They help people buy and sell them, that's all.

Would you like to deal securities? Would you like to buy 100,000 shares of some stock and then see how much buyers would be willing to pay for them later on?

You'd probably rather just pick up the phone and see if you can help your firm sell some of those nice securities to their nice clients at no risk to yourself, right?

That's why you're going to be an agent. You'll be working for a broker-dealer.

Okay, now that we've belabored that point, let's look at all the folks who look like broker-dealers on the surface, but actually turn out to be excluded from the definition upon closer examination.

The following players are NOT Broker-Dealers, ever:
- Agents
- Issuers
- Banks/trust companies/savings institutions

So, if the test question asks, "Which of the following are broker-dealers?" you can eliminate any choices that start out, "An agent who..." or, "An issuer who..." Agents, issuers, banks, trusts, S&L's...those folks are NOT broker-dealers. If they were broker-dealers, guess what we'd call them?

Broker-dealers.

So those folks aren't broker-dealers by definition. You have to look a little closer to find the others, who sure look like broker-dealers but end up escaping the definition.

Let's say the firm is properly registered as a broker-dealer in the state of Wisconsin. They have no office in Illinois, so at this point, what does the state securities Administrator for Illinois care about this broker-dealer in Wisconsin?

Not a rip, right?

So, this Wisconsin firm then wants to do business with some folks in Illinois.

Okay, now the Illinois securities Administrator looks up from his desk and asks an assistant exactly whom this Wisconsin firm wants to sell to in Illinois. Turns out the only folks the Wisconsin firm wants to deal with are banks, S&Ls, trust companies, insurance companies, investment companies, and pension plans in Illinois.

Hmm, those folks usually have millions of dollars to invest and hire professional investors to manage their risk. Pretty sophisticated and able to smell fraud a mile away, right? Do I, as the securities Administrator for the state of Illinois, really have to spend my time protecting sophisticated institutional investors like that?

No.

If I find out somebody's been defrauding these institutional investors, I'll get involved in a heartbeat. But, if this firm properly registered in Wisconsin only wants to deal with these big multimillion-dollar institutional clients, I don't see any need to make them register in my state. So, they're exempt from registration, which means they don't have to register and are very happy about that.

The Administrator licenses people so he can monitor them in order to protect the average investor from fraud. The big guys don't need the same level of protection. Doesn't mean that folks can sell fraudulently to institutionals; just means that the institutionals don't have to be protected quite as much. No different from how closely a parent would watch a 2-year-old child as opposed to a 13-year-old child. Bottom line is that nobody messes with your children, but you have to watch out for the 2-year-old at all times, whereas, the 13-year-old can watch out for himself to a certain extent. So, if the broker-dealer wants to have non-institutional clients, they'll have to register in the state; if the clients are all institutional, they won't have to.

Just like with agents, if a broker-dealer is properly registered in Wisconsin and wants to sell to an existing customer just visiting in Illinois, the Illinois securities Administrator isn't going to define the firm as a broker-dealer in Illinois and therefore undergo the painful and expensive process of registration. Those existing customers are only in the other state for 30 days maximum, remember. More than 30 days, and now we've got a different situation entirely.

So if you're an issuer, right there you are NOT a broker-dealer by definition, because broker-dealers aren't issuers, and issuers aren't broker-dealers. Agents aren't broker-dealers, ever, as we've pointed out a couple of times. And, if you're a bank you are, therefore, NOT defined as a broker-dealer.

Are we having fun yet?

Good! ☺

PRACTICE QUESTIONS

14. Which of the following are broker-dealers?
- A. an issuer of non-exempt, unregistered securities maturing in 270 days or less
- B. a bank that invests more than 20% of total assets in securities
- C. a firm that trades securities for its own account or the accounts of its customers
- D. an agent who represents a broker-dealer in a non-exempt transaction

15. Which of the following broker-dealers must register in the state of Kentucky?
- A. a broker-dealer properly registered in Ohio who sells securities to 17 pension plans located in Kentucky with more than $5,000,000 in assets
- B. a broker-dealer registered in New Mexico who sells securities to 100 banks, trust companies, and S&Ls in Kentucky.
- C. a broker dealer with an office in Kentucky who effects transactions only with banks and insurance companies located in Kentucky
- D. a broker dealer with no office in the state of Kentucky who sells to an existing customer not a resident of the state

16. Which of the following persons would be defined as broker-dealers in the state?
- A. an agent selling promissory notes maturing in more than 12 months
- B. a bank selling products insured by the FDIC
- C. a firm with no office in the state that effects transactions with 7 pension funds in the state
- D. a firm with no office in the state that effects transactions with non-accredited investors who are residents of the state

ANSWERS

14. ANSWER: C

WHY: the other three are excluded from the definition of B/D.

15. ANSWER: C

WHY: how many had offices in the state? Just one.

16. ANSWER: D

WHY: if the firm is out of state, the number of <u>institutional</u> investors is immaterial.

DISHONEST OR UNETHICAL PRACTICES

THIS IS THE ACTUAL DOCUMENT REPRINTED WITH PERMISSION FROM NASAA (an explanation in Plain English immediately follows).

DISHONEST OR UNETHICAL BUSINESS PRACTICES OF BROKER-DEALERS AND AGENTS

[Adopted May 23, 1983]

[HIGH STANDARDS AND JUST PRINCIPLES.] Each broker-dealer and agent shall observe high standards of commercial honor and just and equitable principles of trade in the conduct of their business. Acts and practices, including but not limited to the following, are considered contrary to such standards and may constitute grounds for denial, suspension or revocation of registration or such other action authorized by statute.

1. BROKER-DEALERS

a. Engaging in a pattern of unreasonable and unjustifiable delays in the delivery of securities purchased by any of its customers and/or in the payment upon request of free credit balances reflecting completed transactions of any of its customers;

b. Inducing trading in a customer's account which is excessive in size or frequency in view of the financial resources and character of the account;

c. Recommending to a customer the purchase, sale or exchange of any security without reasonable grounds to believe that such transaction or recommendation is suitable for the customer based upon reasonable inquiry concerning the customer's investment objectives, financial situation and needs, and any other relevant information known by the broker-dealer;

d. Executing a transaction on behalf of a customer without authorization to do so;

e. Exercising any discretionary power in effecting a transaction for a customer's account without first obtaining written discretionary authority from the customer, unless the discretionary power relates solely to the time and/or price for the executing of orders;

f. Executing any transaction in a margin account without securing from the customer a properly executed written margin agreement promptly after the initial transaction in the account;

g. Failing to segregate customers' free securities or securities held in safekeeping;

h. Hypothecating a customer's securities without having a lien thereon unless the broker-dealer secures from the customer a properly executed written consent promptly after the initial transaction, except as permitted by Rules of the Securities and Exchange Commission;

i. Entering into a transaction with or for a customer at a price not reasonably related to the current market price of the security or receiving an unreasonable commission or profit;

j. Failing to furnish to a customer purchasing securities in an offering, no later than the due date of confirmation of the transaction, either a final prospectus or a preliminary prospectus and an additional document, which together include all information set forth in the final prospectus;

k. Charging unreasonable and inequitable fees for services performed, including miscellaneous services such as collection of monies due for principal, dividends or interest, exchange or transfer of securities, appraisals, safekeeping, or custody of securities and other services related to its securities business;

l. Offering to buy from or sell to any person any security at a stated price unless such broker-dealer is prepared to purchase or sell, as the case may be, at such price and under such conditions as are stated at the time of such offer to buy or sell;

m. Representing that a security is being offered to a customer "at the market" or a price relevant to the market price unless such broker-dealer knows or has reasonable grounds to believe that a market for such security exists other than that made, created or controlled by such broker-dealer, or by any such person for whom he is acting or with whom he is associated in such distribution, or any person controlled by, controlling or under common control with such broker-dealer;

n. Effecting any transaction in, or inducing the purchase or sale of, any security by means of any manipulative, deceptive or fraudulent device, practice, plan, program, design or contrivance, which may include but not be limited to;

(1) Effecting any transaction in a security which involves no change in the beneficial ownership thereof;

(2) Entering an order or orders for the purchase or sale of any security with the knowledge that an order or orders of substantially the same size, at substantially the same time and substantially the same price, for the sale of any such security, has been or will be entered by or for the same or different parties for the purpose of creating a false or misleading appearance of active trading in the security or a false or misleading appearance with respect to the market for the security; provided, however, nothing in this subsection shall prohibit a broker-dealer from entering bona fide agency cross transactions for its customers;

(3) Effecting, alone or with one or more other persons, a series of transactions in any security creating actual or apparent active trading in such security or raising or depressing the price of such security, for the purpose of inducing the purchase or sale of such security by others;

o. Guaranteeing a customer against loss in any securities account of such customer carried by the broker-dealer or in any securities transaction effected by the broker-dealer or in any securities transaction effected by the broker-dealer with or for such customer;

p. Publishing or circulating, or causing to be published or circulated, any notice, circular, advertisement, newspaper article, investment service, or communication of any kind which purports to report any transaction as a purchase or sale of any security unless such broker-dealer believes that such transaction was a bona fide purchase or sale or such security; or which purports to quote the bid price or asked price for any security, unless such broker-dealer believes that such quotation represents a bona fide bid for, or offer of, such security;

q. Using any advertising or sales presentation in such a fashion as to be deceptive or misleading. An example of such practice would be a distribution of any nonfactual data, material or presentation based on conjecture, unfounded or unrealistic claims or assertions in any brochure, flyer, or display by words, pictures, graphs or otherwise designed to supplement, detract from, supersede or defeat the purpose or effect of any prospectus or disclosure; or

r. Failing to disclose that the broker-dealer is controlled by, controlling, affiliated with or under common control with the issuer of any security before entering into any contract with or for a customer for the purchase or sale of such security, the existence of such control to such customer, and if such disclosure is not made in writing, it shall be supplemented by the giving or sending of written disclosure at or before the completion of the transaction;

s. Failing to make a bona fide public offering of all of the securities allotted to a broker-dealer for distribution, whether acquired as an underwriter, a selling group member, or from a member participating in the distribution as an underwriter or selling group member; or

t. Failure or refusal to furnish a customer, upon reasonable request, information to which he is entitled, or to respond to a formal written request or complaint.

2. AGENTS

a. Engaging in the practice of lending or borrowing money or securities from a customer, or acting as a custodian for money, securities or an executed stock power of a customer;

b. Effecting securities transactions not recorded on the regular books or records of the broker-dealer which the agent represents, unless the transactions are authorized in writing by the broker-dealer prior to execution of the transaction;

c. Establishing or maintaining an account containing fictitious information in order to execute transactions which would otherwise be prohibited;

d. Sharing directly or indirectly in profits or losses in the account of any customer without the written authorization of the customer and the broker-dealer which the agent represents;

e. Dividing or otherwise splitting the agent's commissions, profits or other compensation from the purchase or sale of securities with any person not also registered as an agent for the same broker-dealer, or for a broker-dealer under direct or indirect common control; or

f. Engaging in conduct specified in Subsection 1.b, c, d, e, f, i, j, n, o, p, or q.

[CONDUCT NOT INCLUSIVE.] The conduct set forth above is not inclusive. Engaging in other conduct such as forgery, embezzlement, nondisclosure, incomplete disclosure or misstatement of material facts, or manipulative or deceptive practices shall also be grounds for denial, suspension or revocation of registration.

ONCE AGAIN, IN ENGLISH, PLEASE...

The following explanation should help to de-code some of the previous legalese.

NASAA Adopted Statement of Policy   5/23/1983
Dishonest or Unethical Business Practices of Broker-Dealers and Agent

This policy statement looks like extremely fertile ground for harvesting test questions. Business practices make up the biggest section on the exam, and this policy statement lists a whole bunch of prohibited practices that can lead to a registration for a broker-dealer or agent being denied, suspended, or revoked.

Which is bad.

The policy statement starts with the conduct of broker-dealers. Item A says, "Don't be dragging your feet when your customer buys or sells securities." Send them their securities or their money within a reasonable time frame. What's reasonable? Would you like to hold a hearing to determine what's reasonable?

Didn't think so.

Item B demonstrates how 24 big words can be easily boiled down into just one word: churning.

Don't do that.

And if you do do that, please make sure you don't get caught. As of January 11, 2004, churning is punishable by 7 years in federal prison and/or public caning.

Seriously.

Also, notice how churning is not just excessive *frequency*, but excessive size, too. So, don't pressure customers into making bigger trades just cuz it leads to bigger commissions or markups for the firm. Item C is just a reminder to perform due diligence when determining suitability. Your recommendations don't have to be profitable—no one can predict the future—but they do have to make sense given each customer's situation. Item D reminds the firm not to buy or sell securities for a customer if the customer hasn't authorized the broker-dealer to do so. You'd think that would not even have to be articulated, but it's actually a surprisingly common occurrence by unscrupulous firms. Nobody's calling to trade? Let's trade *for* them.

No. You have to have discretion over the account to trade without talking to the customer first, and even then you have to buy what's suitable for the client given her investment objectives, risk tolerance, time horizon, etc. Item E is very closely related. Where Item D focuses on the transaction, Item E says "any discretionary power," which could be broken down into the three basic aspects that make an order "discretionary." Choosing the activity (buy/sell), asset (which stock/bond), or the amount (# of shares/bonds) makes an order discretionary. So, if the firm does not have <u>written</u> discretionary authorization from the customer before making any of those choices, they've made a big boo-boo. They can choose time and/or price, because those aspects are not considered discretionary. And—unfortunately—this concept can be tricky. Remember, this statement is talking to <u>broker-dealers</u>, not investment advisers. An IA can actually start using discretion once they've received verbal authorization, provided they get the discretionary authorization in writing within 10 business days. So, be real clear on whether the question is talking to a firm called a broker-dealer or a firm called an investment adviser. I guess an IA, being a "fiduciary," is already expected to act completely for his customer's best interest, so the rule is a little more lax there?

Not that it matters. It's the rule cuz the regulators say so. And it'll remain the rule until, by rule, they change their mind.

Item F reminds the firm not to let a customer start trading on margin unless they have a signed margin agreement promptly after the initial transaction. I would have expected the rule to require the agreement ahead of time, but nobody asked my opinion. This is an example, though, of where your gut feeling could be wrong. You expect the regulators to be uptight about everything, but that's not always the case. The signed margin agreement has to come promptly *after* the first transaction on margin.

Hmm. Oh well. It is what it is.

Point G reminds the firm exactly what the Act of 1934 tried to remind them— commingling is a no-no. Keep the customers' securities separate from the firms' securities. Point H tells the firm to go by the books when pledging customer securities as collateral, which is what you do in a margin account. Point I takes all the fun out of the business by prohibiting the time-honored tradition of sticking it to the customer, gouging him at every opportunity. Point J could also be a test question on the Series 7 or 6—the final prospectus for new offerings must be delivered no later than confirmation of the sale. The customer has already received a preliminary prospectus (Red Herring) but must get the final (or the preliminary plus any additional info) no later than confirmation. See, often the preliminary is so close to the final that they just give an additional statement to it and that serves as the final prospectus.

No, nothing is simple in this business. Except for the simple stuff.

Item K sounds just like the bylaws of the NASD—you can't charge unreasonable fees for services rendered. What makes it unreasonable?

Would you like to hold a hearing?

Point L goes way overboard. Point L has the audacity to dictate to a broker-dealer that they can't tell a customer they'll purchase 1,000 shares of XYZ for $45 a share then try to hand them $22 a share when the deal actually goes down five minutes later.

It's getting to where I don't know how anyone is expected to make a living in this business!

Anyway, item M is little dense. Basically, it's saying that the firm probably shouldn't tell the customer that the firm is purchasing the customer's security "at the market" unless the firm has reasonable grounds to believe that there is, like, an actual "market" for the security outside whatever price the firm decides is fair.

Kind of surprising that some of these rules have to be written, but we don't live in a perfect world.

Item N goes into great detail in explaining that market manipulation will get you into all kinds of trouble. We can't just get together with another firm and start creating the illusion of an active market for a particular stock, no matter how much fun it would be. Words like pegging, capping, painting the tape, matched purchases, and wash sales all fall under this category of market manipulation. Unless you want to lose your license and work in the prison library, I'd recommend staying away from any of that stuff.

Item O reminds the firm not to guarantee the customer against loss. Now there's a rule I can live with, right? Since no one can do it, I don't have to worry about my competitors offering guarantees, either.

Item P is just a dense, legalistic way of saying don't publish in any way, shape, or form that a transaction has occurred unless you actually know it occurred.

Hmm, seems reasonable enough to me.

Item Q reminds the firm not to circulate material that is misleading or deceptive. For example, it might be tempting to put out a flyer that shows how much Company XYZ would be worth if over the next 6 months they simply eliminated $5 billion in debt, increased revenues 10,000% and slashed costs 89% without resorting to layoffs or pay-cuts. You could even show graphs of this wonderful turnaround effort. Trouble is, it's all based on wild conjecture, is so improbable as to be nearly impossible and, therefore, should not be circulated at all. It is "nonfactual," misleading, and probably deceptive.

Don't do that.

Item R is pretty clear as-is. If the firm wants to sell shares of an issuer who just happens to own, control, or be affiliated with the broker-dealer, that should maybe be disclosed to the customer and explained clearly. We aren't just making a commission, markup, or spread on this sale—we're actually directly related to the issuer getting the proceeds. That just might explain our intense enthusiasm for this particular offering.

Item S reminds underwriters not to get greedy when they see the price of an IPO stock start to soar in the secondary market. Might be tempting to withhold the securities just to see how high the price could soar, but that would be "failure to make a bona fide offering" and would get the firm into all kinds of trouble.

Item T is about as clear as NASAA's legalese will ever get. A principal of the broker-dealer has to respond to a customer's written complaint, and has to provide him with any information to which he is entitled. Like a balance sheet, for example. You feel embarrassed by the liabilities on the firm's balance sheet—too bad, the rule says you have to provide the balance sheet to the customer upon the request.

AGENTS. And then the policy statement proceeds to tell agents what's what.

Not sure why you'd want to, but don't act as a custodian for your client. Don't, like, take their cash or stock certificates and, like, put them in your glove box or top desk drawer. Don't borrow or lend money/securities with/to your client. You make recommendations; they buy and sell.

Keep it simple and everybody's happy. Don't start acting like a bank. You're not a bank; you're an agent.

Remember that.

My father was a small businessman who didn't know much about accounting, but he always told me to keep two sets of books as I recall.

Not.

Don't effect (complete) transactions not recorded on the books of your firm unless you have written authorization from the firm to do so. That also sounds bizarre—

that it's okay if your firm puts it in writing. This would be about the *only* place on the exam where I'd say that getting the firm's permission in writing makes it okay.

Item C is self-explanatory. Fictitious accounts?

Wow.

Item D reminds us that, basically, you shouldn't be sharing profits and/or losses with a customer. The only exception is when you're in a joint account with the customer and you've received the customer's authorization as well as your broker-dealer's. Gotta have BOTH the customer's and the B/D's written authorization. If you get any test question on the sharing arrangement, remember that you must share in proportion to your investment in the account.

Item E makes it clear that you can only split commissions with registered agents at your firm or a firm directly related to your firm, as a subsidiary, for example. So, you can split commissions, as long as the agent is registered and works for your firm directly or indirectly.

The policy statement then tells the agent not to do the stuff it told broker-dealers not to do, except for the stuff that would only relate to the firm, like segregation of assets and hypothecation.

And then the policy statement ends with a reminder that these prohibited activities are not inclusive, meaning there's still lots of other stuff that could get you in hot water with the regulators. They just felt like pointing out SOME of the things not to do in this policy statement.

REGISTRATION OF PERSONS: AGENTS, BROKER-DEALERS, IA'S, IA REPS

So we've defined who is and is not considered an agent, broker-dealer, investment adviser and investment adviser representative. We've discussed what these "persons" (legal entities) can and cannot do.

Now let's talk about what they have to do in order to register and keep their registration effective at the state level.

The USA clearly states, "It is unlawful for any person to transact business in this state as a broker-dealer or agent unless he is registered under this act (or excluded/exempted from registration)." And, "It is unlawful for any broker-dealer or issuer to employ an agent unless the agent is registered. The registration of an agent is not effective during any period when he is not associated with a particular broker-dealer registered under this act or a particular issuer." That means NO PARKING. As the USA clearly indicates, if you are not associated with a particular broker-dealer or issuer, your registration as an agent is not effective. Also note that if your broker-dealer employer loses their license, your license as an agent is no good, either.

"When an agent begins or terminates a connection with a broker-dealer or issuer, or begins or terminates those activities which make him an agent, the agent as well as the broker-dealer or issuer shall promptly notify the Administrator." So, if you get a question about who must notify the Administrator when an agent leaves one broker-dealer to go work for another broker-dealer, remember it's all three: both firms plus the agent.

Section 202 of the USA states that, "A broker-dealer, agent, or investment adviser may obtain an initial or renewal registration by filing with the Administrator an application together with a consent to service of process." The law even uses surprising language such as, "Every application for registration under this act and every issuer which proposes to offer a security in this state…shall file with the Administrator…an irrevocable consent appointing the Administrator to be his attorney to receive service of any lawful process in any non-criminal suit, action, or proceeding against him…with the same force and validity as if served personally on the person filing the consent." So, a consent to service of process is a form that gives the Administrator the power to receive court papers on the registrant's behalf, should the registrant get into hot water. In other words, you file this consent to service of process so that if you screw up and flee the state, the other party can still nail you with court papers by serving them on the Administrator and sending a copy to you at your latest known address.

So, what has to be provided to the Administrator in the application?

You guessed it—that's entirely up to the Administrator. As Section 202 states:

The application shall contain whatever information the Administrator by rule requires concerning such matters as:
- the applicant's form and place of organization
- the applicant's proposed method of doing business
- the qualifications and business history of the applicant; in the case of a broker-dealer or investment adviser, the qualifications and business history of any partner, officer, or director
- (4) any injunction or administrative order or conviction of a misdemeanor involving a security or any aspect of the securities business and any conviction of a felony; and
- (5) the applicant's financial condition and history.

The Administrator can also make someone filing an initial application publish an announcement in one or more specified newspapers published in the state. Just like when you start a business of any kind, you publish a notification in a newspaper, right? And, when does the registration become effective? As long as no denial order is in effect and no proceeding is pending (denial, revocation, suspension), the registration becomes effective at noon of the 30th day after an application is filed. The Administrator can also make the application effective earlier than the 30th day, and if any amendments are filed to the application, the Administrator can defer the effectiveness until the 30th day after filing the amendment.

So, it's 30 days, basically, unless the Administrator makes it effective earlier.

And, not surprisingly, when you file an application, you also must pay fees to the state. The exact amount is up to each Administrator.

You might get a question about a "successor firm." Just remember that a broker-dealer or investment adviser may file an application for registration of a successor firm, whether or not the successor firm is then in existence, for the unexpired portion of the year. And, there is no fee to pay in that case—remember there is an "unexpired portion" left on the registration. So, if your broker-dealer was a partnership that is now going to become a corporation, you may register the new entity for the remaining portion of your existing registration without paying a fee…even if the new firm is not yet in existence.

If an agent has discretion over a client's account, the agent may be forced to post a surety/fidelity bond to protect against theft/embezzlement. This can be satisfied by posting the bond or depositing cash and/or securities.

That is not a "minimum net capital" requirement, though. Firms have minimum net capital requirements, and—as we may have pointed out before—an agent is not a broker-dealer and an investment adviser representative is not an investment adviser.

Firms have minimum net capital requirements, not individuals. The USA states, "The Administrator may by rule require a minimum capital for registered broker-dealers and investment advisers." NASAA's "Investment Adviser Net Worth/Bonding Rule," states that an adviser with custody of client funds or securities must at all times maintain a net worth of $35,000. An adviser without custody, but who has discretion (power to choose) over a client's account must maintain at all times a minimum net worth of $10,000. So, there's a higher standard for advisers who have possession of the client's funds/securities than for those who are allowed to choose the Asset/Activity/Amount on any transaction. An Adviser who accepts prepayment of > $500 six or more months in advance must at all times maintain positive net worth, too.

If the firm does not have the required minimum net worth (assets minus liabilities), the firm must post a bond in an amount determined by the Administrator based on the number of clients and the total assets under management. The bonds will be in the amount of the net worth deficiency/shortfall rounded up to the nearest $5,000. Rather than post a bond, the firm can also just deposit either cash or securities, and the Act says the Administrator can not force the firm to deposit cash—the Administrator must accept a deposit of securities, usually Treasury securities rather than, say, E-toys.

Things change in the securities business, so if the firm's net worth falls below the minimum requirement, the firm must notify the Administrator of the shortfall by the close of business on the next business day. And by the close of business of the next business day following this notification, the firm must file a report with the Administrator of its financial condition. So on Monday at 11 o'clock AM your advisory firm realizes their net worth is deficient. By the close of business on Tuesday they must notify the Administrator. And by the close of business on Wednesday, they must file an updated statement of financial condition.

The USA states:

> Every registered broker-dealer and investment adviser shall make and keep such accounts, correspondence, memoranda, papers, books, and other records as the Administrator by rule prescribes. All records so required shall be preserved for three years unless the Administrator by rule prescribes otherwise for particular types of records.

But remember that investment advisers actually keep their records for five years now, due to a relatively recent update.

So, if the test question asks about a broker-dealer, tell it three years. If it's about an IA—five years.

And then move on with your life.

The Act also goes on to point out that every investment adviser and broker-dealer must file financial reports as required by the Administrator. The Administrator has the power to determine which reports must be filed, what the contents of those reports are, and when they have to be certified by independent or certified public accountants. Financial reports are to be prepared in accordance with Generally Accepted Accounting Principles (GAAP). If any information in any of the documents filed with the Administrator becomes inaccurate or incomplete in any material respect, the Administrator must be informed promptly. And—guess what—the Administrator may send somebody to your advisory firm or broker-dealer who would like to have a little look-see at all your records. Heck, if he/she isn't too busy, the Administrator might even drop by him- or herself.

Surprise! We're here! Sure hope all your files are in order.

This power to inspect is called "visitatorial power," and they don't need a subpoena to get you to, like, open the door for them. If you refuse to allow the inspection, right there you have violated the Act. And that could lead to an injunction, a revocation, or even a criminal prosecution, which is bad. The Administrator can even make firms foot the bill for the expense of performing these inspections, which isn't that surprising, really, given your understanding of the Act at this point.

Administrative Orders

Persons and securities that must register at the state level are subject to the Administrator's power to deny, revoke, or suspend a registration. *Denial, revocation,* and *suspension* imply that somebody has done somebody wrong. The Administrator, remember, is out to protect the average investor, so if it is "in the public interest," meaning it provides needed protection for investors, the Administrator can prevent a security from being offered or a person from setting up shop (deny). Or, the Administrator can make a security's underwriters—or tell an agent—to take a time out (suspend). Or, the Administrator can even take back a security's registration or the license of a broker-dealer (revoke).

Usually, you'd have to do something pretty bad, like lie, cheat or steal for any of that bad stuff to happen. But an agent, broker-dealer, or investment adviser's registration could certainly end up being denied, suspended, or revoked if the Administrator feels it is in the public interest <u>and the person</u>:

- has filed a false or misleading application
- has willfully violated or willfully failed to comply with any provision of this act
- was convicted within last 10 years of any securities-related misdemeanor or any felony
- is enjoined by any court from engaging in the securities business
- is the subject of an order of the Administrator denying, suspending, or revoking registration as a broker-dealer, agent, or investment adviser
- is the subject of an order entered within the past 5 years by the securities administrator of any other state or by the SEC denying or revoking registration as a broker-dealer, agent, or investment adviser
- is the subject of an order of the SEC suspending or expelling him from a national securities exchange or national securities association registered under the Securities Exchange Act of 1934
- has engaged in dishonest or unethical practices in the securities business

- (rep, firm) is insolvent
  - For firms, a formal finding of insolvency required
  - For individuals, as soon as liabilities exceed assets, toast
- isn't qualified because they lack training, experience, and knowledge
  - Lack of experience isn't enough all by itself if the applicant does have training and knowledge
- has failed reasonably to supervise his agents if he is a broker-dealer or his employees if he is an investment adviser
- has failed to pay the proper filing fee (denial only, and the order is vacated as soon as the fee is paid)

So, if a registered rep files a registration with the Administrator, the Administrator can always deny the registration if he discovers that the rep was convicted of knocking off liquor stores 7 years ago, or selling unregistered non-exempt securities within 10 years. Any felony can get the rep in trouble, but a misdemeanor has to be related to money and/or securities. If the rep has been working a few years before the Administrator discovers that the rep filed a false or incomplete application—seems he somehow forgot to mention that little incident as a bank teller—the Administrator can suspend or even revoke the registration. Notice how they made the law nice and vague by using language such as "has engaged in dishonest or unethical practices in the securities business."

Pretty broad, huh? And guess who determines if something is dishonest or unethical?

The Administrator.

You can appeal his/her order to deny, suspend, or revoke, but now you're talking about missing work, paying legal fees, and generally having not too many good days for a while.

So, if a broker-dealer or investment adviser is trying to get registered, they could be denied if they've shown a history of failing to supervise their representatives. And, if the registrant hasn't paid proper filing fees, the registration for a security or license could be denied until the fees are paid—but the order would be vacated as soon as the fees were paid up.

Pay the state. It's easier that way.

Many broker-dealers are also investment advisers. However, if the firm tries to register or renew a registration and the Administrator is convinced they have no business being in business as an investment adviser, he can condition the granting of their broker-dealer license on their *not* acting as an investment adviser.

Hmm, just when you thought this stuff was starting to get a little dry, huh?

The law also says that the Administrator may not institute a suspension or revocation proceeding on the basis of a fact or transaction known to him when registration became effective unless the proceeding is instituted within the next thirty days. I am confident the exam will not ask you about that, unless it does. And, it's possible that the test will ask if the Administrator can make a rule that forces agents or broker-dealers or any class of applicants to take an exam, either oral or written. How would you answer that?

Yes. Remember, the Administrator can do all kinds of stuff. If you memorize the few things he *can't* do, you'll be fine. Can't issue an injunction; can't sentence folks to prison; can't issue the big orders (stop, deny, revoke, suspend) without prior notice, an opportunity for hearing, and written findings of fact and conclusions of law. But other than that...

Okay, now if the Administrator is going to step in and deny, suspend, or revoke somebody's registration, that somebody has to be given prior notice, an opportunity for a hearing, and written findings of fact and conclusions of law. The hearing, by the way, has to be a public hearing, unless all parties agree to keep it behind closed doors.

But the Administrator can "summarily suspend" a registration, with or without prior notice. So, if you're calling an attorney to get some help persuading the state not to revoke your license, your registration could go into a "summary suspension" until the final determination has been made. You would then be given an opportunity for a hearing within 15 days, but that's <u>after</u> the order to summarily suspend has been entered. On the other hand, if we were talking about a denial, suspension, or revocation order, the broker-dealer/agent/investment adviser would have to be given <u>prior notice</u> with an opportunity for a hearing and written findings of fact *before* the order is entered.

You also might see a test question similar to this:

Does the Administrator cancel a registration for the same reasons that he/they would deny, revoke, or suspend a registration?

The answer? No.

If a registration is canceled, that just means the party no longer exists. They've left the state, for example. If the office can't be located, or if the person has been declared mentally incompetent by a court of law, the Administrator can cancel the registration. In other words, if the party no longer appears to exist, either mentally or physically, the registration is canceled. Doesn't imply that somebody did anything wrong.

Finally, a withdrawal occurs when the person filing the registration changes his/their mind. They decide, for example, that they aren't going to do any business in New Hampshire, so why go through the hassle of registering there? We'll just withdraw that one, no big deal. But, the state still has one year to initiate a suspension or revocation if they find out the person was up to some funky stuff that partly explains the sudden urge to flee the state. And, a suspension of the license in State A will usually lead to a suspension/revocation of the license in the new state.

When do registrations of persons expire?

On December 31st of each year, unless properly renewed.

How are they renewed?

By paying your fee.

Practice Questions

17. Criminal penalties under USA include which two of the following?
   I.   five years in jail
   II. three years in jail
   III. $5,000 fine
   IV. $3,000 fine

   A. I, III
   B. I, IV
   C. II, III
   D. II, IV

18. Which of the following actions may the Administrator take without prior notice?
   A. issue an injunction
   B. stop order
   C. summary suspension of a registration
   D. all of the above

19. The Administrator has the authority to do all of the following except:
   A. publish violations in a newspaper and/or website
   B. enforce subpoenas issued by Administrators of other states
   C. investigate in other states
   D. sentence violators to three years in prison

ANSWERS

17. ANSWER: C

WHY: memorize it and keep moving.

18. ANSWER: C

WHY: the Big A can't issue injunctions, and stop orders to deny, suspend, or revoke only come after prior notice and an opportunity for a hearing.

19. ANSWER: D

WHY: the courts get ticked when anybody else tries to sentence folks to prison.

SECURITIES

If your money is secure, it's not a security. It's only a security if your money isn't secure.

Seriously.

If something has a fixed or guaranteed payment, that something is NOT a security. So, a fixed annuity is not a security. A variable annuity, which exposes the investor to the ups and downs of the stock market, now *that's* a security, since the investor's money is no longer secure. A whole life policy, with *guaranteed* cash value, is *not* a security. A variable life insurance policy, where the cash value is subject to market fluctuations that could, hypothetically, take the cash value down to zero...now *that's* a "security," since your money is no longer secure.

Precious metals, commodities...way too tangible to be securities. A bar of gold is a bar of gold. You could call it an "investment," but, then again, you could call buying a six-pack of beer an "investment" based on your hunch that the cans will become collectible items some day. Corn is a commodity, it's a tangible thing. A futures contract for December corn could actually lead to a farmer bringing a certain number of bushels of corn to your doorstep in December. It's a tangible thing; therefore it is not a security.

If you own a cow, guess what you actually own?

A cow.

But if you buy a 10% ownership interest in your cousin's cattle farming operation, that ownership interest can be defined as a "security." The USA specifically names "investment contract" as an example of a security. As determined by the Supreme Court's "Howey Decision," an investment contract is anything that looks like this:

- an investment of money in a common enterprise
- where the investor's fortunes are bound together with others, and the
- investor hopes to gain through the efforts of others

So, if you sell me a 10% ownership stake in your cattle farm, you can see how this would fit the three bullet points above. It's an investment of money, where my fortunes are bound with yours and the other owners, and I'll benefit through your efforts, since I'm not inclined to do chores at 5 AM on a cold, winter morning.

Also, a security has an element of risk, so if there's no money at risk, it's not a security. A CD fully insured by the FDIC—too secure to be a security. A jumbo CD with more than $100,000 face value...that's a security, since the excess above $100,000 is uninsured by the FDIC.

A security does NOT include:
- fixed insurance policy (whole life, term, endowment, universal life)
- fixed annuity
- futures/commodities contract
- precious metals

According to the USA a security IS a:

LESSON FOUR

- note
- stock
- treasury stock
- bond
- debenture
- evidence of indebtedness
- certificate of interest or participation in any profit-sharing agreement
- collateral-trust certificate
- preorganization certificate or subscription
- transferable share
- <u>option</u> on commodity/futures contract
- investment contract (defined further by Howey Decision)
- voting-trust certificate
- certificate of deposit for a security
- certificate of interest or participation in an oil, gas, or mining title or lease or in payments out of production under such a title or lease
- in general, any interest or instrument commonly known as a "security"
- warrant, right, or option for a security
- variable annuity or variable life insurance policy
- whiskey warehouse receipts

Did you see that item "option on commodity/futures contract"? Does that imply that a futures contract is not a security, but a put/call *on* a futures/commodities contract *is* a security?

Unfortunately.

But, of course, the test would never try to split hairs with you on such a minor distinction, right?

Right. And I have a glass house in Florida I'd like to sell you before hurricane season ends—wanna see a brochure?

What the heck is a whiskey warehouse receipt? When a whiskey producer distills a barrel of whiskey, they put it in a warehouse to age and get a warehouse receipt for the deposit. If the holder of the receipt gets tired of waiting for the whiskey to age, he could sell it to somebody else. The value would fluctuate, and there's no guaranteed payment, so—yes—a whiskey warehouse receipt is a security.

Good thing you're learning that, huh?

Also remember that whiskey warehouse receipts are, ironically, *not* very liquid.

There are four ways of referring to an individual who represents a broker-dealer in selling securities: agent, broker, registered representative, or investment representative. What these individuals do for their broker-dealers is make offers and—more importantly—make sales of securities. What's the difference between an "offer" and a "sale"?

An offer is an attempt to sell a security.

A sale only takes place when something is actually transferred to somebody for value. *A contract to dispose of a security for value* would be a common way to define a sale.

Why does the law use such language?

By using phrases such as "dispose of a security for value," rather than writing something precise like, "receiving money for a stock," you cast a wider net. If you did it the second, more precise, way, some weasel could break the law by either selling a *bond* (hey, a bond ain't a stock, and a stock ain't a bond) or rather than taking *money* accept a new Jaguar (hey, a car isn't money, and money isn't a car).

Nope. The folks who write rules and regulations can think of just about everything before they write the rules and regulations, and when things pop up later that expose weaknesses in the rules, they just re-convene and re-write the rules to catch the new stuff, too.

And then you get to sit for some complicated, bizarre test called the Series 65, but that's another matter.

Check this out, an "offer to sell" a security is really the same thing as a "solicitation of an offer to *buy*" a security.

Sounds goofy, but if the law didn't include that phrase, then some smarmy stock operator could come into an Administrative hearing claiming, "Hey, I didn't try to sell him nothin'—I asked him to make me an offer to buy. So he says can I? And I says, 'Sure, you can *buy* these securities from me. But I ain't tryin' to *sell* 'em to you or nothin'.'"

So if a test question says that an agent makes a vigorous effort to sell a variable annuity and fails, he has made an offer. If he actually got somebody to buy it, that would have been a sale.

Also check out a tombstone ad in the *Wall Street Journal* some time—at the very top it will say, "This announcement is not to be construed as an offer to sell or a solicitation of an offer to buy. All offers are made by the prospectus."

So, who the heck cares whether something is an offer to sell? Well, if a security is being offered, it has to first be registered. Therefore if something is *not* defined as an "offer," the security does not (or not yet) have to be registered. Remember, if you're an issuer of securities, the best news you can hear is that you are excused (exempt) from the pain-in-the-neck process of paying fees, filing registration statements, and going back and forth with the regulators until you finally get all the paperwork just right. Or, look at it this way: the definition of "fraud" states that "it is unlawful for any person, in connection with the <u>offer</u>, sale, or purchase of any security…to employ any device, scheme, or artifice to defraud."

Well, if the thing you were involved with wasn't an offer, then you didn't commit fraud. Just like a defensive lineman can't possibly commit a "balk," and the pitcher can't possibly be called for "clipping" or "icing," all of which are different games, different sports altogether.

Now, I would expect the following exciting information to show up more often on the Series 63 than the 65/66, but rather than bet on what will show up on my exam, I simply assume EVERYTHING could show up and prepare accordingly. So, if you get a question about "which of the following are not offers," or, its clever kissing cousin, "all of the following represent offers except," remember that the following are not offers under the Uniform Securities Act:

- Any bona fide pledge or loan
- Any stock dividend if nothing of value is given by stockholders for the dividend

- Any act incident to a class vote by stockholders, pursuant to the certificate of incorporation on a merger, consolidation, reclassification of securities, or sale of corporate assets in consideration of the issuance of securities of another corporation
- Any act incident to a judicially approved reorganization in which a security is issued in exchange for one or more outstanding securities, claims, or property interests

Huh?

Well, it's very tempting to just keep moving and tell you to memorize those bullet points, which may or may not rear their ugly heads on your exam. But, I'm just not built that way. It's a beautiful summer weekend morning here in Chicago, Illinois, and I'm such a geek I can't stop myself from explaining even this sh—I mean—material. Oh well. As long as you get your money's worth, I'll forego all interest in the Cubs versus Sox game for now. Back to offer–not offer.

When you borrow money from a broker-dealer, you can pledge your security as collateral for the loan, or you can loan out your security to another short-seller at the firm. In neither case, are you *offering* your security. You saw in the Series 6 and 7 that a stock dividend is just a way of cutting the earnings pie into more slices that are, by definition, smaller. Used to be long 100 XYZ @50; now you're long 125 XYZ @40. Either way, you own $5,000 of XYZ, and you don't give anything to the issuer. They give *you* more shares of stock, at a lower price. The next bullet point has to do with mergers and acquisitions. When HP bought Compaq, they weren't offering the Compaq shareholders HP stock—they were doing a merger/acquisition. And, the final bullet point has to do with a reorganization connected with a bankruptcy proceeding. See, if a company turns out to be a deadbeat, the creditors will start leaning on them. They want their money, and they want it now. Since they're too dignified to employ a Tony Soprano–style collections effort, it all gets worked out in court. Either the company has to be liquidated, whereby everything that can be sold is sold, the proceeds distributed to the creditors however the judge sees fit, or the deadbeat company simply wipes out all the current shareholders (sorry about that), and does a "judicially approved reorganization in which a security is issued in exchange for one or more outstanding securities, claims, etc." That just means that the bondholders, especially the secured bondholders, become the new shareholders. And maybe the big suppliers who haven't been paid for that $5 million shipment of cornstarch to Frank & Emma's receive stock in the newly organized company. But that isn't an offer.

And, let's face it, if you didn't know that, how could the regulators possibly let you start working in this industry?

Anyway, those are examples of "not offers." The following examples *are* offers:

- Every attempt or offer to dispose of, or solicitation of an offer to buy, a security or interest in a security for value
- Any security given or delivered with any purchase of securities is considered to have been offered and sold for value
- Every sale or offer of a warrant or right to purchase another security, as well as every sale or offer of a security which gives the holder a present

or future right to convert into another security, is considered to include
an offer of the other security
- A purported gift of assessable stock

Okay, these make a little more sense and are, obviously, even more fascinating.
The first bullet point emphasizes the exciting detail I imparted a few paragraphs ago
that "offer to sell" and "solicitation of an offer to buy" are the same thing. When
somebody reads a tombstone for a security and calls you up, so far no offer has been
made. If that somebody requests a prospectus, the moment you send it out, you have
made an offer to sell that security. What if they don't buy it? Then, you wasted your
time, but you definitely made an offer of that security—hope you didn't say or do
anything misleading, right? Remember the "f" word—fraud. Sending the prospectus
was an offer, and if you added a Post-It™ note declaring "you can't possibly lose investing in this fund," you really screwed up.

The second bullet point means that if you offer investors convertible bonds, you
have offered both the bonds and the stock to which the bondholders can convert.
Actually, the second, third, and fourth bullet points are all related. They boil down to
this: if you sell (or even give) somebody a security that lets them purchase or convert
to another security, you have also offered the security that they can snag at a later date.
Rights and warrants allow investors to buy common stock at a set price, and so did
assessable stock, back when human beings actually lived in a world of assessable stock,
whiskey warehouse receipts, and a young, lean Elvis Presley. In case the test completely loses its mind and asks you about "assessable stock," remember that a gift of
assessable stock is both an offer and a sale, while a gift of non-assessable stock is
neither an offer nor a sale. These days, all shares of stock are non-assessable, as you'll
see from a quick glance at a stock certificate. Assessable stock gave the holder the
right to buy more stock at a set price, so we treat it like anything else that sets the
purchase price for another security.

REGISTERING SECURITIES

Remember how we said that the state securities Administrator gets real nervous whenever some company comes into the state and tries to raise capital by issuing securities? Why do the states get so uptight? Well, think how easy it would be to set up the
following fraud. A partner and I know the owner of a strip mall with a couple of vacant
storefronts. We get a key to one of them. Next door is a Kinko's. We stop in and buy
some nice paper with a fancy blue border. We print up something that looks like this:

Hi-Techtronics, Inc

10,000 shares common stock
fully paid and non-assessable, no-par value

We set the offering price at $10 a share, and we start calling for suckers willing to give us $100,000 for the above certificate. Trouble is, there is no such company and the "shares" aren't worth the paper they're printed on.

Oh well, if we can sell ten of these certificates and get the heck out of the state before the first customers begin to notice and complain, I'd say it was a pretty good scam.

Well, the states aren't into that kind of thing, and, of course, I can't think of a better example of criminal fraud that would lead to the maximum 3 years and $5,000 penalty, not to mention we'd have to give investors their money back plus interest.

If they ever caught us.

So, since the potential damage to investors could be huge, state regulators make issuers register their securities and follow many bureaucratic steps before issuing/ selling them to investors. The states often make issuers set up an escrow account so that when investors start paying for the securities, the proceeds go into escrow and won't be released to the issuers until the specified amount of capital is raised. That way, had we tried to do our little scam in a more "legitimate" way, we could have filled out a registration statement for the securities and told the state we planned on raising $10,000,000. Actually, though, we planned to flee the state after collecting the first $1 million. Trouble is, all the proceeds are impounded in an escrow account, and this isn't going to work the way we planned.

The state is always trying to provide necessary protection to investors, and since there are actually people out there who have already tried and succeeded in pulling off a scam no more sophisticated than our little vacant-strip-mall operation, the regulators want everything to go by the book.

So, do all securities have to be registered before they can be offered and sold to investors?

Absolutely. Turns out, all securities have to be registered.

Except all the securities that don't.

Some securities are exempt from the filing requirements under the Securities Act of 1933. Government securities, munibonds, church bonds, etc., all have exemptions from the filing requirements. Those are called exempt securities. The word "exempt" means "ex-cused." You could try to make the statement that in high school everybody had to take gym class. Actually, though, everybody had to take gym class, except for everybody who didn't. Some students had medical problems that qualified for an exemption (excuse) from the gym-class requirement. So, while you put on your hideous polyester gym suit, they went to study hall. Why?

They were exempt.

You were non-exempt.

Non-exempt?

Yep. You had no excuse, so you were *non-exempt*.

Requirements don't apply to exempt securities or persons. Requirements only apply to those without an excuse…the non-exempt.

You're sure you want to get your state securities license, right?

Just checking.

Okay, so let's not lose track of what we're talking about. A fixed annuity is not a security, just like I'm not an NFL lineman. But, an exempt security is still a security; it just doesn't have to register. The high school student exempt from gym class requirements was still a high school student. She was simply excused from taking gym class. So a whole life policy is not a security, period. It's an insurance product, and we have plenty of insurance regulators to deal with that. A U.S. Treasury bond is definitely a security—its market price fluctuates and some people are such pathetic investors that they've managed to lose money on a U.S. Treasury bond. How? Rates went up, and they sold with the price of their security down.

Sad, but it happens.

So a U.S. Treasury bond is definitely a security. But it doesn't have to register with the SEC because it is exempt from the registration requirements of the Securities Act of 1933. See, if the SEC says the security is exempt from registering at the federal level, the states almost always play along and say the security is exempt from registering at the state level, too. For the Series 6 or 7 you learned that the following securities are exempt from the registration requirements of the Securities Act of 1933:

- Treasury ecurities, GNMA
- Municipal bonds
- Bank securities (not bank *holding companies*, but banks)
- Debt securities maturing in 270 days or less (i.e., commercial paper, banker's acceptance)
- Small business investment companies (venture capital)
- Non-profit/church securities

This isn't just some random list—there are good reasons why the above don't need to register with the SEC and provide a prospectus. You need a prospectus when some corporation is selling you stock or a bond—what's the company's business plan, what is their financial condition, what are the risks involved? But, why would you need a prospectus for a T-bond, T-note, T-bill, or STRIP? It's a direct obligation of the U.S. Government—there is zero default risk. Only way you could lose money is if you got impatient and sold the thing on the secondary market after interest rates have risen. So, why would you need some 150-page prospectus? Give the government your money—they pay you interest and give you your money back. Pretty simple story, right? Not to mention that the Treasury Department and SEC are on the same team. Munibonds are often backed by the taxing power of the states/counties/cities—the federal government saw no reason to regulate munibonds. Bank securities are regulated by bank regulators—why be redundant? A short-term debt that matures in 9 months or less—base it on the company's credit rating and get a rate of return commensurate with that credit rating. You don't need a prospectus to buy GE commercial paper—their credit rating is stellar, and you'll be getting your money back very, very soon.

So, all the exempt securities that you learned for your Series 6 or 7 are exempt at the state level. And, the USA spells out other securities that are exempt from the state's requirements to register the security and file sales literature/advertising used in the offering. These include:

- Any security issued by or guaranteed by any federal savings & loan, building & loan, or similar association
- Any security issued by any insurance company (this means their stock or debt securities, does *not* cover variable annuities or variable life policies)
- Any security issued/guaranteed by any federal credit union or any credit union organized and supervised under the laws of *this* state
- Any security issued/guaranteed by any railroad, common carrier, public utility, or holding company subject to jurisdiction of the Interstate Commerce Commission. Any security issued/guaranteed by a registered holding company under the Public Utility Holding Company Act of 1935
- Any investment contract issued in connection with an employees' stock purchase, savings, pension, profit-sharing, or similar benefit plan
- Any security issued by ANY Canadian government
- Any security issued by a foreign government with diplomatic relations

We mentioned NSMIA earlier, which stands for the National Securities Markets Improvement Act of 1996. The goal of NSMIA was to eliminate the need for some securities to register with the federal government and also then register with all the states. For some securities this dual registration (fed and state) makes no sense. For example, securities that trade on any national exchange (NYSE, AMEX) or trade on NASDAQ's National Market System are really a federal concern, as are registered investment company securities—mutual funds, for example. Since these are being sold and/or traded inter-state, it's a federal concern, so NSMIA created a class of securities that are covered at the federal level. And they very cleverly named these securities covered at the federal level federal covered securities.

A federal covered security is not necessarily exempt from registering with the SEC. GE is an NYSE-listed stock. It has to be registered with the SEC. Mutual fund securities must be registered with the SEC, as must variable annuities. But the SEC (federal) has them covered, so we call them "federal covered," and the SEC will handle these registrations. The mutual funds don't register with the states—they do provide a "notice filing," which is just what it sounds like—a filing of notice. They notify the states that their shares will be sold in the states. They don't actually register with the states; they register with the federal regulators, the SEC.

Federal covered.

And, let's take a look at the federal covered securities again, since repetition is key to passing the 65. This is just copied and pasted from the exciting text known as NSMIA (National Securities Markets Improvement Act):

COVERED SECURITIES.—For purposes of this section, the following are covered securities:

(1) EXCLUSIVE FEDERAL REGISTRATION OF NATIONALLY TRADED SECURITIES.—A security is a covered security if such security is—

(A) listed, or authorized for listing, on the New York Stock Exchange or the American Stock Exchange, or listed on the National Market System of the Nasdaq Stock Market (or any successor to such entities);

(B) listed, or authorized for listing, on a national securities exchange (or tier or segment thereof) that has listing standards that the Commission determines by rule (on its own initiative or on the basis of a petition) are substantially similar to the listing standards applicable to securities described in subparagraph (A); or

(C) is a security of the same issuer that is equal in seniority or that is a senior security to a security described in subparagraph (A) or (B).

(2) EXCLUSIVE FEDERAL REGISTRATION OF INVESTMENT COMPANIES.—A security is a covered security if such security is a security issued by an investment company that is registered, or that has filed a registration statement, under the Investment Company Act of 1940.

(3) SALES TO QUALIFIED PURCHASERS.—A security is a covered security with respect to the offer or sale of the security to qualified purchasers, as defined by the Commission by rule. In prescribing such rule, the Commission may define the term "qualified purchaser" differently with respect to different categories of securities, consistent with the public interest and the protection of investors.

So, if a security is granted "federal covered" status, it's covered by the federal government, and it doesn't have to register with the states.

So, who *does* have to register with the states?

Any security that is not granted an exemption by the USA, or not granted "federal covered" status. This really boils down to stocks and bonds issued by companies whose securities are not listed on an exchange or on NASDAQ. Remember from the Series 6 or 7 that the "OTC" or "Over The Counter" market includes not just NASDAQ stocks, but also "Non-NASDAQ" stocks. That means if you get a test question about an OTC Bulletin Board or Pink Sheet stock, you need to remember that these get no excuse from the states. So, if a Bulletin Board company wants to do an offering of stock, they first register with the SEC, and then also deal with the state's requirements.

A security that has to register with the states can use one of three methods: coordination, filing, qualification. Registration by coordination is the most common method for inter-state Initial Public Offerings (IPOs). As the name implies, the issuer *coordinates* the state-level registration with the federal (SEC) registration. In order to use this method, the issuer must have a registration statement filed with the SEC. Otherwise, what would they be "coordinating," right? The issuer files the same paperwork with the state Administrator that they filed with the big guys at the SEC, including copies of the prospectus, articles of incorporation, underwriter agreements, and a specimen of the security.

Registration by coordination is effective concurrently/simultaneously with the federal registration, provided that paperwork has been on file for 10 days. Be careful here, though. The test question might say something like, "Registration by coordination is effective 10 days after the effectiveness at the federal level."

Not. Nothing is effective a specific number of days *after* anything. The registration for the security is effective either concurrently with the federal or whenever the Administrator says so. The paperwork must be on file for 10 days, but as long as that requirement is met, the effectiveness coincides with the federal release.

If an issuer has already done their IPO and would now like to sell additional shares to the public, they will most likely use registration by filing. This is the most common method for additional offerings, called "subsequent primary distributions."

In order to qualify for this method, the issuer must have a registration statement filed with the SEC. If they've been in business for 25 months, they don't qualify, because they must have been in continuous operation for 36 consecutive calendar months. They also must not have failed to pay bond interest or a preferred dividend and their stock must be trading for at least $5 per share. The issuer files with the state the same paperwork they filed with the SEC, and as long as the paperwork has been on file for 5 days, the registration is effective concurrently or simultaneously with the federal registration. Again, watch out for a statement such as, "Registration by filing becomes effective 5 days after the effectiveness of the federal registration." That ain't right— it's effective concurrently with the federal, provided that the information has been on file for 5 days. Again, nothing is effective a certain number of days after anything else.

The least desirable method for filing securities is called registration by qualification. Here you're on the state Administrator's home court, and your securities will only be effective if and when the Administrator says so. There is no set time frame. The securities are effective "when so ordered by" the Administrator. The issuer has to file any paperwork the Administrator wants to see. Why does the Administrator have so much power under registration by qualification? Because the SEC isn't involved. If the issuer hasn't filed a registration statement with the SEC, the issuer has to file with the state. Remember that coordination and filing both require filing with the SEC. Well, if you don't file with the SEC and you have no exemption from the registration process, you'll have to file with the state Administrator. If an Alabama issuer is only going to sell securities to Alabama residents, the issuer would only file with the state of Alabama. Or maybe they're ready to do a subsequent primary distribution but have only been in continuous operation for 27 months. That doesn't meet the requirements for registration by filing, so the issuer will have to register by qualification. Registration by qualification is the only method that requires a specific response from the Administrator. When you use coordination or filing, your securities can be sold when the SEC greenlights them—unless you've heard from the Administrator that he has a problem with you.

No matter which method the issuer uses (coordination, filing, qualification), these are the general provisions for registering securities at the state/Blue Sky level:

- A registration statement may be filed by the issuer, any other person on whose behalf the offering is to be made, or a registered broker-dealer
- Every registration statement shall include:
  - a filing fee
  - amount of securities offered in their state
  - names of other states where securities will be offered (not total $ amount)
  - any adverse order, judgment, or decree entered by a court, the securities agency or Administrator in any state, or the Securities and Exchange Commission in connection with the offering.
- Registrations are effective for one year
- Securities offered by coordination or qualification may require an escrow account whose proceeds are impounded by the Administrator and not released to the issuer/underwriters until they have raised the specified amount
- The securities registration statement must include a consent to service of process

Remember, even though shares of a mutual fund are "federal covered," the investment company usually does what's called a "notice filing," which is exactly what it sounds like. It's just a filing of notice. They might have to provide the same documents filed with the SEC, and pay a fee, but, again, they're really on the federal turf, as opposed to the state turf. At www.nasaa.org under "NASAA Library/Uniform Forms" you can actually print a uniform notice filing for investment company shares.

Should you be so inclined.

SECURITIES EXEMPT FROM STATE-LEVEL REGISTRATION

Again, the following securities are exempt from the state's registration and filing of advertising requirements:

- any security issued/guaranteed by U.S. Treasury/U.S. Government
- municipal securities
- any security issued by ANY Canadian government
- any security issued by a foreign government with diplomatic relations (national/federal only...except Canada, ey?)
- bank, savings institution, trust company security (not bank holding company)
- savings & loan, building & loan securities, credit union securities
- insurance company securities (stocks and bonds in insurance company, not variable annuities/variable life)
- securities issued by railroad or other common carrier, public utility, or holding company subject to Interstate Commerce Commission, or issued by registered holding company under Public Utility Holding Co. Act 1935
- federal covered security (exchange-listed, NASDAQ)
- non-profit, religious organization securities
- commercial paper maturing in 9 months/270 days or less
- at least $50,000 denomination
- rated in top 3 credit tiers by a nationally recognized statistical ratings organization (i.e., Moody's, S&P, Fitch)
- investment contract issued in connection with pension/employee benefit program

NOTE: the Administrator can revoke the exemption for
- non-profit, religious organization security
- investment contract in connection with pension/benefit program

PRACTICE QUESTIONS

20. Which of the following are not securities?
  A. whiskey warehouse receipts
  B. interests in multilevel distributorships
  C. fixed annuities
  D. all of the above

21. In which of the following instances has an agent sold a security?
  A. a broker-dealer transfers a treasury note for value
  B. an investment representative donates securities to a charitable organization
  C. an investment representative sells a variable annuity to a high-net-worth client
  D. all of the above

22. An agent unknowingly sold an unregistered non-exempt security to a high-net-worth individual who could easily afford the risks involved. This action is
  A. prohibited and fraudulent under USA
  B. not prohibited but fraudulent under USA
  C. prohibited but not fraudulent for high-net-worth individuals
  D. prohibited but not fraudulent under USA

23. Which of the following securities must register at the state level?
  A. Common stock of an insurance company
  B. Common stock in SWLDY, an OTC Bulletin Board security
  C. General obligation bond of the Government of Montreal, Canada
  D. Secured bond issued by a company whose common stock trades on NYSE

24. All of the following securities are exempt from state registration requirements except
  A. Building & Loan security
  B. Security issued by a railroad subject to the Interstate Commerce Commission
  C. Common stock of a local manufacturer trading on the Pink Sheets
  D. Commercial paper issued by a company not listed on NYSE maturing in 6 months

Answers

20. ANSWER: C

WHY: whiskey warehouse receipts and interests in multilevel distributor-ships are securities, but fixed annuities are not. To answer these questions, just remember what a security is NOT. It does not have a fixed payment, is not a commodity/precious metal. So, if it's not a fixed payment or a commodity, it IS a security.

21. ANSWER: C

WHY: variable annuities are securities (fixed annuities are not). In "A" we might be talking about a security, but B/D's are not agents. Donating is not the same thing as selling, which is why choice B is not in the answer.

22. ANSWER: D

WHY: fraud is the willful/intentional attempt to deceive. Selling un registered securities that have no exemption (non-exempt) is prohibited, but since the agent didn't mean to do it, it's not fraudulent. It is prohibited but not fraudulent under USA; the fact that the client is a high-net-worth individual is irrelevant.

23. ANSWER: B

WHY: a stock that doesn't trade on a recognized exchange, such as NYSE, AMEX, or certain regional exchanges, and doesn't trade on NASDAQ's National Market System does not get an exemption at the state level. So "bulletin board" and "pink sheet" stocks are still required to register at the state level.

24. ANSWER: C

WHY: a stock that doesn't trade on a recognized exchange, such as NYSE, AMEX, or certain regional exchanges, and doesn't trade on NASDAQ's National Market System does not get an exemption at the state level. So "bulletin board" and "pink sheet" stocks are still required to register at the state level.

EXEMPT TRANSACTIONS

The U.S. Government is an exempt issuer—whatever they issue is exempt from registering with anybody. Commercial paper is an exempt security. That means that even though GE would have to register their common stock with the SEC, they would not have to register their commercial paper with anyone, because that is an exempt security.

Well, unfortunately, there is a third type of excuse/exemption called an exempt transaction. That means that if securities are sold in a particular way, they do not have to be registered with the states and are not subject to the requirement to file their sales literature/advertising with the states.

The basic "logic" behind these transactions comes down to the fact that regulations always provide more protection up front to the average investor than they provide to institutional investors. It also comes down to the fact that securities need to be registered for the offering period/primary market. Once those shares are "outstanding," the regulators can relax a little bit.

Anyway, the following <u>transactions</u> are exempt and, therefore, the securities sold in these transactions do not have to be registered with the state Administrator:

- isolated nonissuer transactions in outstanding securities
- unsolicited nonissuer orders effected through a broker-dealer
- transactions with or among underwriters
- transactions by fiduciaries: executors, administrators, sheriffs, marshals, receivers/trustees, conservators
- pledges
- transactions with financial institutions (banks, S&Ls, trust companies, insurance companies, investment companies, pension plans, institutional buyers, broker-dealers)
- private placements
  - IF no more than 10 non-institutional buyers in the state per 12-month period
  - No commissions paid to anyone for soliciting the non-institutional buyers
  - Non-institutional buyers hold for "investment purposes"
- offerings of pre-organization certificates to no more than 10 persons
  - No payment may be accepted yet from any subscriber
  - No commissions paid for soliciting any subscriber
- offerings to existing shareholders
- nonissuer transactions in securities traded publicly at least 90 days
- nonissuer transactions in securities subject to reporting requirements of the Exchange Act of 1934 that have publicly traded 180 days

If a security is sold in any of these exempt transactions, it doesn't matter if it's registered or not.

Let's say you're the registered representative. Somebody calls you up and wants to buy 1,000 shares of a small manufacturing company headquartered in Terre Haute, Indiana. As an agent in San Antonio, Texas, you don't know too much about this manufacturing company in Indiana, but the numbers look right, and you aren't in the habit of refusing orders in the first place. So, you sell the stock to your customer and pocket a decent commission. Later that day, the compliance department informs you that the stock was only registered in Indiana, because it was originally sold in an "intrastate" offering, going only to Indiana residents.

Oops. That stock was never registered in Texas, where your client lives and you do business.

Oh well. First, it's a nonissuer order, meaning the proceeds don't go to an issuer raising capital in the primary market. Second, the sale wasn't your idea to begin with. It was all your customer's notion. Your customer called you, so it's an "unsolicited nonissuer transaction."

Bingo—that makes it an exempt transaction, so it doesn't matter that the stock wasn't registered. You'll probably get the customer to sign an acknowledgment of the fact that the order was unsolicited and keep it on file, because the one claiming the exemption has the burden of claiming/showing why he gets the excuse.

Now, if this had been your idea—ouch! That's a prohibited practice that could get your license suspended or revoked by the Administrator in Texas. Because you do not want to solicit orders for unregistered, non-exempt securities.

But unsolicited nonissuer transactions are exempt, meaning if the stock isn't registered, oh well.

See, the Administrators are more nervous about agents trying to SELL than they are about customers trying to BUY. As Elvis's bodyguard said, "How do you protect a man from himself?"

You can't. You have to let people do pretty much what they want to do, as long as it ain't hurtin' nobody.

But, if somebody is trying to SELL something to a resident of the state, that's when the state gets all nervous and regulatory, because sales reps can and do hurt people all the time.

Other transactions are exempt, so if the security turns out to be unregistered, oh well. Doesn't have to be registered, since the transaction qualifies for an exemption. If an issuer sells to an underwriter, the security doesn't have to be registered yet. It has to be registered before the public buys it, not before the underwriters take possession of it. Any transaction between an issuer and a financial institution or an institutional buyer is an exempt transaction, since these are sophisticated, professional investors. Financial institutions include bank, savings institution, trust company, insurance company, investment company, pension plan, broker-dealer. If a fiduciary is selling off assets (sheriff, marshal, trustee, executor), the security doesn't have to be registered. Those folks aren't securities dealers; they're just liquidating assets because somebody got arrested, went bankrupt, or went to meet that final margin call in the sky.

And since the Administrator is such a regular guy, he's even going to let each broker-dealer do one or two transactions per year in the secondary market even when the stock isn't registered in the state. Those are called isolated, nonissuer transactions. No one is raising capital for a business—just selling stock between two investors. As long as it doesn't happen more than once or twice a year per firm, we're okay with it. The exam might ask you to equate "nonissuer" with the word "secondary."

So, yes, there are plenty of times when a stock doesn't have to be registered, but if it *does* have to be registered—because it just can't find an exemption—then woe unto he or she who tries to sell it in the state! Of course, if you can't find an exemption from registration, chances are, you just aren't trying hard enough, but that's a different matter.

Also remember that the Administrator—if he has a real good reason—can revoke any of the exemptions granted those exciting transactions we just looked at. And, he can even revoke the exemption from state filing requirements for two specific types of otherwise exempt securities: non-profit securities and securities issued in connection with an employee benefit plan. Another testable point is that the burden of proof is always on the party claiming the exemption.

Basically, just remember that on the exam, all securities have to be registered in all cases, except in all the cases when they don't.

Are we having fun yet?☺

PRACTICE QUESTIONS

25. All of the following transactions are exempt except
  A. a broker-dealer sells Treasury bonds to a retail customer
  B. a marshal liquidates securities at public auction
  C. a sheriff liquidates securities at public auction
  D. an issuer sells common stock to an S&L or bank

26. All of the following are exempt transactions except
  A. isolated nonissuer transaction in outstanding securities
  B. private placement
  C. municipal bonds
  D. unsolicited orders

Answers

25. ANSWER: A

WHY: a Treasury bond might be an exempt *security*, but this is not an exempt *transaction*.

26. ANSWER: C

WHY: a municipal bond is a security, not a *transaction*.

DENIAL, SUSPENSION, REVOCATION OF A SECURITY'S REGISTRATION

So, if the issuer, the security, or the transaction does not qualify for an exemption, the security does, in fact, have to be registered with the state. And, don't assume that you'll automatically be allowed to sell the security in the state. See, the Administrator has the power to deny, suspend, or revoke the effectiveness of any registration statement if he finds that the order is in the public interest and:

- The registration statement contains any statement that is incomplete, misleading, or false.
- Any provision of the USA, or any rule or order by the Administrator, has been willfully violated in connection with the offering.
- The security registered or sought to be registered is the subject of an administrative stop order or a court injunction entered under any other federal or state act applicable to the offering.
- The issuer's enterprise includes or would include activities that are illegal where performed.
- The offering has worked or tended to work a fraud upon purchasers (or would so operate).
- The offering has been or would be made with unreasonable underwriter compensation or excessive promoters' profits, or unreasonable amounts or kinds of options.
- A security seeking to be registered by filing is not eligible for such registration.
- A security seeking to be registered by coordination has failed to comply with the requirements of that process.
- The proper filing fee has not been paid (but only a denial order can be entered and shall be vacated once the fee is paid).
- The Administrator may not institute a stop order proceeding against an effective registration statement on the basis of a fact known to him when the registration statement became effective unless the proceeding is instituted within the next 30 days.

As with registrations of persons, a security's application or registration may be denied, suspended, or revoked *only* after the big three things have been provided:

1. Prior notice
2. Opportunity for a hearing
3. Written findings of fact, conclusions of law

And, as with registrations of persons, the exception here is called a "summary postponement" or "summary suspension" pending final determination of an Administrative proceeding. Here, the Administrator summarily postpones the registration before giving prior notice. The notice is then given along with the reasons behind the action, and the affected party may request a hearing and receive one within 15 days.

SCOPE OF THE ACT, ADMINISTRATOR'S POWERS

The Uniform Securities Act gives the Administrator the power to regulate "persons." Which of the following are persons?

- Cleveland, Ohio
- The United States Government
- The State of Missouri
- New York City

The answer?

All of them. They are all legal entities able to open an investment account; therefore, the USA refers to them all as persons.

Some guy riding the commuter train is an *individual*. He's probably a person, too, but the term *person* is much larger than that. A person could be an individual, but it could also be a firm, or a government. It's easier to remember what a person isn't. A person is not:

- Dead
- Mentally incompetent
- A minor

So, as long as they're not dead, crazy, or a child, they're a person. So if a definition uses the word "person," it could be referring to an individual, a firm, or basically any legal entity. An individual is just an example of a person—a broker-dealer, investment adviser, and an issuer are all persons, too. The test might call an individual a "natural person," because the test knows no limits when it comes to harassing you.

Or, think of it this way: Elvis Presley is dead. I know some readers will become all shook up by that news and, no, I don't want to be cruel, but the fact is Elvis Presley is dead. So, Elvis Presley is not a person. But, the Estate of Elvis Presley IS a person. This entity called an estate has a Federal Employer Identification Number (FEIN) just like a corporation. It has investment accounts, bank accounts, etc. So it's a "person" in the same sense that GE and Morgan Stanley are "persons."

Guess what we call the official or agency designated by state legislature or governor to ADMINISTER the securities laws of the state?

Yep, the ADMINISTRATOR.

How much power does the state securities Administrator have?

A lot.

The securities Administrator of the state of Illinois can actually investigate fraud both inside and outside the state of Illinois. Also, if he/they receive a subpoena from the Administrator of Wyoming, they can enforce it there in Illinois, too. In other words, crossing a state border will not shield anyone from the consequences of violating the securities laws of a state.

The Administrator loves to publish the names of folks who violate the state's securities laws, like a teacher writing the names of unruly children on the chalkboard. So if you get caught churning an account, borrowing from a customer, or making unsuitable recommendations, maybe you'll see your name in the papers or up on a website with a searchable database that all future employers can check.

So, the Administrator has a lot of power. However, the securities Administrator is not a court of law, so he/they cannot sentence violators to prison or issue judicial injunctions—only courts can do that. But, they probably have some influence over getting somebody sent to prison or slapped with a judicial injunction, right? Administrators can make you come into their office, raise your right hand, swear to tell the truth, the whole truth, etc. Even if you've invoked your privileges under the Fifth Amendment, the Administrator can make you come in and give a statement under oath, anyway. Nothing you say can be used to incriminate you, but if the Administrator thinks you have something relevant to say, you'll have to talk to him/them at your earliest convenience.

If you commit a prohibited practice, like churning or making unsuitable recommendations, the Administrator can suspend or revoke your license. You have the right to receive prior notice and an opportunity for a hearing, but if the Administrator hears your side of the story and isn't impressed, your license can be denied, revoked, or suspended, which is bad. The hearing has to be a public hearing except in rare cases, and you can appeal the decision arrived at through the hearing to a court within 60 days, but that doesn't sound like much fun, right? Sounds like the Administrator has lots of power, right?

The exam kinda' wants to make that impression on you.

If you don't obey the Administrator's instructions, he will spew big ten-dollar words at you, like "contumacy," which means "failure to comply with an Administrator's order." Contumacy. If you commit the dreaded act of contumacy, the Administrator can go to the proper court of law and ask it to issue an order against your insubordinate little attitude, and neither the court nor the Administrator will be in a good mood next time they see you. If you fail to recognize the court's authority, now you're talking about contempt of court, which is *really* bad.

The Administrator can deny or suspend your license, but the Administrator turns criminal violations over to the courts. If somebody violates the state's securities laws, a court of law can fine them up to $5,000 and/or stick them in jail for up to three years, which is bad.

Three years, five grand. Memorize that. Those are the criminal penalties for violations of the Uniform Securities Act. If something is alleged to have happened more than five years ago, though, guess what? It's too late for anything to be done about it, since the statute of limitations has now expired. And, if a person can prove that they had no knowledge of a particular order they ended up violating, that person cannot be put in prison. In other words, this is one case where ignorance of the law *is* an excuse. Of course, the burden of proof is on the person claiming ignorance, and who wants to be that guy?

The Administrator can issue a *cease and desist* order. This is basically an official warning that the regulators know what you did and ain't too thrilled about it. You now have a regulatory order issued against you, which you'll have to disclose to clients before somehow getting them to sign on the dotted line anyway. And, if you keep it up, you'll most likely end up having your license suspended or denied, which is bad. Now, you've got even more stuff to disclose to future clients, presuming against all odds that any other state would let you set up shop. The USA also says the Administrator can issue a "cease and desist" even in anticipation of a violation, which is like a time-out for a registered rep or a firm. It looks like they might be doing something wrong, so the Administrator issues a cease and desist order to make them stop what they're doing while he takes a closer look at the matter. Sort of like the principal at an elementary school taking a kid aside and saying, "Sorry, Johnny, I'm afraid I'm going to have to give you a time-out because I think it's likely you might smack somebody today after school. It's not a detention, mind you, just a time out to protect one of my kids from getting hurt by a little thug like you."

Cease and desist.

A *stop order* is a formal order stopping somebody from doing something permanently, or possibly stopping them from operating as a broker-dealer in the state. Basically, it's the category under which the words *deny, suspend,* and *revoke* belong. To deny/suspend/revoke basically means that the Administrator is "stop"-ping the security or person from doing what they were registered or are trying to get registered to do. To issue a "stop order," the Administrator has to give the party prior notice and an opportunity for a hearing.

So, if the exam got real funky on you and started babbling about cease & desist versus stop (which I highly doubt), just remember that a cease and desist can happen even without prior notice, while the more serious "stop" order requires prior written notice, et cetera. Also, a registration can be "summarily suspended" even without prior notice, pending final determination of a proceeding against it. So, if the exam has nothing better to talk about, remember that a summary suspension and a cease & desist order can happen without prior notice. The stop orders (deny, suspend, revoke) happen only after prior notice, opportunity for a hearing, yada yada.

The Administrator's orders can always be appealed to the appropriate court of law, but, not surprisingly, judicial reviews are final. The person affected has 60 days to file the appeal, by the way.

At what point does the Administrator's/USA's powers "kick in"?

Whenever an offer to sell is made in this state—meaning the offer either originated in the state or was directed into the state. So if an offer originates in the state of Washington and is directed into the state of Oregon, the Administrators of both states have authority should something funny take place. Remember, if an agent in Washington calls a customer who lives in Oregon trying to sell securities, an offer to sell securities has been made in both Washington and Oregon.

Which actually makes so much sense it's scary.

And if the customer drives to California before calling back and discusses the offer with the rep before accepting the offer to sell, now the state of California has power, too, because the offer was made and accepted in that state. How does one "accept" an offer? By communicating her acceptance of the offer, or of her intention to now buy or sell the securities pursuant to said offer.

Oops, sorry. A little legalese just leaked out that time.

So, if an offer to sell comes from State A and is directed to a client in State B, an offer to sell has now been "made" in both states. And the Administrators of both states have jurisdiction over any funny stuff.

If it's an offer to *buy*, however, the offer would have to be accepted before that state's securities Administrator has authority. Not surprisingly, the regulators get more nervous when somebody tries to sell something (offer to sell) than when somebody tries to buy (offer to buy) something.

An offer has been directed into/received in a state if mail is sent to a post office in the state. So if a registered rep sends the offer by mail, and the offer is delivered to a post office box in Kentucky, the offer has now been directed into/received in the state of Kentucky, even if the owner of the PO box is on vacation in another state at the time or has since moved to Tennessee.

CIVIL LIABILITIES

A registered rep or broker-dealer can also be subject to civil liabilities. If a broker-dealer sells a customer an unregistered, non-exempt security, the customer could sue to recover damages, including reasonable attorney fees and court costs. The seller of that security is liable for the price the customer paid, plus interest, but minus any dividend or interest payment the customer might have received from the security in the meantime. In other words, if the unregistered, non-exempt security were sold for $10, the firm would have to repurchase the stock at $10, plus interest. If the stock had paid $1 in dividends, the firm would deduct $1 from what they pay the customer. Same thing if it turned out the agent sold a security when *he* wasn't registered.

The statute of limitations for money disputes/civil matters is a little tricky. It's basically two years from the date of the unlawful sale, so if the customer knew about it for 25 months, it's too late to sue. If the seller concealed the illegality from the customer, or the customer could not reasonably be expected to know something funky was afoot, there would be another year tacked on, but after three years it's too late to sue.

So, for criminal violations, the statute is five years. For civil liability, the statute is two years from discovery, or three years from the event, whichever comes first.

If the registered rep realizes her mistake of selling a client a non-exempt security that should have been registered, she can make what's known as an offer of rescission. Sort of like a "do-over" that satisfies the requirements of the USA. Here, the rep offers to repurchase the stock for the price paid, plus interest, minus any dividends or interest income that may have been received. If the customer receives the written offer and 30 days have gone by, it's too late to sue. So the customer either accepts the offer, or decides to sue. She has 30 days to do something.

SECURITIES
PRODUCTS

EQUITY SECURITIES

Let's say you own a small, growing business. You're convinced you could turn it into a much bigger company if you only had $100,000. Trouble is, you don't seem to have an extra hundred grand lying around.

However, you do have a friend who could provide some financing. You ask if you can borrow the money, but your friend has a better idea. Rather than borrow money from him, why not let him buy into your company as an equity investor? This way you print up a certificate and sell this piece of paper to him for $100,000, which you will use to grow your business. He'll use the paper as evidence of his status as a proportional owner of your company. If the company does well, so do you and so does he. His piece of paper or "equity stake in the company" is worth more money, and maybe you feel so gosh-darned generous you start cutting him a check every three months and call it a "dividend," which is sort of a thank-you note you can actually cash at the bank. And everybody's happy.

That's basically the deal with equity securities. It's all about corporations selling paper to raise money. The folks who buy the paper don't get interest payments, because they aren't lenders. They're investors who think the company's chances for success are reasonably good. So good, in fact, that they choose to become part-owners of the company, owning exactly as much of the enterprise as their equity stake entitles them to. If they want a bigger stake, guess what they have to do—buy more equity.

COMMON STOCK

The most basic form of this "equity" or "ownership" is known as common stock. Common stock is easily transferable, which means it can be sold without breaking a sweat. If investors get tired of looking at the stock certificates, they can sell them to other investors. That's how common stock works. You get tired of it, you sell it. You start to miss it, you buy it back. It's generally very "liquid," meaning it's easy to sell for a reasonably fair price, unlike trying to unload your house, like, *this afternoon*.

Owners of common stock enjoy several important rights the exam wants you to know about. The first right is the right of common stockholders to vote for any major issue that could affect their status as a proportional owner of the corporation. Things like stock splits, mergers, acquisitions, board elections, and changes of business objectives all require shareholder approval.

Shareholders vote their shares. If you own 100 shares of common stock, you have 100 votes to cast. Let's say there are three seats up for election on the Board of Directors. There are two ways that your votes could be cast for the election. Under statutory voting, you can only cast the number of shares you own for any one seat. So, you could cast up to 100 votes for any one seat, representing a total of 300 votes for three seats.

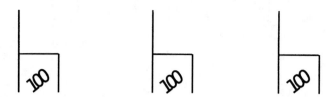

Under cumulative, you could take those 300 votes and split them up any way you wanted among the three candidates. You could even cast all 300 votes for one candidate and give nothing to the others.

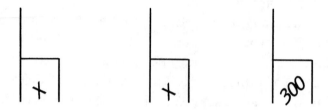

Shareholders may attend the annual meeting in order to cast their vote, but most votes are cast by proxy. Perhaps you yourself have received proxy cards asking you to vote for certain issues at the corporation. Heck, maybe you even bothered to open it up and read the proxy statement? And if only you could have found a darned stamp, you might have actually gone so far as to cast your vote and mail it in.

Maybe.

Beyond voting, common stockholders also have the right to inspect the list of shareholders and copies of the minutes from shareholder meetings. Shareholders have the right to receive stock certificates to show proof of ownership. A stock certificate would state the name of the issuing corporation, the owner's name, and the number of shares the stockholder owns. A shareholder can transfer his shares freely, too, by selling them, giving them away, donating them to charities, or bequeathing them to his heirs when he finally goes to meet that great margin call in the sky. The issuing company pays a bank or other firm to keep track of all these transfers of ownership, and guess what we call them?

The *transfer agent*. The transfer agent is a record keeper who has a list of all the shareholders. The transfer agent cancels old shares and issues new ones when they're lost, stolen, or destroyed. The *registrar* is another outside firm that audits the transfer agent and makes sure the company doesn't accidentally issue more shares than their corporate charter authorizes.

Should a corporation go belly-up and have to be liquidated, common stockholders get in line for their piece of the proceeds. Unfortunately, they are last in line. They are behind all the creditors, including bondholders, and also behind preferred stock holders.

But, at least they are in line, and if there are any *residuals* left, they get to make their claim on those assets. That's known as a "residual claim on assets," by the way, because they like to get real creative in this industry.

Buying common stock is really all about owning a piece of the corporation's earnings. If you remember from the balance sheet, we listed liabilities before listing anything about common or even preferred stock. That's because bondholders are creditors, who have a claim that ranks much higher than stock holders. All stock holders can hope for is that the company can not only pay its bond interest but also end up with a profit, called "earnings." So, common stockholders have a claim on those earnings. As the earnings increase, usually, so does the price of the common stock. That's why we have the phrase "Microsoft Millionaire" in our vernacular. If you own a share of Microsoft's earnings, your share price goes along for the same ride as the earnings, increasing maybe 10,000 percent in a decade.

Which is known, technically, as a *good thing*.

So, an increase in earnings generally makes the stock price rise. High tax-bracket investors often prefer to see their returns in this form of "capital appreciation," since those long-term gains are taxed at a maximum of 15% these days (assuming they want to sell someday). The other way to get a return from your common stock is to receive a piece of those earnings *now*, in the form of a dividend.

Is it better to get the dividend or to have the company reinvest the earnings toward more profits/earnings?

Basically, it depends on how wisely the corporation deploys its earnings. If they can get superior returns when they buy more equipment or hire more engineers, maybe that's better for the shareholders than getting a dividend. But, if the company's earnings aren't going to grow as fast as the overall market for some time, maybe it's better that they pay out some of those earnings now and let the investors get a better return on somebody else's stock or bond.

So, what would you vote for as a shareholder?

Trick question—shareholders don't get to vote on dividends. That's right, if a corporation's board of directors doesn't declare a dividend, the dividend doesn't get paid.

End of story.

But, if the board *does* declare a dividend, the board gets to decide three dates. The NASD decides the fourth one. Here's how it works. The day that the Board declares the dividend is known as the declaration date. The board wonders who should receive this dividend—how about investors who actually own the stock as of a certain date? We call that the record date because an investor has to be the owner "of record" on or before that date if she wants to receive the dividend. The board decides when they'll pay the dividend, too, and we call that the payable date.

Now, since an investor has to be the owner of record on or before the Record Date to receive the dividend, there will come a day when it's too late for investors to buy the stock and also get the dividend.

Why?

Because stock transactions don't settle until the third business day following the trade date. To "settle" means that the buyer has become the new official owner of the stock. If a stock is sold on a Tuesday, the trade doesn't actually settle (ownership doesn't officially change) until Friday, the third business day after the trade. This is known as regular way settlement, T + 3.

So, if an investor has to be the owner of record on the record date, and it takes three business days for the buyer to become the new owner, wouldn't she have to buy the stock at least <u>three</u> business days prior to the record date?

Yep.

So, if she buys it just <u>two</u> business days before the record date, her trade won't settle in time. We call that day the ex-date or "ex-dividend" date, because starting on that day investors who buy the stock will <u>not</u> receive the dividend. On the ex-date, it's too late. Why? Because the trades won't settle in time, and the purchasers won't be the owners of record (with the transfer agent) on or before the record date.

The NASD sets the ex-date, as a function of "regular way" or "T + 3" settlement. The ex-date is two business days before the record date.

So, remember DERP. <u>D</u>eclaration, <u>E</u>x-Date, <u>R</u>ecord Date, <u>P</u>ayable Date. The board sets all of them except the Ex-Date, which is set by the NASD.

Another way an investor could receive a "dividend" is by receiving more shares from the issuer. This is called a "stock dividend," and it's easy to get excited about getting 1,000 new shares of stock, until you realize that you didn't, like, win the lottery. If you got 10% more, everybody got 10% more. That's how a 10% stock dividend would work. Everybody would get 10% more shares. If you had 1,000 shares, now you'll have 1,100.

So, the big idea here is that when the investor ends up with more shares, the total value of his investment is unchanged. His cost basis changes, that's all. More shares, at a lower price. So, when a corporation does a 2:1 stock split, the investor would have twice as many shares. How much would they each be worth?

Half as much.

A stock split and a stock dividend are different events, but both end up doing the same thing to an investor's cost basis—more shares at a lower price. Also, a stock split has to be voted on by shareholders, while a stock dividend does *not* have to be voted on, because shareholders don't vote on dividends.

Just remember "more shares at a lower price." Stock dividends always work that way, because you're always getting more shares from the issuer.

Stock splits always work this way, too.

Except when they don't.

What we were discussing were "forward splits," where you end up with more shares at a lower price. Unfortunately, there are also "reverse splits," where just the opposite happens. Yep—*fewer* shares at a *higher* price. If a company's stock price drops too low, they might be in danger of getting their shares kicked off the NYSE or NASDAQ. Or maybe they know that most institutional money managers won't touch a stock trading below, say, $5. One way to get that embarrassing share price up would be to, like, become a more profitable company.

But that takes a lot of time and hard work.

So, another way to get your share price up is to effect a reverse split. The split has to be approved by the shareholders, who are usually seduced by the notion that a $5 stock could become a $30 stock after a reverse split.

Wow—the stock's going UP!

If you were long 100 shares @$1, what would your cost basis be after a 1:10 reverse split?

You'd have just 10 shares now, but each one would be worth $10.

Wow, a $10 stock.

Yep. Won't you look smart around the water cooler tomorrow?

Instead of paying dividends out to shareholders, some companies use the cash to repurchase outstanding shares and hold them in the "treasury." Treasury stock is just the stock that's been repurchased by the issuer. If the earnings stayed the same and there were suddenly fewer shares to divide the earnings among...see where this is going? It's generally a *good thing* when an issuer decides to buy back shares. It usually signals that they think the stock is worth more than the fools out on the secondary market do, and it usually raises the earnings per share. Larry Ellison at Oracle can't seem to bring himself to pay out dividends to shareholders, but he doesn't seem to mind using the cash that could have been paid out to buy back shares for the treasury.

Not that he's a control freak or anything.

RIGHTS AND WARRANTS

Another feature common stockholders enjoy is the right to maintain their proportionate ownership in the corporation. The corporation can sell more shares to the public, but they have to give the existing shareholders the right to buy their proportion of the new shares before the public gets to buy theirs. Sort of a "first dibs for current investors" thing happening here. For every share owned, an investor receives what's known as a right. It's an equity security with a very short life span. It works like a coupon, allowing the current shareholders the chance to purchase the stock below the market price over the course of a few weeks. If a stock is trading at $20, maybe the existing shareholders can take two rights plus $18 to buy a new share. Those rights act as coupons that give the current shareholders two dollars off the market price. So, the investors can use the rights, sell them, or let them expire in a drawer somewhere, like most coupons.

Another type of special security is called a warrant. It has nothing to do with shareholder rights; it's just easier to learn about warrants and rights together. A warrant is a long-term equity security. There are no dividends attached to a warrant. If you own a warrant, all you own is the opportunity to purchase a company's stock at a predetermined price. If you have a warrant that lets you buy XYZ for $30 per share, then you can buy a certain number of shares at that price whenever you feel it makes sense to do so, like when XYZ is trading for a lot more than $30 per share. When issued, the price stated on the warrant is above the current market price of the stock. It usually takes a long time for a stock's price to go above the price stated on the warrant. But, they're good for a long time, typically somewhere between two and ten years.

Warrants are often attached to a bond offering. Corporations pay interest to borrow money through bonds. If they attach warrants, they can "sweeten" the deal a little and maybe offer investors a lower interest payment.

PREFERRED STOCK

Another equity security tested on the Series 65 is preferred stock. This stock gets preferential treatment during liquidation, and always receives dividends before owners of common stock. The preferred dividend is printed right on the stock certificate. The par value for a preferred stock is always $100. The stated dividend is a percentage of that par value. Six-percent preferred stock would pay 6% of $100 per share, or $6 per share per year.

We hope.

See, dividends still have to be declared by the Board of Directors. Preferred stock-holders aren't creditors. They're just proportional owners who like to receive dividends. If the board doesn't declare a dividend, do you know how much an owner of a 6% preferred stock would receive?

Nothing.

However, if the investor owned cumulative preferred, that might be different. They wouldn't necessarily get the dividend now, but the company would have to make up the missed dividend in future years before it could pay dividends to any other preferred or common stockholders. If the company missed the six bucks this year and wanted to pay the full six bucks next year, cumulative preferred stockholders would have to get their $12 before anybody else saw a dime.

This 6% works more like a maximum than a minimum. If an investor wants the chance to earn more than the stated 6%, he'd have to buy participating preferred, which would allow him to share in dividends above that rate, if the company has the money and feels like distributing it.

Callable preferred may be repurchased by the issuer as of a certain date for a certain price. When interest rates go down, the issuer might get tired of kicking out generous 6% dividends every year. If so, they can buy the things back and put them to bed. Or replace them with new preferred paying stingier dividends that reflect the new lower interest rate environment. So, if the exam asks when preferred stock or bonds get called, tell it that it happens when rates are falling…same time that homeowners refinance. Also, if you give the issuer this type of flexibility, they'll usually pay you a higher rate of return. So, callable preferred tends to pay the nicest rate of return.

A truly wild type of preferred stock is called convertible preferred. This type lets an investor exchange one share of preferred for a certain number of common shares whenever the investor wants to make the switch. Say the convertible preferred is convertible into 10 shares of common stock. Therefore, the convertible is usually worth whatever 10 shares of common stock are worth. If so, they trade at "parity," which means "equal." Just multiply the price of the common stock by the number of shares the investor could convert into. That gives you the preferred's parity price.

So, if the convertible preferred were convertible into 10 shares of common and the common stock went up to $15 a share, how much would the convertible preferred be worth at parity?

10 X $15, or $150.

The test question will either tell you how many shares the investor can convert into, or it will make you take the par value and divide it by the conversion price given. If the question says the convertible is convertible at $10, just take $100 of par divided by that $10, and you'll see that the investor can convert to 10 shares of common. Convertible at $20 would be $100 divided by $20 = 5 shares. Either way, if it's convertible at 10, you have a 10:1 relationship. If it's convertible at $20, you have a 5:1 relationship. Use those 10:1 and 5:1 relationships as your tool. If they give you the common stock price, multiply by the first number to get the parity price of the preferred. If they give you the preferred's market price, *divide* by the first number to get the parity price of the common.

If a security has a fixed payment, the market compares that fixed payment to current interest rates. Current interest rates represent what investors could receive if they bought fixed income securities. If fixed income securities are paying 4%, and your preferred stock pays you a fixed 6%, how do you feel about your preferred? Pretty good, since it's paying a higher rate than current interest rates. If somebody wanted to buy it, they'd have to pay a higher price. But, if interest rates shoot up to 10%, suddenly your 6% preferred doesn't look so good, right? In that case the market price would go down. Not the par value—par value is etched in stone. It's the market price that fluctuates.

Market prices adjust for interest rates: rates up/prices down, rates down/prices up. That's because the value is really determined by a comparison of the fixed rate of return to current interest rates.

But, if we add another variable, now the security's price isn't so sensitive to interest rates. Convertible preferred has a value tied to interest rates, like other preferred stock, but its value is also tied to the value of the common stock into which it can be exchanged or converted. If rates are up, preferred prices drop. But if you're holding a convertible preferred while the common stock is skyrocketing, the price of the preferred would skyrocket right along with it. Remember, it's worth a fixed number of common shares. If the value of the common goes up, so does the value of the convertible preferred. So, the exam might want you to know that convertible preferred stock is less sensitive to interest rates than other types of preferred.

ADR/ADS

Then you've got your ADRs. That stands for American Depository Receipt, and like many of the acronyms you'll need to know for the exam, this one means exactly what it says. It's a receipt issued to somebody in America against shares of foreign stock held on deposit in a foreign branch of an American bank. The receipt is what is traded in America. It pays dividends, maybe. But they have to be converted from the foreign currency into U.S. currency, which is partly why ADR owners are subject to currency risk. Or, if we have a strong dollar versus the other currency, the ADR might not be worth as many U.S. dollars as we'd like.

Other than that, it's just another type of stock, a stock that can pay dividends, or not. The exam might also mention that ADR holders have to right to exchange their receipts for the actual underlying foreign shares. And that they allow U.S. investors to give their portfolios international exposure without having to utilize foreign markets.

But, other than that, not too much to know about ADRs. Except that the test might try to freak you out by calling them ADSs. American Depository Receipts/American Depository Shares.

No big deal. A foreign security on a domestic (U.S.) market. If they ask about voting rights, tell 'em, "No, no voting rights."

REITS AND REAL ESTATE LIMITED PARTNERSHIPS

Investing in real estate has many advantages and disadvantages. The advantages are that property values usually go up and that real estate provides nice diversification to an investment portfolio. The disadvantage is that real estate costs like a lot of money.

And, it isn't liquid. It often takes months to get a house sold, or sold for a decent price, so the lack of liquidity keeps many investors from buying real estate, especially commercial real estate (shopping malls, skyscrapers, factories, etc.).

Which is where REITs come in. A Real Estate Investment Trust (REIT) is a company that owns a whole portfolio of properties and sells shares to investors. You could buy into REITs that own apartment buildings, office buildings, shopping centers, hotels, convention centers, self-storage units, you name it. Now, if there were no REITs, it's safe to say that I would probably never be investing in shopping centers or office buildings. But through REITs, I can participate in big commercial (or residential) real estate without having to be rich or putting up with the traditional liquidity problems. I can liquidate my REITs as fast as I can sell most any other stock.

Real Estate Limited Partnerships are different. First, they are extremely *illiquid*. Meaning, if you think you're going to want to sell, think again. Don't buy in. If you buy in as a Limited Partner, you have limited liability. But, you don't get to sell your limited partnership interest. You're in for the long haul. Often, the folks who buy limited partnership interests are looking for tax write-offs. Since the partners take a share of the income and expenses, often a new partnership will generate losses for the first several years that can be used to offset passive income for the partners. But, these partnership losses can *only* be used to offset passive income—not earned income or portfolio income. Passive income is received from partnerships and any rental units an investor might own.

Not all partnerships are about showing a loss. Some provide new construction. Put up a new townhouse development, sell them all real quick, and walk away with a nice profit.

That doesn't sound too bad. Some real estate partnerships are more into owning real estate and making money by renting it out. More income oriented, then, as opposed to new construction, which is more about capital gains.

The disadvantages of investing in real estate partnerships include the fact that the K-1 you receive for taxes is more complicated than a nice, clean 1099 like you'd get for dividends, interest, or mutual funds. You might even have to file additional forms for state income tax purposes. Costs, fees, and expenses can also reduce your returns, so you need to see how much the business plans to deduct for that stuff as opposed to putting it toward something that might enhance your investment.

A fairly likely point on an exam would be that real estate partnerships do pass through losses to the partners, while REITs do NOT pass through losses to the shareholders. REITs pass through income, but not losses. If the company had a loss, that would just push the stock price of the REIT down, like any other company. Also, there are no net worth requirements for REITs, which explains why a schmuck like me has owned them for so long.

MEASURING RETURNS

Measuring the return on equity securities really comes down to two concerns: capital appreciation and dividends. If you buy a stock at $10, and a year later it's worth $20, that's a capital appreciation of 100%. If the stock pays $2 in annual dividends and costs $20 on the open market, that's a yield of 10%. Yield just asks how much an investor has to pay to receive how much in dividends.

$$\frac{\text{Annual Dividend}}{\text{Market Price}} = \boxed{\text{YIELD}}$$

And total return puts both concepts together. If the test question says Joe Schmoe bought a stock for $10, which is now worth $12 and which paid $1 in dividends, Joe's "total return" is 30%. He got $2 of capital appreciation and $1 in dividends. That's $3 outa' (divided by) $10 or 30%.

Online Updates

Do you have the most current updated information? Visit www.passthe65.com to make sure!

PRACTICE QUESTIONS

1. An investor is long 100 shares of XXR @50. After XXR declares a 5:4 split, the investor will be long how many shares at what price?
    I.   100 shares
    II.   125 shares
    III. $50
    IV. $40

    A. I, III
    B. I, IV
    C. II, III
    D. II, IV

2. Which of the following stocks would most likely interest a value investor?
    A. book value $1, CMV $17.50
    B. book value $1, CMV $11.00
    C. book value $1, CMV $5.00
    D. EPS $3, CMV $60

3. XXX convertible preferred stock can be converted into XXX common stock at $10. If XXX common is currently trading at $14.50, what is the parity price for XXX convertible preferred stock?
    A. $104.50
    B. $145.00
    C. $1,450
    D. Not enough information provided in the question

4. An investor of which of the following types of preferred stock might receive more than the stated rate of return?
    A. Cumulative preferred
    B. Participating preferred
    C. Both A and B
    D. Neither A nor B

5. Which of the following statements is true of rights and/or warrants?
    A. Warrants are better
    B. Warrants are sometimes attached to bond offerings to lower nominal yield
    C. Rights are short-term instruments with an exercise price above CMV
    D. Warrants are short-term instruments with an exercise price below CMV

6. Which two of the following statements are true concerning cumulative voting?
    I.   Said to benefit the majority over the minority investor
    II.   Said to benefit the minority over the majority investor
    III. Allows investors to cast only the number of shares owned per item
    IV.   Allows investors to split total votes in any way they choose

    A. II, IV
    B. II, III
    C. I, IV
    D. I, III

7. **A company may pay dividends in which of the following ways?**
   A. cash
   B. stock
   C. shares of a subsidiary
   D. all of the above

8. **Which of the following represents a benefit of owning common stock?**
   A. liquidation priority
   B. predictable returns
   C. inflation hedge
   D. all of the above

ANSWERS

1. **ANSWER: D** - more shares at a lower price

2. **ANSWER: C** - low price-to-book or PE ratios interest value investors

3. **ANSWER: B** - 10 shares X $14.50 = $145

4. **ANSWER: C** - participating preferred often gets increased dividends, and a holder of cumulative preferred might receive current div's plus arrearages

5. **ANSWER: B** - read the other choices carefully; they're deceitful

6. **ANSWER: A**

7. **ANSWER: D**

8. **ANSWER: C**

DEBT SECURITIES

FUNDAMENTALS OF DEBT

Basically, a corporation can raise money by selling exactly two types of securities to investors. One type is called "equity" and, just like the equity you may have built up in your house, this type of equity also gives people ownership. You buy a company's equity securities, you are a part-owner of the corporation.

The other type of security that a corporation can issue is called "debt." The most common name for debt securities is "bond," although we'll also see other names, including *certificate, pass-through, note, debenture,* and *commercial paper.* When a corporation needs money, it can sell investors pieces of paper known as bonds, which represent loans *from* investors <u>to</u> the corporation. Investors buy the bonds, and the corporation then pays them interest on the loan and promises to return the principal amount of $1,000 at the end of the term.

It's like a mortgage. Your family wants to expand, so you decide to acquire a house. Trouble is, you don't seem to have enough cash on hand to buy the thing outright. So, you borrow the money by issuing a piece of paper known as a mortgage. You carry the loan for 15-30 years, returning the principal amount plus interest until the debt is paid in full. In this case, you are just like a corporation selling bonds. You back up the loan with collateral (the property) plus your credit rating. Only difference is you pay back the principal little by little, while a corporation returns the principal all at once, at the end when the bond matures.

A bond has a specific value known as either "par" or the "principal" amount printed right on the face of the certificate. Bonds have a par value of $1,000 (although some are $5,000). This is the amount an investor will receive with the very last interest payment from the issuer. You might think of this as the investor "getting his original money back." Up to that point, the investor has only been receiving interest payments against the money he loaned to the corporation by purchasing their bond certificates. So the bond certificate has "$1,000" printed on the face, along with the interest rate the issuer will pay the investor every year. This interest rate could be referred to as the coupon rate or "nominal yield." Don't let the word "nominal" intimidate you. It means "name." The nominal yield is <u>named</u> right there on the certificate.

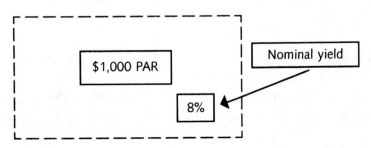

How often does this nominal yield change?

It doesn't. This nominal yield is what is paid to the investor every year. It represents a fixed payment, similar to your fixed-rate mortgage. Since the investor's income is fixed, we got all creative and decided to call bonds fixed income securities.

Rates, yields, bond prices

Interest rates represent what new bonds would have to pay in order to attract new investors. Since the bond we looked at pays a flat 8% interest, whenever interest rates change, they will change the bond's price. When rates on new bonds go up above 8%, the existing bond's price will go down, since new bonds would be issued with coupon rates higher than 8%. When rates go down below 8%, the bond's price will go up, since new bonds would be issued with coupon rates lower than 8%.

And the yields will move right along <u>with</u> interest rates, like this:

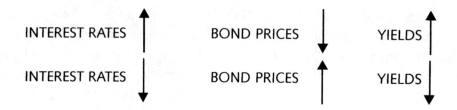

Remember, even though a bond has a par value of $1,000, we don't necessarily expect the bond to <u>trade</u> at $1,000 in the open market. As with a stock, a bond's price fluctuates. Why?

Interest rates.

If a bondholder has a bond that pays a nominal yield of 8%, what is the bond worth when interest rates in general climb to 10%?

Not as much, right? If you had something that paid you 8%, when you knew you could be receiving more like 10%, how would you feel about the bond?

Not too good.

But, when interest rates *fall* to 6%, suddenly that 8% bond looks pretty good, right?

When we take a bond's price into consideration, we're looking at a concept known as current yield. Current yield just takes the annual interest paid by the bond *to* an investor and divides it by what an investor would have to pay *for* the bond. If the bond will pay you $80 a year, would you rather put down $1,000 or $800? You'd probably rather only have to put down $800, leaving you with $200 to invest elsewhere.

$$\text{Current Yield} \cdot = \frac{\text{Annual Interest}}{\text{Bond Price}}$$

It's just how much you get compared to what you put down to get it.

$80/$800 gives us a current yield of 10%.

Notice how "divided by" and "compared to" are really the same thing. If I compare a $1 dividend to the $20 stock price, I'm both comparing 1 to 20 and also dividing

1 *by* 20 to get a dividend yield of 5%. Same thing for the current yield on a bond, which is really the same formula as current dividend yield on a stock.

Let's look at this in detail, since it's one of the biggest concepts in Series Sixty-Fiveland. First of all, we can use the coupon rate of 8% as the fulcrum of our lever below, since the coupon rate doesn't change. It's named right on the bond.

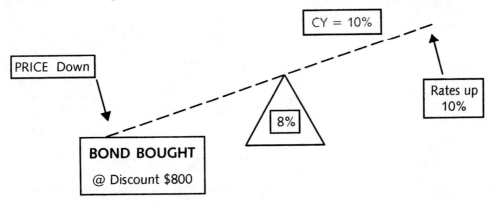

Now, if interest rates on new bonds go up to 10%, suddenly, this bond that pays a fixed 8% isn't worth as much, right? The only motivation for buying this 8% bond sitting out on the open market would be if an investor could get it at a <u>discount</u>. And, if she can get the $80 that the bond pays in annual interest for just $800, isn't she really getting 10% on her money? That's why we say her current yield is equal to 10%, which is why our line from the bond bought at a discount of $800 is going <u>up</u> at a 45-degree angle. The current yield is higher than the coupon rate (the fulcrum), all because interest rates pushed up on the right side of our lever, pushing price down on the other side.

Rates up, price down. But the yields are going up, right along with rates.

As soon as you see a current yield higher than the coupon rate, you know you're looking at a discount bond. But, there are two more yields the test wants you to be comfortable with.

Yield to maturity

The first one is easy. It's the yield to maturity, the theoretical return an investor gets if she holds the bond all the way to maturity. At maturity, an investor receives the par value, which is $1,000. If the investor puts down only $800 to buy the bond and receives $1,000 when the bond matures, doesn't she receive more at maturity than she paid?

Yep. That's why her yield to maturity is higher still. She gets all the coupon payments, plus an extra $200 when the bond matures. If you see a YTM that is higher than the coupon rate, you're looking at a discount bond.

Yield to call

Like homeowners, sometimes issuers get tired of making interest payments that seem too high. That's why some bonds are issued as "callable," meaning that after a certain time period the issuer can buy the bonds back from investors at a stated price. A bond that matures in 10 or 20 years is often callable in just 5 years. Since the investor who bought a bond for less than par is going to make money when the principal of $1,000 is returned, do you suppose he'd rather make his profit sooner or later?

Sooner, right? When you're making money, you want to make it as fast as possible. That's why yield to call is the highest of all for a discount bond.

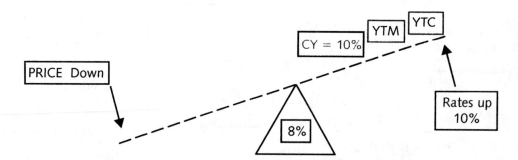

Take a moment and see what our diagram is telling us. What happened to interest rates?

They went up. When they went up, they pushed up on the right side of the lever, pushing the left side—price—down.

Where did the yields go?

Up, right along with the interest rates.

Rates and yields move together.

Prices move the other way. An inverse relationship.

Of course, whatever can go up can also go down. What happens when interest rates fall?

Bond prices RISE.

Here's why.

If you owned this 8% bond and saw that interest rates have just fallen to 6%, how would you feel about your bond?

Pretty good, right? After all, it pays 2% *more* than new debt is paying.

Do you want to sell it?

Not really. But you might sell it to me if I paid you a...that's right, a <u>premium</u>.

If I paid you $1,200, you might be willing to sell it.

From my perspective, I see that new debt is only going to pay 6%, which is too low for my needs. Even though I have to pay more than par for your 8% bond, it will all work out if I can get all those interest payments at a higher-than-prevailing rate.

So, we've just pushed the price of the bond *up* as interest rates went *down*. In this case the rates pushed down on the right side of our lever, which forced the price to go up on the left side. Like this:

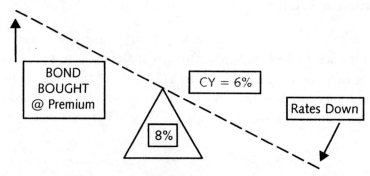

Dividing our $80 of annual interest by the $1,200 we put down for the bond gives us a current yield of 6.7%. That's lower than the coupon rate, which is why the CY is below our fulcrum. Whenever you see a coupon of 8% and current yield of 6.7%, you know you're looking at a premium bond. Remember, the coupon rate doesn't change. Therefore, the only way to get the yield lower than the coupon is to pay <u>more than par</u> for the bond. Just like the only way to get the yield higher than the coupon is to pay <u>less than par</u> for the bond.

Now, when this investor's bond matures, how much does she get back from the issuer? Only $1,000. So, she put down $1,200 and will only get back $1,000 at maturity. Pretty easy to see why her Yield To Maturity (YTM) goes down. So, you can place it where it belongs, <u>below</u> the current yield.

Remember when we decided that a person who buys a bond at a discount wants the bond to return the principal amount sooner rather than later? Well, if you pay more than the par value for a bond, you're going to lose some money when the bond returns your principal, right? So, if you're going to lose money, do you want to do it quickly, or spread it out over time, collecting the higher-than-prevailing-rate interest payments in the meantime?

Pretty clear that we're pushing for the latter, right?

That's why a person who purchases a bond at a premium will have a lower yield to call than maturity. He's going to lose money in either case, so he'd rather lose it over 10 or 20 years (maturity) rather than 5 years (call).

So, yield to call is the lowest yield for a bond purchased at a premium. On the bond seesaw on the previous page, please write "YTM" below "CY" and "YTC" below "YTM." The yields always go in that order: CY, YTM, YTC. For a discount bond, they go UP in that order; for a premium bond they go DOWN in that order.

What about the coupon rate/nominal yield?

It's fixed, which is, again, why we call debt securities "fixed income."

Disclosing yield on customer confirmations

When a customer purchases a bond from you, the registered representative, your firm will have to disclose either the YTM or the YTC on the trade confirmation. Should you disclose the best possible yield or the worst possible yield?

Always prepare your customer for the worst or most conservative yield, so there are no bad surprises, right?

Well, for a discount bond, which yield is lower?

YTM. That's what you would disclose to a customer who purchases a bond at a discount.

For a premium bond, which yield is lower?

YTC. That's what you would disclose to a customer who purchases a bond at a premium.

Callable and convertible

The "callable" concept is easy. Just means that after a certain period of time, the issuer might be able to call up the bondholders and announce that they're buying back the bonds at a certain price already agreed upon. A bond might be callable starting in the year 2005 at 104, meaning that in the year 2005 the issuer can retire the debt by giving each bondholder a check for $1,040 plus any accrued interest.

When might they want to call a bond? Probably when interest rates have fallen, right? Isn't that when homeowners refinance their homes? Works the same way for bond issuers. When rates go down, they start to think maybe the outstanding debt could be replaced with brand-new, much cheaper debt. If interest rates fall to 6%, they reason, let's issue new debt at 6% and use the proceeds to retire the outstanding debt we're currently paying 8% on.

Pretty simple.

Replacing one bond issue with another is called "refunding." It tends to happen when interest rates fall. It allows the issuer to issue less-expensive debt and retire more-expensive debt.

It's not such a great deal for the bondholders, though. What can they do with the proceeds of the call? Reinvest them. At what rate? A lower rate. This is called reinvestment risk. Upon reinvestment, the bondholders will get a lower rate of return, since interest rates have now fallen. And, what happens to bond prices as rates decline?

Right, they go up.

Only they stop going up when the bonds are called away, meaning the bondholder doesn't get the full appreciation in price he would have otherwise gotten.

Then, there are convertible bonds, which can be converted into a certain number of shares of the issuer's common *stock*. Bonds have a par value of $1,000, so the investor applies the $1,000 of par value toward purchasing the company's stock at a pre-set price. When a convertible bond is issued, it is given a conversion price. If the conversion price is $40, that means that the bond is convertible into common stock at $40. In other words, the investor can use the par value of her bond towards the purchase of the company's common stock at a set price of $40. Bonds have a par value of $1,000, so if she applies that $1,000 toward the purchase of stock at $40 per share, how many shares would she be able to buy? 25 shares, right? $1,000 of par value divided by $40 per share of stock tells us that each bond can be converted into 25 shares of common stock. In other words, the two securities trade at a 25:1 relationship, since the big one (bond) can be turned into 25 of the little ones (stock). The company sets the conversion price; they have no control over where their common stock trades on the open market, right? If the price goes up, the value of the convertible bonds goes up. Just like if the price goes down, that drags down the market value of the bonds.

So how much is this particular bond worth at any given moment?

Whatever 25 shares of the common stock are worth.

Just take Par and divide it by the CV price to find out how many shares of common stock the bond could be converted into.

In this case it's 25 shares, since $1,000 would go exactly that far when purchasing stock priced at $40 a share.

Par/CV price = # common shares   1,000/40 = 25 shares

So how much is the bond worth?

Depends. How much are 25 shares of the common stock worth?

Since the bond could always be converted into 25 shares, it generally has to be worth whatever 25 shares of the common stock are worth. If the common stock price goes up, so does the price of the bond. If the common stock falls, so does the price of the bond. We call this relationship "parity," which is just a fancy word for "same" or "equal." Since one's price depends on the other, the two should have a price that is at "parity."

So, if a bond is convertible into 25 shares of IXR common stock, and IXR is trading @50, what is the bond's price at parity?

25 X $50 = $1,250.

And, if the common stock went up to $60 a share, the bond would be worth 25 times that number, right?

25 X $60 = $1,500.

Sometimes the test gets tricky and gives you the bond's market price, asking for the stock's parity price.

Don't sweat it.

It's a 25:1 relationship, so instead of multiplying the stock price by 25, just divide the bond's price by 25. If the bond trades at $1,250, just divide that by 25 to get to the common stock's parity price of $50.

See, once you get that 25:1 relationship determined, you're good to go. If the relationship is 25:1, either multiply the stock's price or divide the bond's price by 25. Just depends on what the question gives you. So, when you see a question on convertibles, look for the conversion price. Divide par by that conversion price, and now you have the relationship. If the bond is convertible at $40, it trades at a 25:1 relationship to the stock. What if the bond were convertible at $50?

20:1.

Convertible at $25?

40:1.

And so on.

Sometimes the question will come right out and say that the bond is convertible into a certain number of shares.

Great, now they've already done the work for you. If it's convertible into 50 shares, it trades at a 50:1 relationship. Usually you have to divide par by the conversion price to get that number. Sometimes the test just gives you that relationship straight up. Either way, just work through the problem step by step. It isn't that difficult really. Just ask yourself how far the par value would go if divided by the conversion price of the stock. Whatever you come up with will allow you to answer the question.

So, all you have to do is find the ratio. $1,000 of par value divided by $40 per share gives us a ratio of 25:1. If the question gives you the stock price, <u>multiply</u> by 25 to find the bond's parity price. If it gives you the bond price, <u>divide</u> by 25 to find the common stock's parity price.

Quotes

Bonds are quoted either in terms of their price, or their yield. Since the coupon rate or nominal yield doesn't change, if you give me the price, I can figure the yield. And, if you give me the yield, I can figure the price. This process is known as "interpolation," by the way, which is just a fancy word for converting bond yields into bond prices, and vice versa. If we're talking about a bond's price, we're talking about bond points. A bond point is worth $10. You'll need to memorize that for the test. So, if a bond is selling at "98," that means it's selling for 98 bond points. With each point worth $10, a bond selling for 98 bond points is trading for $980. A bond trading at 102 would be selling for $1,020. Although fractions have been eliminated from stock and options pricing, they are still very much alive in the world of bond pricing. If a bond point is worth $10, how much is ½ a bond point worth? Five dollars, right? A quarter-point would be worth $2.50, right? An eighth is $1.25, and so on. Therefore, if you see a bond priced at 102 3/8, how much does the bond cost in dollars and cents? Well, "102" puts the price at $1,020, and 3/8 of $10 is $3.75. So, a bond trading at 102 3/8 costs $1,023.75.

$$102 [\$1,020] + 3/8 [\$3.75] = \$1,023.75$$

If we're talking about basis points, we're talking about a bond's yield. Yield to maturity, to be exact. If I say that a bond with an 8% coupon just traded on a 7.92 basis, I'm telling you that the price went up above par, pushing the yield to maturity down to 7.92%. "Trading at a basis of..." just means that the price pushed the yield to maturity to a particular percentage, or number of "basis points." A basis point is the smallest increment of change in a bond's yield. When the media talks about the Fed easing interest rates by fifty basis points, they're talking about ½ of 1 percent. We would write 1% as .01, right? Well, basis points use a 4-digit display system, so .01 is written as:

.0 1 0 0.

Then, we read that figure as "100 basis points." Two percent would be 200 basis points. One-half of one percent would be written as .0050 or "50 basis points." So, a bond trading at a 7.92 basis means that the YTM is 7.92% or 792 basis points.

Fascinating, isn't it?

Municipal bonds are usually issued under a "serial maturity," which means that a little bit of the principal will be returned every year, until the whole issue is paid off. Investors who buy bonds maturing in 2015 will generally demand a higher yield than those getting their principal back in 2007. The longer your money is at risk, the more of a reward you demand, right? If a friend wanted to borrow $1,000 for one month, you'd probably do it interest-free. What if they wanted to take three years to pay you back? You could get some interest on a thousand dollars by buying a bank CD, which carries no risk, right? So, if somebody's going to put your money at risk for an extended period of time, you demand a reward in the form of an interest payment.

Same with bonds. If your bond matures in 2015 when mine matures in 2007, isn't your money at risk for 8 more years? That's why your bond would be offered at a higher yield than mine. If I buy a bond yielding 5.65%, yours would probably be offered at more like 5.89%. The extra 24 basis points is your extra reward for taking on extra risk.

Yield curves

This is how it works under a normal yield curve, where long-term bonds yield more than short-term bonds. Guess what, sometimes that yield curve gets inverted. Suddenly, the rule flies out the window, and folks are getting higher yields on short-term bonds than on long-term bonds. The cause of this is generally a peak in interest rates. When bond investors feel that interest rates have gone as high as they're going to go, they all clamor to lock in the high interest rates for the longest period of time. In a rush of activity, they sell off their short-term bonds in order to hurry up and buy long-term bonds at the best interest rate they're likely to see for a long time. Well, if everybody's selling off short-term bonds, the price drops [and the yield *increases*]. And if they're all buying up long-term bonds, the price increases [and the yield *drops*]. That causes the yield curve to invert, a situation that usually corrects itself very quickly.

Yield spreads

Another yield concept the test might throw at you considers the difference in yields between two types of bonds. Corporate bonds yield more than Treasury bonds, but the difference between the yields isn't always the same. The difference between those yields is called the "yield spread." We could also track the spread between investment-grade and high-yield/junk bonds. Or the spread between Treasury and munibonds. If you get a question telling you that the yield spread has widened between Treasury and corporate bonds or between investment-grade versus non-investment grade bonds, remember that that is generally a negative economic indicator. If folks are demanding a much greater yield on low-rated bonds than on high-rated bonds, that means folks are nervous about issuers' ability to repay and are unwilling to pay up for junk bonds. Remember, if I pay a lower price on a bond, I get a higher yield, and vice versa. If investors don't demand a much higher yield on the low-rated bonds, that means in general they are confident about issuers' ability to repay, which is a positive indicator.

The certificate

There are four different forms that a bond can take in terms of the certificate itself. In the olden days, bonds were issued as **"bearer bonds,"** which meant that whoever "bore" or had possession of the bond was assumed to be the owner. No owner name at all on the certificate; it just said "pay to the bearer," so whoever bore the bond received the principal at maturity. In order to receive the interest, investors holding bearer bonds used to clip *coupons* attached to the bond certificate every six months. There was no name on the interest coupon, either, so the IRS had no way of tracking the principal or the interest income. And you know how much that irritates the IRS. So, bonds haven't been issued in bearer form since the early '80s—that doesn't mean they don't exist. A few are still floating out there on the market, so you have to know about them for the test. Just remember: no name on certificate, no name on payment coupons.

Bonds also used to be registered as to **principal only**. That meant that we had a name on the bond certificate—the person who would receive the <u>principal</u> amount at maturity. But, again, with the silly little unnamed interest coupons. Therefore, only the principal was registered, thus the name "registered as to principal only." See, these vocabulary terms often mean exactly what they say…except when they don't.

Anyway, the bond market got smart in the early 1980s and started registering both pieces of the debt service. Now, the issuer has the name of the owner [principal] and automatically cuts a check every six months for the interest. Therefore, the IRS— who is here to help—can also help themselves to a bit of the proceeds for the interest and principal income. We call these bonds **fully registered**, because both pieces of the debt service (interest, principal) are <u>registered</u>. And you know how that pleases your friends and mine at the Internal Revenue Service.

Book entry/journal entry bonds are still fully registered. It's just that it's done on computer, rather than on paper. The investor keeps the trade confirmation as proof of ownership, but we still have an owner name on computer, and we automatically cut interest checks to the registered owner.

Credit risk

To protect bondholders, Congress passed the Trust Indenture Act of 1939. If a corporation wants to sell $5,000,000 or more worth of bonds in a year, they have to do it under a contract or "indenture" with a trustee, who will enforce the terms of the indenture to the benefit of the bondholders. In other words, if the issuer stiffs the bondholders, the trustee/trust company can get a bankruptcy court to forcibly sell off the assets of the company so that bondholders can recover some of their hard-earned money. Sometimes corporations secure the bonds with specific assets like airplanes, government securities, or real estate. If so, they give title of the assets to the trustee, who just might end up selling them off if the issuer gets behind on its interest payments. Investors who buy bonds attached to specific collateral are secured creditors, the first to get paid should the company go belly up. If the collateral used is real estate, we call it a mortgage bond. If the collateral is securities, we call it a collateral trust certificate. And if the collateral is equipment, such as airplanes or railroad cars, we call it an equipment trust certificate. Since these bonds are the most secure, they offer the lowest coupon payment, too. Remember, you want a big reward, you have to take a big risk. If you take a small risk, you usually only get a small reward.

Most bonds are backed by a promise known as the "full faith and credit" of the issuer. That's why we might want to see what S&P and Moody's have to say about a particular issuer's full faith and credit. If the credit is AAA, we probably won't be offered a huge coupon payment. But if the issuer is rated right at the cut-off point of BBB or Baa for Moody's, then we might demand a bigger pay-off in exchange for buying bonds from an issuer just one notch above junk status. Regardless of the rating, if we buy a bond backed simply by the full faith and credit of an issuer, we are buying a debenture. Debenture holders are general creditors and get paid after secured bondholders. Therefore, debentures pay a higher coupon than secured bonds, since they carry more risk.

"Sub" means "below," as in "submarine" for "below the water," or "subterranean" for "below the ground." <u>Sub</u>ordinated debentures are <u>below</u> debentures when it comes to liquidating a company and paying out money to the bondholders. Since these bonds are riskier, they pay a higher coupon than debentures.

If all the bondholders have been paid and there's still money left over (it could happen, right?), then we start talking about paying out some money to stockholders. <u>Prefer</u>red gets <u>prefer</u>ence, so we pay them first, and common stock is always last in line.

So, if a company goes belly up, interested parties make their claims on the company's assets in the following order of priority:

1. Employees/wages
2. IRS/taxes
3. Secured creditors
4. Debentures/general creditors
5. Subordinated debentures
6. Preferred stock
7. Common stock

Yes, the IRS, an inherently benevolent society, makes sure that employees get paid first...that way they can tax the wages as they come for all the other taxes the corporation has failed to pay.

Warms your heart, doesn't it?

Remember that an "income bond" only pays income if the company *has* income. It's usually issued by a company coming out of bankruptcy and usually offers a high coupon, just in case it ever gets around to making a payment.

U.S. GOVERNMENT DEBT

By far, the safest debt on earth is U.S. Government Debt. This stuff is issued by the folks who also happen to have their hands on the printing press.

Convenient, isn't it? So, if you buy a bill, note, bond, or STRIP from Uncle Sam, you do not have to worry about default risk. You're going to get your money back. You just aren't going to get rich in the process. In fact, you usually need to be rich already to get excited about U.S. Government debt, but that's another matter.

For the test, just remember that U.S. Government/Treasury debt is the safest debt known to humankind. Safe and boring.

T-bills pay the face amount, and investors try to buy them for the steepest discount possible. If the T-bill pays out $1,000, you'd rather get it for $950 than $965, right? In the first case you make $50 interest; in the second case you make only $35. That's why the BID looks higher than the ASK for T-bills. The bid is the discount that buyers are trying to get; the ask is the discount the sellers are willing to give up.

So, the quote might look like this:

BID   ASK
5.0%   4.75%

In other words, the buyers want a 5% discount; the sellers are only willing to give up a 4.75% discount from the par value.

These bills mature in one year or less—4 weeks, 13 weeks, 26 weeks, 52 weeks—so there are no coupon payments. And that's how many short-term debt securities work. Rather than receiving interest on a regular schedule, you simply get back more than you put down, that difference being your interest income. Maybe you've taken out a "note" as opposed to a "loan" at your local bank before. If so, you didn't make regular interest payments. You simply had a short-term deadline upon which you needed to return more than you borrowed. Maybe you borrowed $3,000 and paid back $3,250. If so, your interest rate was $250 divided by $3,000 and then annualized. If they gave you a year, you paid about 8.3% interest plus whatever little fees they buried in the fine print.

Oops—didn't mean to take a swipe at the banking industry.

Anyway, T-bills are the shortest maturity of the Treasuries, and they are offered in minimum denominations of $1,000.

T-notes are offered with 2–10-year maturities. T-bonds go from 10 to 30 years. If you read the *Wall Street Journal, BusinessWeek,* or even the "Money" section of *USA Today®,* you probably see the yields on bills, notes, bonds, or some combination thereof. Since we usually see a normal yield curve, the yields increase from bills to notes and from notes to bonds, right?

As borrowing terms get longer, the yields go up.

Unlike T-bills, T-notes and bonds both make semi-annual interest payments, and are both quoted in 32nds. A quote of 98.16 means $980 plus 16/32nds or ½. So a T-bond priced at 98.16 costs $985. As they say, "Govies are goofy!"

Well, *I* don't say that because, despite what you may have concluded, I'm not really as nerdy as my chosen vocation would imply. I don't actually stand at the front of the classroom singing, "Govies are g-o-o-f-y!" in my best Romper Room voice, although I did used to teach for a company that does. Attend one of their classes, and you'll walk out mumbling about "Grandma's Pies Didn't Sell, Now Please Eat," and wondering why the heck you know that or what the heck you're supposed to *do* with it, assuming against all odds that you actually recall it at the testing center.

Anyway, the Treasury Department can also take T-notes and T-bonds and "strip" them into their various interest and principal components. Like they have a lot of extra time on their hands, what with the whole budget deficit thing and all. But, partly to fund the massive budget deficit the federal government likes to run up, the Treasury does have to get creative in its constant borrowing tactics. Once they "strip" the securities into components, they can sell interest-only or principal-only zero coupon bonds to investors. We call these STRIPS, which stands for the "**s**eparate **t**rading of **r**egistered **i**nterest and **p**rincipal of **s**ecurities." For the test, if an investor needs to send kids to college and needs to have an exact amount of money available on a future date, put him into STRIPS, especially if the question says he wants to avoid reinvestment risk. This way, he'll pay a known amount and receive a known amount on a future date, without having to reinvest coupon payments every six months at varying interest rates. He won't get rich, necessarily, but he won't lose the kid's college fund daytrading debit call spreads, either.

Broker-dealers sell the same basic product, only they call them treasury receipts. For both receipts and STRIPS, just remember that they are purchased at a discount and mature at the face value. T-bills, T-notes, T-bonds, STRIPS, and even Treasury receipts are all taxable only at the federal level.

Finally, as if Treasury securities weren't already safe enough, the government created TIPS, which stands for "Treasury Inflation Protected Securities." When inflation rises, the payout increases, and when inflation drops, the payout goes down. As usual, we use the CPI to measure the rate of inflation.

MORTGAGE-BACKED SECURITIES

The U.S. Government also has agencies that issue debt securities. **Ginnie Mae**, or **GNMA**, is the most testable. Rather than trying to understand Ginnie, Fannie, and

Freddie, let's just remember some key points. They all issue mortgage-backed or "pass-through" securities and all carry "prepayment" risk. That's just the risk that interest rates will drop, folks will pay off their mortgages, and investors will get their money back sooner than they wanted it, re-investing it at a lower rate. Ginnie is the only one backed by the full faith and credit of the U.S. Government, who insures all the mortgages in the pool through VA and FHA loans. Fannie and Freddie are public companies, so you can buy stock in them. No stock in Ginnie. Ginnie Mae requires a $25,000 minimum investment. She pays out a check monthly, since she's just passing through homeowners' mortgage payments [which are made monthly] to the holder of her pass-through certificates.

CMOs are sold by companies, who buy up mortgage-backed securities and create a fancy product called a **collaterized mortgage obligation**, or CMO. Think "tranche" when you think "CMO," and you'll be good to go. Investors get their principal back one "tranche" or "slice" at a time. Prepayment risk is part of this deal. They are usually rated AAA, so default risk is not a major concern. You just never know if you'll get your money back sooner [rates fall] or later [rates rise]. A **TAC (targeted amortization class)** will give you a target date; a **PAC (planned amortization class)** will re-invest your principal automatically. Less risk with a PAC than a TAC.

MONEY MARKET

The money market just refers to debt securities (no stock) set to mature in one year or less. A 30-year bond becomes a money market security once it's about to mature in one year or less. Safe, liquid instruments. They're very liquid and resistant to default risk, but they pay low rates of interest and do not provide inflation protection. The issuers *tend* to be solid, since the SEC will not even let money market mutual funds buy commercial paper rated below S&P/Moody's/Fitch's second credit tier. The exam may refer to money market securities as "cash equivalents," which would be found on the top line of a company's balance sheet. Remember "cash and equivalents"? That represents the money in the bank plus all the money market securities the company owns. And that's generally how I view money market securities: as good as cash. Better, actually, because this stuff that's as good as cash is earning some interest. Not much sometimes, but usually much better than you could make on a bank deposit.

But bank deposits are insured up to 100K by the FDIC.

Good point. But, if you want that level of safety, you make almost nothing. You don't make a ton on money market securities, either, but at least you're putting your cash to work and you're not risking it in the stock market where anything can happen, or the bond market, where interest rates could skyrocket and knock down the value of your holdings.

The following word associations should help here:

- Money market   Matures in 1 year or less, highly liquid, little default risk
- TANs, BANs, RANs   Short-term Municipal Notes, TANs most likely to be used
- Negotiable CDs   "Jumbo's," $100,000 min., excess uninsured by FDIC
- Repurchase Agrmt   We'll buy it right back for more money, agreed?
- Banker's Acceptance   Facilitates Foreign Trade, matures 270 days Max.
- Commercial Paper   Unsecured Note, issued by Corp's 270 days Max

MUNICIPAL BONDS

When the U.S. Government wants to borrow money, they issue Treasury securities and pay folks back out of taxes. When states, counties, cities, school districts, etc., borrow money, they issue municipal bonds and pay investors back either out of taxes or out of the revenues generated by the project being financed by the bonds. If the municipal bonds are paid off through taxes, we call these general obligation bonds, backed by the "full faith and credit" of the issuer. Maybe you've voted on the issuance of school bonds used to expand/improve your local schools. Those are general obligation bonds. They had to ask your permission to use/hike your property taxes in order to pay back the buyers of the bonds used to improve the schools. Your suburb/city/town might also want to build fun stuff like a water park, museum, or convention center. Those projects generate revenue in the form of parking fees, entrance fees, and concession sales. Or, maybe you've never paid a $15 parking fee plus $5 for a watered-down diet soda at McCormick Place here in fast, friendly Chicago, Illinois? Since the revenue can be used to pay the bondholders, we call these revenue bonds. They do not require voter approval, since they aren't backed by your tax dollars. You don't like the idea of McCormick Place?

Cool. Stay home and avoid the traffic on the toll roads, which are also supported by the revenue (tolls) folks like me are willing to pay for the privilege of using roads already supported by the taxes we pay on gasoline.

Guess which bond typically yields more, revenue or "G.O."?

Great Series 65 question—which one carries more risk to the bondholder, the one backed by the full faith and credit/taxing power of the issuer, or the one that is only as solid as the revenues we *hope* are generated?

The revenue bond is riskier, so it yields more. Check the second-to-last page of any *BusinessWeek*, and you'll see the slight difference in yields, plus the tax-equivalent yields for both insured revenue bonds and general obligation bonds.

Municipal bonds generally pay tax-free interest at the federal level. See, the federal government wants states/counties/cities to have good schools, roads, sewers, etc. If they don't tax the interest the issuer pays on the bonds, the issuer can pay lower nominal yields to investors, meaning the issuer can borrow money on the cheap. Why would investors take lower coupon payments? Because the coupon payments aren't taxed by the federal government. Therefore, if you're in the 30% tax bracket, a munibond could pay you 5%, and you'd still come out better than if you'd bought a corporate bond paying 7%. Just take the .05 the muni pays and divide by the "other side" of your tax bracket (.70) to get the munibond's tax-equivalent yield of 7.14%. The corporate would have to yield 7.14% to be equivalent to the muni paying just 5%. This munibond puts $50 cash money in your pocket; a corporate bond paying 7% ($70) each year, would leave you with just $49 after Uncle Sam took his 30% of that $70. That's called tax-free equivalent yield, meaning that if we take the 7% the corporate bond pays and multiply that by the percentage you actually keep (70%), we get a 4.9% tax-free equivalent yield.

So, either way we look at it, the investor in the 30% tax bracket comes out better on a 5% munibond than on a 7% corporate. And, the issuing municipality, therefore, gets to borrow money at 5% rather than at 7%, which makes them as happy as you would be getting a 5% mortgage as opposed to a 7% mortgage.

So, munibonds are tax-free, right?

Whoah, careful now. Depends on what your meaning of the word *is* is.

First, the only thing that could be tax-free is the interest payment; capital gains are fully taxable, so if you buy a munibond at $908 and sell it at $950, you pay a capital gain on the $42 difference. Second, if the munibond pays tax-free interest, that's at the federal level. Your state and local government could tax the interest if you buy the bond from an issuer outside the state or locality. If you live in Mississippi and buy a bond issued by Birmingham, Alabama, the state of Mississippi can tax the interest, as can your local government. If you live in Tupelo, Mississippi, and buy a bond issued by Biloxi, Mississippi, the state won't tax you, but Tupelo could, if they happened to have a local tax on bond interest.

Just to keep things nice and simple. So, if you buy a munibond that qualifies for tax-exempt interest at the federal level, you'll only get a break at the state level if the bond is issued inside your home state, and your local government can tax the interest in any case, unless they happen to be the issuer of the bond. So a New York City resident who buys a general obligation bond issued by New York City gets a break from the federal government, the state of New York, and the government of NYC.

Third, not *all* municipal bonds are tax-free. The ones that provide an essential service (e.g., schools) tend to get the break. But Industrial Development Revenue (IDR) bonds are often fully taxed. And any municipal bond that provides what the IRS considers an inessential service (private purpose) is subject to AMT taxes. Chicago's fifth convention center or first domed sports stadium might not seem as essential to the IRS as it does to the mayor and the city council. In that dispute, guess who generally wins the argument?

The IRS, who, as always, is here to help.

Therefore, all munibonds pay tax-free interest at the federal level, except all the munibonds that don't. Bonds issued to fund schools and necessary infrastructure get the break; those that build parking garages and convention centers often don't. And, that's not even taking the state/local tax into consideration.

Who buys munibonds? Investors looking for income, safety, and tax advantages. You need those objectives plus their state of residence before making recommendations, and—most of all—you need their tax bracket. Low-bracket investors do not buy muni's.

PRACTICE QUESTIONS

1. MMY Corporation has convertible debentures that can be exchanged for shares of MMY common stock at a set price of $40. If MMY common is currently trading at $57 dollars, what is the parity price of the MMY convertible debentures?
   A. $1,017
   B. $1,425
   C. $1,000
   D. $1,765

2. Which of the following statements is true of bonds issued in bearer form?
   A. They no longer exist
   B. They are no longer issued in this manner
   C. Interest coupons are detached from the bonds
   D. Proof of ownership is required at maturity

3. What is true about a bond with an 8% coupon trading at a 10% Yield to Maturity?
   A. It is trading at a discount
   B. The price of the bond went up
   C. Interest rates have risen
   D. The bond is trading at a premium

4. Which of the following bonds are trading at a premium?
   A. 8% coupon, 9.10 basis
   B. 8% coupon, 9.50 basis
   C. 8% coupon, 7.70 basis
   D. 8% coupon, 8.00 basis

5. All of the following statements is true concerning zero coupon bonds except
   A. interest is received at maturity
   B. interest is taxed annually
   C. reinvestment risk is eliminated
   D. taxes paid do not raise the investor's cost basis

6. Which of the following are associated with falling interest rates?
   I. Bond prices rising
   II. Bond prices falling
   III. Coupon rates rising
   IV. Coupon rates falling

   A. I, III
   B. I, IV
   C. II, III
   D. II, IV

7. Which of the following represent money market securities?
   A. ADRs
   B. Short-term equity instruments maturing in one year or less
   C. Preferred stock
   D. Commercial paper

8. **If a company is liquidated, interested parties will be paid in which order?**
   A. Preferred, secured, common, employees
   B. Employees, secured, preferred, common
   C. Secured, employees, preferred, common
   D. Employees, preferred, secured, common

9. **Which of the following investors are considered to have an equity position?**
   A. Owners of callable preferred stock
   B. Owners of debentures
   C. Owners of subordinated debentures
   D. All of the above

10. **All of the following investments come with a guarantee of interest and principal payment by the U.S. Treasury except**
    A. T-bills
    B. GNMA
    C. T-bonds
    D. Treasury receipts

11. **Which of the following represent a benefit of owning fixed-income securities?**
    A. inflation protection
    B. liquidation priority
    C. capital appreciation
    D. growth

12. **Which of the following is probably the least significant risk of owning a municipal bond?**
    A. inflation risk
    B. default risk
    C. interest rate risk
    D. reinvestment risk

Online Updates

Do you have the most current updated information? Visit www.passthe65.com to make sure!

Answers

1. ANSWER: B - 25 shares X $57 per share

2. ANSWER: B

3. ANSWER: A

4. ANSWER: C

5. ANSWER: D - taxes paid always increase cost basis

6. ANSWER: B - coupons on new bonds ARE interest rates

7. ANSWER: D

8. ANSWER: B

9. ANSWER: A - stock = equity

10. ANSWER: D - created by broker-dealers, backed by Treasuries

11. ANSWER: B - choices C and D are the same thing

12. ANSWER: B - muni's are generally safe, especially compared to corporates

MUTUAL FUNDS MADE EASY

As we've discussed, all securities involve risk, so any one security in a portfolio is always subject to the risk that its price will plummet. That's why most investors spread their risk among several stocks or bonds, often from several different industries. That way, if one security loses value, maybe another one will increase in value and offset the loss. While it makes good sense to use this practice of diversification, it also takes a lot of time and money to buy stocks and bonds from many different companies in many different industries, doing all your own research, receiving annual reports from, like, 20 different companies, and sweating all the details yourself. So, instead of trying to assemble a large, diversified portfolio on your own, you can buy shares of a large, already diversified portfolio managed by a professional. That's what a mutual fund is. It's a big portfolio of many securities managed by a professional and packaged as a complete set to the investor. Think of a mutual fund as a big portfolio pie that can serve up as many slices as investors care to buy:

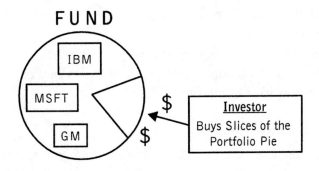

Investors send in money to buy slices of the big pie; the fund uses the money to buy ingredients, like IBM, MSFT, and GM. When an investor sends in, say, $10,000, the pie gets bigger, but it also gets cut up into more slices—however many she is buying with her $10,000. That way each slice stays the same size. The only way for the slices to get bigger is for the pie to get sweeter, which happens when securities in the fund go up in value.

Su-weet!

NET ASSET VALUE (NAV)

Like any portfolio, when the stocks or bonds inside the portfolio appreciate, so do the shares of the mutual fund owned by investors. Mutual fund shares are worth the net asset value or NAV per share. If the fund has $10 million in assets and $500,000 in liabilities, that leaves net assets of $9.5 million. If the pie is worth $9.5 million on net, and there are 1 million slices (shares) of the pie, each slice is worth exactly $9.50. So the NAV of this fund would be $9.50. The net asset value fluctuates with market fluctuations and is re-figured every trading day. Mutual funds will repurchase or redeem their shares whenever an investor gets tired of looking at them. The fund pays investors the NAV per share, which is computed the next time the fund computes it. This is known as forward pricing. If an investor has 1,000 shares to redeem, and the NAV is $9.50 when the fund next computes it, how much do you suppose the investor receives for redeeming her shares?

Yep, $9,500. And, the fund has 7 days in which to redeem the shares, whether they want to or not.

Let's make sure we understand that *when mutual fund investors buy shares of the fund, NAV per share is not affected*. Let's say the fund has $10,000 in net assets: 1,000 shares with a NAV of $10. Tomorrow they sell 100 more shares for the NAV of $10. So, they take in $1,000 and net assets go up to $11,000. They also now have 1,100 shares, so what's the NAV now?

The same ol' $10.

If that same fund had redemptions from rather than sales to customers, the NAV would also have stayed the same. They had $10,000 in net assets: 1,000 shares with a NAV of $10. Tomorrow, investors redeem 100 shares for the NAV of $10. So, the fund pays out $1,000 and net assets drop to $9,000. But there are only 900 shares left, too, so what's the NAV?

Same ol' $10.

Net assets might go up when customers buy and down when customers sell, but the NAV *per share* stays the same.

Anyway, mutual funds are open-ended, meaning that they will issue new shares whenever investors feel like buying them. They will also buy back or redeem shares whenever investors feel like selling them.

OPEN- VS. CLOSED-END FUNDS

On the other hand, we have closed-end funds, which do an initial fund-raiser and that's it. A fixed number of shares are sold, unlike an open-end fund that issues an unknown number on a continuous basis. Another major difference is that closed-end funds can raise money or "capitalize" by issuing common stock, preferred stock, and even bonds. Open-end companies can only issue common stock to investors. That's a big difference between open- and closed-end funds and a highly testable point. It might seem confusing, so let's look a little closer. An open-end fund can definitely invest *in* bonds. Those that do are called, oddly enough, "bond funds." The fund buys bonds from the U.S. Government, municipalities, or corporations as ingredients for the portfolio pie. When investors buy slices of the pie, they are buying an ownership stake in this portfolio of bonds. As we've discussed earlier, ownership = equity, and equity = stock.

The fund isn't borrowing money from investors and paying them back an interest rate. The fund is simply buying bonds en masse and selling little pieces of all the bonds to the mutual fund investors. We all mutually own pieces of these bonds, some owning big pieces and others owning little tiny pieces. The bonds themselves make interest payments to the fund, and the fund, after paying expenses, distributes what's left to the investors as dividends.

Dividends on bonds?

No, remember the investors own shares of common *stock*. That's why we call the income distributed to them *dividends*.

So, if you buy shares of ABC Corporate Bond Fund, you're not buying bonds in the ABC Corporation. The ABC Corporate Bond Fund is buying a portfolio of other companies' bonds and selling you little slices of the bond pie. As the value of the bonds goes up, so does the NAV. And, as the bonds make interest payments to the fund, the fund—after paying expenses—distributes what's left to investors in the form of dividends.

Probably more detail than you ever wanted on that topic, but welcome to the Series 65.

In some ways closed-end funds are very similar to open-end funds. They both have investment advisers sticking to clearly defined investment objectives. They are both investment companies whose chief activity is making investments. The big differences include the fact that closed-end funds can and do *issue* bonds to investors. They can also issue different classes of common stock that give some more voting power than others. They can issue preferred stock, too. Unlike open-end funds, closed-end funds also don't redeem their own shares. Investors buy and sell them on exchanges and OTC, just like individual stocks. Unlike an open-end fund, whose shares are always worth the NAV per share, closed-end funds are worth whatever the market says they're worth. So, for the test, if you see that a fund has a net asset value of $9 per share and is currently trading for only $7.50, you know it's a closed-end fund. Doesn't mean that closed-end funds trade below the NAV. It means that open-end funds do *not*, right? Closed-end funds can also trade at a *premium* to the NAV.

Why?

Supply and demand. If buyers really want the shares of your closed-end fund, they may pay you more than you ever thought possible. Or less. That's the deal with the closed-end fund; you have to trade it just like any other share of stock. You may have heard of ETFs (Exchange-Traded Funds). These are simply closed-end index funds. The difference between an S&P 500 Index Mutual Fund and a "Spider" (Standard & Poor's Depository Receipt) is that you have to redeem the mutual fund version at the next calculated NAV, while you can trade in and out of the SPDR® (spider) throughout the day. So you can't make money when the S&P goes up 50 points and then drops 75 points with the S&P 500 mutual fund, but, with the closed-end fund (ETF) version, you can buy and sell the shares throughout the day, hoping to catch the daily movements of the index.

As if the markets didn't have enough volatility already.

OPEN-END	CLOSED-END
Continuous offering	Initial offering only
Issues common stock only	Issues common, preferred, bonds
Investors redeem shares to fund	Investors sell shares OTC/exchange
Investors pay sales charge	Investors pay commissions
Priced by formula	Priced by supply/demand
Mutual Funds	Exchange-Traded Funds (ETF)

SALES CHARGE

A mutual fund (open-end) will always redeem or buy back its shares at the NAV per
share. Guess what, if you want to buy shares in the fund, you often have to pay a little
more than that. The "extra" that investors pay to buy the shares is called a sales charge
or sales load. If a fund has a NAV per share of $9.50 and costs $10.00, how much is the
sales charge?

Fifty cents.

What is the sales charge as a percentage? Well, how much of ten bucks is the
sales charge? Right, fifty cents. Fifty cents divided by ten dollars equals 5%. The sales
charge is 5% of the public offering price.

Now, the trickiest part here is that the test might give you the NAV and the sales
charge percentage, asking you to calculate the public offering price (POP). Remember
the sales charge is a percentage of the POP. If the test doesn't tell you the POP, how can
you figure it? Just take the NAV—which the test has to give you—and divide it by the
"complement of the sales charge." That sounds like a fancy math term. It just means
that some number plus 8.5% would equal 100%. In this case that number would be
91.5%, right? Or, just take 100% minus the sales charge. Either way you get 91.5%, so
divide the NAV by that number.

If the NAV is $9.15 and the Sales Charge is 8.5%, we would divide $9.15 by .915
(91.5%) to get our POP of $10.00.

$$\frac{9.15}{.915} = \$10.00$$

PRACTICE QUESTIONS

1. **Which of the following must be a closed-end fund?**
   A. NAV = $9.00, POP = $9.25
   B. NAV = $9.00, POP = $9.00
   C. NAV = $9.00, POP = $8.50
   D. NAV = $9.00, POP = $9.10

2. **The maximum sales charge for a mutual fund is**
   A. 8.5%
   B. 9.0%
   C. 10%
   D. 5%

3. **Which of the following statements are true concerning open- and closed-end funds?**
   I.   open-end funds may invest in debt securities
   II. closed-end funds may invest in debt securities
   III. open-end funds may issue debt securities
   IV. closed-end funds may issue debt securities

   A. I only
   B. II only
   C. I, II, IV only
   D. I, II, III, IV

ANSWERS

1. **ANSWER: C** - if the POP is below the NAV, it has to be closed-end. You can never buy mutual funds below the NAV, unless you're a distributor of the fund

2. **ANSWER: A** - memorize it. It's 8.5% of POP, by the way, not NAV.

3. **ANSWER: C** - mutual funds may buy/invest in debt securities, but they can't sell/issue them to investors

REDUCING THE SALES CHARGE

Ever noticed that in general the more you want to buy of something, the better the deal? Doesn't a small bottle of laundry detergent at the convenience store cost a lot more per ounce than a massive, industrial-sized container at Sam's Club®?

Breakpoints

Same with mutual funds. If you want to invest $1,000, you're going to pay a higher sales charge than if you want to invest, say, $30,000. For mutual funds, investors are rewarded with breakpoints. Let's say that the L & H Fund had the following sales charge schedule:

INVEST	SALES CHARGE
$1,000–$25,000	5%
$25,000–$49,999	4%
$50,000–$74,999	3%
$75,000–$99,999	2%

That means that an investor who buys $50,000 worth of the fund will pay a much lower sales charge than an investor who invests $10,000. In other words, less of her money (as a %) will be deducted from her check when she invests $50,000 as opposed to, say, $10,000. A breakpoint means that at this *point* the fund will give you this *break*. A lower sales charge means that an investor's money ends up buying more shares. For mutual funds, we don't pick the number of shares we want; we send in a certain amount of money and see how many shares our money buys us. With a lower sales charge, our money will buy us more shares. Keep in mind that fractional shares are common. For example, $1,000 would buy 12.5 shares if the POP were $80.

Letter or statement of intent

So, what if we didn't have the $75,000 needed to qualify for the lowest sales charge? We could write a letter of intent explaining to the mutual fund our intention to invest $75,000 in the fund over the next 13 months. Now, as we send in our money, say, $5,000 at a time, the fund applies the lower 2% sales charge, as if we'd already invested the full amount. The lower sales charge means we end up buying more shares, right? So, guess what the fund does? It holds those extra shares in a safe place, just in case we fail to invest that $75,000 we intended to. If we don't live up to our letter of intention, no big deal. We just don't get those extra shares. In other words, the higher sales charge applies to the money actually invested.

Also, that letter of intent could be backdated up to 90 calendar days in order to cover a previous purchase. If an investor bought $1,000 of the L & H fund on March 10, he might decide in early June that he should write a letter of intent to invest $75,000 over 13 months. He could backdate the letter to March 10 to cover the previous investment and would then have 13 months from that date to invest the remaining $74,000.

Breakpoints are available to individuals, husbands & wives, parents & minor child, corporations, partnerships, etc. Husband and wife get to combine their investments for the purpose of achieving reduced sales charges. A parent and minor child in a custodial arrangement also get to combine their purchases. So, if the mom puts in $15,000 and also puts in $15,000 for her minor child's UGMA account, that's a $30,000 investment in terms of achieving a breakpoint. The child cannot be an adult; he/she must be a minor. Corporations and other businesses qualify for breakpoints. About the only folks who *don't* qualify for breakpoints are investment clubs.

Another important consideration for breakpoints is that a sales rep can never encourage an investor to invest a lower amount of money in order to keep him from obtaining a lower sales charge offered at the next breakpoint. That's called breakpoint selling and is a violation punishable by death. Well, not death, but if the NASD had their way, who knows? Likewise, if a rep fails to point out to an investor that a few more dollars invested would qualify for a breakpoint, that's just as bad as actively encouraging him to stay below the next breakpoint. Remember, sales reps (broker-dealers) get part of the sales charge. It would definitely be to their advantage to get the higher sales charge. Unfortunately, they have to keep their clients' interests in mind, too. Yes, they take all the fun out of this business!

Rights of accumulation

If an investor's fund shares appreciate up to a breakpoint, the investor will receive a lower sales charge on additional purchases. In other words, when an investor is trying to reach a breakpoint, new money and account accumulation are counted the same way. So, if an investor's shares have appreciated to, say, $42,000 and the investor wanted to invest another $9,000, the entire purchase would qualify for the 3% breakpoint that starts at $50,000. $42,000 of value plus an additional $9,000 would take the investor past the $50,000 needed to qualify for the 3% sales charge. This is known as rights of accumulation.

Concurrent purchases

Most "funds" are part of a "family" of funds. Many of these fund families will let you combine your purchase in their Income Fund with, say, their Index or Growth Fund in order to figure a breakpoint. They call this, very cleverly, a combination privilege. So, if the individual invests $20,000 in the Income Fund and $30,000 in the Growth Fund, that's considered a $50,000 investment in the family of funds, and that's the number they'd use to figure the breakpoint.

Just trying to keep everybody in our happy family.

Conversion/exchange privileges

The fund might also offer a conversion/exchange privilege. This privilege allows investors to sell shares of, say, the L & H Growth Fund, in order to buy shares of the L & H Income Fund at the NAV, rather than the higher POP. If we didn't do that, the investor might get mad enough to leave our happy family, since there would be no immediate benefit to his staying with us. I mean, if he's going to be charged the POP, why not look for a new family with a growth fund that might actually, you know, *grow?* But remember that buying the new shares at the NAV is nice for the investor, but the IRS still considers the sale a taxable event. So if you get a test question on the tax treatment, tell the exam that all gains or losses are recognized on the date of the sale.

And then move on with your life.

Purpose of the Sales Load

What the heck is this sales charge/sales load for, anyway?

Let's say that you and your friends want to start a mutual fund. How would you get the shares sold to investors? First, you'd have to pay someone to print the prospectus. Then, you'd have to pay to mail the thing out to new investors. Who found those investors for you? Broker-dealers throughout this great land of ours, and guess what? They expect to be paid. You also need to do some advertising in newspapers, magazines, TV, and/or radio.

Guess you and your friends won't be starting that fund, after all, huh?

But, wait, there is an NASD member firm with a big, fat checkbook interested in sponsoring/underwriting/distributing/wholesaling your fund for you. They're so nice, they're willing to bear all those costs we just mentioned, known as "distribution expenses." Why are they being so nice? Because they're going to charge customers a sales load/sales charge to not just cover those expenses but, like, make a profit.

A profit motive, in the mutual fund industry?

No way!

Way.

So, how much of an expense is the sales load to the mutual fund?

It isn't an expense to the fund at all. It's an expense to the investor. The underwriter/sponsor/distributor bears the distribution costs up front, then covers them (plus a profit) by tacking on a sales charge to the customer. The fund takes the NAV; the distributors take the amount above that (the load) and share it with the broker-dealers who sold the shares. Some distributors even cut out the middlemen and sell to the investors directly. And—as we'll see later—some funds cut out everybody and act as their own distributor. If they do that, they don't charge a "load" per se. They call it a 12b-1 fee, which will be explained later.

For now, just remember that a sales charge/load covers distribution/marketing expenses and is not an expense to the fund. It's an expense to the investor. And it cannot cover management fees, which are deducted from the fund's assets.

THE A,B,C'S

These sales loads/charges can be charged when a customer buys the shares or when the customer sells the shares. "A" shares charge a front-end load when the investor acquires them. **A = "acquire."** "B" shares charge a back-end load when the investor sells them. **B = "back end."** For a "B" share, the investor pays the NAV, but she will leave a percentage behind when she sells. The percentage usually starts to decline in the second year, and after several years (6 to 8), the back-end load goes away completely—effectively, the "B" shares are converted to "A" shares. That's why they call "B" shares "contingent deferred sales charges." Break down those words. The sales load is deferred until the investor sells, and the amount of the load is contingent upon when the investor sells. Redemptions are a pain in the neck for a mutual fund, so they'll reward investors who can sit tight a few years. For a test question on the proceeds of a B share redemption, just take the NAV and deduct the appropriate percentage from the investor's proceeds. If the NAV is $10, the investor receives the $10, minus the percentage the fund keeps on the back end. So, if she sells 100 shares and there is a 2% back-end load, she gets $1,000 minus $20. B shares almost always have higher quarterly/annual expenses than A shares, so at some point, the load you avoid on the front end—and the back end after 6 to 8 years—could be outweighed by the higher expenses.

Just to make the decision harder, there are also C shares, which may charge both a load (or not) and a 12b-1 fee. **C-shares** are sometimes called **"level load."** They may or may not charge a small front-end load, but they almost always charge a 1% 12b-1 fee. Some also charge a contingent deferred sales charge if the investor sells in less than 1 year or 1½ years, just to keep things nice and simple.

So, which type of share should an investor buy? Although I think this concept is a little too subjective (like what makes something "small cap" versus "mid cap"), I'd recommend the following answers.

Long-term investor (7+ years)	A shares
Intermediate term investor (3–6 years)	B shares
Short-term investor (<3 years)	C shares

Whether you buy A, B, or C shares, there are different methods of making your purchases. Most funds have a minimum investment that might be different for a retirement plan as compared to a taxable account. Maybe it's $1,000 for an IRA and $3,000 for a taxable account.

Investors can choose to reinvest dividend and capital gains distributions (explained next), and if they do, they reinvest at the NAV, avoiding the sales charge. They get the effect of "compounding" that way, which is why most folks do this. They can certainly take the distributions in cash if they want, as we'll explain in a second. Some investors set up "voluntary accumulation plans," which means they let the fund automatically deduct a set amount of money each month from their bank account or paycheck.

If they're putting in a set dollar amount each month, they are "dollar cost averaging." This way, they buy fewer shares when the NAV is expensive, and they load up on cheap shares when the NAV is down. Like this:

Invest	Share Price	Shares Acquired
$1,000	$50	20 shares
$1,000	$20	50 shares
$1,000	$75	13.33 shares
		83.33 shares

Avg. Price $48.33
Avg. Cost $36 ($3,000 / 83.33 shares)

Had the investor bought equal numbers of shares each month, her average cost would have been $48.33. Since she, instead, put in equal dollar amounts, her average cost was only $36. Why? She bought 50 of her 83.33 shares at just $20. Only 13.33 were acquired at $75. And only 20 shares were purchased for $50. So, she bought most of her shares on the cheap, and only a few at higher prices.

I would not be surprised if you had to calculate an average cost just like we're doing above on your exam; in fact, I'd be more surprised if you didn't have to.

TAXATION

Dividend/income distributions

Of course, some of the stocks owned in the fund portfolio will pay dividends to the fund. Almost all funds have at least a percentage of assets in fixed-income/debt securities, too, so there will be interest payments coming in, as well.

Remember, there are only TWO ways to make money with securities: 1) the securities go UP in value; 2) the securities pay the investor some income.

So, receiving dividends/interest is a *good thing*.

The fund takes this "gross income" and uses it to cover expenses (board of directors, investment adviser, etc.). After covering expenses, the fund then distributes a percentage of what's left (net income) to the shareholders. Investors can elect to receive the dividends in cash or automatically reinvest the dividends into more shares of the fund. Although an investor pays the higher public offering price (POP) when buying into the fund, with dividends investors can buy new shares at the lower NAV. Either way your friends and mine at the IRS tax the dividends. Still, it is an advantage to be able to buy new shares at the NAV rather than at the POP. A test question could focus on the effects of electing to receive dividends in cash versus automatic reinvestment. Just remember that taking the dividends in cash will cause the investor's proportional ownership of the fund to shrink. If her husband is automatically reinvesting dividends into more shares of the fund while she takes hers in cash, he'll maintain his proportional ownership, while hers will decrease. Both of them, however, will be taxed on the dividends.

The fund doesn't want to be taxed at the fund level on income, so they distribute as much as possible to investors. If a fund distributes 90% of its net income to investors, it only pays tax on the remaining 10%. This way it qualifies for conduit tax treatment. A fund figures its income by adding dividends and interest paid from the stocks and bonds it owns, then subtracting expenses. If the fund receives $1 million in dividends, $500,000 in interest and has $500,000 of expenses, on net the fund has income of $1 million.

$1,000,000	DIVIDENDS
+ $500,000	INTEREST
= $1,500,000	GROSS INCOME
minus $500,000	EXPENSES
equals $1,000,000	NET INCOME

The fund then distributes $900,000 (90%) or more of their net income to investors, who pay tax on their share of the income. If a fund distributes at least 90% of its net income it is considered a regulated investment company (RIC) under IRC Subchapter M, but now we're really getting geeky. Still, you just never know what kind of mood the exam might be in on test day. By the way, REITs pass out 90% of their net income to shareholders, which is why you'll find some amazingly sweet yields on REITs. In fact, I just bought one this morning for my Health Savings Account, since all money coming out of that is tax-free and REIT income would otherwise be taxed as ordinary income.

But, I digress, just like the Series 65.

Capital gains

Once a year the fund may distribute capital gains to investors. Capital gains are realized when the fund sells securities for more than they paid for them. Mutual fund investors are then sent a capital gains distribution, which is taxed at the long-term capital gains rate. If the fund realizes a short-term capital gain, it identifies it as such, and investors are taxed at the ordinary income rate. Either way, though, the long-term vs. short-term treatment has nothing to do with how long the investor was in the fund. It's only based on how long the mutual fund held the securities they sold. So, if the question says the investor has owned the fund for only three months, chances are the capital gains distribution she receives will still be a long-term gain, because the fund probably held those shares longer than one year. Remember, the investor didn't sell anything—she simply received her proportionate share of the gains that everybody is "mutually" entitled to. So, when the fund distributes capital gains, investors pay taxes on their share of the distribution (even if the price of the fund's shares has gone down).

When the investor re-invests either the dividend or the cap gains distribution, that adds to her cost basis. So, if she puts in $10,000 and reinvests distributions of $1,000, her cost basis is now $11,000 in this fund.

If the test starts talking about "unrealized gains," just break down the words. An "unrealized gain" is just a "paper gain." It means that the securities the fund owns are worth more on paper. They bought GE at $20, and it's now worth $35. That's known, technically, as a "good thing." How would it affect the investor? It would probably make him feel pretty good, especially if most of the other securities are going up in value. In fact, that's the name of the game. "Unrealized gains" simply implies that the NAV of the fund has gone up because the securities inside the portfolio have gone up. How would that affect the investor?

It wouldn't. Not until she sold her shares. If she bought the shares for $10 and sold/redeemed them for $15, the IRS—who is here to help—would like to help her out of some of that $5 capital gain. They call it a capital gains tax, and the more Republican you are, the more you hate it. Not that Democrats cheer wildly when they get their 1099s, either, but that's another matter.

So, there are two types of "capital gains." The first type is the capital gains distribution that the fund sends to investors, no more than once per year. Those come from all the gains the investment adviser took when selling shares for more than she paid for them. Doesn't matter if the NAV for the fund is up or down, and it doesn't matter how long the investor was in the fund. Here comes her distribution, her proportional share of the gains, and she pays her capital gains rate on that distribution, whether she cashes the check or reinvests it into new shares at the NAV.

The other type of capital gain is when the investor sells her shares for more than she paid for them. If she realized that gain within one year, she pays her short-term capital gains rate, which is really her ordinary income rate. If she waits more than 1 year, she only pays her long-term capital gains rate, which is lower. In fact, at the time of this writing it's a maximum of 15%. What a difference a day makes, huh? A wealthy investor could pay, say, 35% tax on a gain realized in 365 days. Had he waited one more day, the rate would drop to 15%. The holding period is determined by the trade date, meaning the date that she buys and the date that she sells her shares. Also, since all the dividends and capital gains distributions are taxed, if the investor reinvests them, they add to her cost basis. If she bought the shares for $10 and reinvests a $1 dividend distribution, her cost basis is now $11. She would simply take the proceeds from the redemption/sale (NAV minus any redemption fees or back-end loads) minus her adjusted cost basis. If she receives $13 from the redemption and her cost basis is $11, she has a capital gain of $2.

Practice Questions

4. **In order to qualify for special tax treatment, a mutual fund must distribute**
   A. at least 90% of capital gains to investors
   B. at least 90% of investment income to the board of directors
   C. at least 90% of net investment income to shareholders
   D. at least 95% of net investment income to shareholders

5. **A letter of intent**
   A. may be backdated 90 days to cover a previous purchase
   B. is a non-binding agreement
   C. covers a period of 13 months
   D. all of the above

6. **In order to reach a breakpoint new money is counted the same way as account value appreciation under**
   A. exchange privilege
   B. rights of accumulation
   C. Breakpoint Act of 1915
   D. combination privilege

7. **For a mutual fund with a POP of $10.00, the maximum sales load is**
   A. 85¢
   B. $1
   C. 50¢
   D. 25¢

8. **Mutual funds redeem their shares**
   A. immediately, on demand
   B. next business day
   C. within 7 calendar days
   D. whenever convenient to the investment adviser

Answers

4. ANSWER: C - memorize it and don't let 'em send it to the Board of Directors, who already average about 100K a year to sit on the board!

5. ANSWER: D - memorize

6. ANSWER: B - doesn't it sort of sound like "rights of accumulation"? If the account value *accumulates*, you get the *right* to pay a lower sales charge, a breakpoint.

7. ANSWER: A - 85 cents outa' $10 is the maximum of 8.5%

8. ANSWER: C - memorize

TYPES OF FUNDS

We talked about diversification at the beginning of this discussion. Mutual funds can be as diversified as they want to, but if the fund wants to advertise itself as being diversified, it has to follow the 75-5-10 rule. That means that at least 75% of the fund's assets have to be diversified so that no more than 5% of the fund's assets are invested in any one stock. The 10 means that the fund can not own more than 10% of a company's outstanding shares. What happens if a particular stock appreciates and now represents more than 5% of the fund's assets?

Nothing. They just can't buy any more of it.

Mutual funds have to clearly state their investment objectives. Sales representatives like you have to match your investor's objectives with those of a particular fund. If your investor is interested in long-term growth, you need to find a mutual fund that invests for long-term growth. The stocks in this fund might pay dividends, but that's not the main objective. This fund wants to buy stocks low and hold them until they appreciate significantly in value. The prospectus I'm looking at says "dividend income, if any, is incidental to the objective of capital appreciation." Of course, "capital appreciation" and "growth" are two ways of saying the same thing. If your client wants income from stocks, you need to find a fund that invests in stocks that pay regular income: utilities, preferred stock, blue chip stocks. They refer to these funds as "**equity income funds**" for obvious reasons.

Some funds invest for both growth and income. Guess what we call them?

That's right, we call them reversionary contrarian volatility-weighted back-end-loaded unit investment vehicles, which are detailed in pages 675-842.

Just kidding.

They're called **growth and income funds**, because of the whole growth and income thing. The equities purchased for the portfolio represent both growth opportunities and opportunities to collect nice dividend checks. Of course, you're trying to get the best of both worlds here, which means you might not get as much growth as a pure growth fund or as much income as a pure income fund. But, if you're going for a little of both, this is the fund for you. These funds will normally hold a bigger "cash" or money market position to make sure they can provide that income they've inserted into their name.

A fund that concentrates its investments in a particular sector of the market is called a **sector** or **specialized fund**. If most of the investments are in pharmaceutical companies or financial companies, we might be looking at a sector fund. The name of the fund usually tips you off that it's a sector fund. An "aggressive growth" fund refers to a style of investing—it doesn't say which industry the companies are in. But, a "science and technology" fund or a "financial services" fund pretty well tip us off that the fund is concentrating in a particular sector, right? The exam may want you to know that sector funds involve high risk-reward ratios. If you invested in any "Internet funds" back in the late '90's, that concept should be pretty easy to remember.

International funds come in a few flavors. They might concentrate in a single country, or a particular region (Latin America, Pacific Rim, etc.). Usually the fund concentrates in companies outside the U.S. A global fund would invest all over the globe, including the U.S. International funds require a higher risk tolerance than purely domestic funds, but they also provide potential returns an American investor would otherwise miss out on and allow the investor to diversify away from the U.S. economy. A particularly volatile type of international fund would be an **emerging market fund**.

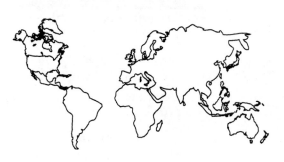

As the name implies, these markets are, you know, emerging, just getting started. Lots of wild ups and downs in an immature economy. And if the insurgents take over...well, you get the idea. High risk-reward ratios offered by international funds, especially emerging market funds. Basically, the economies are transforming from agricultural-based to industrial (Brazil, for example) or from socialist systems to free market systems (Russia, Eastern Europe, China).

Some funds invest in bonds, and we very cleverly call them **bond funds**. Remember that mutual funds are just massive investment pies that serve up slices to investors, so anything that was true of corporate bonds individually is true of a big pie baked from many corporate bonds. So, for maximum income, recommend **corporate bond funds**. For safety or "capital preservation," recommend **government bond funds**. Also remember that the longer the term on the bonds, the more susceptible the fund is to a rise in interest rates, known, cleverly, as "**interest rate risk**." So a long-term bond fund has more interest rate risk than a short- or intermediate-term bond fund, and that could easily be factored into a test question. In other words, don't expect the question to say "capital preservation" with choice "A" as "government bond fund." It *could* be that easy, but more likely there will be something about interest rate risk in the question and then there will be "short-term Treasury fund," "intermediate-term Treasury fund" and "long-term Treasury fund." Typical Series 65 stuff there—you thought all you had to know was the word "Treasury"? Oh no—let's put some more spin on this one, if you don't mind.

Or, even if you do mind.

Income investors looking for tax advantages should buy **municipal bond funds**. Municipal bond funds get income from interest payments, which may be tax-exempt. So, if an investor wants some tax-free dividends, he will get that from a munibond fund. Remember that munibond funds might pay tax-free dividends, but capital gains are still taxable, just as they are on munibonds purchased a la carte.

Some funds invest in a mixture of stocks and bonds. We call those **balanced funds**. If it looks like a good year for bonds, the investment adviser switches the concentration to bonds, and vice versa when it looks like a bull market for stocks. A subtle difference arises when the exam talks about **asset allocation funds**. These funds, as their name implies, allocate the assets according to the perfect mix of stocks, bonds, and "cash," which is like a hip way of saying "money market securities." So the only real difference I see is that a balanced fund has stocks and bonds, while the asset allocation fund goes one better by throwing in the "cash" or "money market" component. Also, the % mixture is probably more rigid in asset allocation.

Some funds write calls against stocks held in the portfolio. We call these **option income funds,** and if you get a question on those, please avoid ladders, black cats, and broken mirrors that day, as your luck is running dangerously low.

Money market mutual funds invest in money market instruments. They are no-load and maintain a stable value of $1 per share. They credit interest to the account every 30 days. Big, exciting vehicles, these money market mutual funds. There is a management fee but no sales charge for money market funds. If they let distributors tack on a 5% load when short-term interest rates are at about 1%, all investors would be guaranteed to lose money.

Which is bad.

Can they lose money to the management fees?

What are you, a traitor to the industry? Stop asking questions like that and just study, darn it.

Also remember that there are **tax-exempt money market funds**. These funds buy short-term municipal obligations (BAN, TAN, RAN, TRAN), or munibonds that are set to mature in a year or less.

Keep in mind that mutual funds are just packages made up of many individual securities. So, if there is preferred stock, you know there are **preferred stock funds**. They would be primarily for income investors. If there are GNMAs, then there are, of course, **GNMA funds** for income investors looking for higher income than that offered by Treasuries. Remember that GNMA pass-throughs start at 25K, so a GNMA fund is more practical for most investors than buying GNMAs a la carte. Could there be a **convertible bond fund**?

Absolutely. Whatever an investor could buy a la carte, she could buy as a complete dinner package through a mutual fund. She pays for the expenses of the fund plus sales charges in many cases, but she gets immediate diversification and professional management in return.

So, if you review the different styles of investing, and throw in the market caps, you see why we could really come up with a variety of fund types. For example:

Growth Funds
- Aggressive Growth
- Conservative Growth
- Small Cap Growth
- Mid Cap Growth
- Large Cap Growth
- International Growth
- New Economy Growth
- EuroPacific Growth

Value Funds
- Small Cap Value
- Mid Cap Value
- Large Cap Value

Bond Funds
- Investment Grade
- High Yield
- Tax-Exempt (munibonds)
- Short-Term Treasury
- Short-Term Tax-Exempt (muni)
- Short-Term Corporate
- Intermediate-Term (treasury, muni, corporate)
- Long-Term (treasury, muni, corporate)

Growth & Income

Equity Income

Balanced

Sector (pharmaceutical, retail, technology, energy, etc.)

Index (bond indexes, S&P500, Russell2000, etc.)

Money Market
- U.S. Government/Treasury
- Tax-Exempt (muni notes, near-term bonds)

STRUCTURE OF THE FUND COMPANY

So, where are all of these rules coming from? From the NASD and from a major piece of federal legislation known as the Investment Company Act of 1940. This is the act that classified investment companies and laid out all kinds of rules. For example, a mutual fund needs at least 100 investors and $100,000 in seed money to qualify as a mutual fund. The Act of 1940 laid out the structure of a mutual fund, dividing it into: board of directors, investment adviser, custodian, transfer agent, sponsor.

BOARD OF DIRECTORS

A mutual fund has a board of directors that oversees operations of the fund or family of funds. The board's responsibilities include:
- establish investment policy
- select and oversee the investment adviser, transfer agent, custodian
- establish dividends and capital gains policy
- approve 12b-1 plans

Remember, the board of directors does not manage the portfolio; they manage the company. The shareholders of the fund elect and re-elect the board members. Shareholders also vote their shares to approve the investment adviser's contract and 12b-1 fees. Those with enough moxie to open the proxy do, anyway.

INVESTMENT ADVISER

Yes, we're still talking about investment advisers, the folks who need the Series 65/66, just like you. Each fund has an investment adviser, whose job is to manage the fund's investments according to its stated objectives. Shareholders and the board vote to hire/retain investment advisers, who are paid a percentage of the fund's net assets. That's why they try so hard. The more valuable the fund, the more they get paid. Their fee is typically the largest expense to a mutual fund. Investment advisers have to advise the fund (select the investments) in keeping with federal securities and tax law. They must also base their investment decisions on careful research of economic/financial trends rather than on hot stock tips from their bartender.

CUSTODIAN

The fund also keeps its assets in a safe place at the custodian bank. Under very strict rules, some funds do this themselves, but most still let a bank take custody, since banks have vaults and security guards and stuff. The custodian receives the dividends and interest payments made by the stocks and bonds in the fund's portfolio. The custodian is also responsible for the payable/receivable functions involved when the portfolio buys and sells securities.

TRANSFER AGENT

The transfer agent is incredibly busy. This is the bank or other company that issues new shares to buyers and cancels the shares that sellers redeem. Most of these "shares" are simply electronic files (book entry), but it still takes a lot of work to "issue" and "redeem" them. While the custodian receives dividends and interest payments from the portfolio securities, it is the transfer agent that distributes income to the investors. The transfer agent acts as a customer service rep for the fund and often sends out those semi-annual reports that investors have to receive.

DISTRIBUTORS

Some funds are sponsored by underwriters, who bear the costs of distributing the fund up front and then get compensated by the sales charge that they either earn themselves or split with the broker-dealers who make the sales. Underwriters (AKA "wholesalers," "distributors," or "sponsors") also prepare sales literature for the fund, since they're the ones who will be selling the shares, either directly to the public or through a network of broker-dealers.

If a fund wants to distribute itself, it can charge 12b-1 fees to cover the costs connected to landing new customers: printing and mailing the prospectus to new customers, paying sales reps, and buying advertising. In other words, mutual funds charge their customers for marketing costs. They either charge sales loads on the front or back end, or they charge little quarterly deductions called "12b-1 fees."

In fact, many charge *both*.

As long as it keeps the 12b-1 fees to .25% of average net assets, the fund can call itself "no load." You know those "no-load" money market funds. Guess what the 12b-1 fee usually is? Yep—.25%, plus a management fee, all deducted from those stellar short-term interest rates you can earn on commercial paper, banker's acceptances, etc. Also note that to approve and re-approve the 12b-1 fee, we need a majority vote of the shares and the board as a whole. To terminate, though, we would only need a majority of the shares and a majority of just the independent board members.

Would the Series 65 try to split hairs with you on such a minor point? Absolutely.

So, these are the methods of distribution for mutual fund shares:
- Fund/to underwriter/to dealer/to investor (assume sales charge here, a nice big one, probably)
- Fund/to underwriter/to investor (underwriter cuts out the other middleman but still gets a sales charge)
- Fund/to investor (no-load funds, who charge 12b-1 fees, deducted quarterly)

There are many conveniences and services offered to owners of mutual funds:
- Investment decisions made by a professional portfolio manager
- Ease of diversification
- Ability to invest fixed amounts in full and fractional shares
- Ability to liquidate a portion of the investment without losing diversification
- Fund shares provide collateral for a loan (after 30 days)
- Simplified tax information (1099s make tax prep easier)
- Simplified record keeping (rather than getting 50 annual reports from 50 companies, you get two semi-annual reports from one mutual fund)
- Ease of purchase and redemption of securities
- Automatic reinvestments of capital gains and income distributions at NAV
- Safekeeping of portfolio securities
- Ease of account inquiry
- Mutual fund shareholders also have the right to:
  - Vote their shares by proxy on:
    - Board of director positions
    - Investment adviser's contract
    - Changes in investment objectives/policy
    - Changes in policy involving real estate or commodities transactions, borrowing/lending money, underwriting other issuer's securities
  - Receive a semi-annual report and an audited annual report (both have an income statement and a balance sheet)

The disadvantages of investing in mutual funds would be that the individual gives up the ability to pick individual stocks and that funds have expenses including 12b-1 fees and/or sales charges.

PROSPECTUS

The prospectus is how the mutual fund provides full disclosure to prospective investors. See the connection? We send a prospect-us to a prospect-ive investor. Again,
we're getting all creative with the language used in this industry. First thing you'll find
in the prospectus is a statement about risk/reward. This is generally the first page of
information where they describe the investment objectives of the growth, income,
bond, or whatever fund. In case the first few paragraphs don't sufficiently scare the
beejeezus out of you, they often end up making statements that are as clear as the
warnings from the Surgeon General. The prospectus I'm looking at (you should be
looking at a few, too) says:

> Your investment in the fund is not a bank deposit and is not insured or guaranteed by the
> FDIC or any other government agency, entity, or person.

And, in case that didn't hit home, they follow up with a bold-letter warning:

> **You may lose money by investing in the fund. The likelihood of loss is greater if you invest
> for a shorter period of time.**

So mutual funds don't necessarily go up? Hmm.

In the prospectus, we'll find the fund's 1-year, 5-year, and 10-year returns. If the
fund hasn't been around for 5 or 10 years, they report their returns over the life of the
fund. The investment adviser(s) is/are named and discussed. The portfolio's allocation is laid out as a pie chart showing which percentage is in, say, retail or pharmaceutical companies, or how much of the bond fund is generally devoted to BBB- versus
AAA-rated issuers. The top 10 stock holdings are usually shown for equity funds; we
don't get the actual holdings of the portfolio, because those can change every day, but
we do get a pretty good idea of how this portfolio is laid out. The prospectus is really
the "summary prospectus." Few folks actually read it, although everybody should,
especially everybody sitting for a regulatory exam like the 6, 7, 63, or 65/66.

Yes—that includes *you.*

If someone is really an egghead, he can request the Statement of Additional Information (SAI) that provides pretty much what it sounds like. Remember that corporations have to provide a prospectus when they do their IPO. Well, mutual fund companies are in a continuous state of IPO, which is why they have to provide full disclosure
to investors in a prospectus that gets updated annually.

YIELD VS. TOTAL RETURN

Whenever you see a test question about dividend or current yield for a mutual fund,
remember to take only the dividends and divide them by NAV. So, ignore the capital
gains distributions for the test questions. The NASD won't let mutual funds include
capital gains in their current yield calculations.

Regulators are real concerned that registered reps can explain the difference between yield and total return. Again, yield is just the dividend/income distribution
divided by the NAV. Total return takes the dividend distribution and also adds two

things: capital gains distribution and capital appreciation. As usual, that sounds fancy but really isn't. Let's say you get a test question like this:

XYZ funds paid $1.00 in dividends and $1.00 in capital gains distributions for the year. The NAV has increased from $10 to $15. Therefore, what is the total return?

Well, if the fund started out at $10 and moved to $15, it appreciated by $5. If the fund also distributed $2 in capital gains and dividends, there's another $2. What is $7 out of (divided by) the original $10 NAV?

A really awesome fund! One that has a "total return" of 70%.

Buy that sucker!

The fund would then publish average total returns for 1-year, 5-year, and 10-year periods, or over the life of the fund for a new fund. They would publish yield separately from total returns, and you need to keep the two separate for the exam, as well.

In the prospectus, you would also find a detailed explanation of all the features discussed earlier: breakpoints, rights of accumulation, combination privilege, letter of intent (LOI).

Also found in the prospectus is a tabular presentation of fees and expenses. It might look something like this:

	A shares	B shares
Maximum sales charge imposed on purchases	4.00%	None

Annual Fund Operating Expenses (expenses that are deducted from Fund assets)

	A shares	B shares
Management fees	0.60%	0.60%
Distribution (12b-1) fees	0.25%	0.65%
Other Expenses (Shareholder Servicing Fees)	0.25%	0.25%
Other Expenses (All Other)	0.19%	0.19%
Total Annual Fund Operating Expenses	0.89%	1.29%

Expense Examples

These examples are intended to help you compare the cost of investing in a Fund with the cost of investing in other mutual funds. The examples assume you invest $10,000 for the time periods indicated, earn a 5% return each year, redeem your shares at the end of the period and that operating expenses remain constant at the level above for "Total Annual Fund Operating Expenses." Your actual returns and costs may be higher or lower than those shown, but based on these assumptions, your expenses will be:

1 Year	3 Year	5 Year	10 Year
$465	$ 786	$1,081	$1,818

ANNUITIES, INSURANCE, RETIREMENT PLANS

Non-qualified retirement plans are less formal than qualified plans. Qualified retirement plans need IRS approval and must follow all the requirements of ERISA. *Usually,* qualified plans are funded with pre-tax dollars. For example, if an individual contributes $2,000 to a qualified plan, he usually gets to deduct that amount from his $30,000 salary—in order to report an income of just $28,000 that year. In other words, he put in the money before (pre-) figuring his income for tax purposes, deducting his income by the amount contributed to the plan. So, if the money goes in before you figure your annual income, that's "pre-tax" money.

Many non-qualified plans are funded with after-tax dollars. If you figure your annual income and then put some of what you have left into a retirement plan, that's an "after-tax" contribution. This after-tax contribution represents your cost basis. Only the amount you earn *on top of* that cost basis would be taxable, and only when you take receipt of the money, usually in retirement.

ANNUITIES

One type of non-qualified retirement plan is called a **variable annuity**. This is both an insurance product and an investment product, which is why you need both an insurance license and either a Series 6 or Series 7 to sell variable annuities. Investors put after-tax dollars into something called the "separate account." I usually think of a separate account as a "tax-deferred mutual fund," but let's see how the federal government defines this separate account in their page-turning document called the *Investment Company Act of 1940*:

> "Separate account" means an account established and maintained by an insurance company pursuant to the laws of any State or territory of the United States, or of Canada or any province thereof, under which income, gains and losses, whether or not realized, from assets allocated to such account, are, in accordance with the applicable contract, credited to or charged against such account without regard to other income, gains, or losses of the insurance company.

Hmm. Like I said, a "separate account" is sort of a tax-deferred mutual fund. If the separate account (mutual fund) is growing, so is the value of the "accumulation units" the investor has purchased—just like mutual fund shares going up in value as the fund's assets grow, right? Since the investor has already paid taxes on the money going into the non-qualified variable annuity, that contribution comes back tax-free.

It's the growth/earnings that get taxed, but not until retirement. Since the investor's money is allocated to various "sub-accounts," which work just like mutual funds, theoretically, the investments should produce earnings, especially if they've been invested a long time. Again, just like with a mutual fund, the idea is to take out more than you put in. The big difference with the variable annuity is that the growth happens tax deferred, while a mutual fund subjects the investor to taxation every year. So, if an annuitant has contributed $10,000, and the account value grows to $15,000 after a few years, he owes no tax. Not yet. A mutual fund shareholder gets taxed every year on the dividends and capital gains distributed (don't think about mutual funds held within retirement plans–that's another subject, coming up soon). So, if the annuitant puts in $10,000, and over time it grows to be worth $15,000 at retirement, he only has to pay tax when he starts taking the money out, and he only has to pay tax on the $5,000 of earnings.

That's tax-deferral. You pay the tax later, at your ordinary income rate.

When the individual retires, he may choose to receive payments monthly for the rest of his life. Or he might just want to take everything out as a lump sum. If he takes a lump-sum payment, the IRS taxes him on the $5,000, then lets him have the $10,000—his cost basis—tax-free. If he takes the $15,000 in two random withdrawals, they tax the $5,000 earnings first. As soon as that's taken care of, the rest comes back tax-free. They might refer to that system as LIFO, meaning the Last In is the First Out. Earnings would be considered the last in, so they're considered the first out.

See, the IRS doesn't like to wait for their money, and these earnings that have been going untaxed year after year are starting to drive them absolutely crazy. At this point, they just can't wait any longer and absolutely insist that all the money coming out above your cost basis is the earnings part.

Whatever. You've probably enjoyed several years of tax deferral and now it's simply time to pay the piper. With any luck Congress and the President will have cut your ordinary income rate by then, but that's another issue. Although it does bring up a very important point—all distributions that are taxable are taxed at the ordinary income rate, never capital gains. We WISH we could pay the lower long-term capital gains rate, but no such luck. So, never tell the exam that somebody pays cap gains on retirement distributions—it's always ordinary income.

When it comes time to retire, many individuals will choose to receive payments monthly for the rest of their lives. We call this "annuitizing the contract" because anything else would have sounded dumb. When the individual gets ready to throw the switch from paying in to paying out, he tells the insurance company which payout option he's choosing. For the biggest monthly check, he'll choose life only. That means the company only has to make payments for as long as he lives. As soon as he ceases, so do his payments. If that seems too risky, he can buy a unit refund life annuity. This way he is guaranteed a certain number of payments. If he dies before receiving them, his beneficiary receives the balance of payments. If he chooses life with period certain, the company will make payments for the greater of his life or a certain period of time, like 10 years. If he dies after two years, the company makes payments to his beneficiary for the rest of the term. And if he lives longer than 10 years, they just keep on making payments until he finally expires. Joint and last survivor would provide the smallest monthly check, since the company is obligated to make payments as long as either one of the parties is still alive. Covering two persons' mortality risks (the risk that they'll live an inconveniently long time) is an expensive proposition to the insurance company, so those monthly checks are going to be the smallest.

Again, "mortality risk" is the insurance company's risk that the annuitant will live much longer than anticipated. In other words, it's just the opposite of the risk the company has in a life insurance policy. For life insurance, the risk is that the customer will make three payments and then die, taking out exponentially more money than he put in. For an annuity (either fixed or variable) the risk to the company is that the customer will put in, say, $10,000 and end up drawing out, say, $100,000 by living to the ripe old age of 117. The guarantee to make payments for as long as the annuitant shall live is called a "mortality guarantee," not a "payment guarantee." A "payment guarantee" would guarantee a certain rate of return. Variable annuities only guarantee that you'll get something every month for the rest of your life—as long as you are a mortal. But, this "mortality guarantee" comes at a price. The insurance company charges a fee to compensate themselves for shouldering the risk that annuitants could live inconveniently long lives. They call it, very cleverly, a "mortality risk fee." The insurance company also guarantees that it won't raise costs for administering the contract beyond a certain level. They call this an "expense guarantee," but they charge an "expense risk charge" to cover their risk. Sometimes you'll see those two fees combined as a "mortality and expense risk fee."

Whatever. Just know that annuities charge lots of fees, which makes them big fun to sell. The investor's money goes into little mutual funds that we call "sub-accounts" and, just as with mutual funds, an "investment management fee" is deducted from the assets. They also charge administrative expenses to cover the cost of administering the contracts. So, as you can see, variable annuities do offer tax-deferral and inflation protection, but they also involve lots of expenses/fees.

ANNUITY UNITS

So, the annuitant socks some money away for retirement, which means eventually she'll want to take some money out. Once the payout or "settlement" option is chosen, the company takes all kinds of stuff into consideration and determines how many "annuity units" an individual will be paid every month for the rest of his life, or the life of the contract. Basically, they convert accumulation units into annuity units, as they move from the accumulation phase to the annuity phase. Once the number of annuity units has been determined, we say that the number of annuity units is fixed. So, for example, maybe every month he'll be paid the value of 100 annuity units.

Trouble is, he has no idea how big that monthly check is going to be, since nobody knows what 100 annuity units will be worth month-to-month, just like nobody knows what mutual fund shares will be worth month-to-month. Again, the units really are mutual fund shares; we just can't call them that. During the pay-in phase, we call the shares "accumulation units." During the pay-out phase, we call them "annuity units," just to keep things nice and simple.

So, how much is an annuity unit worth every month? All depends on the investment performance of the separate account compared to the company's expectations of its performance.

Seriously.

If the separate account returns are better than anybody expected, the units increase in value. If the account returns are exactly as expected, the unit value stays the same. And if the account returns are lower than expected, the unit value drops from the month before. It's all based on the actuary's best guess, known technically as the "Assumed Interest Rate." If the AIR is 5%, that just means the actuary expects the account to return 5% every year. If the account actually gets a 6% annualized rate of return one month, the individual's check gets bigger. (Remember, during the payout phase, the investor is paid the value of his fixed number of annuity units, so to say that the annuity units have increased in value is the same as saying the individual's check gets bigger.) If the account gets the anticipated 5% return next month, that's the same as AIR and the check will stay the same. And if the account gets only a 4% return the following month, the check will go down.

Don't let the exam trick you on this concept. If the AIR is 5%, here is how it would work:

Actual Return:	5%	7%	6%	5%	4%
Check:	$1,020	$1,035	$1,045	$1,045	$1,030

When the account gets a 7% return, the account gets much bigger. So when it gets only a 6% return the following month, that's 6% of a bigger account, and is 1% more than we expected to get. So, just compare the actual return with the AIR. If the actual return is bigger, so is the monthly check. If it's smaller, so is the monthly check. If the actual return is the same as the AIR, the check stays the same.

Notice how the payout varies and, thus, the clever name "variable annuity." If an individual doesn't like the variable part of the annuity she can buy an insurance product called a fixed annuity. In a fixed annuity, the insurance company invests her payments into its general account and guarantees a certain monthly payment. Maybe the payment is $750. That's a guaranteed $750, but that $750 is also just about guaranteed to lose value to inflation. If you keep getting the same flat payment even as prices rise, your payment won't go very far at Wal-Mart, right?

If you want the guaranteed payout, you subject yourself to this "purchasing power" or "constant dollar" risk. If you want to fight inflation, you buy a variable annuity so you can invest at least part of your money in stocks, which are the best protection against inflation. To combat inflation/purchasing power risk, though, you take on investment risk.

Always trade-offs in this business.

But, since Americans simply have to have it all, the industry has also created "combination annuities," which are a hybrid of fixed and variable. Some of the payments the individual makes are put in the general account to guarantee a certain rate of return; some of the payments are allocated to the separate account to try to beat the rate of inflation.

PURCHASING ANNUITIES

The two major types of variable annuities are "**immediate**" and "**deferred.**" Those terms simply define how soon the contract holder wants to begin receiving payments.

These are retirement plans, so you do need to be 59½ to avoid penalties, unless you qualify for an exemption. So, some customers might want or need to wait 15 or 20 years before receiving payments. We call that a "deferred annuity," because "deferred" means "I'll do it later," the way some readers may have "deferred" their study process for a while before opening the book and realizing there's, like, a lot to know for this exam.

If the individual is already in her 60s, she may want to start receiving payments immediately. As you can probably guess, we call that an "immediate annuity."

Customers can buy annuities either with one big payment or several smaller payments. The first method is called "**single premium**" or "**single payment**." The second method is called "**periodic payment**." If an investor has a large chunk of money, she can put it in a variable annuity, where it can grow tax-deferred. Tax-deferred just means that she won't have to take money out of the account every year to pay taxes on dividends, interest, and capital gains. That means there's more money or principal in the account, which will grow faster and bigger until she's ready to take it all out at retirement age, 59½. If she's putting in a big single premium, she can either choose to wait or to begin receiving annuity payments immediately. She has to be 59½ years old to start annuitizing, but if she's old enough, she can begin the pay-out or "annuity phase" immediately. That's called a **single payment immediate annuity**. Maybe she's only 42, though, and wants to let the money grow another 20 years before taking it out. That's called a **single payment deferred annuity** (SPDA). This way she buys accumulation units with her money and holds them as they—we certainly hope—increase in value, just like mutual fund shares.

Many investors put money into the separate account during the accumulation phase (pay-in) gradually, over time. That's called "periodic payment," and if they aren't done paying in yet, you can bet the insurance company isn't going to start paying out. So, if you're talking about a "periodic payment" plan, the only way to do it is **periodic deferred**. No such thing as a "Periodic Immediate Annuity."

Remember that mutual funds and variable annuities have many similarities. The separate account is actually registered as an investment company. If it's directly managed, it's registered as an **open-end Investment Company**. If it's third-party managed, it's a **unit investment trust** (UIT). Investors in mutual funds and variable annuities have the same rights and advantages either way, with a few differences. Instead of a Board of Directors, variable annuities have a Board of Managers (BOM). Mutual fund investors pay taxes on dividends and capital gains every year; variable annuity income and gains grow tax deferred until retirement. Both investors vote for the board members and the investment adviser managing the money. Mutual fund investors own and vote their shares; variable annuitants own and vote their units. Mutual fund investors can often make additional purchases at no sales charge; not so for variable annuitants. Which is why they're lots of fun to sell: every year, the sales rep probably makes a "trailer" as the customer diligently puts in more money.

So far we've looked at the "separate account," but inside of this account the individual actually allocates money to various sub-accounts. These sub-accounts are just like mutual funds. You can select from the usual smorgasbord of investment objectives: growth, income, aggressive growth, long-term bond, etc. One of these sub-accounts might actually have a fixed rate of return, but I don't see why I'd put much of my money there—if I want a fixed rate of return, I buy a fixed annuity.

But that's just me. Investors do all kinds of stuff I don't understand.

Some, for example, will ignore the consequences and just cancel (surrender) the annuity during the accumulation phase. The consequences can be pretty harsh. The contract does have to pay out the "surrender value," but the insurance/annuity company hits the individual with surrender charges, depending on how long she's been making payments. The prospectus I'm looking at right now shows that the annuity has a surrender charge of 7% in the first year. Guess how far it drops in the second year?

All the way down to 7%.

And in the third year, I see yet another drop, all the way down to...7%.

I also see that at www.nasaa.org the state regulators are reaching out to senior citizens asking if anyone has been pushing variable annuities on them. See, the fact is most senior citizens have liquidity needs to cover medical emergencies. If you put a 72-year-old into a variable annuity, he may very well need some money out in the next three years—you're going to nail him with a 7% surrender charge, after taking a sales load and charging all kinds of fees?

No. On the exam, and in the real world, I'd be very skeptical about pushing variable annuities to senior citizens.

Not only do annuities have surrender charges, but also the IRS—who is here to help—will charge ordinary income rates on the growth/earnings portion. And, unless the individual is at least 59½ or qualifies for an exemption, there will also be a 10% penalty added to the growth portion.

Which is why I think I'd just sit tight, myself.

But, again, that's just me.

People often take loans out against the value of their sub-accounts. If so, the insurance company charges interest against the loan, usually by reducing the number of accumulation units credited to the individual. If the individual pays back the loan in full, the greater number of accumulation units is re-established.

Also, even though annuities are not life insurance policies, they often do allow the annuitant to purchase a death benefit payable to a beneficiary. That way if the individual dies during the accumulation phase, the annuity pays the beneficiary the greater of:

•   All payments made into the annuity
•   Value of the annuity on the date of death

And that looks like a test question to me.

Note that the annuity's value would be included in the annuitant's estate for the purpose of federal estate taxes. The beneficiary would also be required to pay ordinary income rates on anything above the cost basis. Remember, these are non-qualified annuities—the cost basis is the cost basis. Only the earnings are subject to tax and penalties.

PRACTICE QUESTIONS

1. The AIR for a variable annuity is 3.5%. Last month, your client received a check for $1,000 based on actual performance of 6%. If the actual performance is 5% next month, your client
   A. will receive slightly less than $1,000
   B. will receive $1,000
   C. will receive more than $1,000
   D. AIR will be increased

2. Annuities may be purchased in all the following ways except
   A. Single premium immediate
   B. Single premium deferred
   C. Periodic deferred
   D. Periodic immediate

3. The major difference between variable annuities and mutual funds involves
   A. tax deferral
   B. investment objectives
   C. bonds vs. stock
   D. EPS

4. An annuitant requiring the largest possible monthly check should choose
   A. life only (straight life)
   B. periodic immediate
   C. period certain
   D. joint and last survivor

5. Your 60-year-old client contributed $10,000 to a non-qualified variable annuity many years ago. Now that the account is worth $40,000, the client takes a withdrawal of $35,000. If his ordinary income rate is 28%, he will pay
   A. no taxes until age 65
   B. no taxes
   C. $8,400 in taxes
   D. $9,800 in taxes

ANSWERS

1. **ANSWER: C** - it's hard to see how the check will go up if the return next month is lower than the return this month. Don't do that—don't compare next month's return to this month's return. Only compare the returns to AIR. AIR is 3.5%, so anything higher than that makes the check go up. Seriously.

2. **ANSWER: D** - "periodic" means the individual has not finished paying in and will continue to pay in periodically. The word "immediate" means the annuity company starts paying out immediately—not if the annuitant hasn't finished paying in, right? If the individual makes a single payment and is old enough, she can immediately go into the annuitization/pay-out phase, but not if she's still making periodic payments into the contract.

3. **ANSWER: A** - mutual funds give no tax deferral; annuities do. The other three choices don't distinguish the two: either could invest in bonds or stock, and they both have investment objectives. No idea what "EPS" could even mean in this context.

4. **ANSWER: A** - if the company only has to bear one mortality risk, they'll be more generous with the monthly pay-out. As soon as the annuitant ceases, so do the payments, unlike a "period certain" that locks in payments for a minimum number of years.

5. **ANSWER: C** - why would there be a penalty? He's over 59½. Also, remember only the earnings are taxed. He only had 30K of earnings, the difference between his 10K contribution and 40K value.

Online Updates

AN INSURANCE PRIMER

It would be awfully rude of me to die unexpectedly and leave family and friends footing the bill for my funeral. That's why I basically "rent" insurance coverage through something called "term life insurance." It's very cheap, but it's only good for a certain term—maybe it's a 5-, 10-, or 20-year term. The individual pays premiums in exchange for a guaranteed death benefit payable to a beneficiary if the insured dies during that period. If the insured does not die during that period, the policy expires. If the policyholder wants to renew, he can, but he's older now and more costly to insure. In other words, his premiums will go up, even though the death benefit will stay the same. Plus, he's older and more likely to have some medical condition that raises his rates, too. So, as with all products, there are pluses and minuses.

Also note the language used in insurance:

- Policyholder: the owner of the policy, responsible for paying premiums
- Insured: the person whose life is insured by the policy, usually the policyholder
- Beneficiary: the party that receives the death benefit upon death of the insured
- Death benefit: the amount payable to the beneficiary upon death of the insured, minus any unpaid premiums or loan balances
- Cash value: a value that can be partially withdrawn or borrowed against

So, let's say that Joe Schmoe buys an insurance policy with a $100,000 death benefit payable to his wife. He's the policyholder and the insured. If he dies, the death benefit of $100,000 is paid to the beneficiary, his wife. As we'll see, most insurance also builds up cash value, which can be withdrawn or borrowed while Joe is still alive. (Note that term does not build up this cash value, which is also why it's relatively cheap insurance.)

PERMANENT VS. TEMPORARY INSURANCE

Just like with automobiles, some prefer to rent for a term, some prefer to buy. Some feel that if you're going to be putting money aside, you might as well end up with something should you have the misfortune of living. Death benefits are only worth something when you die, and, like they say, you can't take it with you. You can leave it behind for your beneficiaries, but many people end up at age 55 realizing that their home is paid off, they've got a $2 million IRA that already names their spouse as beneficiary, so why do they need a $1 million death benefit? They're covered for the death part. With term, they would really have nothing of value at this point to show for all those premiums. With "permanent insurance," however, there would be something called "cash value" that they could tap. They could borrow against it, or maybe withdraw some of it just for fun. The most common type of permanent insurance is called **whole life insurance**. You pay premiums for your whole life (thus the clever name "whole life"). Some policies have the policyholder stop paying premiums at a certain age, but it's still pretty darned close to his or her "whole life." The premiums are much higher than on the **term insurance** you sort of "rent," but insurance companies will guarantee a minimum cash value, and you can also pretty well plan for an even better cash value than that. This way it works to protect your beneficiaries if you die unexpectedly and also acts as a savings vehicle where the cash value grows tax-deferred. Maybe at age 55 you decide to borrow $50,000 of the cash value and put in a new kitchen with granite countertops, cherry cabinets, and other shockingly expensive amenities. Plus, remember that to renew a term policy means you pay a higher premium. Premiums are "level" in a whole life policy, meaning they don't go up.

So, term is "cheap," but after a few years you end up with nothing. And, to keep it going, you'd have to pay more for the same benefit. Reminds me of how I spent five years paying "cheap" rent to a landlord. It was definitely lower than any mortgage payment would have been, so every month I "saved" at least $300. Only, at the end of this 5-year term, I had forked over 40 g's to the landlord and was left with nothing but the opportunity to renew my lease at a higher rate. I covered myself with a roof over my head for five years, and at the end of the five years I owned absolutely no part of that roof, not even one cracked, loose shingle.

Whole life is more like buying the house, which is exactly what I did after five foolish years of renting. I had to come up with a down payment, and my monthly mortgage is now $200 more per month than my rent was. But, at the end of five years, I'll have some equity in the house that I can tap into for a loan maybe (kind of like cash value). Just like with a whole life policy, I'll be getting at least something back for all those payments I've made over the years.

So, whole life involves premiums that are higher than those for term life insurance, but you end up with something even if you stop paying into the policy. There is a guaranteed cash value, whereas term leaves you with nothing. As with term, the death benefit is guaranteed, too, so this is a very popular product for people who want to protect their families and also use the policy as a savings vehicle, where all that increase in cash value grows tax-deferred. Both term and whole life insurance are purely insurance products, and many readers are not only selling them already, but also could probably tell you infinitely more about insurance products right now. Don't let them—remind them that they, too, are studying for a very difficult securities exam and have no extra time for holding court at this point.

Well nothing is simple in either the securities or insurance industry. Since some clients crave flexibility, the industry bent over backwards to come up with a flexible form of permanent insurance called **"universal life insurance."** Think "flexibility" when you see those words "universal life insurance." The death benefit and, therefore, the premiums can be adjusted by the client. They can be increased to buy more coverage or decreased to back off on the coverage and save some money. If the cash value is sufficient, premiums can actually stop being paid by the client and start being covered by the cash value. The cash value grows at a minimum, guaranteed rate, just like on traditional whole life polices, and if the general account does particularly well, the cash value goes up from there. As mentioned, at some point the policyholder may decide to withdraw part of the cash value, or may usually borrow up to 90% of it.

VARIABLE POLICIES

So, whether it's term, traditional whole life, or universal life insurance, we're talking strictly about insurance products. Death benefits and cash values (term has no cash value) are guaranteed by the insurance company, who invests the net premiums (what's left after deducting expenses, taxes, etc.) into their general account. Once you start attaching cash value and death benefits to the ups and downs of the separate account, however, you have created a new product that is both an insurance policy and a security. Opens a whole new market for the company, but it also means that those who sell them need both an insurance and a securities license.

Hey, doesn't that sound familiar? For many readers, this explains why they're reading a book they otherwise wouldn't touch with an 11-foot pole.

Variable insurance

Whole life and term life insurance policies tell clients exactly how much they will pay out upon death. And, unlike most securities, when an insurance company says a policy is worth $100,000, it's really worth $100,000. If it's a whole life policy with a death benefit of $100,000, $100,000 is the death benefit paid upon death of the policyholder, as long as the premiums are paid and no loans have been taken out.

So, in term and whole life policies, the investment risk is borne totally by the insurance company through their "general account."

Well, with variable insurance products, the death benefit—as well as the cash value—fluctuates just like it does in a variable annuity. That's what they mean by "variable." It all varies, based on the investment performance of the separate account. The separate account, as we discussed under variable annuities, is made up of sub-accounts. The investor chooses from these little quasi-mutual funds trying to meet different investment objectives: growth, long-term bonds, short-term Treasuries, etc. He can even choose to invest some of the premiums into a fixed account, just to play it safe, and he can switch between the sub-accounts as his investment needs change without a tax problem. This stuff all grows tax-deferred, remember.

The cash value is tied to account performance, period. So if the test question says that the separate account grew, it doesn't matter by how much. The cash value increases when the separate account increases. But death benefit is tied to actual performance versus AIR, just like an annuity unit in a variable annuity. So, if the AIR is 6% and the account gets a 4% return, the cash value will increase due to the positive return, but the death benefit will decrease since the account returned less than AIR.

Variable Life Insurance (VLI) policies will pay out the cash value/surrender value whenever the policyholder decides to cash in the policy. But, there's no way to know what the value might be at the time of surrender. If the little sub-accounts have performed well, the cash value might be better than expected. But if the market has been brutal, the cash value could go all the way down to zero. Probably not gonna' happen, but it could.

A minimum or fixed death benefit is guaranteed, however. Some refer to it as the "floor." No matter what the market does, the insurance company guarantees a minimum death benefit that could only be depleted by failure to pay premiums or taking out loans against the policy. Remember that any guaranteed payments are covered by the insurance company's general account. So, the minimum is guaranteed, and the policyholder also has the chance of enjoying an increased death benefit, depending on how well the little sub-accounts (inside the separate account) do. As we said, that's tied to AIR, so if the market is kind, the death benefit increases, but if the market is unkind, it could, theoretically, drag the death benefit all the way down to the floor.

Sound familiar? Sounds a lot like investing in...yep, securities.

Again, that's why many insurance agents have to sit for a securities exam called the Series 6 or Series 7. They have strayed far from the safe, guaranteed territory of term and whole life into the less predictable world of variable insurance.

When the customer pays the premium on a VLI policy, the company can charge a maximum of 9% as a sales charge. From the customer's premium, the insurance company deducts S-A-S. That stands for State premium tax, Administrative fee, and Sales load. The "net premium" is then placed in the separate account, allocated among the little sub-accounts that work like little mutual funds. After the money's been allocated to the little sub-accounts of the separate account, the insurance company charges regular fees, just like they do in variable annuities:

- mortality risk fee
- expense risk fee
- investment management fees

The value of the sub-accounts and, therefore, the cash value is calculated daily. The death benefit is calculated annually. If the separate account has several below-AIR months, it will take several above-AIR months until the customer's death benefit starts to increase.

Remember that flexibility we discussed that separates traditional whole life from universal life? Well, it probably isn't too surprising that somebody eventually crossed that with variable life to get Variable Universal Life. Now, we have the death benefit and cash value tied to the separate account (variable), plus we have the flexible premium thing (universal) going on. Regular old variable life is called "scheduled premium." That means the insurance company puts your premium payments on a schedule, and you better stick to it. Variable Universal or Universal Variable Life policies are funded as "flexible premium." That means the client may or may not have to send in a check. With a VUL policy, the customer has to maintain enough cash value and death benefit to keep the policy in force. If the separate account rocks, no money has to roll in from the customer. If the separate account rolls over and dies, look out. Since that's a little scary, some VULs come with minimum guaranteed death benefits.

The advantages of variable life insurance include the ability to invest some of the premiums into the stock market, which has historically enjoyed relatively high average returns and done very well at beating inflation. A robust investment market can increase the cash value and death benefit, often faster than the rate of inflation. A traditional whole life policy, on the other hand, that promised to pay $50,000 when it was purchased in 1964 represented a lot of money. But if it pays that $50,000 out in 2004, the $50,000 doesn't go very far, due to inflation.

POLICY LOANS

Variable policies make at least 75% of the cash value available to the customer as a loan after three years, and maybe as much as 90%. Never 100%, though. 100% means "game over." Guess what, though—they charge interest on that loan. If the loan is not repaid, that reduces both the cash value and the death benefit of the policy. And, if the customer takes out a big loan and then the separate account tanks, he'll have to put some money back in to bring the cash value back to a sufficient level or risk having the policy lapse. Don't worry, though. Some people take out a loan with absolutely no intention of repaying it. They simply don't need as much death benefit, so why not have some fun with the money right now?

SETTLEMENT OPTIONS

The policyholder can choose from many options concerning the method of payment to the beneficiary. These are called "settlement options." The "lump-sum" method is self-explanatory. "Fixed-period" means that the insurance company will invest the proceeds of the policy into an interest-bearing account and then make equal payments at regular intervals for a fixed period. The payments include principal and interest. How much are the payments? That depends on the size of the principal, the interest rate earned by the insurance company, and the length of time involved in this fixed period.

The "fixed-amount" settlement option has the insurance company invest the proceeds from the policy and pay the beneficiary a fixed amount of money at regular intervals until both the principal and interest are gone. The amount received is fixed, but the period over which the beneficiary receives payments varies.

So, for "fixed-period" versus "fixed-amount," the decision comes down to this: do you want to receive some money for a fixed period of time, or do you want to receive a fixed amount of money for an uncertain period of time? In other words, do you want to be paid something like $25,000 for exactly three years (fixed-period)? Or, would you prefer being paid exactly $25,000 for about three years (fixed-amount)?

In a "life-income" settlement option, the proceeds are annuitized. That means the insurance company provides the beneficiary with a guaranteed income for the rest of his/her life. Just like with annuities, the beneficiary's age expectancy is taken into account to determine the monthly payout, along with the size of the death benefit and the type of payout selected.

There is also an "interest only" settlement option, whereby the insurance company keeps the proceeds from the policy and invests it, promising the beneficiary a guaranteed minimum rate of interest. The beneficiary might get more than the minimum, or not, and may receive the payments annually, semiannually, quarterly, or monthly. He/she also has the right to withdraw all the principal if he/she gets antsy, or change settlement options.

GENERAL FEATURES

Since these variable policies are a little confusing to some, the company has to give the policyholder at least two years (24 months) to switch back to traditional whole life without having to provide proof of insurability. The new whole life policy will have the same issue date as the original variable policy.

If you buy a variable life policy, you have the opportunity to exchange it for a different policy even if issued by a different company. You don't have to pay taxes since you aren't taking the cash value and, like, going on a fly fishing trip to Alaska. You just cash in one policy and exchange it, tax-free, for another insurance policy. Or, believe it or not, you can even exchange a life policy for an annuity. You can't turn an annuity into a life policy, though.

Sorry about that.

This tax-free exchange, by the way, is called a "**1035 exchange.**"

When selling variable insurance policies, the rep needs to remember that these are insurance polices, first and foremost. You can discuss the benefits of investing in the sub-accounts, but you can't present these insurance policies primarily as investment vehicles. Primarily, they're to be sold for the death benefit. They also offer the opportunity to invest in the separate account's little sub-accounts, but they're not to be pitched primarily as investment vehicles.

I would expect a question or two on that topic, whether taking the 6, 7, 63, or 65.

Four federal acts are involved with variable life insurance and variable annuities. The Securities Act of 1933 covers variable life insurance (and annuities). These products must be registered with the SEC and sold with a prospectus. Even though the company that issues these contracts is an insurance company, the subdivision that sells the securities products has to be a broker-dealer registered under the Securities Exchange Act of 1934. The separate account is defined as an investment company under the Investment Company Act of 1940 and is either registered as a UIT or an Open-End Fund as defined under that act. The "money manager" or "investment adviser" has to register under the Investment Advisers Act of 1940.

And, at the state level both securities and insurance regulators are watching these products and those who sell them, too.

The prospectus is intended to fully inform the client and fully disclose all sales charges and expenses. It must be delivered either before or during the sales presentation to the client (which just sounds like the answer to a test question to me). The sales rep must believe that the product is suitable, and that the client understands and can afford any risks associated with it. The sales charges and expenses must be reasonable, as determined by regulations, as well. Such expenses in a variable life policy are deducted from the net premium after it's been invested by the client in the various sub-accounts:

- Investment Management Fee
- Cost of Insurance: based on the policyholder's current age and the amount that the insurance company has at risk (the difference between the death benefit and the policy's cash value)
- Administrative Charges: compensate insurance company for expenses involved in issuing and servicing policies after they are sold, i.e., record keeping, processing death claims, loans and surrenders, sending required reports to policyholders
- Mortality and Expense Risk Charges: the risk that the insured will die earlier than expected (opposite of mortality risk in an annuity)

Most policies have an "expense guarantee provision," which limits the amount the company may raise the administrative charges, no matter what.

Variable life insurance policyholders get to vote their units pretty much like variable annuitants and mutual fund investors. They get to vote for the folks running the show, and would get to approve any major changes to investment objectives.

TAXATION OF LIFE INSURANCE

When you pay your life insurance premiums, you don't get to take a deduction against income, so they are made after-tax. They usually grow tax-deferred, however, which is nice. When the insured dies, the beneficiary receives the death benefit free and clear of federal income taxes.

Whew!

But the death benefit will be added to the insured's estate to determine estate taxes.

It's that simple when the beneficiary has the lump-sum settlement option, anyway. If we're talking about those periodic settlement options that generate interest, some of those payments could be taxed as interest income.

Rather than take a loan, the policyholder can also do a "partial surrender," whereby the policyholder takes out some of the cash value, not enough to make the policy lapse, of course. Depending on how much has been paid in premiums, taxes may be due on the amount withdrawn. Unlike for variable annuities, the IRS uses FIFO here, assuming that the first thing coming out is the cost basis, not the earnings. Only the part taken out above the premiums paid would be taxed.

If a loan is taken out, there are no immediate tax consequences.

PRACTICE QUESTIONS

6. **The AIR for a variable life policy is 4%. If the separate account grows at an annualized rate of 3% next month,**
   I.   cash value will increase
   II. cash value will decrease
   III. death benefit will increase
   IV. death benefit will decrease

   A. I, III
   B. I, IV
   C. II, III
   D. II, IV

7. **All of the following life insurance policies are funded with scheduled premiums except**
   A. VLI
   B. VUL
   C. Term
   D. Whole life

8. **The maximum sales load for variable insurance policies is**
   A. 8.5%
   B. 9.0%
   C. 10%
   D. as stipulated in the prospectus

9. **All of the following build cash value except**
   A. traditional whole life
   B. universal life
   C. variable universal life
   D. term life

10. **All of the following offer tax deferral except**
   A. variable annuity
   B. variable life
   C. open-end fund
   D. universal life

11. **Which of the following are taxable to the beneficiary?**
   I.   portion of death benefit payable to the wife of a deceased annuitant representing cost basis
   II. portion of death benefit payable to the wife of a deceased annuitant representing earnings from the separate account
   III. portion of death benefit payable to the beneficiary representing premiums paid on whole life policy
   IV. portion of death benefit payable to the beneficiary representing excess over premiums paid on whole life policy

   A. I only
   B. II only
   C. I, III, IV only
   D. I, II, III, IV

Answers

6. **ANSWER: B** - cash value has nothing to do with AIR—it's just tied to the separate account. The separate account returned 3% annualized, so cash value increases. Death benefit, on the other hand, IS tied to AIR. The account did worse than AIR, so death benefit goes down. Had this been a variable annuity question, accumulation units would have increased in value, while annuity units would have decreased, right?

7. **ANSWER: B** - Variable Universal Life is a "flexible premium" product—all others are "scheduled premium." In VUL, the insured maintains a certain value and does not have to send in a certain payment on a certain date every month.

8. **ANSWER: B** - 9%, a number to memorize, along with many others

9. **ANSWER: D** - term only has a death benefit, which is partly why it's "cheap"

10. **ANSWER: C** - mutual funds offer no tax deferral, but this can be a tricky question, since many people hold mutual fund shares within a tax-deferred plan. Still, never read something into a question that isn't there

11. **ANSWER: B** - death benefits for insurance policies aren't taxable to the beneficiary. They are added to the value of the estate, but there's nothing about estates in this question.

RETIREMENT PLANS

We don't intend to update the book every six months or so just to catch the new maximums for retirement contributions. Please visit www.passthe65.com for current information, where we'll probably direct you to another site where people make a living keeping up on all these ever-changing numbers.

The two big categories for retirement accounts are **"qualified"** and **"non-qualified."** If a retirement plan is "qualified," that means it has to get IRS approval and must comply with certain rules under "ERISA," which means it has to include all eligible employees and various other stuff we'll look at later. It also involves pre-tax contributions, for the most part. We'll talk about ERISA more later in terms of what the investment advisers for these plans need to do and not do to keep the regulators off their back. Many folks think that if the plan involves pre-tax contributions it is, therefore, a "qualified plan," and if it involves after-tax contributions it is, therefore, "non-qualified."

No.

True, qualified plans generally allow for pre-tax contributions, but you can also put after-tax money into your 401K, which is a qualified plan. Also, even though SEP and SIMPLE IRAs involve pre-tax contributions, neither one is a "qualified plan." See, the fact that the contributions are made pre- or after-tax is not the determining factor between qualified and non-qualified plans. The distinction comes down to ERISA. If the plan needs IRS approval and has to include all eligible employees, it's a "qualified plan." If the plan can be set up with just a written agreement between the employer and employee and allows certain workers to be excluded, that's a non-qualified plan.

NON-QUALIFIED BUSINESS PLANS

If a plan is "non-qualified," it is an informal plan that does not have to comply with ERISA. Qualified plans are generally funded with "pre-tax" dollars, meaning the money goes in and then the investor calculates his income for taxes based on what's left. Non-qualified plans are usually funded with money that the investor has already paid taxes on. When you get your paycheck, maybe some of your money has already gone into a K. That's a pre-tax contribution into a qualified plan. With the money that's left, you could fund a non-qualified variable annuity. Those would be considered after-tax dollars.

All employees do not have to be covered by a non-qualified plan. Common examples include deferred compensation and the workplace savings plan or payroll deduction. In either case, the employer runs the plan and basically just puts some of the employee's money in a safe place, where it will be held until retirement. And, as we said a few pages ago, variable annuities are often non-qualified or funded with after-tax dollars. You can do one of those without any help from an employer. Or, sometimes the variable annuity IS the investment vehicle that you use through your employer plan. Nothing is ever simple in this business, which is why you'll always have clients.

Small business owners

A small business can establish a SEP-IRA, which stands for "Simplified Employee Pension" IRA. This allows the business owner to make pre-tax contributions for herself and any eligible employees. SEP contributions are not mandatory on the part of the business owner. It's just that if the business makes *any* contributions, they have to be made to all eligible employees as stipulated in the plan agreement. To establish a SEP, the employer uses a model agreement put out by the IRS (download it at www.irs.gov) that they and the employee sign. It does not have to be filed with the IRS, who does not issue an opinion or approval. That's another sign of a non-qualified plan—more informal, no IRS sign-off required.

Another type of plan for small businesses is called the SIMPLE IRA plan. This is for businesses with no more than 100 employees. The SIMPLE IRA may allow participants to put more money away than the SEP. Of course, that depends on how much they earn. If they earn a lot, a SEP might be better. But, if the participant made only, say, $15,000 and wanted to sock a bunch of cash away for retirement, the SIMPLE would allow her to put up to $9,000 for 2004 and $10,000 for 2005. In a SEP, her allowed % of $15,000 would have been much less than either $9,000 or $10,000. So, SEPs allow high earners to save more than they could save in a SIMPLE IRA, while SIMPLE IRAs allow lower earning employees to save more than they would be able to put away in a SEP, should the exam really feel like harassing you. Both provide for pre-tax contributions, meaning all the money will be taxable when it's distributed during the golden years.

In a SIMPLE plan business owners must match the employee's contributions up to 3% of compensation or contribute 2% of the employee's compensation, whether he contributes or not. There is also a funky thing about SIMPLE IRAs in the first two years. During that time, the participant could only roll the money into another SIMPLE IRA to avoid tax. During this phase, if she tried to roll it into a Traditional IRA, she'd get dinged with a 25% penalty (not 10%), plus ordinary income tax on all of it, plus it could be treated as an excess IRA contribution (6% penalty), so, all in all, not a real good idea. Once the two years have passed, everything's fine. Go ahead and transfer it to a 401K, traditional IRA, 403b, etc.

QUALIFIED BUSINESS PLANS
Defined contribution
401K plans are considered defined contribution plans, because an employer defines how much they will contribute on behalf of the employee. Employers generally match all or part of an employee's contributions up to a certain level, as stipulated in their plan literature. But, remember, they are not *required* to make matching contributions. Since this plan is qualified, it has to follow all the guidelines of ERISA, covering all eligible employees, whether the company wants to or not. Profit-sharing is also a "defined contribution" plan, but the contributions can be very flexible. It's based on corporate profits, so in a year of no profits, guess what?

No sharing.

Defined benefit
Defined benefit plans are the opposite of defined contribution. For a defined contribution plan, the employer says something like, "We'll match your contributions up to 10% of your salary." For a defined benefit plan, the employer has to get sufficient returns on their investments to pay a defined benefit, such as 70% of your average salary over the last three years of service. So, they either define how much they'll put

in on your behalf (contribution) or how much you'll receive (benefit) when you retire. If they define the benefit, they bear the investment risk. If they only define the contribution, you bear the investment risk, which I'm sure they mentioned in the little brochure.

Sole proprietors

Keogh Plans, sometimes referred to as HR-10's, are for the self-employed. Not for S-corps, C-corps or other entities, only sole proprietors. If the individual in the test question has side income or is self-employed, he or she can have a Keogh. They can contribute a certain percentage of their self-employment income into the Keogh.

How much?

A lot.

A self-employed individual can contribute 20% of whatever she makes up to the current maximum. Keoghs are more difficult to establish than SEPs or SIMPLE IRAs and, unlike the other two, Keoghs are qualified plans that must follow all the rules of ERISA. If you go to www.irs.gov and read Publication 560, you'll see that the title doesn't even use the word "Keogh." It just calls them "qualified plans for the self-employed."

That's what they are.

Qualified plans offered by businesses are covered by ERISA, which stands for Employee Retirement Income Security Act. It governs retirement plans in the private sector. It spells out things like vesting, funding, disclosure, etc. Vesting means that at some point even the employer's contributions belong to the employee. Or, at least some percent of those contributions. If you're in a 401K and your employer has put in $10,000 in matching contributions, you'd walk away with only $3,000 if you were only 30% vested. If you were 70% vested, you'd probably forego the temptation to accidentally key your supervisor's car in the parking garage as you walk out with $7,000. And, if you were 100% vested, you might even go back to meet a former colleague for lunch once in a while. The vesting schedule has to be laid out. And it can't take longer than 7 years for an employee to become fully or "100% vested." There has to be money in the plan and the contributions are governed by the section on "funding." The section on "reporting" makes sure that employees are provided regular updates on the account. I get my 401K statements quarterly; ERISA says the reporting to plan participants has to be done at least annually. The employee also gets to choose a beneficiary under ERISA.

Who is eligible for these qualified plans? Gotta be 21 years old and work at least 1,000 hours a year.

That's ERISA in a nutshell, a really small nutshell.

Non-profit plans

TSAs are "tax sheltered annuities." Since everything needs at least two names, they are also called TDAs or "tax-deferred annuities." They are for school and other non-profit organization employees. Non-profit organizations are tax-exempt and called either "403b" or "501c3" organizations, so the exam can refer to these plans by those labels, too. In one class a student said, "Aren't these kind of like 401K's for non-profits?"

Basically. Only the investments are limited to only mutual funds and annuities, thus the name tax-deferred or tax-sheltered annuity. On the exam, assume that these plans are funded with a pre-tax contribution, and the employees will pay ordinary income tax on all the money when they pull it out at retirement. Students don't qualify; janitors at the school do. Gotta be an employee. This is also a true qualified plan because the school or hospital can not exclude certain types of employees from the plan.

INDIVIDUAL PLANS

The first thing you need to remember is: The I stands for INDIVIDUAL.

An IRA is an Individual Retirement Account, so don't let the exam trick you into saying a husband and wife should open a "joint IRA." There is no such thing. If a spouse is non-working, an individual can contribute on his or her behalf in the spouse's INDIVIDUAL Retirement Account. They can do this if they file jointly for income taxes. But under no circumstances can two people jointly own an IRA.

Who can have a Traditional IRA? Anyone with earned income. How much can they contribute? 100% of earned income up to the current maximum. They might not get to deduct their contributions, but if they have earned income, they can have an IRA, so don't let the exam trick you into saying a wealthy executive with a 401K is somehow prohibited from having an IRA.

There are two types of IRAs, Traditional and Roth. Traditional IRAs can be funded with pre-tax dollars. That means if you make $25,000 a year and contribute $4,000 to your traditional IRA, you're only taxed on the remaining or "post-contribution" amount of $21,000. Of course, when you pull the money out at retirement, you'll pay ordinary income tax on all of it. See, with retirement plans, you either pay tax before it goes in, or when it comes out. Luckily, you don't have to pay tax on both ends. You can't have your money until you're 59½ years old. If you take it out before then, you'll pay a 10% penalty. Luckily, there are a few ways to avoid the penalty:

- Die
- Become disabled
- Buy a first home for residential purposes (up to the current maximum amount)

An individual can't have the money until he's 59½ without paying a penalty; he also has to start taking it out by the time he's 70½. If not, the IRS will slap a 50% insufficient distribution penalty on him, which seems a little harsh but is unfortunately how it is. To keep things nice and simple, it's not the year in which the individual turns 70½ (like anybody actually celebrates or notices their 70½th birthday). It's April 1st (not the 15th, which would have made too darned much sense) of the year following the year in which the individual turns 70½.

Gives you a whole new respect for CPAs and retirement specialists, doesn't it?

The test might refer to this situation as "required minimum distributions," which just means that when the investor turns 70½ it's time to ask the IRS the minimum he/she is required to take as a distribution.

Overfunding an IRA (same for SIMPLE, and SEP) results in a 6% penalty on the amount above the maximum contribution and "any earnings associated with the excess contribution." How do they determine which earnings are associated with the overfunded contribution? I have a better idea—don't overfund your retirement account.

The Roth IRA is funded with after-tax dollars. Therefore, the money comes out tax-free as long as the individual is 59½ years old and has had the account for at least 5 years. For the Roth there is no requirement to start taking the money out at 70½. Since the IRS isn't going to tax that money, they couldn't care less when it starts coming out. In fact, they don't even care if you keep putting money in. It's a Roth. Whatever, dude.

The contribution limits for both the Traditional and the Roth are 100% of earned income up to the current maximum. For people 50 and older, an additional $500 is allowed as a "catch up" provision, as in, "Social Security ain't lookin' so secure, so let's everybody try and catch up." Of course, that catch-up amount will probably change just as often as the contribution limits, so, again, please consult an online resource, which can be easily updated. If an individual has both a Traditional and a Roth IRA, the contribution limit would be the total allocated between the two accounts. For this past tax year, the limit was $3,000/$3,500, so that would be the amount you could have split up between the Roth and the Traditional—not $3,000 in the Roth and $3,000 in the Traditional. Next year it will be $4,000/$4,500, but, again, we're not getting into that game of changing the whole book every few months just because those numbers are ever-changing. Those numbers will be a big part of your career, so it's time to find out where to keep track of them.

Income limits

In the "real world" there are income limits for Roth IRAs, but I would not expect the exam to hit you with those. If it does, it's even more evil than I give it credit. Do remember, though, that there are no income limits for the Traditional IRA. Don't worry about how much money somebody makes in the test question, or if she's covered by an employer plan. All that would change is the amount she can deduct from her contribution. See, nothing is simple. We'd like to say that all contributions to a Traditional IRA are pre-tax, but, if the individual is covered by an employer plan or makes what the IRS deems a high salary, she might only get to deduct some of her contribution, or even none of it.

So what?

Either way, she can make her maximum contribution. She'd just have to keep track of how much went in after-tax or her "cost basis," so she doesn't get taxed twice on that money when it comes out with everything else. So, it's a hassle, but if she has earned income, she can contribute to her Traditional IRA. She might not deduct 100% or even any percent of it, but it can still go in there. Some of her distributions will represent a tax-free return of her after-tax cost basis and the rest will be fully taxable, sort of like an annuity, and it will be kind of a pain to make sense of it/keep track of it, but it can and does happen. And I could *easily* see the test going there, and let me drill down on *why*. See, the test is extremely mean. It isn't just hardball, it's beanball. They're aiming at your head with some of these questions. And, that's how I'd do it if they were paying me to write beanball questions. I'd take an IRA, something all of you are fairly comfortable with, and I'd get you assuming that this one will be easy. Then, I'd put this nasty spin on the question and have the individual making after-tax contributions to her *Traditional* IRA. Huh? That's not what you're expecting—that doesn't even sound right. Okay, maybe she can do it, but this question actually wants you to tell it how the distributions will be treated, and you've probably never met anyone who's actually dealing with this problem.

Harsh.

Yep.

Doesn't mean you'll get that question—it means you'll get tons of questions that start with something familiar and then end up putting weird spins on what *used to be* familiar concepts.

It's great fun, this Series 65, trust me.

But, you can win, as long as you understand what you're up against.

Back to the non-deductible contributions to the Traditional IRA. See, whether you deduct or not, the real beauty of these plans is that the earnings grow tax-deferred. In a regular old investment account if an individual is in the 35% tax bracket, that means every time he sells stock held less than a year for a profit, he has to give up 35% of the gain to the federal government. However, if the stock is owned inside an IRA, there are no capital gains taxes to pay. Buy a stock at $20 and sell it for $50 three months later? Fine. When you retire, you'll pay taxes on all the money in your account at your ordinary income tax rate, which should be pretty low when you retire.

Right?

So tax-deferred earnings provide a major benefit to the individual.

Investors who write covered calls in taxable accounts have to pay short-term capital gains on the premiums received. Not in an IRA, though. You receive $2,000 in premiums, fine. Keep the money in the account. When you retire, you'll be paying ordinary income tax on all of it, and you'll probably be in a much lower tax bracket at that point.

Investment restrictions

Not that you were planning to, but I must inform you that you can not put life insurance or collectible items into your IRA. No beanie babies, or Barry Bonds rookie cards, or rare art work. U.S. minted coins are okay, but nothing else that looks like a collectible item is allowed. And no munibonds. Munibonds pay tax-exempt interest, which is why their coupon payments are so low. All money coming out of the IRA is taxed, so the muni's tax-advantage is destroyed and all the individual is left with is a lower coupon payment and a registered rep ducking his phone calls.

Back to options—not only can you write covered calls, but these days, you can even buy calls and puts in your IRA. You can't do spreads, straddles, or combinations, and you can't write naked options, but you can write covered calls and buy calls or puts in your *retirement account*.

I'm not making this up, I swear. In fact, I've put it to the test in my own IRA.

Finally, don't let the test trick you into thinking you can't put REITs into your IRA. There is absolutely no reason why you couldn't—they're shares of stock, end of story.

Rollovers and transfers

If you want to move your IRA from one custodian to another, your best bet is to do a transfer. Just have the custodian cut a check to the new custodian, nice and simple. You can do as many of these direct transfers as you want. If, however, you do a *rollover*, things get tricky. First, you can only do one per year, and, second, it must be completed within 60 days. Plus, the custodian withholds 20% of the money, and that will become a huge hassle, so, if at all possible, do the transfer. In a rollover, the custodian cuts a check in your name. You cash it and then send the money to the new custodian, but you have to make up the 20% that was withheld. Otherwise, what they withheld is treated as an early distribution, and now the 10% penalty thing plus ordinary income, plus much heartburn and lost sleep, etc. Imagine rolling over a $100,000 IRA, where you receive a check for only $80,000 and then have to come up with an additional $20,000 within 60 days or get penalized and taxed.

No thanks.

So, since the difference between a transfer and a rollover is so painful to the individual, this seems like fertile test question ground to me.

SAVING FOR EDUCATION

Educational Savings Accounts (ESAs) can also be referred to as "Coverdell Accounts" or "Education IRAs." Why the heck they used the phrase "IRA" here, since no one is retiring, I have no idea, but I do know that they allow adults to invest $2,000 per year per child (and that number will surely rise like all others, so do a check-up to see if that's still the current maximum contribution). That's per child, notice, not per donor. It's funded by after-tax dollars and will all come out tax-free, as long as it's used for educational expenses of the child. There are also 529 or "Section 529" Plans that allow larger after-tax contributions that can also be taken out for purposes of education tax-free at the federal level. The states? Well, that depends. Some tax the withdrawals, some don't.

Read the fine print first.

HEALTH SAVINGS ACCOUNTS

First, notice that all of these tax-deferred accounts started out as retirement accounts, but nowadays, we've added similar plans for educational savings, and now health savings. The Coverdell has been referred to as an "educational IRA," which actually makes no sense. I mean, what does the "R" in "IRA" stand for? Retirement, dude—this is a KID going to college, primarily—why is the "r-word" in there at all?

Whatever.

So, the 529 plans and the Coverdells (ESAs) are similar to Roth IRAs in that they allow for *after*-tax contributions and tax-free distributions. Well, the new HSAs (Health Savings Accounts) go it even one better: tax-<u>deductible</u> contributions, and tax-free distributions.

No, that's not a typo. The money goes in pre-tax (reduces ordinary income) and comes out tax-*free*. Self-employed folks like me are also getting into these exciting vehicles, which work like this: Step 1, buy a high-deductible health insurance plan. My health insurance comes with a $2,000 deductible, so all I have to do is rack up $2,000 in routine medical expenses each year, and after that, baby, it's smooth sailing. Just how many electrodes I plan to have attached to me this year and how many vials of bodily fluids I aim to submit, I haven't figured out yet, but I know I'm covered after that first $2,000 comes out of my pocket.

Well, not surprisingly, a $2,000 deductible policy can be purchased for a fairly small premium. As usual, when you don't get much, you don't pay much, either. So, the exam might refer to these as "high-deductible, low-premium health insurance plans," if they refer to HSAs at all.

Step Two is to establish a Health Savings Account at one of the handful of financial institutions offering these plans. Most plans seem to like the idea of money market funds, but after poking around I was able to find one that allows me to invest in stocks.

So, I pay my premium to the insurance company, and then I can also fund my Health Savings Account up to the current maximum, which can be used if I ever have the misfortune of actually going to the doctor. The contributions into the HSA are tax-deductible, so whatever your marginal tax bracket is, you save that percentage of the money you put in. And, when you cut checks or use the little debit card they provide you for medical expenses, those are tax-*free* withdrawals.

If the test asks what types of investments are allowed, remember that you can invest in stocks, bonds, money market accounts, and mutual funds, just like in an IRA. So, if the question implies that there are special investment restrictions on HSAs, it's messing with you. No different from an IRA. What's in my HSA? A Real Estate Investment Trust, as I indicated earlier. Remember how REITs pay ordinary dividends? Well, since my dividends are paid into the HSA, they will come out tax-free. And that, so far, is about the only benefit I've been able to uncover from these exciting plans.

PRACTICE QUESTIONS

12. Your client is self-employed (organized as a sole proprietor, not an S-corporation), has a Keogh plan in effect, and makes a profit of $85,000 this year with her web design business. How much may she contribute to her IRA?
    A. $42,500
    B. $40,000
    C. $4,000
    D. 20% of pre/25% of post, whichever is greater

13. When will a participant in an IRA be fully vested?
    A. 3 years
    B. 5 years
    C. 7 years
    D. immediately

14. Which of the following do mutual funds and variable annuities have in common?
    A. Right to vote for the investment adviser
    B. Right to vote for the board of directors
    C. Tax-deferred growth
    D. Current taxation of all dividends, interest, capital gains

15. Your 58-year-old client has invested a total of $30,000 into a non-qualified variable annuity. The value of the separate account is now $68,000. If your client withdraws $20,000, what will be the result?
    A. 10% taxed at short-term capital gains rate
    B. 10% taxed at long-term capital gains rate
    C. 10% of growth taxed at ordinary income
    D. growth taxed at ordinary income, plus 10% penalty on growth portion

16. Your client, who is 60 years old, has invested a total of $10,000 into a qualified variable annuity. The value of the separate account is now $57,000. If your client withdraws $25,000, what will be the result?
    A. Ordinary income on excess over cost basis
    B. Capital gains on excess over cost basis
    C. 10% penalty on entire amount
    D. Entire distribution taxed at ordinary income rate

17. You are about to sell your Uncle Harry a variable annuity. What is the most important factor in determining suitability?
    A. Number of accumulation units may vary
    B. Educational level
    C. Value of annuity units varies
    D. Uncle Harry's got plenty of money

18. Which of the following risks does the investor retain in a fixed annuity?
    A. Market risk
    B. Investment risk
    C. Mortality risk
    D. Purchasing power/constant dollar risk

19. **Your client's wife does not work. How would you advise him to make IRA contributions this year?**
    A. 100% of earned income, up to $3,000 for the couple
    B. $2,000 for him, $1,000 for her
    C. $6,000 in a joint IRA if filing jointly
    D. $4,000 each, in separate IRAs

20. **You work for the ABC Corporation and participate in the company's defined contribution plan. If you make in excess of $50,000, how much may you contribute to your IRA?**
    A. $1,000
    B. 50% of pre-contribution income
    C. 100% of post-contribution income
    D. $4,000

21. **When must you present a prospectus to a client considering the purchase of a variable annuity?**
    A. At the time of contract delivery
    B. As soon as you say the word variable
    C. As soon as you say the word annuity
    D. Before or at the time of solicitation

ANSWERS

12. ANSWER: C - the current maximum contribution to an IRA is $4,000. For folks 50+, the maximum is $4,500. And this will change again and again and again over your career.

13. ANSWER: D - "vesting" and "IRA" don't really go together. It's your money, so you're "vested," whatever that means. Vesting has to do with becoming entitled to an employer's contributions on your behalf.

14. ANSWER: A - kind of nitpicky, but there is no Board of Directors for an annuity—they call 'em a "Board of Managers" just to keep things nice and simple. Individuals have the same voting rights with both products: the board, the adviser, investment objectives. The two products also have different tax treatments. Mutual funds are currently taxed—annuities are only taxed at retirement, called "constructive receipt."

15. ANSWER: D - gotta be 59½, and note that only the growth/earnings would ever be subject to ordinary income tax or penalties. The cost base belongs to the investor, end of story.

16. ANSWER: D - one word can turn a question upside down. The word "qualified" was pure evil. Usually the annuities on the exam are "non-qualified," but if the question says it's "qualified," you have to roll with it. Qualified annuities (like all qualified plans) are funded with pre-tax dollars, so all distributions are fully taxed.

17. ANSWER: C - see what Uncle Harry says about the variable checks he'll receive. If he gasps, sell him a fixed annuity instead.

18. ANSWER: D - only risk in a fixed annuity is that the fixed payment will never increase, even if inflation does. The annuitant bears no investment risk, but maintains this "purchasing power" or "constant dollar" risk.

19. ANSWER: D - no such thing as a "joint IRA." There are no JRAs, right?

20. ANSWER: D - if you have earned income, you can contribute to a traditional IRA. You might not get to deduct the full contribution, but you can still make it.

21. ANSWER: D - a lay-up. Make all the lay-ups on this exam since there are no 3-pointers.

Options Made "Easy"

NOTE: the NASAA study guide indicates that TWO questions on derivatives may show up on the exam. Derivatives are options, but also include swaps and forwards. So, if you're running out of time at this point, please keep in mind that the following fascinating chapter might be good for TWO questions.

Plus a certain amount of side-splitting mirth.

Concept of an Option

A guy steps into a tavern. After a hard day at the office, he's full of attitude. He plops down at the last open stool and slaps a stack of twenties on the bar, just loud enough to get the bartender's attention. The bartender, an attractive redhead in a pressed, white oxford shirt and bright green tie, looks up from the pitcher of ale she's pouring.

"Just a sec'," she says, afraid to take her eyes off the thick head of foam gathering at the top.

"No hurry," the guy says, although it's clear he's not in the mood to wait.

Bartender finally comes up and takes his order. Bourbon and Pepsi. Not Coke—Coke's for losers. He wants *Pepsi* with his Bourbon.

The waitress shrugs and mixes him his drink.

Three guys sitting to his right heard the crack about Coca-Cola and decide to take the bait.

"You don't like Coke, huh, buddy?" says the dark-haired guy in the denim shirt.

"Nope," the guy says. "Don't like the drink, don't like the stock."

"What, you're a trader?" the blond dude with the big shoulders says, wiping foam from his blond mustache.

"Just a guy who says Coke is headed where it belongs—down the toilet."

The three friends all raise their chins to the same level at the same time.

"That's a bold statement," the dark-haired guy says. "My dad drove a route for Coke twenty years."

"Good for him," the guy says. "Used to be a decent company—that's history, though. I say Coke is a dog, and I'll bet anybody at this bar it won't go above twenty-five bucks the rest of the year."

He says the last part loud enough to get everyone's attention. Even the jukebox seems to quiet down at this point.

"Oh yeah?" somebody shouts from a corner booth. "I'll take that bet."

"Me, too!" somebody cries from over by the pool tables.

Pretty soon the guy has over a dozen loud-talking, well-lubed happy hour customers standing in line to bet the cocky newcomer that Coca-Cola common stock will, without a doubt, rise above $25 a share at some point between today (March 1) and the rest of the year.

How do they make this bet?

The guy breaks out a stack of cocktail napkins and on each one he writes the following:

```
BUY
100 SHARES
COCA-COLA
$25 EACH
GOOD THROUGH 3RD FRIDAY DECEMBER
```

Anybody who thinks Coca-Cola stock will rise above $25 a share has to pay the guy $300. That's called the "premium," and once the buyer of the contract pays it, it's gone. Once the seller takes it, that's as much as he can make. So, the guy takes $300 from 15 different customers and walks out with $4,500 in premiums.

What's his risk as he steps onto the rainy sidewalk outside?

Unlimited.

See, no matter how high Coca-Cola common stock goes between today and the 3rd Friday of December, this guy would have to sell it to any holder of the cocktail napkin for $25 a share. Theoretically, his risk is unlimited, since there's no limit to how much he'd have to pay to get the stock.

What if the stock never makes it above $25 in the next 9 months?

That's what he's hoping! If it never makes it above $25, nobody will ever call him up and ask to buy the stock for $25. In *short*, he'll walk away with the $4,500 in premiums, laughing at all the suckers at the bar who bet the wrong way.

CALLS

What the guy sold everybody at the bar was a Coca-Cola Dec 25 call @3. As the writer of that option, he granted any buyer willing to pay $300 the *right to buy* Coca-Cola stock for $25 per share any time between today and the end of the year. When would the person holding that option want to use or *exercise* it?

Only if Coca-Cola were actually worth more than $25 a share. In fact, since they each paid $3 a share for this right, Coca-Cola will have to rise above $28—their breakeven point—before it ever became worth the trouble of exercising the call.

Either way, the guy who sold/wrote the calls gets the $4,500 in premiums. If Coke never makes it above $25, he'll never have to lift a finger. Just smile as the calls expire on the third Friday of December.

Think of a call option as a bet between a buyer and a seller. The buyer says the price of a particular stock is going up. The seller disagrees. Rather than argue about it all day, they put their money where their mouths are by buying and selling call options.

The buyer pays the seller a premium. Because he pays some money, he gets the <u>right</u> to buy 100 shares of a particular stock for a particular price within a particular time frame. If the buyer has the right to buy the stock, the seller has the obligation to *sell* the stock to the buyer, if the buyer chooses to exercise his right.

Buyers have *rights*. *Sellers* have *obligations*.

The buyer pays a premium, and he receives the right to buy a particular stock at a particular price. That particular price is known as the strike price. So you can probably see why call buyers make money when the underlying stock goes <u>up</u> in value.

That's right. Call buyers are betting that the stock's market price will go up <u>above</u> the strike price. That's why they're called "bulls." Bull = up. If you hold an Aug 70 call, that means you're "bullish" on the stock and would like to see the underlying stock go UP above 70. How far above?

As far as possible. The higher it goes, the more valuable your call becomes. Wouldn't you love to buy a stock priced at $190 for only $70?

That's what call buyers are hoping to do.

So for a call, just compare the strike price to the stock's market price. Whenever the underlying stock trades above the strike price of the call, the call is said to be in the money. A MSFT Aug 70 call would be in the money as soon as MSFT began to trade above $70 a share. If MSFT were trading at $80 a share, the Aug 70 call would be in the money by exactly $10.

Online Updates

Do you have the most current updated information? Visit www.passthe65.com to make sure!

PRACTICE QUESTIONS

1. **A MSFT Jun 50 call is in the money when MSFT trades at which of the following prices?**
    A. $49.00
    B. $50.00
    C. $51.00
    D. $49.05

2. **How far is a MSFT Jan 90 call in the money with MSFT trading at $85?**
    A. $5
    B. $90
    C. $87.50
    D. none of the above

3. **How far are the IBM Aug 70 calls in the money if IBM trades at $77?**
    A. $77
    B. $7
    C. $0
    D. none of the above

Answers

1. **ANSWER: C**

2. **ANSWER: D**

3. **ANSWER: B**

THE PREMIUM

The money you pay for your life or auto insurance policy is called a "premium." That's also what we call the money paid for an option; in fact, as you'll see with hedging, options can be used as insurance policies to protect against the risk of owning securities.

How much does an investor have to pay in premiums for an option?

Depends.

Option premiums really just represent the probability that a buyer could win a particular bet. If the premium is cheap, it's a long-shot bet. If the premium is expensive, the bet is probably already working in favor of the buyer with time left for things to get even better. As with everything else, you get what you pay for when trading options.

Time and intrinsic value

There are only two types of value that an option can possess: intrinsic value, and time value. For calls, intrinsic value is another way of stating how much higher the stock price is compared to the strike price of the call. If the underlying stock is trading at $75, the MSFT Aug 70 call is how far in the money? Five dollars. The stock price is above the call's strike price by $5; therefore, the call has intrinsic value of five dollars. That just means that an investor could save $5 by owning that call and using it to buy the underlying stock.

But, if the stock is trading *below* the strike price, the option is out of the money. With MSFT trading at $65, the Aug 70 call would have absolutely no intrinsic value. So, if there is a premium to be paid for this "out-of-the-money" call, it's only because there's plenty of time for things to improve. In other words, if the option doesn't expire for another three months, speculators might decide that the stock could easily climb more than 5 points in that time period. If so, the market will attach time value to the call. Time value simply means that the option could become more valuable given the amount of time still left before expiration.

Whenever a call is out of the money, the premium represents time value. Whenever a call is in the money, you can find the time value attached to it by subtracting intrinsic value from the premium. Let's say MSFT is trading at $72, and the Aug 70 calls are selling for a premium of $5. That means the call is in the money by $2 ($72 market vs. 70 strike price), yet an investor has to pay a premium of $5. So, where is that extra three dollars coming from?

Time value. If there is still plenty of time on the option, speculators might gladly pay an extra $3, even if the stock is only above the strike price by $2 at this point.

Premium of $5 minus intrinsic value of $2 = time value of $3.

PREMIUM	5
- INTRINSIC VALUE	-2
TIME VALUE	3

So for calls, intrinsic value is a way of stating how much <u>higher</u> the stock price is than the strike price. Time value equals whatever is left in the premium above that number.

What if MSFT were trading at $69 with the MSFT Aug 70 calls @5—how much time value would that represent?

PREMIUM	5
- INTRINSIC VALUE	-0
TIME VALUE	5

All time value. In other words, with the stock trading at only $69, the right to buy it at $70 has NO intrinsic value. (If you disagree, please call us at your earliest convenience; we have some options we'd like to sell you here in fast, friendly Chicago, IL). In fact, if the stock were trading right at the strike price of 70, there would still be no intrinsic value to the MSFT Aug 70 call, right? If you want to buy a $70 stock for $70, do you need to buy an option?

No. You only buy the call because you want to end up buying the stock for LESS than it's currently trading, which will happen if the stock moves above the strike price. So, if you pay $5 for a MSFT Aug 70 call with the stock trading at $70 or below, you're paying purely for the time value on the option.

Remember that options go in-the-money or out-of-the money. <u>People don't do that</u>. People have gains and losses, based on how much they paid for an option versus how much they received for the option. So, terms such as *time value, intrinsic value, in-the-money, out-of-the-money,* and *at-the-money* refer only to <u>options</u>. Terms such as *gains, losses,* and *break-even* refer to the options <u>investor</u>.

Only three things can happen once an option contract has been opened:
- Exercise
- Close Position
- Expire

If the call goes in the money, the investor could choose to exercise it. That means he buys at the strike price and sells at the current market price. The investor could also close his position for the intrinsic value. To close the position, remember that if he bought to open, he sells the option to close. If he sold to open, he buys the option back to close. And, finally, the option could expire worthless. The exam questions will give clues as to which of the three events has occurred. Just make sure you read the question carefully so you'll know what the exam expects.

The language makes it fun

It would be a lot easier if we could just refer to the two parties in the options contract as the buyer and the seller. Unfortunately, we have other ways of referring to each. The exam might talk about the *buyer* of an option, or it might refer to him as being "long the option." Or, maybe he is referred to as the owner of the option.

It's all the same thing.

To sell an option is to write an option. If you sell an option, you are said to be "short" the option.

All means the same thing.

Why would they use the word "hold" instead of "buy" or "own"? Think back to our guy in the tavern. When he sold the little cocktail napkins, the buyers were now *holding* the option in their hands. And, we call the seller the "writer," because, as you remember, our guy in the tavern literally *wrote* the terms of the contract on each cocktail napkin.

Buyer-holder-owner.

Seller-writer.

Why would we call the buyer "long" and the seller "short"?

Because it blows people's minds and, therefore, makes us the experts.

So far, we've been talking about calls, which give investors the right to buy stock. Let's take a look at puts now, which give investors the right to sell stock at the strike price before expiration.

PUTS

Back to our tavern. It's Monday after that third Friday in December, and our hero is back at the bar buying all the call buyers cheap beer just so they'll stick around long enough for him to rub it in.

Yes, unfortunately, for everyone but the seller/writer of the calls, Coca-Cola only made it to $22, and the calls all expired worthless. So, with the $4,500 still in his pocket, the guy is in a pretty good mood. He's in such a good mood that he can't keep himself from not only dissing Coca-Cola but talking up his favored Pepsi. Pepsi is such an awesome stock, he swears, stirring his Bourbon and Pepsi, that it couldn't possibly fall below $70 a share in the next nine months. He's so confident his favorite stock won't fall below $70 that he'll take a bet with anyone who says the stock is a loser. You have to pay him three hundred dollars to make the bet, but it gives you the right to sell him 100 shares of PepsiCo for $70, no matter how low it goes in the next nine months. Even if the stock drops to ZERO dollars, you can make him pay you $70 a share.

The 15 losers look at each other and decide the temptation is just too great. They imagine how much fun it will be to see the dude's face when they all make him give them $70 a share for a worthless stock. What if they're wrong? Then, just like before, they lose part or all of their premium. But that's *all* they can lose, too.

How much can our Pepsi-loving dude make? Same as before—just the premium. That's all a seller of an option can ever make. How much can he lose on this Pepsi put?

The good news for him as the writer/seller/short dude of a put (as opposed to a call) is that his maximum loss is NOT unlimited. In fact, you won't see the word "unlimited" associated with puts. A stock can only go down to zero, which caps the maximum loss for the seller and the maximum gain for the buyer. If this guy collects $3 a share ($300 total) from these argumentative happy hour drinkers for the right to sell him stock at $70 per share, the worse that could happen is that he'd pay $70 for a stock worth zero and would have only collected $3 per share. A maximum loss of $67 per share, and it could only happen if PepsiCo, like, went out of business in the next nine months. Which could never happen, unless it did.

So, like before, the guy lines up the same 15 buyers and takes $300 from each one. He takes out a cocktail napkin for each buyer and writes:

```
┌─────────────────────────────────────────┐
│                                           │
│                 SELL                      │
│             100 SHARES                    │
│               PEPSICO                     │
│                 $70                       │
│      through 3ʳᵈ Friday of September      │
│                                           │
└─────────────────────────────────────────┘
```

So, after finishing his drink and buying the house another round, the guy walks out with $4,500 and the obligation to buy PepsiCo for $70 a share, no matter what it's actually worth at the time.

Oh well. He's confident that the stock will remain at $70 or above. If so, those Pepsi puts will end up just as worthless as the Coke calls did.

But, if Pepsi drops to, say, $40 per share, he would have to pay $70 a share when the put buyers put (sell) the stock to him.

And that would kind of suck.

HEDGING

Let's say one of your favorite stocks looks like it's about to do a belly flop. What should you do about it?

Sell the stock?

Yes. You *could* sell the stock, but that's a drastic measure, especially when it's also possible that the stock will rally, and you'd sure hate to miss out if it did.

So, instead of taking a drastic measure, maybe you could buy an option that names a selling price for your stock.

Let's see, which option gives an investor the right to sell stock at a particular price?

That's right, a PUT.

So, if you thought one of your stocks might drop sharply, you could buy a put, giving you the right to sell your stock at the put's strike price, regardless of how low it actually goes.

It's like a homeowner's insurance policy. If you own a home, you buy insurance against fire. Doesn't mean you're hoping your house burns down, but, if it does, aren't you glad you paid your *premium*?

Buying puts against stock you own is a form of insurance. Insuring your downside, you might say. In Series Sixty-Fiveland we call it "protection."

A question might look like this:

Vito Marcello purchases 100 shares of QSTX for $50 a share. Mr. Marcello is bullish on QSTX for the long-term but is nervous about a possible downturn. To hedge his risk and get the best protection, which of the following strategies would you recommend?

    A.   Sell a Call
    B.   Buy a Call
    C.   Sell a Put
    D.   Buy a Put

Okay, first of all, when we say "hedge," all we mean is "bet the *other* way." If an investor buys stock, he is bullish, or betting the price will go up. To hedge, he'd have to take a bearish position, betting that the stock might go down. There are two "bearish" positions he can take in order to bet the other way or "hedge." He could sell a call, but if the test wanted you to recommend that strategy, the question would have said something about "increasing income" or "increasing yield."

And this one doesn't. This one gives you the key phrase:

and get the best <u>protection</u>

Whenever you see the word "protection," remember that the investor has to BUY an option. If an investor is long stock, he would buy (or go "long") a put for protection.

Let's see how the protection might work for Mr. Marcello. Let's say he bought that stock for $50 and paid $3 for an Oct 45 put. That Oct 45 put gives him the right to sell the stock for $45, regardless of how low the stock actually drops. Downside insurance for a premium of $3. With a "deductible" of how much? $5 (buy stock at $50; right to sell for a loss of only $5).

That's what we mean by "protection."

But, the question might have looked like this:

Barbara Bullbear purchases 100 shares of QSTX for $50 a share. Ms. Bullbear is bullish on QSTX for the long-term but is nervous about a possible downturn. To hedge her risk and increase income, which of the following strategies would you recommend?
A.   Sell a Call
B.   Buy a Call
C.   Sell a Put
D.   Buy a Put

Well, as we saw, you don't increase your income by buying a put. When you buy something, money comes *out* of your wallet. In this case, Barbara Bullbear has to <u>sell</u> an option. What's the only bearish option she could sell?

A call. Call sellers are bearish. Since Barbara already owns the stock, this would be a covered call. Let's say she bought the stock at $50, then writes a Sep 60 call at $3. If the stock shoots up to the moon, what would happen? Ms. Bullbear would be forced to honor her obligation to sell the stock at the strike price of $60. Well, she only paid $50 for the stock, so she just made ten bucks there. And, she took in $3 for writing the call. So, she made $13, which represents her maximum gain.

So, the upside is limited, and the maximum loss is much larger than the investor who bought the put in the preceding question. In this case Ms. Bullbear has not purchased a sale price for her stock. All she did was take in a premium of $3. That is the extent of her downside insurance. She paid $50 for the stock and took in $3 for the call. So, when the stock falls to $47 she has "broken even." But after that she can lose the full $47.

Covered calls, obviously, are not about protection. They generate some income. If the stock goes nowhere, at least you made the premium.

QUICKFACTS ON OPTIONS

- Transactions settle T + 1 (next business day)
- Last opportunity to trade or exercise is 3rd Friday of the month
- Options officially expire 11:59 PM Saturday following 3rd Friday
- 100 shares per contract
- Premium is given "per-share" just like stock prices
- New customer must receive OCC Disclosure Document at the time, or before, ROP (registered options principal) approves account
- Customer may trade as soon as ROP approves account
- American exercise = "any time up to expiration"
- European exercise = "exercise at expiration only"
- Buyers have the right to buy or sell something at a set price
- Sellers are obligated to the buyer
- Buyers EXERCISE the option, Sellers are ASSIGNED the option
- A MSFT July 50 call is NOT issued by MSFT—listed options are issued by the Options Clearing Corporation
- Options are "derivatives" because they derive their value from the value of the underlying instrument (stock, index, foreign currency, etc.)

Trading Securities

Every investor wants to buy low and sell high, right?

Well, some investors prefer selling <u>high</u>, *then* buying back low. It's the same principle; they just do it in reverse.

Short Sellers

We call these investors "short sellers," because calling them high-risk lunatics wouldn't be polite.

It works like this. You go to your friend's house and see that she has a new mountain bike that she paid *way* too much money for. Mind if I borrow your mountain bike, you ask, to which your friend agrees. On the way home you run into another friend, who admires the bike very much. She likes it so much, in fact, that she offers you two thousand bucks for it.

Two thousand bucks? Sold! You take the two thousand bucks and put it in your pocket.

Wait a minute, that wasn't even your mountain bike!

No problem. All you have to do is replace it with an identical machine. A few weeks later you go to the bike store to replace the borrowed bike, expecting to find that prices have once again dropped. Only this time it doesn't work that way. For whatever reason, that mountain bike you sold for two thousand bucks now costs *three* thousand bucks.

Ouch.

Your friend's bike has to be replaced, so you'll have to pay $3,000 for a machine you already sold for only $2,000. You <u>lost</u> when the price went <u>up</u>.

That's the risk you take by selling short. You would have made a profit if you could have replaced the borrowed item for $1,000. If so, you would have kept the difference between the $1,000 you paid and the $2,000 you received for the transaction.

Okay, so instead of selling bicycles, short sellers could sell <u>stocks</u> of the companies that *make* bicycles (or any other stock for that matter). If an investor feels that the price of XXR has gone as high as it's going to go for the next 90 days, he can sell it short at what he feels is the top, then buy it back when it falls to what he feels is the bottom. If he sells it higher than he buys it back, he ends up with a profit, just like the guy who buys it low first, then sells it high later. Either way, more money comes in than goes out, which is, after all, the whole point of investing.

Every transaction involves a T-chart, with a debit and a credit. If an investor goes "long," that means he starts with a debit. If an investor goes "short," he starts with a credit. Eventually, the long position will be sold and the short position will be bought back, completing both sides of the transactions. For either investor, the objective is to have more in the credit column than in the debit column when it's all said and done. If so, the investor ends up with a profit, regardless of which side of the transaction was performed first. Buy at $40, sell at $60 is the same thing that a short seller is hoping to do, except he'll sell at $60 and buy it back at $40.

He hopes.

Short sellers make money when the price of a stock goes *down*. According to the NYSE uptick rule, however, they can only execute the short sale when the price is moving <u>up</u>. A stock's price has to be at an "uptick" or a "zero-plus tick" for the short sale to be executed. The following prices show where short sales could occur:

			+	0+	+			+	+
20.01	19.75	<u>20.00</u>	<u>20.00</u>	<u>20.25</u>	20.03	19.68	<u>19.75</u>	<u>20.05</u>

After "19.75," "20.00" is an uptick. The next "20.00" is a repeat of the last uptick, which we call a "zero-plus tick." 20.25 is another uptick, but after that we see two down ticks in a row (20.03, 19.68). Only when the price moves from 19.68 to 19.75 do we see another plus-tick at which a short sale could occur, followed by another at $20.05. For your test, remember that a one-penny increment is a "tick," so if the stock moves up one penny, that's an uptick.

SECONDARY MARKET

A big focus of trading securities has to do with four different markets. First of all, you have to remember that "primary" and "secondary" are different terms altogether. <u>The primary market refers to a situation whereby an issuer receives the proceeds of a transaction.</u> In the secondary market, other folks buy and sell securities, at no direct financial benefit to the issuer.

EXCHANGE/FIRST MARKET

Within the secondary market, there are four separate components. Let's start with the exchange market. Imagine a clanging bell and the roar of frantic buyers and sellers in funny-looking jackets all day long until the bell rings again at four o'clock eastern standard time. That's the New York Stock Exchange, the exchange or "first" market. There are also regional exchanges in Chicago, Philadelphia, Boston, and elsewhere that are based on the NYSE. They tend to focus on regional stocks, but they still gather at trading posts, and they still sell NYSE-listed securities. If it's a physical location where buyers and sellers gather to bid and offer, we're talking about the first market. Lots of shouting and shoving going on down there, like an NBA playoff game. The exam wants you to know about four different players who can play down on the floor. The first one is called the **commission house broker**. He works for a brokerage house and fills orders for a commission. The more orders he can fill, the more money he can make, which explains why he's always in such a hurry. If he's too busy to fill an order, he can enlist the services of a **two-dollar broker**, who gets a commission to help out when the commission house broker is too busy. Then there are the big power forwards who compete for themselves only. These **registered floor traders** make a fortune if they can buy low and sell high, in either order, more often than not. The exam is probably most inclined to talk about the specialist. The **specialist** trades for his own account, carrying an inventory. The specialist is an exchange member whose responsibility is to maintain a "fair and orderly market" in a particular listed security. The specialist decides where a stock opens during an opening rotation. The specialist also keeps a book of stop and limit orders, which we'll explain later in the chapter. The exchange market includes both the NYSE and the regional exchanges in Boston, Philly, Chicago, and the Pacific (San Francisco).

THE OTC MARKET

The over-the-counter market is sometimes called the second market. It's not a physical marketplace, but it's definitely a market. Also known as the **"interdealer"** or **"negotiated market."** Market makers put out a bid and ask and stand ready to take either side of the trade, for at least one round lot. For stocks a round lot is 100 shares. So if a dealer or market maker says their quote is 20.00 - 20.11, they stand ready to buy 100 shares at $20.00 or sell 100 shares at $20.11. The difference between where they buy and where they sell is called the "spread," just like the difference between what a car dealer will *pay* for your trade-in, and what you'll pay for the new car he wants to sell you. Over-the-counter stocks have more than three letters in their symbols, by the way. So if you see a symbol like "IBM," you know that one's on the first market; whereas if you see "PSFT," you know that one is considered "OTC."

People trade OTC stocks by computer rather than gathering at a big building on Wall Street. Quotes are entered and viewed through an electronic quotation system known as NASDAQ, which stands for National Association of Securities Dealers Automated Quotation system. There are three levels of NASDAQ quoting that the test wants you to know about. The first is called **Level 1**. From the customer's perspective, Level 1 would represent the best bid and the best ask. Customers want to pay the lowest ask price and receive the highest bid price when they sell, which is what Level 1 displays to a registered rep. Among all market makers, Level 1 displays the highest bid and the lowest ask. That makes up a very important concept known as the "inside market" or "inside quote." Everything is based on that. When a dealer sells a security, they have to be close to that inside market, which might look like this:

Bid	Ask
19.75	20.00

Those two prices represent the highest bid and the lowest ask among all market makers currently quoting the stock. If any particular market maker wants to sell higher than 20 or buy lower than 19.75, they have to remain somewhere within 5% in order to conform to the 5% markup rule.

Let's say there are three market makers quoting this stock and their quotes look like this:

	Bid	Ask
Dealer 1	19.11	20.00
Dealer 2	19.75	20.50
Dealer 3	19.23	20.25

Among the three market makers, we find the highest bid at 19.75 and the lowest ask at 20.00. That's what makes up the inside quote, the price that firms will trade among themselves. When a customer wants to buy or sell it, the dealer has to base their markup (ask) or markdown (bid) on that inside quote. If a dealer sells too far above the inside ask, or pays too far below the inside bid, they could be violating the 5% markup policy. If Dealer 2 actually does sell some stock at their 20.50 ask, how far above the inside ask of 20 is that? Well, .50 divided by 20 would be 2.5%, which is well within the 5% guideline. Dealers can also charge higher markups for riskier securities, securities that are hard to locate, securities with a low sticker price, and small orders. If it's a big order and the stock costs $100 per share, the markup/markdown percentage should be lower as compared to the markup/markdown on an order for 22 shares of a stock trading at 2.75.

So, **Level 2** identifies each market maker's quote, from which Level 1 pulls the highest bid and lowest ask to provide the "inside market."

Level 3 has input fields that market makers use to enter their quotes. If you're not a market maker, you don't have Level 3. Levels 1 and 2 report quotes. Level 3 lets market makers provide quotes; it's interactive, rather than just a display.

Remember that when a broker-dealer acts as a "broker" or "agent," they tack on a commission. When acting as a principal/dealer/market maker, they make their money on a markup or markdown. As much as they'd like to, they can't charge both a commission and a markup/markdown on the same trade.

3RD MARKET

The third market is just a term used when an exchange-listed security gets sold OTC. Maybe an institutional buyer can get a better, negotiated price for an order of 10,000 IBM, a listed security, so they decide to buy it over-the-counter. When a listed security trades OTC, we refer to that situation as the "third market."

4TH MARKET

The "fourth market" is easy to keep separate. It involves direct trading between institutional investors, completely bypassing brokers by using a telecommunications system called INSTINET. Institutions…INSTINET.

TYPES OF ORDERS

MARKET ORDER

The exam will ask you to work with market orders, limit orders, stop orders, and even the dreaded stop-limit order. Well, market orders are easy. You want to buy 1,000 shares quickly, you place a market order. It will get filled as quickly as possible. We don't know exactly the price it will be filled at, but if we fill it fast enough it will probably be the same price we're looking at right now. *Now* is always the best time to fill a market order, which is also why those players down on the floor are running around like crazy people most of the day.

LIMIT ORDER

Sometimes customers like to name their price. If a stock is at 43, maybe they're starting to get interested in selling it. They'd be a lot more interested if they could sell it for $45, so they enter a sell limit order above the current market price. Sell limit @45 means the investor will take 45 or better (*more* is better for a seller). If he can get 45 or 45.15, or even higher, he'll sell his stock.

Another investor is interested in buying a stock currently trading at 30. He'd be a lot more interested in buying it at $25, so he places a buy limit order below the current price. That means he'll buy the stock if he can get it for $25 or better (*less* is better for a buyer). If the ticker comes in like this, he'll get filled at $25, his limit price:

$$30.00, 29.25, 28.75, 27.00, 26.25, 25.25, 25.00$$

And, if the last two prices had been 25.25, 24.50, he could have been filled at 24.50, which is "or better" than 25.00 when you're a buyer.

Sometimes the stock's price fails to perform like an investor wants it to. If it's entered as a day order, the limit order either gets executed that day or it goes away. If the investor is going on vacation for three weeks and doesn't want to look at his stocks while he's gone, he can leave the order open by entering it GTC, which stands for good 'til canceled. If the order doesn't get filled and the investor doesn't cancel it, the order remains open.

STOP ORDER

Stop orders are even more fun. Let's say a technical analyst sees that a particular stock is trading in a narrow range, between 38 and 40. The technical analyst sees no reason to tie up his money in a stock that is stuck in a narrow trading range, known as consolidation. He decides if the stock can break through resistance (40), it will probably continue to rise, which is why he'd like to buy it on the way up. So he places a buy stop above the current market price. Buy stop @41 means that the price first has to reach 41 or higher, at which point the order is triggered. It will be <u>executed</u> at the <u>next available price</u>, whatever that is. Stop orders have a trigger price, at which point they become market orders. So if the ticker came in like this:

40.00, 40.50, 40.75, 41.00...his order would now be triggered or "elected" at 41.00. It would then be filled at the next available price, regardless of what that is. And, if the last two prices had been 40.75, 41.50, the order would have been triggered at 41.50, at which point the price has passed through the stop price of 41. Notice that stop orders don't guarantee a price for execution. The price named as the stop is just the price that triggers or elects the order. The order—now a market order—is filled at the next available price.

A day trader decides to take a large position in a high-risk security, because, well, that's what day traders do before flaming out. But this particular day trader decides to play it safe and limit his loss. He buys 10,000 shares at $50 a share and immediately enters a sell stop order at 49. This means that as long as the stock stays above $49 he's in. As soon as it slips to 49 or lower, though, he's out. A sell stop at 49 would be triggered as soon as the stock's price hit 49 or lower, at which point it would be sold at the next available price. The exam might tell you that a customer is bullish on a stock but fears a possible downturn in the short-term. What should she do?

Well, if she originally bought in at $20 and the stock is now at $50, you should tell her that making more than $30 would be great. At this point, however, she should make sure she doesn't lose too much of the $30 dollar profit she has within her grasp. We'll give up one dollar from here, you tell her, but if it falls to $49 or lower, you're selling and taking your profit. So, if it goes up, great, and if it goes down, you take a profit.

If somebody wants to get really tricky, they can enter a stop-limit order. Now their stop order also names the most they'll pay or the least they'll accept for a particular stock. A buy stop @50, limit 52 would start out as a stop order. The stock has to hit 50 or higher before it's triggered, but the investor also won't pay more than $52 for it. A sell stop @30, limit 29 would be triggered if the stock hit 30 or lower, but the investor will not take less than $29 a share. If the order gets triggered and then the price falls lower than 29, this sell order simply won't get executed, and the investor will end up holding a loser that would have otherwise been sold with a sell-stop (not a stop-limit) order.

These orders can also be entered as "specialized orders." A fill or kill order has to be executed immediately or the whole thing is killed. Fill it or kill it. An immediate or cancel order also has to be filled immediately. If the whole thing can't be filled immediately, fill what you can and cancel the rest. So this is the only one that will take a partial execution. An all or none order will *not* take a partial execution. Fill all of it or none of it. You don't necessarily have to fill it right away, though. Just don't come back here with half of it filled, okay?

At-the-open and at-the-close orders are filled, surprisingly enough, near the open of trading and near the close of trading, respectively.

To bypass brokers for NYSE trades, SUPERDOT is used. All you have to know is that it is an electronic system for direct-to-post-and-back trading of listed securities.

STOPS AND LIMITS REVIEWED

Let's drill down on the stop and limit orders a littler harder, since I suspect you'll be hit with at least three questions on this stuff, and I know from experience just how much most people enjoy working with these concepts. Right now, XYZ's last reported price is $25. The BID is $24.90, the ASK is $25.10. Notice how the bidders (buyers willing to let you sell to them) want to buy your stock for 10 cents less, and the offerors/askers would like an extra 10 cents if you want to buy from them. You could certainly enter a market order to buy and pay $25.10, or you could enter a market order to sell and receive $24.90.

Or, you could get fancy. If you want to buy this stock for less, enter a buy-limit order below the inside ASK/offer price. The ASK is $25.10, but you aren't willing to pay one penny more than $24. Fine, enter a buy-limit @24. Nothing will happen unless and until the ASK/offer price drops to $24.

Three hours later, the ASK price does, in fact, drop to $24, and your order is filled. Congratulations, you just bought a stock whose price is dropping faster than a big league curve ball. But, this time you get lucky, and the stock turns around and starts going up in your favor. Well, heck, you're not greedy or anything, so as soon as this stock could be sold for $30, you'd be okay with a 25% profit, and you enter a sell-limit @30. So, if/when the BID price moves up to $30, you'll sell it to the bidder. You've concluded that this stock isn't likely to move above $30, anyway, so you might as well take your profit at $30. This isn't going to happen in the space of an afternoon, so you mark the order GTC, or "good 'til canceled."

Three weeks later, XYZ begins to move conveniently in your favor. The BID finally rises to $30, and you sell your stock for a $6 profit, minus commissions. Great, that was all the upside there was in the stock, anyway, right?

Wrong. As soon as you sell the stock, it starts to *really* take off, leaving you behind like the sad child nobody ever waits up for. Ouch! This stock is going up without you. But, maybe it's a temporary blip. Maybe there are only a few more points of upside on this stock—let's find out. How? Let's assume that it could easily go to $35 and then drop. But, if it goes above $35, it will keep going. How do we know that?

We don't. Remember, nobody really knows anything when it comes to trading stocks. But, we figure if XYZ breaks through resistance @35 it will continue to go up, which means if the stock goes UP to a certain level, we'll buy it. What kind of weird order is that?

A buy-stop. Let's place a buy-stop @36. That way, if the stock breaks through resistance of $35, we'll buy it just as it's about to make a real break. What if it never makes it to $36?

Then, we never really wanted it.

Now, stop orders aren't based on the BID/ASK the way limit orders are. They're based on actual trades or the "last trade" price. Just means there will have to be an actual transaction at $36 or above before our order gets thrown into the game.

It takes a while, but after a few days, XYZ does break through resistance, and we end up buying shares at $36.15. Remember, stop orders aren't filled at the stop price necessarily. If you're that much of a control freak, you need to add the word "limit" to your buy-stop. But we didn't do that, because we just wanted to make sure we got the stock.

And we did. Turns out, we were exactly right—this stock is a rocket ship headed nowhere but up. But then, in a moment of clarity, we remember that they said the same thing about CSCO, JDSU, and QCOM. Yes, stocks do occasionally reverse directions and go the wrong way on us, so just in case that happens here, let's have a sell-stop. The stock has gone from our $36.15 purchase price to $45, which is known, technically, as "a real good thing." Let's not let this real good thing slip away, though. If it continues to go up, we want to hold it. But if it starts to drop, we want to walk away with a profit. So, we enter a sell-stop @44. Remember, we bought at $36.15, and we're sitting on a profit of $8.85 at this point because the stock is trading at $45. With our sell-stop @44, we will only sell if the stock drops. If it goes up, we continue to hold it and enjoy the upside. If it starts to drop, we walk away with a profit.

Turns out, three days later, the stock opens at $43, which triggers our sell-stop (triggered at or below the trigger price of 44). The stock is sold a few ticks later at

$42.95, and we walk away with a decent paper profit, while everybody else is in denial, talking about "doubling down," "lowering their average cost," and various other clichés often uttered before disaster finally strikes.

And, disaster does finally strike. Two weeks later, the CEO is indicted for fraud, the company re-states earnings for the past five years, and the whole thing makes the Worldcomm debacle look like mild by comparison.

Only, it doesn't really affect us. We protected our paper profit and got out with a sell-stop.

You may recall that a certain television personality claimed that she didn't actually dump her shares due to insider trading. Rather, her broker and she had an "agreement" to sell the stock if it dropped below a certain price. Right, the broker was walking around the office with dozens of these "agreements" in his head, ready to spring into action if any one of 175 stocks ever dropped to a certain price.

Could be why no one believed her. This so-called "agreement" would be known as a "sell-stop" order, so where is the order ticket the broker filled out?

Uh, well…

Anyway, if after reading the preceding ramble on stops and limits you still need help, send us an email or give us a phone call. This stuff isn't easy, but it sure is testable.

FIRM AND SUBJECT QUOTES

When a registered rep calls a market maker, he asks for a quote. If the market maker responds, "It's 20-20 and a half," that's a firm quote. There were no hedging words or qualifiers attached. If the market maker had said words like "around," "near," or "subject," we would know he's only giving a subject quote. Subject quotes are for sharing information. Firm quotes imply that the market maker stands ready to trade at those prices. He has to honor his bid and ask for at least one round lot, or 100 shares. If the registered rep had asked for a quote on 500 shares, and the market maker gave a firm quote, the market maker would have to honor the quote for 500 shares.

CASH AND MARGIN ACCOUNTS

Stocks and bonds can be purchased in "cash accounts" or "margin accounts." A cash account or "special cash account" indicates that the buyer has to pay the full price of the security (within 5 business days under Reg T). A margin account allows him to put down just half the amount, gaining leverage. A margin account is basically like taking a cash advance on your credit card and putting it into the market. Much riskier than a cash account. What's the collateral in a margin account used to secure a loan for 50% of a stock's price?

The current market value (CMV) of the stock.

What happens if the CMV starts to drop?

Your telephone starts to ring, and ring, and ring. Suddenly, that agent you haven't been able to reach for two weeks will be calling your home phone, work phone, cell phone, and any other phone he can think to dial. That's a "maintenance call," by the way. You always have to maintain at least 25% of the CMV as "equity." So, you start out with at least 50% equity, but you only have to maintain 25%. When these maintenance calls start to come in, you either have to pay down your debit balance with cash, or they'll liquidate enough securities to pay down the debit. They're real flexible that way.

Or, let's say things actually work out for you—it could happen. Instead of dropping, the stock rises. Here's where margin accounts are cool. See, you only borrowed half the purchase price from the broker-dealer; any advance in the stock is 100% yours. That means that if you buy $50,000 of stock, you typically borrow $25,000 from the broker-dealer. But, if the stock rises to $80,000, that $30,000 movement is yours. You could even sell it, pay the broker-dealer the $25,000 they loaned you and walk away with $5,000.

Or, you could use this increase in equity (equity = ownership, remember) to get yourself even deeper into your broker-dealer's pocket. Your equity started out at $25,000, but it has now risen to $55,000. Just take the CMV of the stock minus the debit of $25,000—the difference between $80,000 and $25,000 is $55,000. Reg T is 50% and we use it as a measuring stick here. On an $80,000 position, Reg T (50%) would be only $40,000. So, if you have $55,000 of equity with Reg T at just $40,000, you have $15,000 of "excess equity," which we quickly label "SMA." SMA is a line of credit in a margin account. This $15,000 of credit can be borrowed, meaning they'll cut you a check for $15,000, and you'll pay it back, you reason, when the stock price keeps advancing conveniently in your direction. Or, since you only put down half in a margin account, that 15K of funny money can be used as the margin requirement for a $30,000 stock purchase. Yes, you can use borrowed money (SMA) to borrow more money from your broker-dealer.

Now, perhaps, we see why margin accounts have sort of a reputation and are only suitable for high-risk, speculative investors. Also, retirement accounts can not be set up as margin accounts, thankfully. Long-term retirement savings and short-term speculation on borrowed funds don't really go together, right?

Other things to remember about margin accounts:

- Reg T's margin requirement is set by FRB
- To open a margin account, customer needs to put down at least $2,000 and/or 50% of the security's value
- The 50% above is set by FRB; the $2,000 is set by SROs (NYSE, NASD)
- Act of 1934 gave FRB power to regulate margin
- Reg T does not apply to exempt securities (muni's, Treasuries, etc.)
- Options can be bought in the account, but you pay for them in full.
- Mutual funds can be bought in the account, but you pay for them in full.
- IPOs can be bought in the account, but you pay for them in full.
- Options, mutual funds, IPOs can be pledged as collateral after holding them fully paid for 30 days.
- Penny stocks are not "marginable."
- All short sales take place in margin accounts, not cash accounts.

Practice Questions

1. An investor originally purchased 100 shares of INTC at $20 a share. Now the stock is at $60. The investor is still bullish on the stock for the long-term but fears a possible downturn in the short-term. As her registered rep, you would tell her to place a:
   A. Market order to sell
   B. Sell limit order at $59
   C. Buy stop order at $61
   D. Sell stop order at $59

2. A sell stop order would be elected when:
   A. The stock price passes through the trigger price
   B. The stock price hits or passes through the trigger price
   C. The stock price hits the trigger price and conforms with the NYSE uptick rule
   D. The specialist receives a signed, notarized affidavit

3. On which of the following prices would a buy stop at 45 be triggered?
   A. 44.00
   B. 44.37
   C. 44.87
   D. 46.00

4. A market maker tells a dealer his quote on XYZ is 20.00 – 20.25. At the time the inside market is 19.00 – 19.35. If the market maker sells XYZ to a retail customer, on what price will he base his markup?
   A. 20.00
   B. 20.25
   C. 19.00
   D. 19.35

5. What is the "first market"?
   A. The primary market
   B. The first report over the consolidated tape
   C. The exchanges
   D. The first market to which an institutional buyer presents an order

6. Which of the following orders would be used to protect against a loss in a long position?
   A. Buy limit
   B. Sell limit
   C. Sell stop
   D. Sell stop-limit

7. Which of the following orders would be used to protect a profit in a short position?
   A. Buy limit
   B. Sell limit
   C. Buy stop
   D. Buy stop-limit

8. **Which of the following orders would not be found on the specialist's book?**
   A. Buy limit
   B. Sell stop
   C. Market
   D. Sell stop-limit

9. **Which of the following persons would be found on the floor of the NYSE?**
   A. Block trader
   B. Registered rep
   C. Alan Greenspan
   D. Specialist

Answers

1. **ANSWER: D**

2. **ANSWER: B**

3. **ANSWER: D**

4. **ANSWER: D**

5. **ANSWER: C**

6. **ANSWER: C**

7. **ANSWER: C**

8. **ANSWER: C**

9. **ANSWER: D**

PRACTICE FINALS

Online Updates

DO YOU HAVE ENOUGH PRACTICE QUESTIONS? DUE TO SIZE CON-STRAINTS, WE CAN ONLY PRESENT THREE OF OUR PRACTICE FINALS IN THIS BOOK, BUT THERE ARE ADDITIONAL PRACTICE QUESTIONS AVAILABLE AT WWW.PASSTHE65.COM. AND, BELIEVE IT OR NOT, WE THINK YOU DESERVE A "SECOND OPINION," SO WE RE-SELL A CD-ROM FROM ANOTHER VENDOR WITH 800+ PRACTICE QUESTIONS. THE COMBINATION OF OUR QUESTIONS AND THE CD-ROM IS AMAZINGLY POWERFUL.

PLEASE VISIT WWW.PASSTHE65.COM FOR MORE PRACTICE QUESTIONS NOW. ALSO, IF NEW MATERIAL STARTS APPEARING ON THE ACTUAL EXAM, WE CAN ADDRESS IT IN REAL TIME ON THE WEBSITE, SO, PLEASE VISIT FREQUENTLY FOR ANY UPDATES!

PRACTICE FINAL 1—SERIES 65

1. **What is the difference between an offer and a sale?**
   A. an offer comes from the customer; a sale from the registered representative
   B. an offer is the attempt to sell; a sale is a binding contract to dispose of a security for value
   C. an offer must be approved by a supervisory analyst
   D. an offer is binding; a sale is inherently non-binding

2. **All of the following are considered securities except**
   A. Investment contract
   B. Roth IRA
   C. Mutual fund
   D. Variable annuity

3. **Which of the following investment advisers would not have to register in the state?**
   A. adviser with no office in the state who advises 7 high net-worth individuals who are residents of the state
   B. adviser with an office in the state who advises 5 non-institutional clients who are residents of the state
   C. adviser with an office in the state who advises 11 pension funds located in the state
   D. adviser with no office in the state who advises 11 pension funds located in the state

4. **Which of the following persons are excluded from the definition of "investment adviser"?**
   A. certified financial planners
   B. sports agents
   C. banks
   D. broker-dealers

5. **All of the following are investment adviser representatives except**
   A. individual hired by an IA to help determine recommendations to clients
   B. individual hired by an IA to sell the advisory services
   C. individual hired by an IA to do filing and clerical work
   D. individual who supervises a staff of solicitors for the firm

6. **All of the following are exempt transactions except**
   A. A marshal liquidates securities held by a convicted felon
   B. A receiver in bankruptcy liquidates securities to pay creditors
   C. A CFP sells NYSE-listed securities to high-net-worth individuals
   D. An issuer offers securities in a Reg D private placement to 9 investors in the state

7. **A person in the business of effecting transactions for the accounts of others or its own account is defined as a(an)**
   A. agent
   B. broker
   C. investment adviser
   D. broker-dealer

8. All of the following professionals qualify for an exemption to registration as an IA provided their advice is not an integral component of their practice except
   A. lawyer
   B. accountant
   C. teacher
   D. economist

9. As a result of NSMIA, the SEC is responsible for overseeing all of the following except
   A. listing standards for regional exchanges
   B. capital formation
   C. competition in the securities industry
   D. improvement and oversight of market efficiency

10. All of the following are excluded from the definition of "investment adviser" by the Investment Advisers Act of 1940 except
    A. bank
    B. bank holding company
    C. financial planner
    D. person whose advice pertains solely to direct obligations of the U.S. Treasury

11. Joan Jarvis terminates her employment as an agent with Broker Dealer A in order to take a position at Broker Dealer B—also located in the state—as a registered representative. Who must notify the Administrator?
    A. Joan only
    B. Broker Dealer A
    C. Broker Dealer B
    D. Joan, Broker Dealer A, Broker Dealer B

12. For how long must state-registered investment advisers maintain business records?
    A. indefinitely
    B. 5 years
    C. 3 years
    D. 7 years

13. The purchaser of a fixed annuity would be affected most by
    A. GDP
    B. CPI
    C. Systematic risk
    D. Non-systematic risk

14. Which of the following interest rates is the most volatile?
    A. discount
    B. broker call loan
    C. prime
    D. fed funds

15. If the GDP has declined two consecutive quarters, the appropriate monetary policy would include all of the following except
    A. Buy Treasury securities from primary dealers
    B. Lower the discount rate
    C. Decrease reserve requirements
    D. Raise the discount rate

16. All of the following are listed as assets on the balance sheet except
    A. money market securities
    B. accounts receivable
    C. accounts payable
    D. patents, copyrights

17. Which of the following represents a corporation's working capital?
    A. Assets minus Liabilities
    B. Total Assets minus Total Liabilities
    C. Liabilities divided by Assets
    D. Current Assets minus Current Liabilities

18. In which of the following cases would the Administrator most likely cancel a person's registration?
    A. it is in the public interest to do so
    B. the individual can not be located
    C. the individual lied on an initial application
    D. the individual lied on a renewal application

19. If a security is "guaranteed," an investor may conclude that
    A. there is no chance of sustaining an investment loss
    B. a third party promises to pay if the issuer can not
    C. the security has been approved by the SEC
    D. the security has been approved by the Administrator

20. Which of the following is a true statement concerning registration of a successor firm?
    A. this practice is illegal in a majority of states
    B. the successor firm's registration is good for the unexpired portion of the year
    C. this practice is illegal in a plurality of states
    D. the successor firm must be in existence at the time of registration

21. Which of the following is a true statement concerning minimum net capital requirements?
    A. the Administrator must require minimum net capital at least as high as the federal requirement
    B. the Administrator may require net capital requirements in excess of federal requirements
    C. rather than using a fixed dollar amount, some states use the ratio of net capital to aggregate indebtedness when determining minimum net capital requirements
    D. minimum net capital requirements are only for those firms with discretion or custody

22. Carmen Cragen purchased shares of GE @20. Four years later, the shares are worth $25. Her holding period return is
    A. 5%
    B. 25%
    C. 6.25%
    D. 10%

23. An individual representing an issuer of which of the following securities would be required to register as an agent?
    A. State of Ohio Revenue Bond
    B. State of New Jersey Turnpike Bond
    C. General Electric preferred stock
    D. Treasury bonds

24. An investor is in the 30% marginal tax bracket. If a Chicago General Obligation bond yields 7%, she would receive an equivalent yield from a debenture yielding
    A. 4%
    B. 7.3%
    C. 10%
    D. 5%

25. Karen just passed her Series 6 and Series 63 exams. She may begin to sell securities within a state as soon as
    I.   she likes
    II. she receives written permission from a principal
    III. she is granted a license by the Administrator
    IV. she is affiliated with a broker-dealer

    A. I only
    B. I, II only
    C. II, IV only
    D. III, IV only

26. All of the following investments may be subject to the state's requirements of registration and filing of advertising materials except
    A. whiskey warehouse receipt
    B. whole life policy
    C. debenture
    D. ADR

27. Michele's new job is to set appointments for money managers by using an approved list of prospects. Michele must register as
    A. an agent of the broker-dealer
    B. a principal of the investment adviser
    C. an investment adviser
    D. an investment adviser representative

28. One of your customers is very concerned with risk. If his portfolio appreciated 10% last year, which of the following beta coefficients would give him the highest risk-adjusted return?
    A. .5
    B. .7
    C. 1.0
    D. 1.5

29. Which of the following best describes the activities of an investment adviser?
    A. individual charging commissions when selling non-exempt securities
    B. firm charging commissions when selling exempt securities
    C. firm dispensing specific investment advice on securities for a flat fee
    D. firm dispensing advice on real estate purchases

30. Which of the following statements is true?
    A. in order to register as an investment adviser, the person must also be registered as a broker-dealer
    B. an investment adviser may not also register as a broker-dealer
    C. the Administrator may condition the registration for broker-dealer on the person not acting as an investment adviser if the person is not qualified to do so
    D. all of the above

31. A company considering investing in capital equipment would most likely be concerned with
   A. Net present value
   B. Beta
   C. Systematic risk
   D. Non-systematic risk

32. Which of the following statements by a registered representative is accurate and permissible?
   A. All mutual funds with 12b-1 fees are also "no load"
   B. If a mutual fund charges a 12b-1 fee, it cannot be referred to as "no load"
   C. This federal covered security is obviously safer than other securities, or they wouldn't have given it federal covered status
   D. A Treasury note has no default risk but does carry interest rate risk

33. XYZ Growth Fund had a NAV of $10 at the beginning of the year, ending with a NAV of $12. The fund also paid dividends of $1 and capital gains of $1. The total return is
   A. 20%
   B. 40%
   C. 25%
   D. not determinable

34. All of the following represent prohibited activities of investment advisers except
   A. exercising any discretionary power in placing an order to purchase or sell securities for a client after receiving verbal authorization
   B. placing all client transactions through a broker-dealer that compensates the adviser with commissions without disclosing this arrangement to clients
   C. trading opposite of recommendations given to clients
   D. revealing client affairs, transactions, account balances, etc., in the absence of a court order

35. Investment advisers are expressly prohibited from engaging in all the following activities except
   A. inducing clients to trade frequently
   B. inducing clients to engage in transactions that are excessive in size given the client's financial resources and risk tolerance
   C. recommending agency cross transactions to both sides of the transaction
   D. recommending tax-exempt revenue bonds to high-net-worth clients

36. Maria Hernandez is a sole practitioner set up as an investment adviser. Maria studies financial statements, focusing primarily on target companies' cash flow, earnings acceleration, and revenue generation metrics. Which of the following is the most accurate way for Maria to describe her approach to rendering investment advice?
   A. I use the technicals of a company from a technical analysis approach
   B. I use the technicals of a company from a fundamentalist approach
   C. I use fundamental analysis to determine which companies represent strong investment opportunities
   D. I am certified by the state securities Administrator to perform fundamental analysis in rendering advice/recommendations

37. A customer of Q & R Investment Advisers calls an adviser representative to inquire what the "wrap fee" charged on her account represents. Which of the following represents the best response from the IA representative?
A. A wrap fee is the same thing as a commission
B. A wrap fee is just like a sales load
C. A wrap fee is charged when the account achieves a certain level of return
D. A wrap fee combines charges for advice as well as execution of a transaction

38. A value investor typically buys
I.   stocks with low PE ratios
II.   stocks with high PE ratios
III. stocks with low price-to-book ratios
IV. stocks with high price-to-book ratios

A. I, III
B. I, IV
C. II, III
D. II, IV

39. Which of the following is a true statement concerning reports and recommendations in the investment advisory business?
A. An adviser may not use published reports and/or statistical analyses provided by other sources when rendering investment advice
B. An adviser may not use published reports and/or statistical analyses provided by other sources when rendering investment advice without disclosing the source to clients
C. An adviser may not present a client with an investment recommendation prepared by someone else without disclosing the source to the client
D. An adviser may provide clients with reports prepared by outside sources without disclosure for discretionary clients

40. Which of the following yields would be associated with a bond trading at a premium?
A. Nominal 8%, Current Yield 9%
B. Current Yield 9%, Yield to Maturity 9.50 basis
C. Nominal 8%, Current 7%
D. Current Yield 9%, Yield to Call 9%

41. John Jacobs is an investment adviser who happens to hold 1,000,000 warrants on XYZ common stock. Whenever large numbers of purchase orders on XYZ hit the market, John notices that the stock tends to rise sharply. Therefore, John
A. must refrain from recommending XYZ
B. must refrain from recommending XYZ to non-institutional clients
C. must provide disclosure to clients on the potential conflict of interest
D. may recommend XYZ freely, provided he rebates a reasonable percentage of the commissions to his clients

42. In order to improve sales and customer satisfaction, QRZ Advisers have implemented a policy whereby clients are rebated 85% of their advisory fees whenever their accounts lose to the S&P 500 by more than 2 percentage points. What is true of this arrangement?
A. it is fraudulent
B. it is prohibited
C. it is allowable for clients with more than $25,000 under management
D. it is permissible with prior approval from a principal

43. All of the following statements are true of investment advisory contracts except
   A. they must be in writing
   B. they must state that no assignment of contract can occur without client consent
   C. they must explain the basis for compensation
   D. they must disclose the results of the most recent inspection performed by the state

44. Noting that advisory clients are increasingly demanding results, XYZ Advisers has drafted an agreement that allows clients to compensate the firm as a basis of capital appreciation above the rate of quarterly S&P 500 index appreciation. This type of waiver
   A. is fraudulent
   B. is prohibited
   C. is permissible for clients with $10,000 or more under management
   D. is a prohibited practice known as "selling away"

45. An investor most concerned with purchasing power would least likely purchase
   A. variable annuities
   B. small cap stock
   C. large cap stock
   D. debentures

46. Sarina Sanborn is an investment adviser set up as a sole proprietor. Sarina would like to share the gains and losses in client accounts. What is true of this situation?
   A. it is fraudulent
   B. Sarina must get the clients' written consent first
   C. Sarina must get the clients' written consent and the consent of SEC first
   D. this is prohibited

47. What is true of material facts?
   A. omitting or misstating them is unlawful and fraudulent
   B. they need not be disclosed to large, institutional clients
   C. the agent must choose which material facts to include and exclude from presentations to clients
   D. they must not be disseminated or acted upon

48. An investor most concerned with interest rate risk would least likely buy
   A. T-bills
   B. T-notes
   C. T-bonds
   D. Money Market Mutual Funds

49. Which of the following are true concerning criminal penalties under the USA?
   A. there is no statute of limitations for securities fraud
   B. the statute of limitations for securities fraud is 7 years
   C. the maximum penalty is 3 years in jail, $5,000 fine or both
   D. ignorance of the law/rule has no bearing in criminal proceedings

50. Stock of a corporation operating in a highly competitive, emerging industry is most susceptible to which of the following risks?
   A. inflation
   B. interest rate
   C. business
   D. liquidity

51. All of the following are prohibited practices except
   A. An investment adviser is compensated as a share of capital gains
   B. An agent feels it is likely that a company like GRZ will be NYSE-listed and so she indicates to her clients and prospects that GRZ is a listed company
   C. An investment adviser takes custody of client funds in the absence of a rule against custody, informing the Administrator in writing
   D. An investment adviser representative tells a prospect that she has been approved by the Administrator to provide both technical and fundamental analysis on NYSE-listed securities

52. Capital gains distributions may be combined with income distributions when calculating yield for an investment company share
   A. for 3 years
   B. for 5 years
   C. for up to 10 years
   D. under no circumstances

53. Why is churning a violation?
   A. because the SEC mandates only 11 trades per week for non-institutional investors
   B. because the SEC allows only 11 trades per week for non-institutional investors
   C. because the practice yields commissions to agents and firms, often at the expense of customers
   D. because the Securities Act of 1929 defined it so

54. All of the following represent prohibited practices for IAs except
   A. entering into or renewing contracts that provide for compensation as a share of capital gains
   B. entering into or renewing contracts that provide for compensation as a percentage of total assets under management
   C. entering into or renewing contracts that provide for assignment of contract without client consent
   D. entering into verbal contracts with non-institutional clients

55. An investor holding a large percentage of investable assets in cash and equivalents is least susceptible to which of the following risks?
   A. opportunity cost
   B. purchasing power
   C. interest rate
   D. default

56. A stock listed on the NYSE is not exempt from which of the following requirements of the Uniform Securities Act?
   A. filing of advertising materials
   B. registration
   C. anti-fraud provisions
   D. progress reports

57. All of the following securities might be found in a money market mutual fund except
   A. T-bills
   B. Commercial paper
   C. Banker's Acceptances
   D. Preferred Stock

58. A client informs you that she would like to receive maximum current income. Your risk profile determines that she has moderate risk tolerance. You would recommend
   A. Large cap stock
   B. T-bills
   C. T-bonds
   D. Investment-grade corporate bonds

59. An investment adviser in Chicago would like to record a testimonial by Oprah Winfrey, a client of the firm. Ms. Winfrey will explain how satisfied she is with the results she has achieved through the advisory firm. This
   A. is unacceptable
   B. is permissible with prior principal approval
   C. is allowable with approval by the State Administrator
   D. is exempt from SEC rules given Ms. Winfrey's accredited investor status

60. Which of the following debt securities subjects investors to phantom tax exposure?
   A. preferred stock
   B. STRIPS
   C. General Obligation bonds
   D. Revenue bonds

61. An investment adviser may have custody of client funds and securities
   I.   if the adviser files a consent to service of process
   II.   if the Administrator does not, by rule, prohibit custody
   III. if the Administrator is informed of the custodial arrangement
   IV.   if the adviser is registered with the SEC

   A. I, II, III, IV
   B. I only
   C. II, III only
   D. II, III, IV only

62. Pete Best, after tragically being ousted as drummer for the Beatles, has decided to start an investment advisory firm. His firm's business cards may be printed in all of the following ways except
   A. Peter A. Best, Investment Consultants
   B. Pete Best & Associates
   C. Best Investment Advisers
   D. Best & Associates, LLC

63. ABC 4.5% preferred stock is convertible @$20. Currently, ABC common is @30. Therefore, the parity price of the preferred stock is
   A. $100
   B. $104.50
   C. $1,500
   D. $150

64. In an agency cross transaction, the investment adviser
   A. may advise both the buyer and the seller
   B. may advise both the buyer and seller provided that fees are reduced on both sides
   C. must provide prior disclosure that such a transaction may be a conflict of interest
   D. need not provide annual statements to each client with the total number of agency cross transactions and commissions collected

65. Omitting material facts in the solicitation or rendering of investment advice is
A. fraudulent for institutional customers
B. fraudulent for non-institutional customers
C. fraudulent for retail customers
D. fraudulent and prohibited by the USA

66. To be considered an "insider" for purposes of insider trading rules, the person in question
A. possesses material, non-public information
B. must be a vice-president of a public company or higher-level executive
C. must be CEO or CFO of a large, publicly traded company
D. must be CEO or member of the Board of Directors

67. An investor holding a large percentage of her portfolio in GNMA pass-through certificates is most susceptible to
A. default risk
B. credit risk
C. prepayment risk
D. fiduciary risk

68. All of the following facts must be disclosed to advisory prospects and clients except
A. regulatory actions against the firm
B. any securities-related misdemeanors committed by the firm in the past 10 years
C. any injunctions issued against the firm for violations of securities regulations
D. conviction of the founder's wife for embezzlement of Treasury securities from a bank

69. Before the Administrator enters an order to deny, suspend, or revoke a license, what must the affected party be given?
I. consent to service of process
II. prior notice
III. opportunity for a hearing
IV. written finding of fact, conclusions of law

A. I only
B. I, II only
C. II, III only
D. II, III, IV only

70. Holders of common stock may vote on all the following except
A. stock splits
B. members of the BOD
C. objective changes
D. dividends

71. A customer is sold an unregistered, non-exempt security in violation of the USA. What is the customer entitled to receive?
A. three times the amount paid for the security
B. original purchase price, plus interest, less income received
C. original purchase price, plus unspecified damages for pain and suffering
D. contumacy

72. **When does the registration for a person become effective?**
    A. immediately
    B. immediately if accompanied by a signed and notarized affidavit
    C. at noon on the 30th day after filing the registration, provided no stop orders are pending
    D. within 15 days of filing

73. **Which of the following securities is most susceptible to interest rate risk?**
    A. straight preferred
    B. convertible preferred
    C. convertible debentures
    D. common stock

74. **The Administrator has the power under the USA to**
    I. force testimony over 5th Amendment objections
    II. publish violations
    III. sentence sales representatives to up to 3 years in prison
    IV. require federal covered advisers to pay fees to the state

    A. III, IV only
    B. II only
    C. I, II only
    D. I, II, IV only

75. **Under the USA, the statute of limitations for criminal violations is**
    A. three years
    B. five years
    C. two years from discovery, three years from occurrence
    D. three years from discovery, two years from occurrence

76. **Under the USA, the statue of limitations for civil action is**
    A. three years
    B. five years
    C. two years from discovery, three years from occurrence
    D. three years from discovery, two years from occurrence

77. **An investor most concerned with purchasing power would most likely invest in**
    A. money market securities
    B. fixed annuities
    C. common stock
    D. investment-grade corporate bonds

78. **An agent in Arkansas calls a customer residing in Louisiana to try and interest her in some 5 3/4s Little Rock Revenue Bonds of '13. The customer is uncertain and does not make her decision until three days later, when she calls the representative from a cell phone while playing slot machines in Biloxi, Mississippi, and says she will buy 100 of the Little Rock Revenue Bonds. The Administrator(s) of which state(s) has/have jurisdiction over this transaction?**
    A. none because municipal bonds are exempt securities
    B. Mississippi
    C. Louisiana
    D. all three states

79. Which of the following stocks would tend to have the highest risk/reward ratio?
    A. large cap
    B. blue chip
    C. mid cap
    D. small cap

80. All Administrative orders to deny, suspend, or revoke must
    I.   be in the public interest
    II. provide protection to investors
    III. be approved by state legislature
    IV. be approved by the Securities and Exchange Commission

    A. I, III only
    B. II, III only
    C. I, II only
    D. II, IV only

81. If it is in the public interest and provides necessary protection to investors, the Administrator may deny, suspend, or revoke an investment adviser representative's license for all the following reasons except
    A. the rep has filed a false or misleading application
    B. the rep failed to disclose her suspension from the NASD four years ago
    C. the rep is insolvent
    D. the rep lacks a college degree or equivalent training in finance/economics

82. A fundamental analyst is least concerned with
    A. Earnings trends
    B. PE ratios
    C. Price-to-cash ratios
    D. Advance/Decline Line

83. All of the following Administrative orders generally stem from violations in the securities industry except
    A. suspension
    B. revocation
    C. withdrawal
    D. denial

84. What is the purpose of a consent to service of process?
    A. it insures against theft or embezzlement
    B. it acts as a fidelity/surety bond
    C. it gives the Administrator the authority to receive service of process against the applicant in non-criminal proceedings
    D. it certifies that the applicant has attained the highest level of training available

85. An analyst focusing on volume and chart patterns is called a
    A. fool
    B. navigational analyst
    C. technical analyst
    D. fundamental analyst

86. An investment adviser with custody of client funds must send account statements to customers
    A. promptly
    B. monthly
    C. quarterly
    D. annually

87. Brooks & Baker Broker-Dealers would like to get into the investment advisory business. When they apply to do so, the Administrator determines that the firm simply is not qualified to act as an investment adviser. Therefore, the Administrator will most likely
    A. revoke the firm's license as a broker-dealer
    B. revoke the firm's license as an investment adviser
    C. condition the application for broker-dealer on the firm not engaging in the investment advisory business
    D. suspend the firm's license as a broker-dealer

88. All of the following represent expenses to a mutual fund except
    A. Board of Director salaries
    B. Management fees
    C. Sales Loads
    D. 12b-1 fees

89. If a registered representative in California attempts to sell securities to a resident of Oregon via telephone, where has an offer to sell been made?
    A. California
    B. Oregon
    C. Neither state
    D. Both states

90. What must an investment adviser established as a partnership do if one or more members are admitted to the partnership?
    A. incorporate
    B. notify all clients promptly
    C. notify all institutional clients promptly
    D. sign a waiver of noncompliance

91. Which of the following might be purchased below NAV?
    A. Open-End Fund
    B. A shares
    C. B shares
    D. Closed-End Fund

92. If your license is suspended, you may appeal the Administrator's decision to the appropriate court within how many days?
    A. 15
    B. 30
    C. 60
    D. 90

93. What is the main effect of NSMIA?
    A. provides better insurance protection for non-institutional investors
    B. supplants SIPC up to $5,000,000 per separate account title
    C. federal law has precedence over state law
    D. agents now receive better, fairer compensation

94. **Which of the following types of funds is associated with low expense ratios?**
    A. Aggressive Growth
    B. Overseas Opportunities
    C. Value
    D. Index

95. **Which of the following statements is correct concerning securities registrations?**
    A. a stop order issued by the state of Kansas may not affect the effectiveness of the securities' registration in Oklahoma
    B. the Administrator may not initiate a proceeding to deny a security's registration based on a fact known to him for more than 30 days
    C. all securities registered with the SEC must also be registered with the states
    D. all securities registered with the SEC are automatically registered with the states

96. **An investor long stock would receive protection by**
    A. Selling puts
    B. Selling calls
    C. Buying puts
    D. Buying calls

97. **An agent has just received formal notice of the Administrator's intention to revoke her license. If she requests a hearing, one will be granted within how many days?**
    A. 60
    B. 30
    C. 15
    D. 10

98. **Buying puts on a broad-based index protects against which of the following risks?**
    A. Systematic
    B. Liquidity
    C. Regulatory
    D. Non-systematic

99. **All of the following are true of ADRs/ADSs except**
    A. They represent foreign stock on a domestic market
    B. They are priced in U.S. dollars
    C. Investors are shielded from foreign exchange risk
    D. They represent equity securities

100. **The Administrator has the power to do all the following except**
    A. deny a non-exempt security's registration
    B. arrest violators
    C. issue subpoenas
    D. publish violations

101. **REITs are associated with all of the following except**
    A. Pass-through of income
    B. Portfolios of operating real estate
    C. High dividend yields
    D. Pass-through of capital losses

102. An investor who buys a limited partnership interest will benefit from all of the following except
    A. Accelerated Depreciation
    B. Tax Deferral
    C. Depreciation Recapture
    D. High Internal Rate of Return

103. Which of the following is most susceptible to constant dollar risk?
    A. Fixed annuities
    B. ADRs
    C. Convertible preferred
    D. Variable annuities

104. Rebalancing a portfolio for an older investor by reducing the percentage of equities and increasing the percentage of fixed-income investments is called
    A. strategic asset allocation
    B. buy and hold
    C. tactical asset allocation
    D. random walk theory

105. All of the following are true of dividend reinvestment in a mutual fund except
    A. Investors may defer taxes on the reinvestment for one calendar year
    B. Investors buy new shares at a net asset value basis
    C. Investors avoid paying sales loads on reinvestments
    D. Cost basis is increased by the amount of the reinvestment

106. Non-systematic risk is mitigated best through
    A. diversification
    B. selling short
    C. writing puts
    D. arbitrage

107. Why would dollar cost averaging result in a lower average cost per share?
    A. As the share price rises, investors buy more shares
    B. Time value of money
    C. More shares are purchased at lower prices
    D. Parity

108. All of the following taxes are progressive except
    A. gift
    B. estate
    C. sales
    D. income

109. All of the following taxes are regressive except
    A. gasoline
    B. excise
    C. estate
    D. sales

110. **All of the following plans are funded with after-tax contributions except**
   A. 529 Plans
   B. Roth IRAs
   C. 403b
   D. Deferred compensation

111. **Your client is a small business owner saving for retirement via a SEP-IRA. If she withdraws the entire value of her account at age 47, she will**
   A. be charged with intent to defraud
   B. pay a 10% penalty plus capital gains on any earnings above cost basis
   C. pay a 10% penalty plus ordinary income on any earnings above cost basis
   D. pay a 10% penalty plus ordinary income on the entire withdrawal

112. **All of the following subject the participant to market risk, AKA "systematic risk," except**
   A. 401K
   B. 403b
   C. Keogh
   D. Defined benefit pension plan

113. **The manager of a pension fund may be allowed to do all the following except**
   A. buy bonds rated below Baa/BBB
   B. buy stocks in companies without solid earnings history
   C. allocate 40% of the fund to equities when the statement of investment policy limits the allocation to 30%
   D. buy index puts

114. **What is the primary concern of a fiduciary managing pension fund assets?**
   A. achieving the highest yield possible
   B. achieving maximum growth
   C. staying out of high-risk investments
   D. managing the tradeoffs between risk and reward

115. **Which of the following represents a major thrust of the Uniform Prudent Investors Act?**
   A. an executor of an estate is held to the same standards as a pension fund manager
   B. bonds rated below BBB/Baa may not be purchased by fiduciaries
   C. penny stocks are inherently too risky for pension funds
   D. no individual investment can be accurately labeled "risky," but, rather, the risk of the overall portfolio is to be considered when selecting investment opportunities

116. **All of the following bear capital risk on a transaction except**
   A. specialist
   B. dealer
   C. market maker
   D. broker

117. **Which of the following may be purchased in a customer's margin account?**
   A. listed stocks
   B. junk bonds
   C. options
   D. all of the above

118. **Which of the following may be purchased on margin?**
    A. options
    B. IPO shares
    C. mutual fund shares
    D. listed stock

119. **What must a dealer use to determine the fairness of a markup?**
    A. what the firm was currently quoting
    B. the inside BID
    C. the inside ASK
    D. what the firm originally paid for the security

120. **Which of the following is a true statement concerning BID/ASKed prices?**
    A. customers buy at the BID, sell at the ASK
    B. market makers buy at the ASK, sell at the BID
    C. customers buy at the ASK, sell at the BID
    D. market makers must honor quotes up to 5 round lots

121. **If your customer is interested in buying a stock away from the market, he might enter all of the following except**
    A. Buy limit
    B. Buy stop
    C. Buy stop-limit
    D. Sell limit

122. **What must be disclosed on the trade confirmation for all stock transactions?**
    A. price the dealer originally paid for the security
    B. name of the contra party
    C. amount of the commission
    D. amount of the markup

123. **ABC 5s debentures trading @103 have a current yield of**
    A. 5.5%
    B. 5.8%
    C. 4.35%
    D. 4.85%

124. **Which of the following investments have historically enjoyed the highest inflation-adjusted returns?**
    A. T-bills
    B. T-bonds
    C. Common stock
    D. Preferred stock

125. **A customer with a low risk tolerance would most likely invest in**
    A. small cap funds
    B. large cap funds
    C. GNMA pass-throughs
    D. Investment-grade corporate bonds

126. Choosing all of the following aspects of a transaction is considered discretionary except
   A. the security to be purchased
   B. the number of shares to be purchased
   C. whether to buy or sell
   D. the time of day to execute the order

127. All of the following actions are anti-inflationary except
   A. raising reserve requirements
   B. selling Treasuries to primary dealers
   C. raising income tax rates
   D. cutting the discount rate

128. Sharon Sherman is finally ready to start investing. She makes a good income and would like to begin saving for retirement. She has a moderate risk tolerance, is 35 years old, and is planning to make a $20,000 down payment on a condominium in 13 months. If she has $100,000 to invest, how would you recommend that she allocate her investments?
   A. 100% in MMN Aggressive Growth fund
   B. 50% in MMN Aggressive Growth fund, 50% in GGG Government Bond fund
   C. 50% in MMN Aggressive Growth fund, 50% in AAA high-yield fund
   D. 40% BRZ Growth & Income fund, 40% Aggressive Growth fund, 20% AZZ Money Market fund

129. Jeff Jacobs is 45 years old. He would like to accumulate as much money as possible for retirement but would also like to begin supplementing his current income in order to scale back the hours he spends running his own accounting firm. Given his moderate risk tolerance, which of the following funds would you likely recommend?
   A. MMM Municipal Bond Fund
   B. G & I Growth and Income Fund
   C. AAA Aggressive Growth Fund
   D. CCC Corporate Bond Fund

130. Which of the following investments tends to have the highest dividend yield?
   A. T-bonds
   B. Corporate bonds
   C. REITs
   D. Money market mutual funds

131. A portfolio analyst concludes that a portfolio has a 20% chance of appreciating 30% and a 10% chance of appreciating 50%. Therefore, the expected return is
   A. at parity
   B. incongruous
   C. 11%
   D. 110%

132. An advocate of the Efficient Market Theory would most likely invest in
   A. actively managed mutual funds
   B. aggressive growth funds
   C. index funds
   D. variable annuities with high sales loads and redemption fees

133. **Josh and Jeb are fraternal twins. Josh recently purchased all 100 stocks in the S&P 100 Index, while Jeb purchased an S&P 100 Index Mutual Fund. What is true of this situation?**
    A. both are highly susceptible to non-systematic risk
    B. both are highly susceptible to default risk
    C. Josh is an equity investor, while Jeb is a creditor
    D. Neither is highly susceptible to non-systematic risk

134. **All of the following represent derivatives except**
    A. CMOs
    B. Puts
    C. Calls
    D. Common stock

135. **A mutual fund share that is purchased at the NAV and has gradually declining sales charges is referred to as**
    A. a front-end load
    B. an A share
    C. a B share
    D. an annuity unit

PRACTICE FINAL 1—SERIES 65

ANSWERS

1. ANSWER: B

WHY: because the other three answer choices were really lame. That's the best reason to choose any answer on the exam—try to find two or three that really suck. Eliminate them. If you're guessing, it has to be an educated guess between two likely choices.

Look at choice "D." That's not tempting—the word "sale" sounds more final than the word "offer," so why would the sale be "inherently non-binding"?

Sure, there are some goofy concepts on the 65, and, no, you probably never figured you'd have to know about whiskey warehouse receipts or purported gifts of assessable stock. But that doesn't mean everything is goofy. Most of this stuff is fairly logical and intuitive.

If you chose "A," in my opinion you made a better guess than if you chose "C" and "D." Does that sound subjective? Welcome to the Series 65! ☺

2. ANSWER: B

WHY: a retirement plan is a protective layer that you wrap around your securities. That way when you take any capital gains or receive interest/dividends, they all stay in the account, growing tax-deferred. But the plan itself is not a security, so if you saw the following choices, you would have to exclude them from the definition of "security," too: SEP-IRA, Keogh, 401K, defined benefit plan. The securities are the stocks, bonds, and mutual funds that you buy inside a retirement plan so that the income grows tax-deferred.

3. ANSWER: D

WHY: it's easy to forget whether you're looking for who does have to register or who doesn't. The difference is critical. Here, you're looking for those who do not have to register, but a common tendency is to grab the one who does. Anyway, you're looking for the one example where the IA does not have to register.

The ones with offices in the state have to register—unless it said their only clients were investment companies, but I don't think your test will be that mean.

Your test wants you to know that, in general, if a firm has an office in the state, they have to register in the state. Except when they don't. So choices B and C do have to register. That leaves it up to A and D. In choice A the IA is over the "5" allowed for an out-of-state "de minimus" exemption. In choice D the IA is dealing with institutional investors, so the number is irrelevant. The IA in choice D does not have to register. Aren't you glad you know that?

4. **ANSWER: C**

WHY: of these four choices, only banks are specifically excluded. Broker-dealers are often registered as advisers, too, just like many individuals have a Series 6/7 and a 65/66, making them both an agent and a registered investment adviser representative. If a broker-dealer is purely a broker-dealer and never gets compensated for advice, that firm is excluded from the definition of "investment adviser."

Why?

Because they're not investment advisers.

Just like I'm not an NFL defensive lineman. I'm excluded from that definition by the obvious facts that I'm slow, pain-averse, and tip the scales at about 180. Therefore, I can break all the training rules of the NFL and never get in trouble.

Why?

I don't quite fit the NFL's definition of "defensive lineman."

So if a broker-dealer isn't acting like an investment adviser, guess what?

They're not an investment adviser.

I'm not pumping iron five hours a day or crashing into 295-pound men with intent to maim or kill, so I'm not an NFL defensive lineman.

Remember that SEC Release IA-1092 sort of went out of its way to bring CFPs and sports agents into the fold—quite unwillingly on the part of the CFPs and sports agents, actually. They didn't catch all of them, but the test sort of makes the impression that most of them really oughta' register and save themselves a big headache. But banks are banks. They're part of the Federal Reserve System, which is all the regulators any business should ever have to deal with.

5. ANSWER: C

WHY: the test might use the words "clerical" or "ministerial." Those are the individuals at the IA firm who are not considered "investment adviser representatives." The folks they want to register are involved with selling the services, making recommendations, and managing accounts, plus those who supervise them.

Makes perfect sense to me—those are the folks who directly impact each customer, so let's define them, regulate them, and make them sweat through some nightmare of a test called the Series 65 or 66.

6. ANSWER: C

WHY: I can't think of any reason why a CFP selling stock to individuals would be an exempt transaction. Can you?

7. ANSWER: D

WHY: broker-dealer is a hyphenated word for this very reason: they either broker transactions, or they deal directly with the customer. Broker (accounts of others). Dealer (or its own account). Broker-Dealer.

What else could we call them?

8. ANSWER: D

WHY: "economist" makes a real nice trick answer, as it makes so much more sense than "engineer." Oh well. The law is not required to make sense. It's just the law.

9. ANSWER: A

WHY: the exchanges do that—but the point of a practice question like this isn't to teach you choice "A." It uses choice "A" to help you remember the other three. Just in case you get a question like that on the test, which you probably won't.

Unless you do.

10. ANSWER: C

WHY: SEC Release IA-1092 specifically mentions CFPs and sports agents in its attempt to bring them into the warm, friendly regulatory family.

11. ANSWER: D

WHY: now this one just looks like a boilerplate exam question to me. Both broker-dealers and the agent have to let us know about this change of employment—that's something the regulators are trying to tell you. Really, the whole point of the test is just to remind you that you're under the state's regulatory authority, you have to register and keep your registration current and updated—just as you do your driver's license— and if you screw up, you can have your license suspended and revoked by your current state and denied in every other state except New Jersey.

12. ANSWER: B

WHY: on the Series 65/66 there are a handful of pure memorization questions. This is one of them. It requires no explanation; it's just a lay-up. Put it through the hoop and keep moving.

13. ANSWER: B

WHY: you can read "CPI" as "inflation," since that's what the index measures. The price of stuff, the "consumer price index."

In a fixed annuity, you're guaranteed a minimum rate of return, so the market risk is really shouldered by the insurance company. Your only risk is that the payout will be fixed at, say, 5%, with inflation at more like 8%. You'd be losing purchasing power, so they call it "purchasing power risk." It's the only risk to a fixed annuitant.

14. ANSWER: D

WHY: it's basically the rate banks charge each other for overnight loans, so it's not surprising that it can change…overnight.

15. ANSWER: D

WHY: never raise interest rates during a recession if you can help it. When the economy is stuck in the mud, we give it a little gas by lowering interest rates. We only raise rates on purpose to fight inflation, which is a nasty byproduct of too much economic growth as far as we know. Which ain't too far, really. If inflation is the result of rapid economic expansion, how come in the '70s and early '80s we had inflation with a shrinking economy?

Instead of answering that, they just called it "stagflation" and kept moving.

Just like we should keep moving about now—remember, it's only a test. You just have to get about 70% of these things right. A long, long way from perfection.

16. ANSWER: C

WHY: a good test taker would probably surmise that accounts receivable and accounts payable must be on opposite sides of the balance sheet, right? So, a good test taker starts with a 50% chance, which is where you always want to start. An asset represents money coming toward you; a liability is the money you have to pay out. So "accounts payable" are liabilities, while "accounts receivable" are assets.

17. ANSWER: D

WHY: a good one to memorize. It's the capital that keeps them working in the short term: Current assets need to cover current liabilities. Otherwise, we got ourselves a major cash crunch, just like a consumer with a $30,000 credit card balance and a $25,000-a-year job.

18. ANSWER: B

WHY: the Administrative orders to deny, suspend, revoke, or cease & desist are all issued because they are "in the public interest and provide necessary protection to investors." In other words, somebody apparently did something wrong, like lying on their registration/application, or forgetting to mention the speculative nature of their many recommendations on penny stocks to senior citizens living on fixed incomes. But "cancel" just means the firm is no longer in business, appears to have moved, or appears to have gone to meet that final margin call in the sky.

Withdrawal is another order that does not imply anybody did anything wrong. You could register in Louisiana, for example, then realize you don't speak the language and withdraw your registration.

19. ANSWER: B

WHY: for example a bond could be issued by one of GE's subsidiary companies and "guaranteed" by the parent, GE. GE is like a really affluent parent cosigning for a child's loan. It's not an absolute money-back-guarantee, but it sure makes the lender sleep better at night than they would after getting the kid's signature on the loan all by itself.

20. ANSWER: B

WHY: nothing illegal about this. It just means that, for example, your advisory firm is changing from a partnership to an S-corporation. Therefore, your firm's name is going to change. So, you register the new firm even before it's in existence and you can use the unexpired portion on your current registration. No fees required, either. They'll get those when your registration expires with everybody else's, on December 31st unless properly renewed.

21. ANSWER: C

WHY: now that's a tough question. The USA grants the state securities Administrator the power to require a minimum net capital for firms based on their activities, but it doesn't say the Administrator has to. NSMIA definitely set the record straight that the states can't have higher requirements than federal. And the discretion/custody thing is related to minimum net capital—if a firm is doing that stuff, they're taking on more risk, so they either need to maintain a certain net capital or they buy bonds in $5,000 increments to cover the shortfall.

But, even firms who don't have custody/discretion will have minimum net capital requirements. The riskier their activities, the higher their minimum net capital requirement.

That's to protect them from going bankrupt over a few lousy trades in their proprietary account, or a firm commitment underwriting that leaves them holding millions of shares nobody wants, least of all their creditors.

Agents and IARs don't have minimum net capital requirements, but if they have discretion over a customer account, they'll need to buy "fidelity" or "surety" bonds. And promise not to take anything home over the weekend, even when they fully intend to reimburse the client after winning the trifecta.

22. ANSWER: B

WHY: her stock has gone up 25% over the time she has held it—holding-period return. If we annualize that rate, we divide by the 4 years it took to get it, but that's a different calculation.

23. ANSWER: C

WHY: if the individual represents the issuer of the security—the folks whose names are on the stock or bond certificates—he/she only has to register if the issuer, security, or transaction has not been granted an excuse. Treasuries, agencies, municipal bonds, and short-term debt, along with bank and small business investment company securities, have been granted excuses.

GE got no special exemption. They might issue some exempt commercial paper, and they might do an exempt transaction from time to time, but when they offer their preferred stock, common stock, or bonds to investors, they have to file registration statements with the SEC. Big difference between a "federal covered" security and an "exempt" security. A federal covered security has to be registered, with the SEC. An exempt security is excused by the SEC.

24. ANSWER: C

WHY: a munibond yielding 7% is effectively putting $70 in the investor's pocket. If she's in the 30% bracket, she'd need to receive $100 in order to end up with $70 after sharing with Uncle Sam. 10% yield taxable would be the same as 7% tax-free for this investor.

What about state taxes?

That ain't in the question, so don't put it in there.

25. ANSWER: D

WHY: tell the regulatory exam exactly what a regulator would want to hear. And don't assume a principal at the firm has a magic pen he/she can wave around to make bad stuff okay. You're going to be held responsible for your conduct. You might pull your supervisor down with you, but his/her involvement will in no way make what you did any less appalling or egregious in the eyes of the regulators. That's the point of the exam, to make you aware of what can get you in trouble. That way, if you do it anyway, they can hold you fully accountable, fine you, and take your license away.

But you'd have to really give them a reason to do any of that stuff.

26. ANSWER: B

WHY: whole life, term life, fixed annuities...those aren't even securities.

27. ANSWER: D

WHY: she represents the investment adviser by selling the services of the firm, a perfect definition of an investment adviser rep who must register. Michele gets to sit for her Series 65/66, in other words, just like you.

28. ANSWER: A

WHY: "beta" means "risk" in the sense of wild up and down movements. The bigger the number, the bigger the up and down movements, called "volatility" or "beta." So, ".5" is the least amount of volatility, which would make a risk-sensitive investor much happier than a beta larger than 1 or, God forbid, 2 or 3.

29. ANSWER: C

WHY: choice A describes an agent, choice B describes a broker-dealer.

30. ANSWER: C

WHY: that's one of those stodgy phrases pulled verbatim from the Uniform Securities Act. Lots of broker-dealers are also IAs—although it can certainly be an either-or situation, too. If your firm is clearly not qualified to act as an investment adviser, the Administrator will grant your initial or renewal application for a broker-dealer license on the condition that you do NOT act as an investment adviser. That's not meant as an insult to a "mere broker-dealer," I don't think. It's just a way to let broker-dealers still operate as broker-dealers, rather than going for the big "IA" registration and ending up losing their broker-dealer license if the IA license is denied. Doesn't really sound reasonable or necessary for the protection of investors, does it? Which is why they wrote the law that way. The USA is all about providing necessary protection to investors. If it doesn't do that—forget about it.

31. ANSWER: A

WHY: if you get a tough question on net present value, your luck is running pretty thin that morning. It has to do with "discounting the future cash flows" of an investment. Should we build the factory in Indianapolis? We calculate the investment's "net present value" by projecting the cash flows it would provide and then "discounting them to their present value." If the cost of the investment is lower than the net present value, we go for it. If not, we table the idea.

32. ANSWER: D

WHY: a mutual fund loses the ability to refer to itself as "no load" if the 12b-1 fee exceeds .25% of average net assets. Most "no load" funds still have 12b-1 fees; in fact, they sort of have to. Somebody has to pay the marketing expenses of the fund, and it's the shareholders. They either pay for them through a sales load, a 12b-1 fee, or—in the real world—usually both.

33. ANSWER: B

WHY: just take all the "positives" and add them together. Then divide by where you started. $2 of share price appreciation plus $2 coming your way is a "positive" of $4. $4 out of $10 = 40% total return.

34. ANSWER: A

WHY: remember the inherent difference between a broker-dealer and an investment adviser.

Broker-dealers make commissions or markups every time somebody trades. So, there's too much temptation for them to start buying stuff for a client in order to increase their income. Therefore, they can't make any discretionary trades until they have that authority granted to them in writing.

An IA, on the other hand, is often just getting a percentage of the assets or a flat fee for their services—what personal benefit would they really get in making trades for clients? In fact, if they put $100,000 of the client's money into lousy investments, the firm's %-based fee will drop right with the account value. Therefore, they can execute a discretionary order with only verbal authorization from the client, as long as they get the written authority within 10 business days.

Choices B and C represent potential conflicts of interest that have to be disclosed, and never reveal your client's personal affairs unless forced to by court order or granted permission from the client.

35. ANSWER: D

WHY: nothing wrong with recommending munibonds to high-tax-bracket investors. That's who buys munibonds. An IA can perform "agency cross transactions," but they can never advise both sides. They advise one client and act as a broker to the other. And, they also disclose to each advisory client how many purchases and sales were executed as "agency cross transactions" each year.

36. ANSWER: C

WHY: she's a fundamental analyst, and the Administrator doesn't certify or approve anything. If we're real lucky they "allow," and, if not, they "disallow."

37. ANSWER: D

WHY: that's what a wrap fee is. Not the same thing as a commission or sales load—it combines a fee for advisory services as well as executing transactions.

38. ANSWER: A

WHY: even if you're guessing, you should be able to equate "value" with "low price," no matter how we gauge that price.

39. ANSWER: C

WHY: if somebody else actually made the recommendation, that has to be disclosed.

IAs use reports and analyses produced by experts all the time to make the recommendations that they, themselves, present to the client. Now, if they just hand the client a report prepared by someone else, that has to be disclosed. But that's a different story from using somebody's expertise to help the IA make a good recommendation for the client. Maybe you like to short stock of companies about to get busted for accounting irregularities, so you hire a forensic accountant to uncover potential fuzzy-math financial reports. You pay the accountant for the report and tell certain clients which stocks to short.

That's fine.

Just don't sell the report as your own, right?

40. ANSWER: C

WHY: if the yield is down, the price is up. Only way for a bond to be trading at a lower yield than the coupon/nominal yield printed on the certificate is if it's trading at a higher (premium) price.

41. ANSWER: C

WHY: what other choice really looks tempting here? Maybe "A," but then you remember the general idea about disclosing potential conflicts of interest, and you choose C.

42. ANSWER: B

WHY: can't do that/it's prohibited. It's not fraudulent—there's no deception of clients going on here. It's just not allowed. The principal doesn't have a magic pen to make everything okay with his/her approval. And $25,000 under management is about $725,000 shy of being able to do performance-based compensation.

43. ANSWER: D

WHY: choice D should look like the least likely thing, even if you aren't sure. Remember, you're looking for the most likely answer when you're not sure.

44. ANSWER: B

WHY: no waivers of any provision allowed. And, if you take the trouble to pay an attorney to draft a waiver, it won't be worth the paper it's printed on, much less the legal fees you paid for a contract deemed "null and void" by the regulators.

45. ANSWER: D

WHY: fixed-income securities are lousy for fighting inflation. Why? As inflation rises, the coupon payment stays exactly the same. Not to mention that its market price also drops as interest rates inevitably rise. Buy stock or variable annuities, not fixed-income investments, when trying to hedge against purchasing power risk.

46. ANSWER: D

WHY: an agent might get to do this, but an IA never gets to do this. But, even if you tried to answer this question as if Sarina were an agent, you can't choose B or C. Agents need customer's written consent and the consent of the broker-dealer. The SEC is way too busy to deal with an issue like that.

47. ANSWER: A

WHY: if you chose any other answer, you probably misread the question. Don't do that if you can help it.

48. ANSWER: C

WHY: long-term bonds carry more interest rate risk. T-bonds are longer-term than any of the other choices.

49. ANSWER: C

WHY: at the state level, it's 3 years/5,000 or both. Memorize that.

50. ANSWER: C

WHY: a risky business or industry carries "business risk." Go figure.

51. ANSWER: C

WHY: choice C describes exactly how an IA should proceed when taking custody of clients' funds/securities.

52. ANSWER: D

WHY: capital gains are part of "total return." Yield is dividends compared to NAV only.

53. ANSWER: C

WHY: choice D is bogus—no such Act exists. The SEC doesn't have a magic number for trades—they just get upset when brokers encourage customers to trade frequently, which benefits the broker but usually harms the client.

54. ANSWER: B

WHY: that's why the business is often called "asset-based management." Also, no verbal contracts are allowed.

55. ANSWER: D

WHY: about the only good thing you could say about the money market is that it's "safe" in terms of default risk. It's horrible for fighting inflation, and when you see that you made 1.75% on your short-term debt securities while your buddy, Brad, made 11.75% on common stock, you'll feel all 10% of your "opportunity cost" and you won't feel like buying Brad-buddy a beer any time soon.

56. ANSWER: C

WHY: some securities don't have to register, but no one is exempt from anti-fraud provisions.

57. ANSWER: D

WHY: it has to be a debt security. Remember, a bond can only start with a 30-year maturity. Next year it's 29 years away, and 28 years away the next. Eventually, it will be 1 year away from maturity, right? So, a T-bond or T-note can definitely end up in a money market mutual fund during its last year of existence.

58. ANSWER: D

WHY: maximum current income = corporate bonds. We're dealing with the moderate risk tolerance by steering her toward investment-grade issues.

59. ANSWER: A

WHY: the question provides its own answer.

60. ANSWER: B

WHY: you don't get your interest income until maturity, but you get taxed on this "phantom income" every year. STRIPS/Receipts/Zeroes...all the same thing.

61. ANSWER: C

WHY: many state-registered IAs take custody; as long as there's no rule against it and the Big A is informed, it's okay. Everybody files a "consent to service of process," even those registering securities for sale in the state.

62. ANSWER: C

WHY: isn't "C" the most misleading name of the four?

63. ANSWER: D

WHY: preferred stock has a par value of $100. $100 will buy 5 shares if the conversion price is set at $20; therefore, the preferred should be worth whatever 5 shares are currently worth. $30 times 5 = $150.

64. ANSWER: C

WHY: prior disclosure and annual statements as to how many of the advisory client's purchases and sales were done as "agency cross transactions." The IA can NOT advise both sides, any more than a divorce attorney can represent both the wife and the husband.

65. ANSWER: D

WHY: if something is fraudulent, it's fraudulent irrespective of how large the client is.

66. ANSWER: A

WHY: it's exactly that simple. Just ask Martha.

67. ANSWER: C

WHY: GNMA ain't gonna default, and there's no such thing as "fiduciary risk." As usual, you get the right answer by eliminating the wrong ones.

68. ANSWER: D

WHY: who cares about the founder's wife? The customer needs to know what's up with this advisory firm.

69. ANSWER: D

WHY: if you included "consent to service or process" in your answer, you got it backwards. It's the IA, the agent, the broker-dealer, etc., who provide a consent to service of process TO the Administrator, not the other way around.

70. ANSWER: D

WHY: letting shareholders set dividend policy would be about as wise as letting your 14-year-old set her allowance, her curfew, and the nights on which she may borrow the family car.

71. ANSWER: B

WHY: you don't get "pain and suffering" or "treble damages." You get "made whole" by receiving the original purchase price plus interest, as established by the Administrator. And, the seller who goofed may deduct the dividends you received on the stock from what he pays you for this "rescission" of the trade.

72. ANSWER: C

WHY: just something to memorize. And, remember, you can not afford to miss any question where you merely have to memorize. You'll be taxing your brain plenty by reasoning and making educated guesses on the others. The memorization questions simply have to be answered successfully. Make the few lay-ups the test gives you.

73. ANSWER: A

WHY: fixed-income securities are most susceptible to interest-rate risk. Rates up—price down, end of story.

But, it's NOT the end of the story if the security is convertible—now it would have a second factor, the price of the common stock. If rates go up, convertibles might not get smacked down as hard, not if the common stock is rising.

Straight preferred has one factor—the rate of return vs. interest rates. Rates up, price down, end of story for that one.

74. ANSWER: D

WHY: the Administrator is not a court of law. Only courts can issue injunctions and sentence people to prison. Remember, the Administrator can make you talk over 5th Amendment objections—he/they just can't use the information to incriminate you.

75. ANSWER: B

WHY: another lay-up. Memorize it and don't even allow yourself to miss a question this easy.

76. ANSWER: C

WHY: memorize it and keep moving.

77. ANSWER: C

WHY: common stock might suffer the biggest price fluctuations (volatility), but it's also your best way of maintaining purchasing power. The other three choices are fixed income securities, which are safe from default risk, but lousy for fighting inflation.

78. ANSWER: D

WHY: the offer originated in Arkansas, was directed into Louisiana, and was accepted in Mississippi.

79. ANSWER: D

WHY: small companies have the highest potential to grow and the highest potential to flame out. For an even higher risk/reward ratio, try micro cap. And pick up plenty of Maalox.

80. ANSWER: C

WHY: that's exactly what all Administrative orders are about.

81. ANSWER: D

WHY: who says a college degree will help somebody sell the services of the firm, or even pick stocks? Plenty of Ph.D.'s bought YHOO for over $100 a share, and plenty of high school dropouts didn't. Also, good test-taking skills would allow you to determine that this fact is the least important to a regulator.

82. ANSWER: D

WHY: a technical analyst would watch the advance/decline line and pretend to draw a meaningful conclusion from it. It would tell a fundamental analyst nothing about the value of the company or the state of its industry. It's just the number of stocks that went up vs. the number that went down.

83. ANSWER: C

WHY: both withdrawal and cancellation are unrelated to bad behavior. Deny, suspend, revoke, and cease & desist are related to bad stuff.

84. ANSWER: C

WHY: doesn't "C" just look like the right answer?

85. ANSWER: C

WHY: many technical analysts call themselves "chartists." Personally, I like choice "A," but that's not going to be the answer on a Series 65/66 question.

86. ANSWER: C

WHY: memorize it.

87. ANSWER: C

WHY: they can still be a broker-dealer, as long as they don't try to act as an IA. They don't lose their broker-dealer license just because they tried to get an IA license. That would be like going for a promotion and getting fired if you don't get it.

88. ANSWER: C

WHY: sales loads aren't deducted from a fund's income. They're deducted from a customer's check, either when they buy or when they sell.

89. ANSWER: D

WHY: both states, for sure.

90. ANSWER: B

WHY: not sure why the clients would care, but the law says they must be notified promptly.

91. ANSWER: D

WHY: open-end mutual funds are never purchased below NAV.

92. ANSWER: C

WHY: memorize it.

93. ANSWER: C

WHY: memorize it.

94. ANSWER: D

WHY: they really have no business running high expenses when all they're doing is buying the same stocks in a particular index and holding them.

95. ANSWER: B

WHY: while renewing my driver's license by mail the other day, I noticed that I couldn't do it if I had a license in trouble with another state. In other words, if Missouri suspended my driver's license, Illinois sort of has a problem with me, too. And, in IL, the secretary of state who grants driver's licenses is also the state securities Administrator who grants and/ or takes away securities licenses.

Choice "C" contradicts what you know about federal covered securities, which register with the SEC but not the states. And choice "D" ignores the fact that unlisted, Non-NASDAQ companies register with the SEC and with the states, by coordination, or filing.

96. ANSWER: C

WHY: for protection you have to BUY the option. And you have to "bet" the other way from your stock. Long stock is bullish—you need to go bearish with the option.

97. ANSWER: C

WHY: and if she doesn't request the hearing, so much the better and easier for the Administrator to go ahead and issue the order against her.

98. ANSWER: A

WHY: if the whole market (systematic) goes down, the index should drop, too, making the put more valuable. Making money when the market drops? What could be more fun?

99. ANSWER: C

WHY: investors bear foreign exchange risk. If the dollar is strong, the ADR won't be worth as many dollars, and dividends are declared in the foreign currency, then converted to the dollar.

100. ANSWER: B

WHY: he has no power to arrest. He could get a court to issue an order against you, and if you blew that off, the judge could issue a bench warrant. That oughta' get your attention, huh?

101. ANSWER: D

WHY: you don't take a share of the company's losses from a REIT, any more than you would from a share of GE or MSFT. Only real estate partnerships (not REITs) pass through losses.

102. ANSWER: C

WHY: depreciation is a benefit, but the part the IRS "recaptures" is not good. Except for the IRS.

103. ANSWER: A

WHY: if you narrowed it down to the two fixed-income securities, you then had to remember that "convertible" preferred or bonds are less sensitive to interest rates than straight preferred or regular ol' bonds.

104. ANSWER: A

WHY: it would be considered "tactical" allocation, if we were switching into bonds because we felt it was going to be a good year for bonds. Which would mean we're heretics in the high church of the Efficient Market Theory or EMT, as in "empty."

105. ANSWER: A

WHY: mutual funds offer no tax deferral ever, end of story.

106. ANSWER: A

WHY: the risk that any one stock could drop is called "non-systematic risk." The more stocks you hold, the less any one stock could hurt you. Diversify.

And, remember, this test thinks it's sophisticated, so expect to see fancy words like "mitigated" or "concurrently," although the words "lugubrious" and "abstruse" are unlikely to appear.

107. ANSWER: C

WHY: if a larger percentage of the stocks is purchased at a lower cost, the average cost will drop, right?

108. ANSWER: C

WHY: sales tax is flat, regardless of who's buying the stuff being taxed. The others get bigger as the thing being taxed gets bigger—progressive.

109. ANSWER: C

WHY: only the estate tax of these four would rise with the size of the estate.

110. ANSWER: C

WHY: 403b's are funded with pre-tax dollars, so if you get a question asking on what amount the teacher will be taxed...all of it. No cost basis.

111. ANSWER: D

WHY: nothing fraudulent about taking your money out of the retirement plan. You never pay capital gains rates on retirement money. And, you have no cost basis, since the SEP is funded with pre-tax (tax-deductible) contributions.

112. ANSWER: D

WHY: go out on a limb here. If the plan has defined your benefit, it doesn't sound like you have to worry about the market risk, right?

113. ANSWER: C

WHY: always follow the policy statement, unless it's in violation of ERISA.

114. ANSWER: D

WHY: choice "D" should just sound like the right answer. If not, keep working on improving your test-taking skills.

115. ANSWER: D

WHY: that's the major thrust of this Act. Modern portfolio theory says that risks on one stock can be mitigated by investing in others. The Act even mentions that in 1973 an investor could have offset the losses in international oil stocks by purchasing domestic oil stocks—which actually benefited from a rise in oil prices. Therefore, no one stock or bond is considered "too risky" for a fiduciary to buy. The risk is looked at in terms of the portfolio as a whole. And, if your aunt names you the executor of her estate, you aren't held to the same standards as the professional pocketing $500,000 a year and passing himself off as an expert to the pension fund he manages, right? An amateur fiduciary is held to the standard of what a prudent amateur would do. A professional fiduciary is held to the standard of what a prudent professional would do.

Some of this stuff makes so much sense it's scary.

116. ANSWER: D

WHY: a "broker" just arranges a trade between a buyer and a seller.

117. ANSWER: D

WHY: you can purchase whatever you want within your margin account. You might have to pay in full for things like IPOs, mutual funds, and options, but they're still purchased within your margin account.

118. ANSWER: D

WHY: NYSE-, AMEX- and NASDAQ-listed stock is "marginable," but IPOs, options, and mutual funds are not.

119. ANSWER: C

WHY: to determine the fairness of a markup, the firm compares the price they're selling the stock for to the inside or lowest ASK price. A markdown would be compared to the inside BID.

120. ANSWER: C

WHY: the customer pays the higher price when he buys and receives the lower price when he sells.

Shocking, isn't it?

A market maker's quote must be honored for one—not 5—round lots.

121. ANSWER: D

WHY: he wants to buy, not sell. "Away from the market" means at some price either above or below the current market price. Not a "market" order, in other words.

122. ANSWER: C

WHY: the amount of the commission must always be disclosed. The amount of the markup only has to be disclosed on certain transactions.

123. ANSWER: D

WHY: just divide the $50 of annual income by the $1,030 paid to get it. Yield.

124. ANSWER: C

WHY: common stock does the best versus inflation.

125. ANSWER: C

WHY: GNMAs have no default risk.

126. ANSWER: D

WHY: time of day and price to pay are NOT discretionary.

127. ANSWER: D

WHY: cutting the discount rate speeds up the economy. To fight inflation, we need to slow the beast down a little.

128. ANSWER: D

WHY: pretty clear that $20,000 needs to be parked in the money market, right?

129. ANSWER: B

WHY: he needs growth to save for retirement and income to supplement his other income. Growth & Income.

130. ANSWER: C

WHY: they have to pass out 90% of their net income to shareholders, so they tend to have really sweet dividend yields. And, of course, neither A nor B would ever pay "dividends."

131. ANSWER: C

WHY: according to this wacky theory, the portfolio has an expected rate of 11%. It is literally 20% of 30 plus 10% of 50 = 11.

Hmm.

132. ANSWER: C

WHY: the market is so efficient, there's no way to beat an index. If you can't beat the index, join it.

133. ANSWER: D

WHY: they each own 100 stocks, so non-systematic risk has been diversified away to some extent. They're susceptible to systematic risk.

134. ANSWER: D

WHY: why would common stock be a "derivative"? The others derive their value from something else.

135. ANSWER: C

WHY: also called "contingent deferred sales charge." It's deferred until you sell, and the charge is contingent upon when you sell it—the load goes down over time.

Online Updates

PLEASE VISIT WWW.PASSTHE65.COM FOR ADDITIONAL PRACTICE QUESTIONS AND FOR ANY UPDATES THAT MAY HAVE BEEN ADDED TO THE MATERIAL.

PRACTICE FINAL 2—SERIES 65

1. Sharon Shumacher would like to share in the gains and losses of her client's account. As a registered representative of Berkley Broker-Dealers, what is true of this arrangement?
   A. this arrangement is fraudulent and unethical
   B. Sharon must obtain the client's written consent
   C. Sharon must obtain both the client's and the firm's written consent
   D. Sharon needs only her firm's written consent

PLEASE VISIT
WWW.PASSTHE65.COM
FOR ADDITIONAL
PRACTICE QUES-
TIONS AND FOR ANY
UPDATES THAT MAY
HAVE BEEN ADDED
TO THE MATERIAL.

2. None of the following represent violations of securities regulations by registered representatives except
   A. choosing the price paid or the time of execution for a security in the absence of discretionary authority
   B. effecting transactions not recorded on the regular books of the broker-dealer with advance written authority from the firm
   C. choosing the amount of shares of GE to be purchased for a non-discretionary client
   D. referring to VLI as primarily an "insurance product"

3. Jose Jiminez would like to share commissions with Carlos Cordoba. Jose is a licensed agent of XYZ Broker-Dealers. Carlos is a licensed representative of ABC Broker-Dealers. What is true of this situation?
   A. sharing commissions is an unethical business practice
   B. the sharing arrangement must be approved by the Administrator
   C. the agents must get permission from their respective firms
   D. the agents must get permission from their respective firms, and the firms must be affiliated directly or indirectly

4. Which of the following statements by a registered representative is accurate and permissible?
   A. All mutual funds with 12b-1 fees are also "no load"
   B. If a mutual fund charges a 12b-1 fee, it can not be referred to as "no load"
   C. This federal covered security is obviously safer than other securities, or they wouldn't have given it federal covered status
   D. A Treasury note has no default risk but does carry interest rate risk

5. XLY Broker-Dealers has been charging customers commissions and mark-ups that average 15% more than the industry average. What is true of this situation?
   A. it is fraudulent and deceptive
   B. it is permissible with prior NASD approval
   C. it is prohibited if deemed to be excessive and/or unreasonable
   D. all customers over the past 90 days are due full refunds, plus court costs, minus any income received from recommended purchases

6. ABC Broker-Dealers charges 35% more than the industry average for collecting and transferring dividends and interest payments on behalf of clients. What is true of this practice?
   A. it is perfectly acceptable, as these services are not covered by NASAA policy statements
   B. it is fraudulent
   C. firms may not charge excessive or inequitable fees for services performed, including these services
   D. it is prohibited to charge customers who have had accounts more than 12 months inequitable and/or excessive fees for such services

7. **All of the following represent prohibited activities of investment advisers except**
   A. exercising any discretionary power in placing an order to purchase or sell securities for a client after receiving verbal authorization
   B. placing all client transactions through a broker-dealer that compensates the adviser with commissions without disclosing this arrangement to clients
   C. trading opposite of recommendations given to clients
   D. revealing client affairs, transactions, account balances, etc., in the absence of a court order

8. **Investment advisers are expressly prohibited from engaging in all the following activities except**
   A. inducing clients to trade frequently
   B. inducing clients to engage in transactions that are excessive in size given the client's financial resources and risk tolerance
   C. recommending agency cross transactions to both sides of the transaction
   D. recommending tax-exempt revenue bonds to high-net-worth clients

9. **Maria Hernandez is a sole practitioner set up as an investment adviser. Maria studies financial statements, focusing primarily on target companies' cash flow, earnings acceleration, and revenue generation metrics. Which of the following is the most accurate way for Maria to describe her approach to rendering investment advice?**
   A. I use the technicals of a company from a technical analysis approach
   B. I use the technicals of a company from a fundamentalist approach
   C. I use fundamental analysis to determine which companies represent strong investment opportunities
   D. I am certified by the state securities Administrator to perform fundamental analysis in rendering advice/recommendations

10. **A customer of Q & R Investment Advisers calls an adviser representative to inquire what the "wrap fee" charged on her account represents. Which of the following represents the best response from the IA representative?**
    A. A wrap fee is the same thing as a commission
    B. A wrap fee is just like a sales load
    C. A wrap fee is charged when the account achieves a certain level of return
    D. A wrap fee combines charges for advice as well as execution of a transaction

11. **Which of the following is a true statement concerning reports and recommendations in the investment advisory business?**
    A. An adviser may not use published reports and/or statistical analyses provided by other sources when rendering investment advice
    B. An adviser may not use published reports and/or statistical analyses provided by other sources when rendering investment advice without disclosing the source to clients
    C. An adviser may not present a client with an investment recommendation prepared by someone else without disclosing the source to the client
    D. An adviser may provide clients with reports prepared by outside sources without disclosure for discretionary clients

12. **John Jacobs is an investment adviser who happens to hold 1,000,000 warrants on XYZ common stock. Whenever large numbers of purchase orders on XYZ hit the market, John notices that the stock tends to rise sharply. Therefore, John**
    A. must refrain from recommending XYZ
    B. must refrain from recommending XYZ to non-institutional clients
    C. must provide disclosure to clients on the potential conflict of interest
    D. may recommend XYZ freely, provided he rebates a reasonable percentage of the commissions to his clients

13. In order to improve sales and customer satisfaction, QRZ Advisers have implemented a policy whereby clients are rebated 85% of their advisory fees whenever their accounts lose to the S&P 500 by more than 2 percentage points. What is true of this arrangement?
    A. it is fraudulent
    B. it is prohibited
    C. it is allowable for clients with more than $25,000 under management
    D. it is permissible with prior approval from a principal

14. All of the following statements are true of investment advisory contracts except
    A. they must be in writing
    B. they must state that no assignment of contract can occur without client consent
    C. they must explain the basis for compensation
    D. they must disclose the results of the most recent inspection performed by the state

15. Noting that advisory clients are increasingly demanding results, XYZ Advisers has drafted an agreement that allows clients to compensate the firm as a basis of capital appreciation above the rate of quarterly S&P 500 index appreciation. This type of waiver
    A. is fraudulent
    B. is prohibited
    C. is permissible for clients with $10,000 or more under management
    D. is a prohibited practice known as "selling away"

16. Sarina Sanborn is an investment adviser set up as a sole proprietor. Sarina would like to share the gains and losses in client accounts. What is true of this situation?
    A. it is fraudulent
    B. Sarina must get the clients' written consent first
    C. Sarina must get the clients' written consent and the consent of SEC first
    D. This is prohibited

17. All the following activities are prohibited except
    A. sharing commissions with other agents at the firm
    B. pegging
    C. capping
    D. indicating that the Administrator has approved a security

18. All of the following are prohibited activities except
    A. matched purchases
    B. arbitrage
    C. selling away
    D. front running

19. One of your customers is extremely persistent and perturbed. After sending several hostile letters to complain of your handling of the account, the customer refuses to return your next several phone calls. When you receive another angry letter, you decide to discard the letter as well as the others you have received. This practice
    A. is fraudulent
    B. is prohibited because all written customer complaints must be forwarded to the SEC within 5 business days
    C. is prohibited because all written customer complaints must be forwarded to the Administrator within 5 business days
    D. is prohibited because all written customer complaints must be brought to the attention of your employer

20. **A registered representative may split commissions with his secretary**
    A. if the principal approves it
    B. if the secretary is registered as an agent
    C. if the split is at least 75/25
    D. never

21. **Your customer's investment objective is steady income without taking on significant default risk. As the registered representative you have discretion over the account. If you purchase penny stocks in companies without positive earnings, this is known as**
    A. an unauthorized trade
    B. misuse of material inside information
    C. churning
    D. fraud

22. **What is true of material facts?**
    A. omitting or misstating them is unlawful and fraudulent
    B. they need not be disclosed to large, institutional clients
    C. the agent must choose which material facts to include and exclude from presentations to clients
    D. they must not be disseminated or acted upon

23. **All of the following business practices are prohibited except**
    A. failing to state all facts about a security
    B. commingling
    C. failing to state all material facts about a security
    D. failing to obtain customer financial information prior to providing recommendations

24. **All of the following are prohibited practices except**
    A. An investment adviser is compensated as a share of capital gains
    B. An agent feels it is likely that a company like GRZ will be NYSE-listed and so she indicates to her clients and prospects that GRZ is a listed company
    C. An investment adviser takes custody of client funds in the absence of a rule against custody, informing the Administrator in writing
    D. An investment adviser representative tells a prospect that she has been approved by the Administrator to provide both technical and fundamental analysis on NYSE-listed securities

25. **All of the following statements by investment representatives are unacceptable except**
    A. "Treasury Bills are riskless securities guaranteed by the U.S. Government."
    B. "Treasury Notes are riskless securities guaranteed by the U.S. Government."
    C. "Treasury Bills are guaranteed by the U.S. Government, but do retain interest rate risk."
    D. "If you invest in the Long-Term Treasury Mutual Fund right now, you can benefit by receiving the upcoming dividend."

26. **Which of the following represents an acceptable sharing arrangement with clients?**
    A. an investment adviser shares the gains and losses in a joint account with a client after receiving written client consent
    B. an investment representative, after receiving client consent and approval from the branch manager, establishes a joint account with an immediate family member and shares the gains/losses/appreciation 60/40
    C. an investment representative shares the gains and losses of each transaction within a discretionary account
    D. an investment representative shares the gains and losses of each transaction within a non-discretionary account

27. Capital gains distributions may be combined with income distributions when calculating yield for an investment company share
   A. for 3 years
   B. for 5 years
   C. for up to 10 years
   D. under no circumstances

28. An investment representative is registered in State A. She sells an unregistered, exempt revenue bond issued by State B to a customer who is a resident of State A. This activity
   A. is fraudulent
   B. is prohibited
   C. is prohibited without prior principal approval
   D. is not prohibited

29. Yesterday you told a customer via telephone that reinvesting all dividend and capital gains distributions from the Oswald Aggressive Growth Fund will insure against a loss of principal. This statement is
   A. irrelevant
   B. immaterial
   C. misleading
   D. prohibited unless accompanied by a prospectus

30. If a customer asks you to place Post-It® notes on the most important pages of the preliminary prospectus, with your own succinct explications, you should
   A. have your explanations proofread by a supervisory analyst
   B. have your explanations approved by a compliance officer
   C. refuse to comply with this request
   D. only comply with this request with prior principal approval

31. The practice of promising clients to re-sell one of their securities in 3 months for 35% more than they purchase it for today is
   A. allowable only with prior principal approval
   B. prohibited
   C. a violation referred to as frontrunning
   D. a violation referred to as repurchase reciprocation

32. One of your customers is a retired widow living on a modest fixed income. She calls one afternoon and insists that she needs to sell her government bonds and put the money into small-cap technology stocks trading on the OTC Bulletin Board. What should you do?
   A. inform the SEC
   B. petition the appropriate court to schedule a hearing to determine mental competence
   C. tell the customer you feel the action is unsuitable and only execute the transactions after obtaining written acknowledgment that they are "unsolicited"
   D. inform the Administrator

33. Why is churning a violation?
   A. because the SEC mandates only 11 trades per week for non-institutional investors
   B. because the SEC allows only 11 trades per week for non-institutional investors
   C. because the practice yields commissions to agents and firms, often at the expense of customers
   D. because the Securities Act of 1929 defined it so

34. **Which of the following would be an acceptable statement for an agent to make to a customer concerning Treasury securities?**
   A. No one has ever lost money investing in Treasury notes and bonds
   B. No one can lose money investing in Treasury notes and bonds
   C. Treasury securities carry no default risk
   D. Treasury securities carry no interest rate risk

35. **Which of the following securities is most susceptible to interest rate risk?**
   A. Chicago revenue bond maturing in '09
   B. XYZ 6s debenture maturing in '11
   C. GNMA pass-through maturing in '13
   D. T-bond maturing in '17

36. **Which of the following securities is most susceptible to default risk?**
   A. Chicago revenue bond maturing in '09
   B. XYZ 6s debenture maturing in '11
   C. GNMA pass-through maturing in '13
   D. T-bond maturing in '17

37. **How often must IAs send account statements to customers?**
   A. frequently
   B. promptly
   C. monthly
   D. quarterly

38. **All of the following represent prohibited practices for IAs except**
   A. entering into or renewing contracts that provide for compensation as a share of capital gains
   B. entering into or renewing contracts that provide for compensation as a percentage of total assets under management
   C. entering into or renewing contracts that provide for assignment of contract without client consent
   D. entering into verbal contracts with non-institutional clients

39. **A stock listed on the NYSE is not exempt from which of the following requirements of the Uniform Securities Act?**
   A. filing of advertising materials
   B. registration
   C. anti-fraud provisions
   D. progress reports

40. **Which of the following is a true statement concerning material facts?**
   A. omitting material facts is fraudulent in the offer or sale of exempt securities
   B. omitting material facts is fraudulent in the offer or sale of securities
   C. omitting material facts is prohibited when offering or selling securities to retail investors
   D. omitting material facts is prohibited when offering or selling securities to institutional buyers

41. In order to sell an unregistered, non-exempt security you convince your client to sign a waiver of non-compliance, effectively exempting both parties from the registration provisions of the Uniform Securities Act. **This contract between you and the client is**
    A. enforceable only at the federal level
    B. enforceable only at the state level
    C. null and void
    D. punishable up to 7 years in a state prison

42. **Which of the following activities are prohibited?**
    I.   soliciting orders for registered, non-exempt securities
    II. creating the appearance of active trading in a security
    III. soliciting orders for unregistered, exempt securities
    IV. failing to bring written complaints against an agent to the attention of a principal at the employing broker-dealer

    A. I, II, III, IV
    B. I, II, IV only
    C. II, IV only
    D. III only

43. **If a husband wants to open an account in which he trades for his wife, which of the following documents must be completed and signed?**
    A. power of attorney from the wife
    B. new account form
    C. power of attorney for the husband
    D. margin agreement

44. **The Securities Exchange Act of 1934 granted the Federal Reserve Board the power to regulate margin. If an investor wishes to establish a margin account in order to acquire stock through the use of leverage, which of the following is required?**
    A. 50% of the purchase price, $1,000 minimum
    B. 25% of the purchase price, $1,000 minimum
    C. 50% of the purchase price, $2,000 minimum
    D. 55% of the purchase price, $2,000 minimum

45. **An investment adviser may have custody of client funds and securities**
    I.   if the adviser files a consent to service of process
    II. if the Administrator does not, by rule, prohibit custody
    III. if the Administrator is informed of the custodial arrangement
    IV. if the adviser is registered with the SEC

    A. I, II, III, IV
    B. I only
    C. II, III only
    D. II, III, IV only

46. **Pete Best has decided to start an investment advisory. His firm's business cards may be printed in all of the following ways except**
    A. Peter A. Best, Investment Consultants
    B. Pete Best Portfolio Management, Inc.
    C. Best Investment Advisers
    D. Best & Associates, LP

47. In an agency cross transaction, the investment adviser
   A. may advise both the buyer and the seller
   B. may advise both the buyer and seller provided that fees are reduced on both sides
   C. must provide prior disclosure that such a transaction may be a conflict of interest
   D. need not provide annual statements to each client with the total number of agency cross transactions and commissions collected

48. Omitting material facts in the solicitation or rendering of investment advice is
   A. fraudulent for institutional customers
   B. fraudulent for non-institutional customers
   C. fraudulent for retail customers
   D. fraudulent and prohibited by the USA

49. While selling securities for a broker-dealer located on the premises of a retail bank, a registered representative tells a prospect that SIPC and FDIC are basically the same thing. This statement is
   A. not prohibited
   B. misleading and prohibited
   C. accurate but still prohibited
   D. an example of selling away

50. Just before placing a large buy order for your customer on a thinly traded Bulletin Board stock, you buy calls and go long the stock yourself. This is an example of
   A. good market timing skills
   B. frontrunning, a violation
   C. frontrunning, not a violation
   D. matching

51. What is the difference between an offer and a sale?
   A. an offer comes from the customer; a sale from the registered representative
   B. an offer is the attempt to sell; a sale is a binding contract to dispose of a security for value
   C. an offer must be approved by a supervisory analyst
   D. an offer is binding; a sale is inherently non-binding

52. Which of the following is not considered a person under the USA?
   A. child
   B. corporation
   C. city government
   D. state government

53. All of the following are considered securities except
   A. investment contract
   B. Roth IRA
   C. mutual fund
   D. variable annuity

54. All of the following are considered securities except
   A. whiskey warehouse receipt
   B. interests in multilevel distributorships
   C. ownership interests in prize-winning thoroughbreds
   D. Keogh plan

55. **Which of the following investment advisers would not have to register in the state?**
    A. adviser with no office in the state who advises 7 high-net-worth individuals who are residents of the state
    B. adviser with an office in the state who advises 5 non-institutional clients who are residents of the state
    C. adviser with an office in the state who advises 11 pension funds located in the state
    D. adviser with no office in the state who advises 11 pension funds located in the state

56. **Which of the following persons are excluded from the definition of "investment adviser"?**
    A. certified financial planners
    B. sports agents
    C. banks
    D. broker-dealers

57. **All of the following are investment adviser representatives except**
    A. individual hired by an IA to help determine recommendations to clients
    B. individual hired by an IA to sell the advisory services
    C. individual hired by an IA to do filing and clerical work
    D. individual who supervises a staff of solicitors for the firm

58. **A person in the business of effecting transactions in securities for the accounts of others or its own account is defined as a(an)**
    A. agent
    B. broker
    C. investment adviser
    D. broker-dealer

59. **Which of the following is a non-issuer transaction?**
    A. private placement
    B. initial public offering
    C. secondary offering
    D. subsequent primary distribution

60. **All of the following professionals qualify for an exemption to registration as an IA provided their advice is not an integral component of their practice except**
    A. lawyer
    B. accountant
    C. teacher
    D. economist

61. **All of the following are excluded from the definition of "investment adviser" except**
    A. bank
    B. savings institution
    C. sports agent
    D. trust company

62. **For how long must state-registered investment advisers maintain business records?**
    A. indefinitely
    B. 5 years
    C. 3 years
    D. 7 years

63. **An individual represents an issuer in selling securities to banks and S&Ls. If the individual receives a commission**
    A. she must register as a broker-dealer
    B. she must register as an investment adviser
    C. she is an agent but need not register
    D. she is not an agent and need not register

64. **In which of the following cases would the Administrator most likely cancel a person's registration?**
    A. it is in the public interest to do so
    B. the individual cannot be located
    C. the individual lied on an initial application
    D. the individual lied on a renewal application

65. **If a security is "guaranteed," an investor may conclude that**
    A. there is no chance of sustaining an investment loss
    B. a third party promises to pay if the issuer cannot
    C. the security has been approved by the SEC
    D. the security has been approved by the Administrator

66. **Amber Adams has represented Coca-Cola® for four years, selling Coca-Cola® stock to Coca-Cola® employees and receiving commissions. She has now decided to terminate her employment with the company and take a position at a broker-dealership. Which statement below best describes required procedure at this point?**
    A. because Coca-Cola® is an exempt issuer, no notification must be provided the state Administrator
    B. Coca-Cola®, Amber, and the new employer must notify the state Administrator
    C. only the new employing broker-dealer must provide notification
    D. because Coca-Cola® issues only exempt securities, no notification is required

67. **Which of the following is a true statement concerning registration of a successor firm?**
    A. this practice is illegal in a majority of states
    B. the successor firm's registration is good for the unexpired portion of the year
    C. this practice is illegal in a plurality of states
    D. the successor firm must be in existence at the time of registration

68. **Which of the following is a true statement concerning minimum net capital requirements?**
    A. the Administrator must require minimum net capital at least as high as the federal requirement
    B. the Administrator may require net capital requirements in excess of federal requirements
    C. rather than using a fixed dollar amount, some states use the ratio of net capital to aggregate indebtedness when determining minimum net capital requirements
    D. minimum net capital requirements are only for those firms with discretion or custody

69. **Broker-dealers, investment advisers, and registered representatives share all of the following requirements for registration except**
    A. consent to service of process
    B. surety bonds
    C. minimum net capital
    D. filing fees

70. **A consent to service of process must accompany all the following except**
    A. initial application for an agent
    B. initial application for a broker-dealer
    C. registration form for a security
    D. civil complaint against an investment adviser

71. **Which of the following persons are considered fiduciaries?**
    I.   Investment Adviser for a non-discretionary client
    II. Investment Adviser for a discretionary client
    III. Registered representative
    IV. Broker-dealer

    A. II only
    B. II, IV only
    C. I, II only
    D. I, II, III, IV

72. **An individual representing an issuer of which of the following securities would be required to register as an agent?**
    A. State of Ohio Revenue Bond
    B. State of New Jersey Turnpike Bond
    C. General Electric preferred stock
    D. Treasury bonds

73. **Offerings of which of the following securities may be subject to the filing of sales literature/advertising with the state Administrator?**
    A. Indianapolis General Obligation Bond
    B. Microsoft®
    C. IBM®
    D. Stock trading regularly on the OTC Bulletin Board

74. **All of the following investments may be subject to the state's requirements of registration and filing of advertising materials except**
    A. whiskey warehouse receipt
    B. whole life policy
    C. debenture
    D. ADR

75. **Michele's new job is to set appointments for money managers by using an approved list of prospects. Michele must register as**
    A. an agent of the broker-dealer
    B. a principal of the investment adviser
    C. an investment adviser
    D. an investment adviser representative

76. **Which of the following best describes the activities of an investment adviser?**
    A. individual charging commissions when selling non-exempt securities
    B. firm charging commissions when selling exempt securities
    C. firm dispensing specific investment advice on securities for a flat fee
    D. firm dispensing advice on real estate purchases

77. The president of a bank has been selling securities of the issuer for several months now, receiving commissions. Therefore the president
   A. is guilty of a felony
   B. is guilty of fraud
   C. is an agent and must register
   D. is not an agent and need not register

78. Which of the following statements is true?
   A. in order to register as an investment adviser, the person must also be registered as a broker-dealer
   B. an investment adviser may not also register as a broker-dealer
   C. the Administrator may condition the registration for broker-dealer on the person not acting as an investment adviser if the person is not qualified to do so
   D. all of the above

79. Before the Administrator enters an order to deny, suspend, or revoke a license, what must the affected party be given?
   I.   consent to service of process
   II.   prior notice
   III. opportunity for a hearing
   IV. written finding of fact, conclusions of law

   A. I only
   B. I, II only
   C. II, III only
   D. II, III, IV only

80. If a customer is sold a security in violation of the USA, which of the following is the customer entitled to?
   I.   court costs
   II.   attorneys' fees
   III. original purchase price
   IV. interest less income received

   A. I, II, III, IV
   B. I, II only
   C. III, IV only
   D. II only

81. When does the registration for a person become effective?
   A. immediately
   B. immediately if accompanied by a signed and notarized affidavit
   C. at noon on the 30th day after filing the registration, provided no stop orders are pending
   D. within 15 days of filing

82. The Administrator has the power under the USA to
   I.   force testimony over 5th Amendment objections
   II.   publish violations
   III. sentence sales representatives to up to 3 years in prison
   IV. require federal covered advisers to pay fees to the state

   A. III, IV only
   B. II only
   C. I, II only
   D. I, II, IV only

83. The statute of limitations for criminal violations under the USA is
    A. three years
    B. five years
    C. two years from discovery, three years from occurrence
    D. three years from discovery, two years from occurrence

84. The statute of limitations for civil action under the USA is
    A. three years
    B. five years
    C. two years from discovery, three years from occurrence
    D. three years from discovery, two years from occurrence

85. If it is in the public interest and provides necessary protection to investors, the Administrator may deny, suspend, or revoke an investment adviser representative's license for all the following reasons except
    A. the rep has filed a false or misleading application
    B. the rep failed to disclose her suspension from the NASD four years ago
    C. the rep is insolvent
    D. the rep lacks sufficient experience to work in the highly competitive advisory business

86. All of the following Administrative orders generally stem from violations in the securities industry except
    A. suspension
    B. revocation
    C. withdrawal
    D. denial

87. The Administrator may deny the registration of a security for all the following reasons except
    A. underwriting compensation appears excessive
    B. the order is in the public interest
    C. the order provides protection to investors
    D. the issuing company has failed to pay dividends

88. An investment adviser with custody of client funds must send account statements to customers
    A. promptly
    B. monthly
    C. quarterly
    D. annually

89. What is the purpose of a consent to service of process?
    A. it ensures against theft or embezzlement
    B. it acts as a fidelity/surety bond
    C. it gives the Administrator the authority to receive service of process against the applicant in non-criminal proceedings
    D. it certifies that the applicant has attained the highest level of training available

90.   What must an investment adviser established as a partnership do if one or more members are admitted to the partnership?
   A. incorporate
   B. notify all clients promptly
   C. notify all institutional clients promptly
   D. sign a waiver of noncompliance

91. If your license is suspended, you may appeal the Administrator's decision to the appropriate court within how many days?
   A. 15
   B. 30
   C. 60
   D. 90

92. What is the main effect of NSMIA?
   A. provides better insurance protection for non-institutional investors
   B. supplants SIPC up to $5,000,000 per separate account title
   C. federal law has precedence over state law
   D. agents now receive better, fairer compensation

93. Your investor needs a debt security that bears no reinvestment risk. Which of the following would you least likely recommend?
   A. Treasury STRIPS
   B. Treasury Receipts
   C. Corporate zero coupon bonds
   D. T-notes

94. In order to fight inflation, the FRB/FOMC might do all of the following except
   A. raise the discount rate
   B. raise the reserve requirement
   C. buy T-bills from primary dealers
   D. sell T-bills from primary dealers

95. All of the following investors are bullish except
   A. put sellers
   B. call buyers
   C. put buyers
   D. stock buyers

96. The board of directors for ABC Corporation has failed to declare a dividend on ABC non-cumulative, non-convertible 4.5% preferred stock. Therefore, holders of the preferred stock will be able to
   A. sue the corporation for breach of contract
   B. sue the corporation for breach of fiduciary duties
   C. convert the shares to the underlying ABC common stock
   D. hope for the dividend to be declared in the future

97. All of the following investors are bearish except
   A. call buyers
   B. short sellers
   C. call writers
   D. put buyers

98. Your customer bought a second mortgage bond with a 5% nominal yield at a 7.10 basis. Three years later, she sells the bond at a 4.35 basis. Therefore, she probably
   A. realized a capital gain
   B. acted illegally
   C. performed an arbitrage transaction
   D. realized a capital loss

99. Which of the following represent equity investments?
   I.   participating preferred stock
   II.   non-participating preferred stock
   III. convertible debentures
   IV.   cumulative preferred stock

   A. II, IV
   B. III
   C. I, II, III, IV
   D. I, II, IV

100. Ricardo Ramirez reckons that rates have peaked. Which of the following would be the most suitable investment to recommend?
   A. T-bonds
   B. T-notes
   C. 10-year corporate bonds
   D. money market instruments

101. Which of the following is the lowest investment-grade bond rating?
   A. AAA
   B. Baa
   C. Ba
   D. AA

102. ABT 4 7/8s of '12 debentures are convertible at $20. Currently, XYZ common trades at $30, so the parity price of the bonds is
   A. $1,500
   B. $1,575
   C. $1,000
   D. not determinable

103. Whenever a corporation issues more stock, they must send securities to existing shareholders that allow the shareholders to maintain their proportionate ownership of the corporation. These securities are referred to as
   A. rights
   B. warrants
   C. options
   D. coupons

104. If gross domestic product is declining, Congress and the President might
   A. sell T-bills from primary dealers
   B. raise the reserve requirement
   C. cut spending
   D. increase spending

105. A cellphone manufacturer in Sweden has garnered much interest on the part of American investors, who purchase dollar-denominated
    A. rights
    B. warrants
    C. ADRs
    D. Debentures

106. Which of the following is considered a "negotiated market"?
    A. NYSE
    B. Regional exchanges
    C. NASDAQ
    D. Options

107. What is true of the difference between "BID" and "ASK"?
    A. market makers sell at the bid, buy at the ask
    B. market makers buy at the bid, sell at the ask
    C. customers buy at the bid, sell at the ask
    D. the terms are synonymous

108. All of the following are advantages of closed-end funds over open-end except
    A. shares may be sold short
    B. shares may sometimes be purchased at a discount
    C. investor always receives NAV when selling
    D. shares may sometimes be sold at a premium

109. Open-end funds are allowed to do all of the following except
    A. sell an unlimited number of shares
    B. sell to a n unlim ited number of investors
    C. sell securities short
    D. close off purchases to new investors

110. TRY Fund has a NAV of $10.00 and a POP of $9.50. XLZ Fund has a NAV of $9.00 and a POP of $9.50. Which of the following are true statements?
    I. TRY is an open-end fund
    II. TRY is a closed-end fund
    III. XLZ is an open-end fund
    IV. XLZ is a closed-end fund

    A. I, III
    B. II, III
    C. I, IV
    D. II, IV

111. Your client's objective is maximum current income but she is not comfortable with excessive risk. Therefore, you would most likely recommend
    A. Money market funds
    B. Open-end funds
    C. High-yield bond funds
    D. Investment-grade corporate bond funds

112. Your client's goal is to accumulate money for retirement. She has a good job and no debt beyond a modest mortgage payment. She is not risk-averse. Which of the following funds would you least likely recommend?
    A. Money Market Fund
    B. Aggressive Growth Fund
    C. Overseas Opportunities Fund
    D. Science and Technology Fund

113. A schoolteacher participates in a 403b plan. Over her past 20 years of service the school district has contributed $50,000 to her account, with the account valued at $92,500 at retirement. Therefore, the teacher will be taxed on
    A. $42,500
    B. $92,500
    C. $50,000
    D. none of the above

114. A schoolteacher participates in a 403b plan. Over her past 20 years of service the school district has contributed $50,000 to her account, with the account valued at $92,500 at retirement. Therefore, the teacher's cost base is
    A. $50,000
    B. zero
    C. $92,500
    D. $42,500

115. A client covered under an employer's qualified defined benefit pension plan started an IRA before tax year 1996. What is true of this situation?
    A. the IRA must be closed under Graham-Rudman-Leach
    B. the IRA money must be commingled with the pension money
    C. contributions to the IRA must cease before April 15 of the following year
    D. the client may continue to contribute to the IRA

116. What is normally associated with a 401K plan?
    A. after-tax contributions
    B. employer matching
    C. corporate bonds
    D. munibonds

117. Which of the following are true statements?
    I. an adviser with custody of client funds/securities must maintain minimum net worth of $35,000
    II. an adviser with custody of client funds/securities whose minimum net worth falls below $35,000 must post bonds in the amount of the net worth deficiency rounded up to the nearest $5,000
    III. an adviser with discretion over a client's account who does not have custody of the client's securities/funds must maintain minimum net capital of $10,000
    IV. An adviser who accepts prepayment of >$500 six or more months in advance must at all times maintain positive net worth

    A. I, II, III, IV
    B. I, III
    C. II, IV
    D. I, III, IV

118. **Which two of the following would be defined as investment advisers under the USA?**
  I.   an economics professor with an active consulting business providing regular advice to pension funds as to which money managers to retain for the fund
  II. a federal or state-chartered bank
  III. a property & casualty insurance company
  IV. a lawyer who frequently advises non-accredited investors as to the value or advisability of investing in particular securities

  A. I, II
  B. I, IV
  C. II, III
  D. II, IV

119. **If you determine that a portfolio has a 10% chance of returning 8% and a 20% chance of returning 5%, you are using**
  A. capital asset pricing model
  B. support-resistance theory
  C. expected return
  D. net present value

120. **When a corporation analyzes a potential investment in capital equipment based on discounted cash flows, they are using**
  A. leading indicators
  B. lagging indicators
  C. net present value
  D. future value

121. **If a customer is in the 30% federal tax bracket, a municipal bond yielding 7% would be equivalent to a corporate bond yielding**
  A. 4%
  B. 10%
  C. 7%
  D. 5%

122. **An investment strategy that seeks to maintain an ideal mix of stocks, bonds, money market, REITs, and tax-free fixed-income securities is called**
  A. active management
  B. asset allocation
  C. LIFO
  D. FIFO

123. **A proponent of the efficient market theory would most likely invest in**
  A. actively managed mutual funds
  B. index funds
  C. REITs
  D. DPPs

124. **Advocating tax increases to fight inflation would most likely describe**
  A. Keynesian economics
  B. Supply side economics
  C. Laissez-faire economics
  D. Voodoo economics

125. **Supply side economics is most closely linked to**
   A. Keynes
   B. Laffer
   C. Milton Friedman
   D. Alan Greenspan

126. **If a client's portfolio appreciates 24% over a 3-year period, the holding period return is**
   A. 8%
   B. 12%
   C. 24%
   D. 25.5%

127. **Your investor's portfolio grows 15% this year but was also subject to high volatility. If you express the return as a function of the portfolio beta, you are using**
   A. future value
   B. risk-adjusted return
   C. discounted cash flows
   D. real return

128. **Which of the following bond ratings is most likely attached to a bond with the highest yield?**
   A. Baa
   B. BBB
   C. AA
   D. B

129. **Which of the following securities would be least affected by a change in interest rates?**
   A. GNMA
   B. Preferred stock
   C. Convertible preferred stock
   D. Common stock

130. **An investor short stock could best protect the position with a**
   A. short call
   B. long call
   C. short put
   D. long put

131. **If the yield curve is inverted, which of the following securities would you most likely buy?**
   A. T-bill
   B. T-note
   C. T-bond
   D. STRIP

132. Heather Hanks is a CPA. She frequently puts together financial plans for customers, but—rather than charging a fee for the advice—Heather is compensated by commissions only when the customers buy the insurance policies, mutual funds, and annuities that are presented as part of the plan. What is true of this situation?
   A. as a CPA, Heather is excluded from the definition of "investment adviser" and need not register
   B. Heather is acting as an investment adviser and must register, as stipulated by SEC Release IA-1092
   C. if Heather attains a CFP distinction, she will not have to register as an investment adviser
   D. if her clients are high-net-worth individuals, Heather need not register

133. "Investment adviser representative" is to "investment adviser" as "agent" is to
   A. IAR
   B. Broker-dealer
   C. Federal covered
   D. Parity

134. Which of the following portfolio analysis tools is the least complex?
   A. holding period return
   B. risk-adjusted return
   C. standard deviation
   D. expected return

135. XYZ has EPS of $3.00, pays a dividend yield of 1.9% and has a market price of $30.00. What is the PE?
   A. 1.9%
   B. $10
   C. 10
   D. 1:10

PRACTICE FINAL 2—SERIES 65

ANSWERS

1. ANSWER: C

WHY: boilerplate exam question. Memorize it.

2. ANSWER: C

WHY: in other words, "which one of the four is prohibited?" You can't choose the number of shares a customer buys or sells unless you have discretion. The "price paid" is not a discretionary aspect, so the rep can choose that. Believe it or not, there are rare occasions where a transaction might be effected but not recorded on the regular books of the broker-dealer. I could give you an example, but it wouldn't help you pass the test, and it would take much more effort on both our parts than it's worth. And, finally, VLI is supposed to be sold primarily as an insurance product. The fact that the market makes death benefit and cash value fluctuate also makes it a "security," but it's primarily an insurance vehicle.

3. ANSWER: D

WHY: good one to memorize.

4. ANSWER: D

WHY: most no-load funds have 12b-1 fees. If the fee gets too big, they lose the ability to call themselves "no load." Never imply that a federal covered security is inherently safer than one subject to the state's filing requirements.

    Even if it is.

5. ANSWER: C

WHY: there's no deceit going on. The firm had just better hope the regulators don't decide the firm is unfairly gouging their clients.

6. ANSWER: C

WHY: doesn't "C" just look like the right answer?

7. ANSWER: A

WHY: remember the inherent difference between a broker-dealer and an investment adviser. Broker-dealers make commissions or markups every time somebody trades. So, there's too much temptation for them to start buying stuff for a client in order to increase their income. Therefore, they can't make any discretionary trades until they have that authority granted to them in writing.

An IA, on the other hand, is often just getting a percentage of the assets or a flat fee for their services—what personal benefit would they really get in making trades for clients? In fact, if they put $100,000 of the client's money into lousy investments, the firm's %-based fee will drop right with the account value. Therefore, they can execute a discretionary order with only verbal authorization from the client, as long as they get the written authority within 10 business days.

Choices B and C represent potential conflicts of interest that have to be disclosed, and never reveal your client's personal affairs unless forced to by court order or granted permission from the client.

8. ANSWER: D

WHY: nothing wrong with recommending munibonds to high-tax-bracket investors. That's who buys munibonds. An IA can perform "agency cross transactions," but they can never advise both sides. They advise one client and act as a broker to the other. And, they also disclose to each advisory client how many purchases and sales were executed as "agency cross transactions" each year.

9. ANSWER: C

WHY: she's a fundamental analyst, and the Administrator doesn't certify or approve anything. If we're real lucky they "allow," and, if not, they "disallow."

10. ANSWER: D

WHY: that's what a wrap fee is. Not the same thing as a commission or sales load—it combines a fee for advisory services as well as executing transactions.

11. ANSWER: C

WHY: if somebody else actually made the recommendation, that has to be disclosed. IAs use reports and analyses produced by experts all the time to make the recommendations that they, themselves, present to the client. Now, if they just hand the client a report prepared by someone else, that has to be disclosed. But that's a different story from using somebody's expertise to help the IA make a good recommendation for the client. Maybe you like to short stock of companies about to get busted for accounting irregularities, so you hire a forensic accountant to uncover potential fuzzy-math financial reports. You pay the accountant for the report and tell certain clients which stocks to short.

12. ANSWER: C

WHY: the advice given to the client is supposed to be about helping the client. If the advice, when acted upon, gives a direct benefit to the IA, that's a potential conflict of interest and must be disclosed. Just think along those terms, and you'll be able to spot what an IA can and can't do. They're fiduciaries, which means they put the client's needs first.

13. ANSWER: B

WHY: nothing deceitful in nature here, so there's no fraud. But rebating when you lose to the benchmark is just the flipside of making more money when you beat the benchmark. Performance-based compensation is only allowed when you work with institutions or individuals with $1.5 million net worth, $750,000 under management, plus still more stuff. In other words, $25,000 of assets isn't even close for talking about performance-based compensation. As usual, the principal's pen is not a magic wand.

14. ANSWER: D

WHY: makes sense, doesn't it? If not, give us a call or send us an email.

15. ANSWER: B

WHY: it's prohibited because we can't just get together and grant each other immunity from the law. Imagine if a drug dealer told the cops that it was okay for him to sell crack to that other guy because the two of them drew up a legal document that mutually exempted each other from the state's narcotics laws.

The exam might also say that such waivers/contracts are considered "null and void" in a court of law. In other words, not even worth the paper they're printed on.

16. ANSWER: D

WHY: an agent might get to share gains and losses inside a joint account with a client, but that stuff isn't allowed between advisory firms and advisory clients. Makes the whole fiduciary responsibility thing a lot easier to remember when the IA isn't a co-customer.

17. ANSWER: A

WHY: just like the SEC, the Administrator neither approves nor disapproves. If you're real lucky, they permit. If you're not so lucky, they prohibit. You can share commissions with registered agents of your firm, or a subsidiary. Why not? You're both licensed to do that sort of thing. Don't let this exam make you think EVERYTHING's a violation—it's okay to make commissions.

Really.

18. ANSWER: B

WHY: arbitrage is completely legal, unless you do it the way "arbitrageur" Ivan Boesky did it—by lying, cheating, and deceiving.

19. ANSWER: D

WHY: it's really the only answer choice that makes sense, right? The Administrator grants licenses—they don't supervise reps and settle customer disputes.

20. ANSWER: B

WHY: lots of broker's assistants get their licenses these days. That way the broker has more time to play golf with the rich clients, and the assistant can do all the work for 1/10 the pay.

21. ANSWER: A

WHY: if you have discretion, you are authorized to buy and sell what's appropriate for your customer. If you buy or sell what is inappropriate, they call it an unauthorized trade. You might have thought it was fraudulent, but that just means your definition of "fraud" at this point is too wide. Don't worry, it will be fine-tuned as you work through this meticulous, yea, laborious material.

22. ANSWER: A

WHY: you had to be tempted with A, right? Hope you didn't talk yourself out of an easy answer.

Hate it when that happens.

By the way, don't feel bad if you miss these questions. Sometimes I miss them—and I'm the guy who wrote the questions.

That's how tricky some of these things are—seriously. The traps are very effective at misleading you. Kind of funny that a test that tries to bring home the point that you can't deceive or mislead your clients goes out of its way to deceive and mislead you with tricky questions.

Oh well. We're on their turf, so let's play their game by their rules.

And walk away with lots of our money once the exam is behind us.

23. ANSWER: A

WHY: what are "all facts" about a security? Do you have to tell the customer that the bond certificates will be printed using Arial 12-point font? Does he need to know the paper will be coated or matte? Should you tell him the middle name of the transfer agent?

Only material (relevant, important) facts need to be disclosed.

I wish I could tell the people who sit next to me on the El that, but that's another matter.

24. ANSWER: C

WHY: choice "C" states exactly how an IA should approach the issue of taking custody of client money/securities. The Administrator hates the words "approved" and "certified" as much as the SEC does. If you have any doubts, put up a billboard by O'Hare or Midway with the slogan, "Approved to Sell Investment Advice in Illinois by Jesse White" right after you pass the Series 65.

25. ANSWER: C

WHY: the phrase "riskless security" is an oxymoron, like "jumbo shrimp." All securities have some type of risk. Treasuries have no default risk, but if rates go up, their prices go down. The T-bill would have less of that risk than the T-note, T-bond, or STRIP, but the risk still needs to be disclosed to an investor. In choice "D" the rep is selling dividends, a no-no. You can pitch a security because it pays regular dividends. But you can't pitch it for the upcoming dividend itself. The investor might do just as well to wait a few days and buy the shares for less, also avoiding the taxation of the dividend.

26. ANSWER: B

WHY: advisers don't have joint accounts with their customers, and you can't share per transaction—that's the whole point. They don't want agents going "halvsies" with their clients on a trade. Usually, you'd like to see a proportional sharing arrangement, but with an immediate family member, that's not such a big thing.

Notice how even the right answer can still leave you with a bad feeling. Welcome to the Series 65/66.

27. ANSWER: D

WHY: never combine capital gains with dividend/income distributions when calculating yield. Capital gains is part of total return. Yield is just the dividends divided by the NAV.

28. ANSWER: D

WHY: I don't see any problem here, do you? The agent is registered in the customer's state. The revenue bond doesn't have to be registered because it's exempt.

29. ANSWER: C

WHY: misleading and real dumb.

30. ANSWER: C

WHY: don't highlight or alter the preliminary prospectus.

31. ANSWER: B

WHY: don't promise a specific result to a client. You can't guarantee a customer a profit or guarantee them against a loss.

Nor would you want to.

32. ANSWER: C

WHY: tell the customer she's nuts, but no reason to get the authorities involved.

33. ANSWER: C

WHY: there was no securities act passed in 1929 that I know of. And if there was, I still don't care.

34. ANSWER: C

WHY: Treasury securities will pay the interest and principal, so there's no default risk. But their price will drop if interest rates go up suddenly. In fact, a 30-year Treasury bond's price would be hit harder than a corporate bond maturing in 10 years. Corporate bonds have more default risk than Treasury debt, but interest-rate risk is always greater on long-term bonds of any issuer. If you needed to liquidate your T-bonds for an emergency, you could easily get back less than you paid for them, so people can and have lost money on Treasuries before, I guess. Which is pretty sad if you think about it—to lose money on something with no default risk.

Oh well. No need to rub it in.

35. ANSWER: D

WHY: just look for the longest maturity—that's the bond with the most interest rate risk. It will shoot up higher when rates drop, and drop faster when rates shoot up.

Trust me.

Or, send an email if you need more details.

As if you might crave more details at this point. ☺

36. ANSWER: B

WHY: debentures are corporate bonds, which are more subject to default risk than munibonds. And both are more susceptible to default than Treasuries.

37. ANSWER: D

WHY: at least quarterly, and if there's been any activity in the account, better make it monthly.

38. ANSWER: B

WHY: money managers, called "investment advisers" on the exam, get a % of the assets. It's a great way to motivate them and align their interests with those of their client. Verbal contracts are no good, because advisory contracts are way too complicated for that. Not that verbal contracts are ever a real good idea, but, believe it or not, the Uniform Prudent Investors Act mentions that there could be such a thing as a verbal trust agreement.

Whatever. Advisory contracts need to be in writing. That way when you lose 75% of your client's assets, it will make arbitration much easier for all parties involved.

39. ANSWER: C

WHY: "not exempt" means "not excused," and no one is excused from anti-fraud regulations. GE doesn't have to file advertising materials with the states, but if anybody does anything funny in the state of IL, they can get in trouble by the state of IL, just like so many firms on Wall Street recently got in trouble with the state regulator of New York.

40. ANSWER: B

WHY: painful, huh? Technically, choices C and D are "true," except that they imply it's only fraudulent to omit material facts in those particular cases. The statement in choice B is irrefutable. Doesn't matter who the customer is or what the security is—omitting or misstating material facts in the offer or sale of a security is fraudulent. Only choice B makes that point. And, if you think A, C, or D is true, which one do you pick?

You can't—so you pick the right answer, B.

41. ANSWER: C

WHY: no waivers allowed, and if you try to create one, it won't be recognized in a court of law, other than something for the judge and bailiff to snicker at during recess.

42. ANSWER: C

WHY: nothing wrong with soliciting orders for registered securities, so eliminate "I", which leaves you with C or D. Pretty clear that it's "C" once you do that.

Of course "exempt" securities are "unregistered," since "exempt" means "don't gotta register."

43. ANSWER: A

WHY: the wife would have to grant him that power or authority with a "power of attorney." The customer doesn't have to sign the new account form.

44. ANSWER: C

WHY: good one to memorize. Also a Series 7 question.

45. ANSWER: C

WHY: all persons file a consent to service of process, and many state-registered advisers have custody. Once you make those two judgments, you can eliminate any choice with a "I" or a "IV" in it. And that would leave you with just one answer, the right one.

46. ANSWER: C

WHY: which name would be the most misleading?

47. ANSWER: C

WHY: the IA can't advise both sides of the transaction, any more than a lawyer can represent the husband and the wife in divorce court. The IA needs to make prior disclosure and once a year send out a statement to clients totaling all the purchases and sales they made as "agency cross transactions." Why? Wouldn't you start to wonder why you were talked into a large number of agency cross transactions? Could it have been, pray tell, that the IA liked the commissions they were getting brokering the trade whether it was a good deal for their advisory client or not?

Hmm. Curious, indeed.

48. ANSWER: D

WHY: only D makes the statement clearly and irrefutably. The other three make it sound as if it's only bad when you deceive certain customers.

49. ANSWER: B

WHY: it's misleading and wrong. SIPC covers broker-dealer failure/missing assets. FDIC-insured means your bank CD can't lose value. A stock that goes to zero isn't covered by SIPC or FDIC or anybody.

50. ANSWER: B

WHY: you're getting in front of the order to make an easy profit—that's called frontrunning and it's definitely prohibited.

51. ANSWER: B

WHY: that's just the legal definition of offer versus sale.

52. ANSWER: A

WHY: dead—minor—mentally incompetent. Everybody else is a legal person.

53. ANSWER: B

WHY: a retirement plan is not a security. You buy securities within your retirement plan.

54. ANSWER: D

WHY: a retirement plan is not a security. Securities are purchased within a retirement plan.

55. ANSWER: D

WHY: if they're in the state, they basically have to register. If they're not in the state, they can do business with as many institutional investors as they want, like the firm in choice "D." But they can only do business with 5 non-institutional investors—not 7, like the firm in choice "A."

High-net-worth individuals aren't institutions. They're just rich.

56. ANSWER: C

WHY: only the bank, of these four choices, is specifically excluded from the definition. If a broker-dealer is compensated for their advice, they are an IA. But if they don't, they're not. SEC Release IA-1092 mentioned financial planners and sports agents as folks who actually are investment advisers, even if they fail to realize or admit that unfortunate fact.

57. ANSWER: C

WHY: they only want to regulate those who sell the services of the firm to the client, make or give recommendations to the client, or supervise those who do. Who cares about the person doing the filing—if they're sloppy, we'll just punish the firm, anyway, the folks we want to regulate.

58. ANSWER: D

WHY: broker (for the accounts of others), dealer (for its own account). Broker-dealer.

59. ANSWER: C

WHY: the word "secondary" and "non-issuer" are synonymous. In the secondary market, the proceeds do not go to the issuer. That happens in the primary market.

60. ANSWER: D

WHY: an economist? That would make too much sense. The "e" is for engineer.

61. ANSWER: C

WHY: many sports agents actually do end up being defined as investment advisers and hassled accordingly.

62. ANSWER: B

WHY: memorization point.

63. ANSWER: D

WHY: she represents an exempt issuer in an exempt transaction. Not an agent. Not gonna sit for some silly test like this one.

64. ANSWER: B

WHY: if you moved out of the state and never returned their requests to renew your driver's license, they would just cancel it. Same with a securities license. You're not in trouble. You are just, apparently, no longer in need of your license. So it's canceled.

65. ANSWER: B

WHY: it's just like a cosigner. When a parent cosigns for an automobile loan, the bank could still suffer a default. But they definitely sleep better at night knowing the parent's signature is on the document rather than just the kid's all by itself.

66. ANSWER: B

WHY: she was an agent if she got commissions—remember, that transaction with employees is only exempt if the individual does not get commissions. So, the issuer, the agent, and the new broker-dealer all notify the state. Notice of termination from the issuer—notice of the new hire from the new broker-dealer. And the agent, as always, has to let the state know where he/she is or is no longer working.

67. ANSWER: B

WHY: if your advisory business is changing from a partnership to a corporation, you may register the new entity, even before it is in existence. There is no fee to pay if there is still an unexpired portion left on your registration—remember that registrations of legal persons expire on December 31st, unless properly renewed. If it's July, there would be several months left on the registration, which could be used by the new entity.

68. ANSWER: C

WHY: the USA gives the state Administrator the authority to set minimum net capital requirements for firms, based on the risks inherent with their activities. In other words, firms that do lots of underwriting and trading for their own account might need higher net capital than firms that simply broker trades for customers. But, the Administrator does not have to do this, and he may NOT have higher requirements than those set by the "feds" at the SEC. Firms with custody and discretion must maintain a certain minimum net capital, but they're not the only firms that have net capital requirements. By the way, firms with custody need at least $35,000 net capital, and firms with only discretion need $10,000. If they don't have that, they buy surety bonds in $5,000 increments, rounded up to the next $5,000 increment.

I'm confident that the exam will not get this detailed, unless it does.

69. ANSWER: C

WHY: firms have net capital requirements, not individuals. If an agent has discretion over the account, the firm will need to have him/her bonded, but that's a slightly different—even if related—matter. Fidelity/surety bonds would protect against the rare case where an agent accidentally walks out of the firm with $10,000 of bearer bonds on his way to the racetrack.

It happens.

70. ANSWER: D

WHY: agents, IARs, broker-dealers, advisers, and the issuers of securities file a consent to service of process when they register with the state. Wouldn't make sense to file one when you're suing one of those persons— the person you're suing has filed one with the Administrator so that you can serve court papers on the Administrator rather than trying to find the suddenly hard-to-find person you're trying to sue.

71. ANSWER: C

WHY: IAs are fiduciaries. A broker-dealer or agent would only be a fiduciary if they had discretion over an account.

72. ANSWER: C

WHY: where's the exemption for GE preferred stock? It's not commercial paper (exempt security), and it's not an exempt transaction. GE is not an exempt issuer, right? In fact, they're a non-exempt issuer. So, the individual would be an agent and would have to register after sitting for some silly test like this one.

73. ANSWER: D

WHY: basically, the only issuers who file with the states are the ones who get no exemption from the SEC or don't trade on a recognized exchange, like NYSE, regionals such as the Chicago Stock Exchange, AMEX, or NASDAQ. The "bulletin board" and the "pink sheet" stocks are the ones stuck registering at the state level.

74. ANSWER: B

WHY: whole life isn't a security. You wouldn't have to register a whole life policy with a securities regulator any more than you would register a bicycle with those folks.

75. ANSWER: D

WHY: she is, literally, representing an investment adviser...investment adviser representative.

76. ANSWER: C

WHY: if you chose any of the other three, take a second and ask yourself why you did that.

     Don't do that.

77. ANSWER: D

WHY: a bank (not a bank holding company like Citigroup or BankOne) is an exempt issuer—their bank securities are exempt securities. So, if an individual represents a bank, he/she is NOT an agent.

     Don't misunderstand this—it doesn't mean banks are in some wild west atmosphere. Just the opposite. They already have plenty of bank regulators breathing down their necks: FRB, FDIC, Comptroller of the Currency. Securities regulators don't want to regulate banks and insurance companies, since there are already plenty of bank and insurance regulators. Instead, they want to regulate securities. Which is why they call themselves "securities regulators."

78. ANSWER: C

WHY: your firm can be just a broker-dealer, only an IA, or both. But if the Administrator doesn't think you have any business being in the advisory business, he/she/they can condition your registration as a broker-dealer on the understanding that you won't try to act as an adviser. In other words, if a broker-dealer applies for an IA license, they don't end up losing their broker-dealer license if the Administrator doesn't want them in the IA business. That would be like applying for a promotion and getting fired if somebody else gets it.

79. ANSWER: D

WHY: if you included "consent to service of process," remember that it's the other way around—a broker-dealer, IA, IAR, or agent would provide that document to the Administrator when first registering in the state.

80. ANSWER: A

WHY: memorize and move on.

81. ANSWER: C

WHY: memorize and keep moving.

82. ANSWER: D

WHY: they can't issue injunctions or sentence folks to prison. Courts can do that, not the Administrator. What can the Administrator do to you? Take away your license and make your life miserable, that's all.

83. ANSWER: B

WHY: if you were tempted by "C" or "D," you were confusing the criminal statute of limitations with the civil statute of limitations.

84. ANSWER: C

WHY: if the client knew about it for more than two years, it's too late to sue. And, even if they didn't find out about it, after three years it's too late. So, the exam might say, "two years from discovery or three years from occurrence, whichever comes first."

85. ANSWER: D

WHY: if they didn't give you a chance to gain experience, you'd never get a chance to gain experience.

86. ANSWER: C

WHY: both withdrawals and cancellations are "non-punitive" Administrative orders. The word "non-punitive" means "no punishment."

87. ANSWER: D

WHY: heck, even Oracle, with about $7 billion in cash, has never paid a dividend, and they're a NASDAQ stock. Some companies pay 'em, some don't. Reinvesting earnings back into the company can boost your stock price, which is maybe just as good as paying out dividends in terms of helping the investor.

Or not.

88. ANSWER: C

WHY: memorize and keep moving.

89. ANSWER: C

WHY: like most of the phrases in this material, just break down the words: if you give your consent to let the Administrator receive service of court process papers on your behalf…that would be called a "consent to service of process." If the act is designed to keep securities laws uniform, we call it the "Uniform Securities Act." If the individual represents an investment adviser, we call her an "investment adviser representative."

Not many in the securities industry start out in advertising, as you may have guessed.

90. ANSWER: B

WHY: I'm not sure why anyone cares, and I don't care to know. It might be on the test, so be ready for a question on it. Also remember that if the change in partnership structure is due to partners with a minority interest, that is not considered "assignment of contract."

Again, I'm not sure why anyone would have thought it was, and I don't care enough to track it down.

91. ANSWER: C

WHY: memorize it. If the Administrator intends to suspend your license, you will receive a notice of opportunity for a hearing by registered/certified mail. If you're smart enough to request the hearing, you'll get one within 15 days. If you lose the hearing—and you most likely will—the order against you will be entered. You can now appeal to the appropriate court within 60 days.

92. ANSWER: C

WHY: because of NSMIA, wherever federal and state law conflict, the feds trump the state.

Shocking, isn't it?

93. ANSWER: D

WHY: T-notes pay interest every six months, which would presumably be reinvested into new T-notes. What if rates are down at that point?

That's the reinvestment risk, which would be avoided by zero coupons, STRIPS, Treasury receipts, and the like. They don't pay an income stream— you just get back a higher par value than you paid.

94. ANSWER: C

WHY: a good test taker would see two opposites such as "buy" versus "sell" Treasuries and conclude that it must be one or the other. In other words, a good test-taker starts out by doubling her odds from 25% to 50%. If the FOMC buys Treasuries, they push interest rates down and stimulate the economy. That would worsen inflation, not fight it.

95. ANSWER: C

WHY: a good test taker would see two opposites such as "put buyers" and "put sellers" and conclude it must be one of the two. In an option contract, the buyer and the seller have opposite bets.

96. ANSWER: D

WHY: dividends are up to the Board. They aren't an obligation the way bond interest is. And, you can't convert a non-convertible security.

97. ANSWER: A

WHY: you knew it had to be either the call writer or the call buyer, since they have opposite opinions of the market's direction.

98. ANSWER: A

WHY: "basis" is yield to maturity. If the yield dropped from 7.10% to 4.35%, which way did the price go?
    Up.
    Capital gain—she bought low and sold high.

99. ANSWER: D

WHY: stock is equity; bonds are not.

100. ANSWER: A

WHY: when rates are high, lock them in with the longest-term bond available. You'll get the high coupon rates for longer, and the market price (should you care to sell) will rise faster on your long-term bond.

101. ANSWER: B

WHY: Ba would be below investment grade. Read the questions carefully!

102. ANSWER: A

WHY: $1,000 divided by $20 = 50. 50 times $30 = $1,500.

103. ANSWER: A

WHY: you have the right to maintain your proportional ownership. Rights, stock rights, or subscription rights are three names for the same thing.

104. ANSWER: D

WHY: increase spending, hand out contracts for the Department of Defense, and let Boeing and other defense contractors start hiring folks. Pay technology companies to upgrade computers for the Social Security Administration. There are lots of ways politicians can spend our tax dollars, some of which actually help.

105. ANSWER: C

WHY: because.

106. ANSWER: C

WHY: NASDAQ is the main part of the OTC market, which is called a "negotiated market" by regulators who haven't traded a stock since the first Nixon administration.

107. ANSWER: B

WHY: the market maker bids this much if you want to sell to him and asks you to pay this much if you want to buy from him.

108. ANSWER: C

WHY: the customer receives whatever the market is bidding for his closed-end fund, which could be at, below, or above the NAV.

109. ANSWER: C

WHY: a very tiny % of funds actually can sell short, but since the overwhelming majority can't, the test could say that mutual funds don't sell short.

110. ANSWER: B

WHY: if the POP is below the NAV, it's a closed-end fund. You can't buy open-end funds below the NAV.

111. ANSWER: D

WHY: maximum income = corporate bonds. High-yield corporates are too risky for this investor, so we'll put her into the investment-grade corporates. Open-end funds tell us absolutely nothing about what type of investments are IN the fund, and money market will never produce "maximum" current income.

112. ANSWER: A

WHY: you don't get "growth" from a money market mutual fund. You get current short-term interest rates and nothing more.

113. ANSWER: B

WHY: the contributions were made pre-tax (tax deductible), so all the money coming out will be taxed at the teacher's ordinary income rate.

114. ANSWER: B

WHY: no cost base in a qualified plan. You just get taxed.

115. ANSWER: D

WHY: if you have earned income, you can contribute to a traditional IRA. The contributions might not be fully or even partially tax-deductible, but you can still make them.

116. ANSWER: B

WHY: you probably know that from personal experience.

117. ANSWER: A

WHY: memorize and keep moving.

118. ANSWER: B

WHY: lawyers, accountants, teachers, and engineers are excluded from the definition of "investment adviser" only if their advice is incidental to their practice. If they start acting like IAs, then they're IAs and have to register.

119. ANSWER: C

WHY: believe it or not, they pay people to come up with such calculations. They even give egghead professors grants to study such nonsense.

But, as always, I'll keep my opinions to myself.

120. ANSWER: C

WHY: memorize and pray they don't ask you to calculate net present value on the exam.

I don't see why they would do that, unless they've completely lost their minds.

121. ANSWER: B

WHY: it the customer gets $70 from the munibond after zero taxes, how much would a corporate bond have to pay in order to leave him with $70? $100/10% nominal.

This investor would get $100 and share $30 of it with their rich uncle, Uncle Sam, leaving the investor with $70.

We don't factor in state taxes for these questions.

122. ANSWER: B

WHY: sounds like they're allocating money to different assets, right?

123. ANSWER: B

WHY: no one can consistently beat an index because of the transaction costs of actively trading stocks. So, buy a low-cost index fund that will match the index. In other words, if you can't beat the index, join it.

124. ANSWER: A

WHY: Keynesians advocate government intervention, unlike "laissez-faire" economists, who advocate that government get out of the way, and "supply side economists," who advocate cutting taxes no matter what. "Voodoo economics" was what the first George Bush called Ronald Reagan's economic plan. Showing a thick skin and a strong sense of humor, Reagan subsequently made Bush his running mate and vice president, frequently leaving little dolls with pins through the eyes on Vice President Bush's desk, a joke Mr. Bush felt was funnier the first 800 times it was played.

125. ANSWER: B

WHY: Charles Laffer is credited with the "Laffer Curve," which showed that the ideal tax rate was 20%. Even if that sounded like a lower rate of taxation, it would end up pulling in more tax revenues because it would stimulate the economy so much that the tax cuts would "pay for themselves" as incomes and stock prices rose, increasing income and capital gains tax receipts for the government.

Whenever you hear a politician say that a tax cut will pay for itself, you're listening to a "supply sider."

126. ANSWER: C

WHY: it went up 24% over the holding period.

127. ANSWER: B

WHY: beta = risk. If you factor in beta, you're using "risk adjusted return."

128. ANSWER: D

WHY: the lower the rating, the higher the yield.

129. ANSWER: D

WHY: the exam will say that common stock is least susceptible to a change in interest rates, which seems about right to me. The other three are fixed-income securities, so a change in rates always makes that fixed income payment either more or less attractive. Common stock has no set rate of return.

130. ANSWER: B

WHY: protect = buy. Short stock is bearish; hedge by buying the bullish position. Or, think of it this way: you have to buy back the stock you sold short. You can let Mr. Market name the price, or you can name the price by buying a call.

131. ANSWER: A

WHY: have you noticed that many test questions are the mental equivalent of the "two-step" dance? Step one, what the heck is an inverted yield curve? That's when rates on short-term debt are suddenly higher than on long-term. Step two, which one of the four choices has the shortest term? T-bills.

Process these questions and you will win the first time out.

132. ANSWER: B

WHY: not all CPAs are excluded—just the ones who aren't really acting as IAs.

CFPs get no special break; in fact, SEC Release IA-1092 went out of its way to bring them, along with many sports agents, into the happy family of regulated IAs. High-net-worth individuals are not institutions, even though many expect to be treated as such.

133. ANSWER: B

WHY: what is this, an IQ test? Sort of.

134. ANSWER: A

WHY: holding period return is simply the return somebody gets on a stock. There is no adjusting to do for inflation, risk, time, taxes, etc.

135. ANSWER: C

WHY: the PRICE is 10 times as high as the EARNINGS. P to E.

What about the dividend yield?

That was placed in your way as a roadblock.

You're welcome.

Online Updates

PRACTICE FINAL 3—SERIES 65

1. **Which of the following statements is true concerning investment advisers with custody of client securities and/or funds?**
   A. This practice is illegal in all cases
   B. The adviser must send to clients semi-annually an itemized statement showing the funds and securities in the adviser's custody and all debits, credits, and transactions over such period
   C. At least once per year the adviser must schedule an inspection by a CPA or public accountant, who will file a statement with the Administrator promptly afterward
   D. Unless the Administrator specifically prohibits custody of client funds/securities, the adviser may take custody of client funds/securities if written notice is sent to the Administrator

PLEASE VISIT WWW.PASSTHE65.COM FOR ADDITIONAL PRACTICE QUESTIONS AND FOR ANY UPDATES THAT MAY HAVE BEEN ADDED TO THE MATERIAL.

2. **Which of the following are true statements?**
   I. an adviser with custody of client funds/securities must maintain minimum net worth of $35,000
   II. an adviser with custody of client funds/securities whose minimum net worth falls below $35,000 must post bonds in the amount of the net worth deficiency rounded up to the nearest $5,000
   III. an adviser with discretion over a client's account who does not have custody of the client's securities/funds must maintain minimum net capital of $10,000
   IV. An adviser who accepts prepayment of >$500 six or more months in advance must at all times maintain positive net worth

   A. I, II, III, IV
   B. I, III
   C. II, IV
   D. I, III, IV

3. **The DJIA (Dow Jones Industrial Average) is:**
   I. an un-weighted average
   II. a price-weighted average
   III. 30 stocks, mostly industrial companies
   IV. 100 industrial stocks

   A. I, III
   B. I, IV
   C. II, III
   D. II, IV

4. **XYZ common has a yield of 2.95%, EPS of $2.50 and a PE ratio of 10. Its market price is**
   A. 25¢ per share
   B. $25.00 per share
   C. undeterminable
   D. $29.50 per share

5. **If a trader can see the inside market, as well as quotes from all market makers in a particular stock, he has access to**
   A. NASDAQ Level 2
   B. the OTC Bulletin Board
   C. NASDAQ Level 1
   D. inside information

6. **Now that XYZ has filed an S1 with the SEC for a new issue of common stock, which of the following may a registered rep do?**
   A. confirm sales to certain qualified clients
   B. obtain the SEC's approval of the issue
   C. solicit indications of interest
   D. none of the above

7. **The Securities Exchange Act of 1934**
   A. prohibits the use and dissemination of inside information
   B. determines the contents of a prospectus
   C. details approval process of securities registered with the SEC
   D. is the first piece of federal legislation passed on the securities markets

8. **When a customer sells restricted stock via Form 144, she may sell the greater of 1% of the company's outstanding shares or the average weekly trading volume over the four most recent weeks. And, she may sell this amount over which of the following periods?**
   A. 5 days
   B. 5 consecutive trading days
   C. 1 year
   D. 90 days

9. **A customer tells a cold-calling registered representative she is not interested in this offer and does not wish to be contacted again. The Telephone Consumer Protection Act of 1991 states that**
   A. The rep's immediate supervisor must contact the prospect to apologize and offer compensation
   B. The rep's immediate supervisor may contact the prospect to apologize and offer compensation
   C. The rep may send a fax next time, but no more phone calls for 90 days
   D. The firm may not contact the prospect

10. **The Chief Financial Officer of a large, publicly traded company tells a member of his country club that his company is about to be acquired by one of the largest international conglomerates in the world. The country club member astutely purchases convertible debentures and call options on the CFO's company's stock. Who, if anyone, has violated insider trading rules?**
    A. neither has violated the rules
    B. both have violated the rules
    C. only the CFO violated the rules
    D. only the buyer of the securities violated the rules

11. **Which of the following is the least suitable investment for a Traditional IRA?**
    A. Municipal Bonds
    B. Corporate Bonds
    C. Treasury Bonds
    D. Treasury Notes

12. **Which two of the following would be defined as investment advisers under the USA?**
    I.   an economics professor with an active consulting business providing regular advice to pension funds as to which money managers to retain for the fund
    II. a federal or state-chartered bank
    III. a property & casualty insurance company
    IV. a certified financial planner who puts together plans for clients and only receives commissions on the products sold when the client implements the plan

    A. I, II
    B. I, IV
    C. II, III
    D. II, IV

13. **What is the main difference between variable annuities and mutual funds?**
    A. sales loads
    B. tax deferral
    C. stocks vs. bonds
    D. cash vs. bonds

14. **All of the following aspects are discretionary except**
    A. security purchased
    B. amount of security purchased
    C. whether purchased or sold
    D. time of day

15. **Two consecutive quarters of GDP decline signal a**
    A. depression
    B. recession
    C. double-dip recession
    D. fed short wave

16. **Concerning a new issue of securities, the SEC**
    A. guarantees the accuracy of the information disclosed
    B. assesses the merits of the security
    C. approves the security for sale
    D. none of the above

17. **All of the following are tax preference items for AMT except:**
    A. accelerated depreciation
    B. MACRS
    C. straight-line depreciation
    D. interest from private purpose munibonds

18. **Denise Williams deposited $100,000 into her Keogh plan, which has now grown tax deferred to a value of $150,000. At age 53, Denise withdraws $50,000. What are the tax and penalty consequences?**
    A. none
    B. ordinary income on the $50,000
    C. ordinary income plus $5,000 penalty
    D. capital gains rate on $50,000 plus $5,000 penalty

19. **The FOMC is selling Treasury securities to certain primary dealers. What effect will this have on the bond market as a whole?**
    A. coupon rates on new issues will fall
    B. prices on outstanding bonds will fall
    C. yields on outstanding bonds will fall
    D. none of the above

20. **All of the following are leading indicators except**
    A. number of new unemployment claims
    B. inventory
    C. housing starts
    D. S&P 500

21. **Which of the following is a true statement?**
    A. long-term interest rates are more volatile than short-term
    B. short-term bond prices are more volatile than long-term
    C. long-term bond prices are less volatile than short-term
    D. long-term bond prices are more volatile than short-term

22. **The FRB has just raised the reserve requirement. What will be the effect on the bond market?**
    A. bond prices will rise
    B. bond yields will fall
    C. bond yields will rise
    D. coupons on new issues will fall

23. **Your clients are married, in their early 50s, and are planning to retire in the next 10 years. They would both like to reduce their workloads by about 40%, so they need supplemental income but also capital appreciation. Which of the following funds would you most likely recommend?**
    A. money market
    B. small cap
    C. balanced fund
    D. index fund

24. **The Securities Exchange Act of 1934 covers all of the following except**
    A. short sales
    B. 10-Q reporting
    C. 10-K reporting
    D. new issues

25. **All of the following represent benefits to limited partners except**
    A. depreciation
    B. appreciation
    C. depreciation recapture
    D. accelerated depreciation

26. **Losses from DPPs may be used to offset**
    A. ordinary income only
    B. portfolio income only
    C. passive income only
    D. all of the above

27. All of the following are exempt from the Securities Act of 1933 except
    A. bank securities
    B. commercial paper
    C. municipal bonds
    D. common stock

28. All of the following require power of attorney except
    A. buy 1,000 shares of an insurance company
    B. buy as much GE as I can afford today
    C. buy 1,000 shares of GE today
    D. buy insurance company stocks and REITs today

29. Issuers of which of the following securities are exempt from the antifraud provisions of the Securities Exchange Act of 1934?
    A. corporate debentures
    B. common stock
    C. municipal bonds
    D. none of the above

30. All of the following factors may justify a higher markup on a security except:
    A. price dealer paid for the security
    B. dollar amount of the trade
    C. price of the security
    D. whether stock or bond

31. ABC Fund's NAV was $9.50 at the start of the year. The fund paid a dividend distribution of $1.00 and a capital gains distribution of $1.50. What is the fund's total return for the year if the NAV (ending) is $9.00?
    A. 10.0%
    B. 21.0%
    C. 11.1%
    D. 10.52%

32. All of the following are qualified plans except
    A. 401K
    B. 403b
    C. Defined benefit
    D. Deferred compensation

33. All of the following are funded with pre-tax contributions except
    A. Keogh
    B. HR 10
    C. Roth IRA
    D. 403b

34. All of the following are funded with after-tax contributions except
    A. non-qualified variable annuity
    B. Roth IRA
    C. 529 Plan
    D. 401K

35. **All of the following plans pass investment risk to the participant except:**
   A. 401K
   B. defined benefit
   C. 403b
   D. defined contribution

36. **All of the following measures are anti-inflationary except**
   A. raising taxes
   B. decreasing government spending
   C. increasing the reserve requirement
   D. buying T-bills from primary dealers

37. **If the American dollar declines relative to the Japanese yen, all of the following statements are true except**
   A. American tourists to Japan will find their vacation dollars do not go as far as hoped
   B. American imports from Japan would be more competitive with domestically produced goods by American manufacturers
   C. A current trade deficit for the Americans would probably improve
   D. American exports to Japan would be more competitive with domestically produced goods from Japanese manufacturers

38. **The strategy of diversification is used to combat which of the following risks?**
   A. mortality
   B. liquidity
   C. market
   D. non-systematic

39. **Hannah Reynolds purchased 100 XYZ @17 back in 1979. In 2003, Hannah donates the stock to a charitable organization with XYZ @25. She may take a deduction of**
   A. $25,000
   B. 70% of $25,000
   C. $1,700
   D. $2,500

40. **Holders of common stock vote on all of the following except**
   A. mergers
   B. acquisitions
   C. stock splits
   D. stock dividends

41. **If the stock price drops 20% and the dividend paid drops 17%, what will happen to the dividend yield?**
   A. Remain stable
   B. Increase
   C. Decrease
   D. Fluctuate inversely to parity

42. **How could a corporation benefit by attaching warrants to debenture offerings?**
   A. it allows them to offer much higher nominal yields
   B. it allows them to offer lower nominal yields
   C. it is anti-dilutive
   D. it indicates a more sophisticated and, therefore, solid capital structure

43. A member bank borrows from the Federal Reserve Board at which interest rate?
   A. Federal Funds Rate
   B. LIBOR
   C. Discount Rate
   D. Repo plus 50 basis points

44. If the yield curve were inverted, prices of short-term debt securities would be
   A. low
   B. high
   C. unchanged
   D. at parity

45. When preparing the income statement, a corporation would deduct all of the following items pre-tax except
   A. Bond interest
   B. Salaries
   C. Depreciation
   D. Dividends

46. ABC common stock appreciated 8% over a 6-month period. What is the annualized return?
   A. 8%
   B. 8.5%
   C. 16%
   D. 6%

47. ABC and XYZ are two common stocks with a correlation of -.5. If ABC rises 10%, you would expect XYZ to
   A. remain stable
   B. rise 10%
   C. fall 5%
   D. rise 5%

48. Which of the following investment choices is most attractive?
   A. 8% predicted return, standard deviation 5.5
   B. 8% predicted return, standard deviation 6.0
   C. 8% predicted return, standard deviation 6.5
   D. 9% predicted return, standard deviation 5.0

49. An investment with a 50% chance of appreciating 10% and a 20% chance of appreciating 15% has an expected return of
   A. 8%
   B. 25%
   C. 12.5%
   D. 15%

50. Discounting an investment's expected cash flows to present value determines
   A. Book value
   B. Book value per share
   C. Net present value
   D. Standard deviation

51. **Which of the following investors can best withstand a market correction?**
    A. older investor with high risk tolerance
    B. older investor with moderate risk tolerance
    C. younger investor with moderate risk tolerance
    D. younger investor with high risk tolerance

52. **Which of the following bonds has the highest duration?**
    A. 8% coupon, 20-year maturity
    B. 8% coupon, 30-year maturity
    C. 6% coupon, 20-year maturity
    D. 4% coupon, 30-year maturity

53. **Which of the following income statement items appears first?**
    A. Cost of Goods Sold
    B. Revenue
    C. Pre-Tax Income
    D. Preferred Dividends

54. **Which of the following ratios represents the most stringent measure of a corporation's solvency?**
    A. Current Ratio
    B. Quick Ratio
    C. Cash-to-current liabilities
    D. Cash-to-total liabilities

55. **Which of the following debt ratios indicates the most highly leveraged company?**
    A. 30%
    B. 40%
    C. 50%
    D. 65%

56. **What is a company's market capitalization?**
    A. Long-term debt minus cash
    B. Short-term debt plus cash and equivalents
    C. Share price times shares outstanding
    D. Long-term debt plus net worth

57. **Which of the following represents an asset on a corporate balance sheet?**
    A. Accrued taxes
    B. Goodwill
    C. Debentures
    D. Accrued wages

58. **Which of the following represents a liability on a corporate balance sheet?**
    A. Goodwill
    B. Plant, equipment
    C. Debentures
    D. Accounts receivable

59. Which of the following measures imports versus exports and also includes domestic investments in foreign securities versus foreign investments in domestic securities?
   A. Domestic ratio
   B. Xenophobic ratio
   C. Balance of trade
   D. Balance of payments

60. A rise in which of the following would compromise a company's gross margins?
   A. dividend payouts
   B. cost of goods sold
   C. revenues
   D. net worth

61. Which two of the following would cause a company's gross margins to improve?
   I. increased revenues
   II. decreased revenues
   III. increased cost of goods sold
   IV. decreased cost of goods sold

   A. I, III
   B. I, IV
   C. II, IV
   D. II, III

62. An investor is in the 28% marginal tax bracket. Therefore, a debenture yielding 10% would be equivalent to a general obligation bond yielding
   A. 7%
   B. 7.2%
   C. 12.4%
   D. 12.8%

63. Which of the following debt securities has the highest duration?
   A. T-bill
   B. T-note
   C. 30-year T-bond
   D. 30-year STRIP

64. If an investment returns 4% over Q1, what is the annualized rate of return?
   A. 12%
   B. 4%
   C. 16%
   D. 5%

65. Which of the following represents Standard & Poor's lowest investment-grade bond rating?
   A. AA
   B. Baa
   C. BBB-
   D. BB

66. Which of the following represent benefits of corporate bond ownership?
  I.   senior status in liquidation
  II. inflation protection
  III. capital appreciation
  IV. regular income payments

  A. I, II
  B. II, III
  C. I, IV
  D. II, IV

67. Which of the following represent benefits of owning equity securities?
  I.   voting rights
  II. status in liquidation
  III. capital appreciation
  IV. inflation protection

  A. I, II
  B. I, III
  C. III only
  D. I, III, IV

68. Which of the following represent benefits of owning money market mutual funds?
  I.   low volatility
  II. liquidity
  III. capital appreciation
  IV. growth

  A. I, II
  B. I, III
  C. II, III
  D. I, II, IV

69. Construction of a toll road or turnpike would most likely be financed by
  A. debentures
  B. general obligation bonds
  C. revenue bonds
  D. STRIPS

70. Which of the following bond issues requires voter approval?
  A. revenue
  B. general obligation
  C. T-bonds
  D. STRIPS

71. How are the expenses of a mutual fund expressed?
  A. as a quarterly dollar amount paid by each investor
  B. as a quarterly dollar amount paid by the average investor
  C. as a percentage of average net assets
  D. in terms of their standard deviation from a particular fund group

72. This class of mutual fund share has no front-end load. The sales charge declines gradually over time, and the annual expenses tend to be higher than they are for the front-end loaded shares. This describes a(an)
A. A share
B. B share
C. C share
D. I share

73. If an investor sells stock short, he could protect this position with a
A. short put
B. long call
C. short call
D. long put

74. What generally distinguishes an S-Corp from a C-Corp?
A. limited liability
B. profit motive
C. double taxation of dividends
D. sales loads

75. An investor bought shares of ABC when the market was: BID - $9.95 ASK - $10.00. Two years later, she sold the shares when the market was: BID - $12.00 ASK - $12.25. Therefore her
I.   cost basis is $9.95 per share
II.   cost basis is $10 per share
III. proceeds are $12 per share
IV.   proceeds are $12.25 per share

A. I, III
B. II, III
C. I, IV
D. II, IV

76. Which of the following persons is most likely an investment adviser?
A. A bank offering CDs insured by the FDIC
B. An attorney who collects a $200 fee once a year to educate an association on the benefits of equity investment
C. A certified financial planner who designs financial plans and only earns commissions when customers purchase VLI, variable annuities, and/or mutual funds
D. An individual representing a federal covered adviser

77. All of the following are fiduciaries except
A. Trustee
B. Pension fund manager
C. Investment adviser without discretion
D. Agent

78. **Within how many days will the SEC either grant registration to an advisory firm or begin proceedings to determine eligibility?**
    A. 10
    B. 30
    C. 45
    D. 90

79. **When do IAs file their annual updating amendment to renew their SEC registration?**
    A. at the start of each fiscal year
    B. at the start of each calendar year
    C. within 90 days of the end of each fiscal year
    D. within 30 days of the end of each fiscal year

80. **If an IA withdraws SEC registration, it will be effective**
    A. In 30 days
    B. In 60 days
    C. Upon acceptance by the IARD
    D. Retroactively

81. **All of the following statements are true concerning IA disclosure brochures except**
    A. must contain substantially identical information to ADV part 2
    B. may be a copy of ADV part 2
    C. must be delivered 48 hours before contract signing, or at the time of signing if the client has 5 days to cancel
    D. must be delivered to all clients

82. **Janet Johnson is a certified public accountant who also owns an investment advisory firm. She has earned her MBA as well as being certified by the College of Financial Planners. Janet may print all of the following initials after her name except**
    A. CPA
    B. MBA
    C. CFP
    D. RIA

83. **All of the following are allowable forms of soft-dollar compensation except**
    A. research reports
    B. clearing services
    C. custodial services
    D. office equipment

84. **Which of the following statements by a registered representative is accurate and permissible?**
    A. All mutual funds with 12b-1 fees are also "no load"
    B. If a mutual fund charges a 12b-1 fee, it cannot be referred to as "no load"
    C. This federal covered security is obviously safer than other securities, or they wouldn't have given it federal covered status
    D. A Treasury note has no default risk but does carry interest rate risk

85. **All of the following are prohibited practices except**
    A. a registered representative recommends a growth stock with an exceptionally high PE ratio to all 100 of her clients across the board
    B. a broker-dealer effects an opening transaction in a margin account one day before receiving a signed margin agreement from the customer
    C. a registered rep takes an order from a non-discretionary client's wife without 3rd-party trading authorization
    D. a broker-dealer buys REITs for a non-discretionary client before informing the client, because the investment is perfectly suitable

86. **XLY Broker-Dealers has been charging customers commissions and mark-ups that average 15% more than the industry average. What is true of this situation?**
    A. it is fraudulent and deceptive
    B. it is permissible with prior NASD-approval
    C. it is prohibited if deemed to be excessive and/or unreasonable
    D. all customers over the past 90 days are due full refunds, plus court costs, minus any income received from recommended purchases

87. **ABC Broker-Dealers charges 35% more than the industry average for collecting and transferring dividends and interest payments on behalf of clients. What is true of this practice?**
    A. it is perfectly acceptable, as these services are not covered by NASAA policy statements
    B. it is fraudulent
    C. firms may not charge excessive or inequitable fees for services performed, including these services
    D. it is prohibited to charge customers who have had accounts more than 12 months inequitable and/or excessive fees for such services

88. **When must a final prospectus be delivered to a client purchasing an IPO?**
    A. At the time payment is made
    B. No later than the due date for confirmation
    C. No later than T + 5
    D. Just before delivering the Red Herring

89. **TLC Broker-Dealers is a wholly owned subsidiary of General Electric, Inc. If TLC would like to sell shares in a private placement of GE stock**
    A. this is a fraudulent, unethical practice
    B. the Administrator must grant prior approval
    C. full disclosure must be provided to non-institutional buyers
    D. full disclosure must be provided to all buyers

90. **All of the following represent prohibited activities of investment advisers except**
    A. exercising any discretionary power in placing an order to purchase or sell securities for a client after receiving verbal authorization
    B. placing all client transactions through a broker-dealer that compensates the adviser with commissions without disclosing this arrangement to clients
    C. trading opposite of recommendations given to clients without disclosure
    D. revealing client affairs, transactions, account balances, etc., in the absence of a court order

91. **Investment advisers are expressly prohibited from engaging in all the following activities except**
    A. inducing clients to trade frequently
    B. inducing clients to engage in transactions that are excessive in size given the client's financial resources and risk tolerance
    C. recommending agency cross transactions to both sides of the transaction
    D. recommending tax-exempt revenue bonds to high-net-worth clients

92. **Which of the following is a true statement concerning reports and recommendations in the investment advisory business?**
    A. An adviser may not use published reports and/or statistical analyses provided by other sources when rendering investment advice
    B. An adviser may not use published reports and/or statistical analyses provided by other sources when rendering investment advice without disclosing the source to clients
    C. An adviser may not present a client with an investment recommendation prepared by someone else without disclosing the source to the client
    D. An adviser may provide clients with reports prepared by outside sources without disclosure for discretionary clients

93. **John Jacobs is an investment adviser who happens to hold 1,000,000 warrants on XYZ common stock. Whenever large numbers of purchase orders on XYZ hit the market, John notices that the stock tends to rise sharply. Therefore, John**
    A. must refrain from recommending XYZ
    B. must refrain from recommending XYZ to non-institutional clients
    C. must provide disclosure to clients on the potential conflict of interest
    D. may recommend XYZ freely, provided he rebates a reasonable percentage of the commissions to his clients

94. **In order to improve sales and customer satisfaction, QRZ Advisers have implemented a policy whereby clients are rebated 85% of their advisory fees whenever their accounts lose to the S&P 500 by more than 2 percentage points. What is true of this arrangement?**
    A. it is fraudulent
    B. it is prohibited
    C. it is allowable for clients with more than $25,000 under management
    D. it is permissible with prior approval from a principal

95. **All of the following statements are true of investment advisory contracts except**
    A. they must be in writing
    B. they must state that no assignment of contract can occur without client consent
    C. they must explain the basis for compensation
    D. they must disclose the results of the most recent inspection performed by the state

96. **Noting that advisory clients are increasingly demanding results, XYZ Advisers has drafted an agreement that allows clients to compensate the firm as a basis of capital appreciation above the rate of quarterly S&P 500 index appreciation. This type of waiver**
    A. is fraudulent
    B. is prohibited
    C. is permissible for clients with $10,000 or more under management
    D. is a prohibited practice known as "selling away"

97. Sarina Sanborn is an investment adviser set up as a sole proprietor. Sarina would like to share the gains and losses in client accounts. What is true of this situation?
    A. it is fraudulent
    B. Sarina must get the clients' written consent first
    C. Sarina must get the clients' written consent and the consent of SEC first
    D. this is prohibited

98. All the following activities are prohibited except
    A. sharing commissions with other agents at the firm
    B. pegging
    C. frontrunning
    D. indicating that an IA is certified by the Administrator

99. All of the following are prohibited activities except
    A. matched purchases
    B. arbitrage
    C. selling away
    D. front running

100. One of your customers is extremely persistent and perturbed. After sending several hostile letters to complain of your handling of the account, the customer refuses to return your next several phone calls. When you receive another angry letter, you decide to discard the letter as well as the others you have received. This practice
    A. is fraudulent
    B. is prohibited because all written customer complaints must be forwarded to the SEC within 5 business days
    C. is prohibited because all written customer complaints must be forwarded to the Administrator within 5 business days
    D. is prohibited because all written customer complaints must be brought to the attention of your employer

101. What is true of material facts?
    A. omitting or misstating them is unlawful and fraudulent
    B. they need not be disclosed to large, institutional clients
    C. the agent must choose which material facts to include and exclude from presentations to clients
    D. they must not be disseminated or acted upon

102. All of the following business practices are prohibited except
    A. frontrunning
    B. failing to state all facts about a security
    C. failing to state all material facts about a security
    D. recommending municipal bonds to a high-tax-bracket investor within a Keogh plan

103. Which of the following is true concerning criminal penalties under the USA?
    A. there is no statute of limitations for securities fraud
    B. the statute of limitations for securities fraud is 7 years
    C. the maximum penalty is 3 years in jail, $5,000 fine or both
    D. ignorance of the law/rule has no bearing in criminal proceedings

104. **All of the following are prohibited practices except**
   A. An investment adviser places 100% of an IPO allocation to its own account, even though the investment is suitable for several of the firm's clients
   B. An agent offers investment opportunities in her sister's new restaurant to several clients on her book of business without informing her employing broker-dealer
   C. An investment adviser takes custody of client funds in the absence of a rule against custody, informing the Administrator in writing
   D. An investment adviser representative tells a prospect that she has been approved by the Administrator to provide both technical and fundamental analysis on NYSE-listed securities

105. **Which of the following statements by a registered representative is permissible?**
   A. "Treasury STRIPS are riskless securities guaranteed by the U.S. Government."
   B. "Treasury Notes are riskless securities guaranteed by the U.S. Government."
   C. "If you invest in the fund right now, you can benefit by receiving the upcoming dividend."
   D. "Treasury Bills are guaranteed by the U.S. Government, but do retain interest rate risk."

106. **Which of the following represents an acceptable sharing arrangement with clients?**
   A. an investment adviser shares the gains and losses in a joint account with a client after receiving written client consent
   B. an investment representative, after receiving client consent and approval from the branch manager, establishes a joint account with an immediate family member and shares the gains/losses/appreciation 60/40
   C. an investment representative shares the gains and losses of each transaction within a discretionary account
   D. an investment representative shares the gains and losses of each transaction within a non-discretionary account

107. **In order for a registered representative to borrow money from a client**
   A. the client must sign a waiver
   B. the client must be a bank or lending institution
   C. the principal must sign off
   D. the Administrator must grant approval

108. **Which of the following are components of a mutual fund's total return calculation?**
   A. dividends distributed by the fund
   B. capital gains distributed by the fund
   C. growth in NAV
   D. all of the choices listed

109. **An investment representative is registered in State A. She sells an unregistered, exempt general obligation bond of State B to a customer who is a resident of State A. This activity**
   A. is prohibited
   B. is fraudulent, unless the client is accredited
   C. is prohibited without prior principal approval
   D. is acceptable

110. Last week you told a customer that reinvesting all dividend and capital gains distributions from the Hanover Conservative Income Fund will insure against a loss of principal. This statement is
    A. acceptable if prior principal approval has been granted
    B. a non sequitur
    C. misleading
    D. prohibited unless accompanied by a prospectus

111. All of the following are prohibited activities for agents except
    A. failing to state all material facts about a security to a customer
    B. misstating a material fact about a security to a customer
    C. soliciting orders for unregistered, non-exempt securities
    D. sharing commissions with registered agents working at a subsidiary of the employing broker-dealer

112. If a customer asks you to highlight the most important pages of the preliminary prospectus, you should
    A. forward the request to a supervisory analyst
    B. refuse to comply with this request
    C. have your highlights approved by a compliance officer
    D. immediately alert the Securities and Exchange Commission

113. Providing a fictitious quote to a customer is
    A. misleading and fraudulent
    B. a violation known as pegging
    C. a violation known as capping
    D. not prohibited for fictitious accounts established at the firm

114. Promising a client a 20% profit from an investment or their money back is
    A. allowable only with prior principal approval
    B. prohibited
    C. a violation referred to as matched purchases
    D. a violation referred to as frontrunning

115. One of your customers is a widow living on a modest fixed income. She calls one afternoon and insists that she needs to sell her Treasury notes and invest the money into a small cap value fund. What should you do?
    A. inform the NASD
    B. petition the appropriate court to schedule a hearing to determine mental competence
    C. tell the customer you feel the action is unsuitable and only execute the transactions after obtaining written acknowledgment that they are "unsolicited"
    D. inform the SEC

116. Which of the following would not represent an inappropriate recommendation?
    A. recommending growth stocks to investors with income as an objective
    B. recommending municipal bonds to low-tax-bracket investors
    C. recommending frequent trades to long-term investors
    D. recommending stocks on your broker-dealer's preferred list

117. **Why is churning a violation?**
     A. because the NASD mandates only 19 trades per week for non-institutional investors
     B. because the SEC allows only 11 trades per week for non-institutional investors
     C. because the practice yields commissions to agents and firms, often at the expense of customers
     D. because the Securities Act of 1921 defined it so

118. **Which of the following statements may an agent make to a customer concerning Treasury securities?**
     A. No one has ever lost money investing in Treasury notes and bonds
     B. No one can lose money investing in Treasury notes and bonds
     C. Treasury securities carry no default risk
     D. Treasury securities carry no market risk

119. **Which of the following securities is most susceptible to interest rate risk?**
     A. Phoenix, Arizona revenue bond maturing in '09
     B. ABC 6s debenture maturing in '11
     C. GNMA pass-through maturing in '13
     D. T-note maturing in '17

120. **Which of the following securities is probably most susceptible to default risk?**
     A. New York City general obligation bond maturing in '09
     B. XYZ 6s debenture maturing in '11
     C. GNMA pass-through maturing in '13
     D. T-bond maturing in '17

121. **Broker-dealers may charge customers reasonable fees for all the following services except**
     A. transferring dividends
     B. transferring bond interest
     C. safekeeping securities
     D. forwarding proxy statements

122. **All of the following represent prohibited practices for IAs except**
     A. entering into or renewing contracts that provide for compensation as a share of capital gains
     B. entering into or renewing contracts that provide for compensation as a percentage of total assets under management
     C. entering into or renewing contracts that provide for assignment of contract without client consent
     D. entering into verbal contracts with non-institutional clients

123. **An agent is making a sales presentation to a high-net-worth investor. The agent is convinced the particular growth stock is an excellent opportunity and perfectly suitable for the investor's objective of growth and relatively high risk tolerance. All of the following activities on the part of the agent would be prohibited except**
     A. Promising to repurchase the stock if it drops more than 10%
     B. Guaranteeing a specific result
     C. Omitting immaterial information
     D. Refusing to provide a prospectus or other disclosure document

124. Andy Ackerman has been soliciting and filling orders for retail customers even though he is not registered as an agent. What is true of this situation?
   A. it is permissible with prior approval from a registered general securities principal
   B. the broker-dealer can not be subjected to disciplinary actions
   C. it is permissible if the securities are exempt
   D. this represents a violation and customers may recover the original price paid for their securities plus interest

125. A stock listed on the NYSE is exempt from which of the following requirements of the Uniform Securities Act?
   A. filing of advertising materials
   B. anti-fraud provisions
   C. both choices listed
   D. neither choice listed

126. Which of the following statements best addresses material facts?
   A. omitting material facts is fraudulent in the offer or sale of non-exempt securities
   B. omitting material facts is fraudulent in the offer or sale of securities
   C. omitting material facts is prohibited when offering or selling exempt securities
   D. omitting material facts is prohibited when offering or selling securities to qualified buyers

127. In order to sell an unregistered, non-exempt security, you convince your client to sign a waiver of non-compliance, effectively exempting both parties from the registration provisions of the Uniform Securities Act. This contract between you and the client is
   A. permissible
   B. enforceable only at the federal level
   C. null and void
   D. punishable up to 7 years in a state prison

128. Which of the following activities is/are prohibited?
   I.   soliciting orders for unregistered, non-exempt securities
   II.   creating the appearance of active trading in a security
   III. soliciting orders for unregistered, exempt securities
   IV. failing to bring written complaints against an agent to the attention of a principal at the employing broker-dealer

   A. I, II, III, IV
   B. I, II, IV only
   C. II, IV only
   D. III only

129. If a wife wants to open an account in which she trades for her husband, which of the following documents must be completed and signed?
   A. power of attorney from the wife
   B. new account form
   C. power of attorney from the husband
   D. margin agreement

130. The Mayor of Monticello, Minnesota, deliberately omitted material information in a private sale of municipal bonds to an accredited investor. During a heated press conference the mayor states that she has not committed fraud in the securities markets because she is not a securities "dealer" or "agent" as defined under the USA, municipal bonds are exempt securities, and the omission of material information was intentional. What is true of this situation?
    A. it represents a really long, stupid question
    B. the mayor is correct—no fraud can occur if the securities are exempt
    C. the mayor is incorrect—whether the securities are exempt and whether she is defined as agent or dealer are irrelevant facts
    D. the mayor is correct, since the omission was intentional

131. Higher than normal commissions or markups may be charged to customers if
    A. the security is exempt
    B. the security is non-exempt
    C. the higher charges are justified and disclosed to the client after the transaction
    D. the higher charges are justified and disclosed to the client before the transaction

132. Barbara and Betty are customers of your broker-dealer employer in a JTWROS account. Barbara instructs you to sell 1,000 shares of GMRZ from the joint account and cut a check payable in her name. Your firm, instead, makes the check payable to both Barbara and Betty. This action represents
    A. a fraudulent practice on the part of your firm
    B. a fraudulent practice on the part of Barbara
    C. standard operating procedure for joint accounts
    D. selling away

133. Which of the following activities are permissible?
    I.   soliciting orders for unregistered, exempt securities
    II.   soliciting orders for registered, non-exempt securities
    III. buying GE on the NYSE for one price while simultaneously selling it at a higher price on a regional exchange
    IV.   not ignoring a client's explicit instructions to not purchase a security

    A. III only
    B. IV only
    C. I, II, III only
    D. I, II, III, IV

134. In an agency cross transaction, the investment adviser
    A. may advise both the buyer and the seller
    B. may advise both the buyer and seller provided that fees are reduced on both sides
    C. must provide prior disclosure that such a transaction may be a conflict of interest
    D. need not provide annual statements to each client with the total number of agency cross transactions and commissions collected

135. Omitting material facts in the solicitation or rendering of investment advice is
    A. fraudulent for institutional customers
    B. fraudulent for non-institutional customers
    C. fraudulent for retail customers
    D. fraudulent and prohibited by the USA

PRACTICE FINAL 3—SERIES 65

ANSWERS

1. **ANSWER: D**

   WHY: if there's no rule against it, take custody, and remember to inform the Administrator. Once a year a surprise inspection needs to occur, but it can't be "scheduled." Heck no—that would spoil the whole surprise! Anyone who maintains custody of client funds must send statements quarterly, not semi-annually.

2. **ANSWER: A**

   WHY: memorize it.

3. **ANSWER: C**

   WHY: memorize it.

4. **ANSWER: B**

   WHY: PE means "price" compared to "earnings." The price of the stock is 10 times the earnings. EPS = "earnings" per share.

5. **ANSWER: A**

   WHY: that's Level 2. Level 3 is for market makers. Level 1 shows the inside market or "interdealer market."

6. **ANSWER: C**

   WHY: no sales and no advertising. The SEC neither approves nor disapproves.

7. **ANSWER: A**

   WHY: it does lots of stuff, actually. It doesn't cover new issues—that's covered by the Act of 1933.

8. **ANSWER: D**

   WHY: the filing of Form 144 allows the investor to sell a certain amount of a particular stock over a 90-day period.

9. ANSWER: D

WHY: if the customer says "not interested," you have to put them on the firm's don't call list and don't call them, not even to apologize.

10. ANSWER: B

WHY: both the "tippee" and the "tipper" have run afoul of the law.

11. ANSWER: A

WHY: munibonds pay low coupon rates that work out better for some folks because the interest is federally tax-free. So, if you put them in a qualified, pre-tax retirement account, they'll pay tax on the income when they start taking withdrawals at retirement.

And that would be dumb.

12. ANSWER: B

WHY: remember the three-pronged test:
* Does the professional provide investment advice?
* Is he/she in the business of providing advice?
* Do they receive compensation for this advice?

13. ANSWER: B

WHY: annuities grow tax-deferred; mutual funds do not.

14. ANSWER: D

WHY: time and price are not discretionary aspects.

15. ANSWER: B

WHY: and a depression would be 6 quarters/18 months.

16. ANSWER: D

WHY: the best they'll do is allow, never approve/disapprove.

17. ANSWER: C

WHY: memorize it and hope you don't actually see it on your test.

18. ANSWER: C

WHY: since she's not 59½ years old or disabled, she'll pay ordinary income plus 10% of whatever she withdraws.

19. ANSWER: B

WHY: selling Treasuries to banks would pull money out of banks and raise interest rates. Rates up/prices down. Coupon rates and "rates" are the same thing. Bond coupon rates not only reflect current interest rates—they are current interest rates. Yields and rates are also the same thing. Remember, it's only price that moves the other way. Rates/yields up—price down. Rates/yields down—price up.

20. ANSWER: B

WHY: inventory is lagging. You don't know what you just sold or didn't sell in the recent past until you check what's in the warehouse. High inventory levels are bad; low inventory levels are good.

  Why?
  Who cares?

21. ANSWER: D

WHY: short-term interest rates are more volatile than long-term rates, because these are the rates that the FRB manipulates. Fed funds, discount, and money market rates jump up and down frequently, but the rates on 30-year bonds and mortgages are more steady. However, when interest rates overall move, the price of long-term bonds moves the most, either up or down. People pay big premiums for them when rates drop, and they panic-sell when rates go up.

22. ANSWER: C

WHY: rates rise when the reserve requirement is increased, because there is suddenly less money to borrow, and you have to pay more to borrow it. Rates up/yields up/price down. Coupon rates go up—in fact, that's just another way of saying "rates up." Coupon rates on new bonds don't just reflect current interest rates—they are current interest rates.

23. ANSWER: C

WHY: a balanced fund invests in stocks and bonds. They'll get growth from the stocks (we hope) and income from the bonds. Another good answer choice here would have been a "growth & income fund." Those are all stocks, where some produce growth (we hope) and some pay nice dividends.

24. ANSWER: D

WHY: new issues are covered by the Act of 1933, which requires full disclosure from non-exempt issuers.

25. ANSWER: C

WHY: depreciation recapture just sounds bad, doesn't it?

26. ANSWER: C

WHY: passive losses can only offset passive income, not ordinary or portfolio income.

27. ANSWER: D

WHY: don't miss the lay-ups.

28. ANSWER: C

WHY: time of day and the price to pay are NOT discretionary. Equate "discretionary" with "power of attorney" and "trading authorization" because every concept needs at least three names in this business.

29. ANSWER: D

WHY: a security or firm might be exempt from filing requirements, but that's all that the word "exempt" means. Nobody gets a pass when it comes to fraud. Freddie Mac is an exempt issuer that doesn't even have to file quarterly and annual reports (if they do, it's out of the kindness of their hearts). Still, when their accounting practices turn out to be funky, they can all get busted for fraud. Even the Treasury Secretary could get busted for fraud, even though he'd never have to register a T-bond, because he/they are "exempt" from those filing requirements.

30. ANSWER: A

WHY: nobody cares what the dealer paid except the dealer.

31. ANSWER: B

WHY: it went up $2.50 (div's/cap gains) and down $.50. What is "up $2.00" compared to/divided by where it started?

$2 divided by $9.50 = 21% total return.

This is a question I'd expect to see on the exam—something similar, that is.

32. ANSWER: D

WHY: it just is.

33. ANSWER: C

WHY: it just is.

34. ANSWER: D

WHY: that's how the test world sees it. Even though you know you could probably put some after-tax money into your 401K, the fact is, they're really for pre-tax money. And, when you start mixing pre-tax and after-tax contributions, you have a real mess on your hands keeping track of your "basis."

35. ANSWER: B

WHY: if the company defines your benefit, it's up to them to invest smart enough to pay you. It's not your problem. Unless they go bankrupt.

36. ANSWER: D

WHY: putting money into the banks makes the economy run faster, which makes inflation worse. To fight inflation, you have to tap the brakes. Buying Treasuries, lowering the discount rate and reserve requirement would all make the economy run faster, which is what causes inflation, as far as anyone knows.

37. ANSWER: B

WHY: our weak dollars can't buy Japanese imports as easily as they can buy the stuff we make here, priced in our weak dollars. Equate "weak dollar" with "cheaper American goods." Wouldn't that make it easier for Japanese consumers to buy our stuff, and harder for our weak dollars to buy their expensive stuff?

38. ANSWER: D

WHY: memorize it

39. ANSWER: D

WHY: she deducts exactly what the stock is worth, $2,500.

40. ANSWER: D

WHY: we don't ask shareholders what the dividend should be, any more than I'd ask my 15-year-old daughter what her curfew should be and which nights she should get to borrow my Corvette.

41. ANSWER: B

WHY: run some numbers. Take $1.00 over $10.00 and compare that to 83 cents (down 17%) over $8.00 (down 20%). The yield goes up. Be a creative problem solver.

42. ANSWER: B

WHY: the nominal yield they pay on the bond is just like the nominal yield you pay on your mortgage. Lower is better, right? You could probably offer your mortgage lender the right to buy shares in your company for a set price. And, as soon as the laughter subsided, you could get back to discussing your mortgage.

43. ANSWER: C

WHY: "fed funds rate" is what banks charge each other to borrow the money that the Fed allows them to lend out. The other money is locked up as a "reserve requirement."

44. ANSWER: A

WHY: an inverted yield curve means yields are high on the short-term bonds, meaning their prices are low.

45. ANSWER: D

WHY: that's why they passed the new lowered dividend tax rate—the company paying you the dividend already paid tax on the money. Why should you be taxed fully? You pay ordinary income on bond interest, because the company already deducted that from their income pre-tax. Why does the federal government reward companies and homeowners to borrow money?

Because the federal government is the largest borrower on the planet—it's the language they understand best.

46. ANSWER: C

WHY: 6 months is half a year, so double that rate to get an annualized rate of return.

Just don't confuse that with making an actual 16% return. For all we know, the next 6 months will erase all those paper gains. But it's fun to think of it as a 16% return, even if we're sort of kidding ourselves.

47. ANSWER: C

WHY: a very likely question on the exam—something similar, that is. The "-" sign tells you the direction is opposite, and the ".5" tells you the second stock always moves 50% of what the first one does.

Unless it doesn't.

48. ANSWER: D

WHY: the higher the standard deviation the less attractive the investment. So, if you can expect the highest return with the lowest deviation from that return, that would be the most attractive opportunity, even if we have no flippin' idea which investment will actually work out the best. The next-most-attractive investment would be "A," because if the other three all "offer" 8% returns, I want the one with the lowest standard deviation.

49. ANSWER: A

WHY: Just take 50% of 10 (5%) and add it to 20% of 15 (3%) to get 8%. Just don't take out any loans on the street based on this 8% you expect to get. Loan sharks don't just expect returns—they get them.

50. ANSWER: C

WHY: memorize it.

51. ANSWER: D

WHY: no way to miss this one. He's younger and has a high risk tolerance.

52. ANSWER: D

WHY: the highest duration belongs to the bond with the lowest coupon and longest maturity. It will take forever to get your principal back in the form of the $40 per year they pay in interest. In fact, that would take 25 years. And, since it's a 30-year bond, its price is inherently more sensitive to interest rates along the way. Imagine if rates shoot up to 9%. This 4%, 30-year bond is toast!

53. ANSWER: B

WHY: you should know that "revenue" is the top line and "net income" is the bottom line. And, if you get a chance, please explain that subtle difference to Jeff Bezos at Amazon-dot-com.

54. ANSWER: D

WHY: if a company could pay ALL of its debts with its cash reserves, that would be a pretty solid company. It's also nice when all of your current assets cover your current liabilities, but that's not as stringent, as your current liabilities include things you may never turn into cash: accounts receivable and inventory. Let's see how far your cash would go.

In other words, which would make you sleep better: knowing you can cover your credit card debt with this year's salary or having $100,000 in the money market with total bills/liabilities for the year at, say, $10,000. Which situation would lead to a better term on your next loan from the bank?

55. ANSWER: D

WHY: leverage and high debt ratios are one and the same. The percentage refers to the % of capital that was raised by selling debt.

56. ANSWER: C

WHY: it's just the total value of the outstanding shares. Microsoft, as of yesterday, had a market capitalization of $291 billion, which is the share price of about $27 times the 10.8 billion shares outstanding. All those shares are worth about $291 billion, in other words, which is very much a "large cap" stock.

57. ANSWER: B

WHY: process of elimination gets you the answer, since the other three choices represent things that have to be paid out.

58. ANSWER: C

WHY: nobody misses this one. You have to recognize the word "debenture" as a debt/liability at this point. If not, you're getting tired. Take a break. It's just a practice test, no big deal.

59. ANSWER: D

WHY: hope you weren't tempted by "xenophobic ratio." I'm not even sure what "xenophobic" means, but I bet it's a word invented by some lousy foreigner.

60. ANSWER: B

WHY: gross margin is just revenues minus cost of goods sold, divided by revenues. If revenues fall, or if cost of goods sold rises, we have shrinking/ compromised margins.

Hate it when that happens, and so do S&P and Moody's, which is why a company's bond rating can easily be downgraded due to such unfortunate developments.

61. ANSWER: B

WHY: if revenues rise and/or cost of goods sold falls, we have a bigger difference or "margin" between the two. That's just saying that if you sold $90 million of computer parts for $100 million last year, you'd feel better buying those same parts for $80 million next year and selling them for $120 million. Kind of a buy-low–sell-high philosophy of profit making, right?

Your gross margins would have improved based on the $40 million difference, compared to the $10 million difference last year. Only way to improve profits is to raise sales and cut costs. As the company gets bigger, they sell more stuff and beat down their suppliers on price, improving margins.

If that sounds like Wal-Mart or Home Depot, now you know how they became large cap or "blue chip" companies. The bigger they get, the more they sell, and the more bargaining power they have with suppliers.

62. ANSWER: B

WHY: a debenture paying $100 would leave this investor with $72 after she shares $28 with her rich uncle, Sam. If the munibond paid $72, it would be equivalent, since the investor doesn't have to share with her uncle.

63. ANSWER: D

WHY: a zero coupon, such as a STRIP or Treasury Receipt, has a duration exactly equal to the bond's maturity, since you won't get your principal back until then. Interest-paying debt securities have durations that are less than their maturity date. In other words, zeroes have high volatility/durations.

64. ANSWER: C

WHY: 4% times 4 quarters = 16% annualized.

65. ANSWER: C

WHY: after that BBB-, we'll have to call you "junk."

66. ANSWER: C

WHY: inflation kills the purchasing power of the fixed coupon payment and usually leads to higher interest rates, which kill the market value of the bond. Capital appreciation = stock, not bonds, since on a bond you wait years and years just to get the same $1,000 you paid back, which is worth less now due to the time value of money (inflation).

Can you tell how many bonds are in my portfolio at this point?

67. ANSWER: D

WHY: you know common stock is last in line at liquidation, but the other three are benefits, or possible benefits of owning stock.

68. ANSWER: A

WHY: your money won't grow in a money market. If you're real lucky it won't lose all its value to management fees and inflation.

69. ANSWER: C

WHY: if there will be revenue generated by the facility, it's a revenue bond.

70. ANSWER: B

WHY: GOs are backed by taxes paid by taxpayers, who are voters and get to vote before you spend their money building a new school.

71. ANSWER: C

WHY: yep, which is why customers have no idea how much they're paying in expenses.

You think a customer is going to get the "average net assets" and divide that by the average number of shares outstanding over the year to come up with his/her share of the expenses?

Not.

72. ANSWER: B

WHY: also called a "contingent deferred sales charge." It's deferred until you sell, and it's contingent upon when you sell. In the first year(s), the back-end load is huge, and then it declines all the way to zero over time.

73. ANSWER: B

WHY: to protect you BUY/go long an option. To hedge you bet the other way. Short stock is bearish; long call is bullish. Or, think a little harder if you must: You have to buy back the stock at some price. Do you want that price to be a big question mark burning a hole through your esophagus as you toss and turn at night, or would you rather pay a small premium to get the RIGHT to BUY at a set/certain exercise price?

74. ANSWER: C

WHY: if you're an owner of a C-corp, you pay tax on your company's income and then pay yourself dividends, which are then taxed on your individual income form.

Ouch.

An S-corp just gives every owner his/her share of the income, and they get taxed only on their individual tax returns. Both shield you from liability in the sense that your house and individual assets are separate from the business. If the business fails, you keep your house. A sole proprietor could lose the house.

75. ANSWER: B

WHY: this is just another way of saying the customer pays (cost base) the ASKed price and receives (proceeds) the BID price when selling.

76. ANSWER: C

WHY: you have to eliminate the bank and the rep, both of which are never called "investment advisers." Now, you're down to somebody who gets a nominal fee to talk about "equities" and somebody who regularly gives advice, is in the business of giving advice, and gets compensated for that advice…those are the "3 prongs" to the "3-prong test" mentioned in SEC Release IA-1092.

77. ANSWER: D

WHY: agents represent the firm. They have to be ethical when dealing with customers, but they don't put the customers' needs first.

78. ANSWER: C

WHY: a memorization point.

79. ANSWER: C

WHY: a memorization point.

80. ANSWER: C

WHY: a point to memorize

81. ANSWER: D

WHY: if you advise a mutual fund/investment company, you don't have to give them a disclosure brochure. And if you perform "impersonal advisory services," same deal.

82. ANSWER: D

WHY: RIA looks like a certification or credential, when, in fact, it is neither. It just means "registered investment adviser," and could be misleading to a customer if written like an MBA or CFP credential.

83. ANSWER: D

WHY: no furniture, office equipment, travel expenses, or vacations allowed. In other words, none of the good stuff.

84. ANSWER: D

WHY: never imply that a federal covered security is inherently safer than a non-federal covered security. Often they are, but often they aren't, so it would be misleading to say that all federal covered securities are safer. Mutual funds are federal covered, and lots of those lose 50% or more in a year. No load funds usually have 12b-1 fees. If the fee is bigger than .25% of avg. net assets, they lose the ability to call themselves "no load."

85. ANSWER: B

WHY: pretty surprising that they can effect the margin transaction even before they promptly get the margin agreement, but you also had to know the other three are prohibited. You can't take orders from a third party who lacks authorization, and you can't use discretion when you don't have it.

86. ANSWER: C

WHY: doesn't "C" just look like the right answer? There's no fraud going on here—we just better hope we have a convincing reason for charging so much. Maybe our "full service" is so awesome that it's justified.

Or not.

87. ANSWER: C

WHY: another tidbit pulled from the NASAA Statement of Policy for Broker-Dealers and Agents, 1983.

88. ANSWER: B

WHY: memorize it.

89. ANSWER: D

WHY: Gee, why would we want you to buy GE? Because they, like, own us?

GE, by the way, does own or has owned broker-dealers.

90. ANSWER: A

WHY: believe it or not, the IA can use discretion after granted verbal authorization, as long as they get it in writing in 10 business days. In general, IAs don't get paid per transaction, so the temptation to churn wouldn't be there. If they make a dumb purchase, they not only don't get a commission on the trade, they watch their fees go down, since it's now, say, 1% of a smaller amount of assets.

Hate it when that happens.

91. ANSWER: D

WHY: choice "D" looks like a suitable recommendation, doesn't it? The IA can do an "agency cross transaction," but they can't be recommending both sides. They act as broker for both sides and IA to the advisory client, and they disclose the fact that it's an agency cross transaction to their advisory clients.

Which makes sense, given the fact that the commission received for brokering the trade is going to motivate them and could be a conflict of interest—it might be the main reason they're recommending the purchase or sale to their advisory client, who is only supposed to receive advice designed to benefit him/her/them.

IAs are fiduciaries and must always look for potential conflicts of interest, disclosing them ahead of time to their clients.

92. ANSWER: C

WHY: you can definitely use reports and analyses to make a recommendation, but you can't pass off somebody else's report or recommendation as your own. Subtle but important difference.

93. ANSWER: C

WHY: if there's a conflict of interest that could cloud the IA's judgment; it needs to be disclosed. Even without realizing it, the IA might subconsciously favor the stock that tends to go up every time he recommends it, making his portfolio richer and richer. Try to forget smarmy stock cheerleaders like Mary Meeker and Jack Grubman when you read a question like this—or remember that they are the reason this stuff has to be disclosed.

94. ANSWER: B

WHY: that's just the flip side of being paid for performance. Unless you see that the investor is an institution or an individual with $1.5 million net worth, $750,000 under management, and the contract clearly explains the terms of compensation, the IA reasonably believes the client understands those terms, and losses have to be subtracted from gains, yada, yada. Otherwise, no performance-based compensation for your IA.

95. ANSWER: D

WHY: a point to memorize.

96. ANSWER: B

WHY: it's prohibited to do it, since we can't just agree to make each other immune from the law. And the contract is also considered "null and void" in a court of law, meaning "useless." Kind of reminds me of waiting in the lunch line in grade school and watching a kid walk up toward the front and propose to cut in front of a friend, who then cuts in front of him. Cuts–cuts back, I believe this blatant violation of kiddie common law was called.

Like any other such waiver of noncompliance, it isn't worth the paper it's written on.

97. ANSWER: D

WHY: it's not deceitful; it's just not allowed...she's an IA, not an agent.

98. ANSWER: A

WHY: you can share with registered agents at the firm or a firm under common control.

99. ANSWER: B

WHY: arbitrage is very dangerous but totally legal. Unless the arbitrageur's name happens to be Boesky.

100. ANSWER: D

WHY: thought you could just shred the complaint, did you?
   I think not!

101. ANSWER: A

WHY: you don't choose which important facts to disclose—you just disclose the material facts, honestly, accurately, thoroughly.

   Or, you have your license suspended or revoked. Or a court issues an embarrassing injunction on your unethical, fraudulent attitude.

102. ANSWER: B

WHY: what are "all facts about a security"? Do they include the type of paper the certificates are printed on? The font or PMS color used by the printer? What about the average height of the 17 lowest-paid company vice presidents?

103. ANSWER: C

WHY: three years, five grand. Ignorance of the law can actually keep you out of jail and maybe just pay a fine. But you have to publicly make a convincing case for your incredible ignorance. Although if it kept me out of jail, I'd probably show up in a clown suit riding a tricycle.

104. ANSWER: C

WHY: choice C describes exactly how it's supposed to happen.

105. ANSWER: D

WHY: "Riskless security" is a contradiction in terms, like "jumbo shrimp" or "lead zeppelin." All securities have risk, even Treasuries. Treasuries have no default risk, but if rates go up, their prices drop. The T-bonds have more interest-rate risk, in fact, than short-term corporate bonds. Of course the corporate bonds have more default risk. Which one's more important? How about if we just disclose all the risks, and let the client help us determine which risks will keep them up at night and which ones will keep them from clogging our voice mailbox.

106. ANSWER: B

WHY: when it's immediate family, we don't worry about the sharing arrangement, but we still need customer consent and firm consent. IAs don't share, and you never share on a per-transaction basis. Imagine if you let a broker talk you into going halvsies on 10,000 shares of Enron. Now imagine how hard to reach the guy would be after Enron flames out. Who's your daddy now, Mr. Partners-on-the-trade?

107. ANSWER: B

WHY: even if you weren't sure, your test-taking skills need to be sharp enough at this point to lead you to B.

Administrator-approve. Eliminate that evil pairing of words.

Principals don't have a magic pen to make everything okay—eliminate that one.

And you know waivers are not allowed, so eliminate that one, and you're left with the right answer.

That is how you win the game. You see what you can eliminate right off the bat, and keep eliminating until you're left with the most compelling answer.

Heck, that's what I do when I invest. I eliminate companies with too much debt, weak sales, and weak profits. I keep looking for weaknesses in the few that are still left, and the ones I can't eliminate, I buy.

108. ANSWER: D

WHY: that's total return, a concept that WILL be on your exam. Maybe it's total return for a mutual fund, or total return on a stock or bond investment. Just take all the income the investment pays, plus any gain (or loss) on paper. Compare that to where it started, and you've got yourself "total return."

109. ANSWER: D

WHY: break down the words—she did absolutely nothing wrong. She's registered in the state where the customer lives. The municipal bond doesn't have to be registered, period.

110. ANSWER: C

WHY: reinvesting dividends means you can't lose? How?

111. ANSWER: D

WHY: you can share with other registered agents at the firm or a subsidiary of the firm. Maybe your buddy likes to pitch annuities and you prefer mutual funds. So, you refer the annuity sales to him, and he refers the mutual fund sales to you, and everybody's happy.

112. ANSWER: B

WHY: don't add to or alter the prospectus.

113. ANSWER: A

WHY: a gift of a question.

114. ANSWER: B

WHY: don't be doin' that. Can't guarantee specific results, nor would you want to.

Stock drops 50%, and you're stuck buying it for 20% above the original purchase price?

What are you, writing puts with your client? Betting against him?

Don't be doin' that.

115. ANSWER: C

WHY: definitely try to talk her out of it, but it would probably be impolite to turn her over to the authorities or have her declared mentally incompetent, don't you think?

She is a customer, after all.

She has money.

116. ANSWER: D

WHY: backwards sometimes speaks the exam. That's okay—just translate it back to English. Three are inappropriate—which one is okay?

Broker-dealers definitely have preferred lists. Maybe their analysts have decided that 30 stocks represent exceptional value, and now the agents are pitching them to their clients, based entirely, of course, on suitability.

117. ANSWER: C

WHY: because it's the best answer choice of the four. There is no Securities Act of 1921, and neither the NASD nor the SEC limits the number of trades an investor can make. They just make sure the agent isn't talking customers into frequent trading solely to make commissions off them.

118. ANSWER: C

WHY: that's the only true and accurate statement. If somebody has an emergency—like a child being accepted to an Ivy League school—they might have to sell Treasuries. If rates are up, the market price they receive could be less than they paid.

Hate it when that happens.

119. ANSWER: D

WHY: the bond with the longest term has the most interest-rate risk. When rates go up or down, the long-term bond prices rise and fall to a greater degree than shorter-term bond prices.

It's a fact.

You could look it up.

120. ANSWER: B

WHY: debentures are corporate bonds. Some corporate bonds are issued by Kmart, United Airlines, Enron, and Worldcomm.

Any questions?

121. ANSWER: D

WHY: the Act of 1934 says that the issuer has to pay for soliciting proxy votes, so the broker-dealer doesn't charge the customer—they charge the issuer.

122. ANSWER: B

WHY: that's the way it's supposed to be—a % of the assets that the adviser hasn't managed to lose yet.

123. ANSWER: C

WHY: don't do any of the other three.

124. ANSWER: D

WHY: sounds like the firm is violating securities law, doesn't it? Securities sold in violation of securities law sometimes end up being repurchased by the fools who sold them illegally, plus interest.

125. ANSWER: A

WHY: the state securities Administrator can enforce anti-fraud regulations on absolutely anyone.

126. ANSWER: B

WHY: you have to be a careful, patient reader to pass this exam. English majors like me usually have an edge. If you double majored in English and Finance, you really have an edge. Assuming you ever made it to class.

127. ANSWER: C

WHY: it's not worth the paper it's written on, much less the legal fees paid to draft an unenforceable waiver.

No waivers. No way.

128. ANSWER: B

WHY: exempt securities are always unregistered. Read carefully.

129. ANSWER: C

WHY: the new account form does not have to be signed by the customer. Why anybody ever thought that was, like, a good test question, I've no idea.

130. ANSWER: C

WHY: not everybody has a license that could end up being suspended or revoked, but anybody could get busted for fraud if they deceive someone in connection with the offer or sale of any security, even exempt ones.

131. ANSWER: D

WHY: get the client's consent before the deal goes down.

132. ANSWER: C

WHY: all distributions must be made payable to all names on the account, exactly as registered.

133. ANSWER: D

WHY: absolutely nothing wrong going on in any of the four choices, is there? Exempt securities are, by definition, unregistered, and as long as the non-exempt ones are registered, we're cool with that, too. Choice III describes "arbitrage," which is high-risk but still allowed, like skydiving or rock climbing or running into a south-side bar and yelling "White Sox suck!" Choice IV has it right—not ignoring your customer's instructions.

134. ANSWER: C

WHY: there's a potential conflict of interest when your adviser is telling you to buy a stock that he's going to make a commission on from the seller, so it has to be disclosed. The adviser cannot advise both sides of a transaction any more than a divorce lawyer can represent the husband and the wife in the same proceeding.

135. ANSWER: D

WHY: just another reading question. Read carefully, patiently, analytically.

PLEASE VISIT
WWW.PASSTHE65.COM FOR
ADDITIONAL PRACTICE QUES-
TIONS AND FOR ANY UPDATES
THAT MAY HAVE BEEN ADDED
TO THE MATERIAL.

ACRONYMS

ADR	American Depository Receipt
AIR	assumed interest rate
B/D	broker-dealer
BOD	board of directors
BOM	board of managers
CMO	collaterized mortgage obligation
CMV	current market value
COP	code of procedure
CPI	consumer price index
CY	current yield
DERP	**D**eclaration, **E**x-Date, **R**ecord Date, **P**ayable **D**ate
EPS	earnings per share
ERISA	Employee Retirement Income Security Act
FHLMC	Federal Home Loan Mortgage Corporation, Freddie Mac
FIFO	first in, first out
FNMA	Federal National Mortgage Corporation, Fannie Mae
FOMC	Federal Open Market Committee
FRB	Federal Reserve Board
GDP	Gross Domestic Product
GNMA	Government National Mortgage Association, Ginnie Mae
GO	general obligation
IPO	initial public offering
IRA	individual retirement account
JTIC	joint tenants in common
JTWROS	joint tenants with rights of survivorship
LIFO	last in, first out
LOI	Letter of Intent

MSRB	Municipal Securities Rulemaking Board
NAC	National Adjudicatory Council
NASAA	North American Securities Administrators Association
NAV	net asset value
OTC	over the counter
POP	public offering price
PPI	producer price index
REIT	Real Estate Investment Trust
SAI	Statement of Additional Information
SAR	suspicious activity report
SEC	Securities and Exchange Commission
SEP	simplified employee pension
SIPC	Securities Investor Protection Corporation
SPDA	single payment deferred annuity
SRO	self-regulatory organization
STRIPS	separate trading of registered interest and principal of securities
TDAs	tax deferred annuities
TOD	Transfer on Death
TSAs	tax sheltered annuities
UGMA	Uniform Gifts to Minors Act
UTMA	Uniform Transfer to Minors Act
UIT	unit investment trust
VC	venture capital
VLI	variable life insurance
VUL	variable universal life
YTC	yield to call
YTM	yield to maturity

GLOSSARY

A

Accrued Interest: the amount of interest that the buyer of a debt security owes the seller. The buyer pays the seller for daily interest starting with the last payable date up to the day before settlement.

Active Management: a style of investing where the investor actively selects certain securities over other alternatives. Based on the premise that information is not immediately acted upon and that markets are not perfectly efficient.

Agent: an individual (natural person) who represents either an issuer or a broker-dealer in effecting transactions in securities.

Alpha: the difference between an investment's actual return and its expected return. Excess returns = "positive alpha."

Annualized Rate of Return: a stock's increase or decrease measured in annual increments. For periods of less than 1 year, multiply the return by the appropriate number, i.e., a 6-month return is doubled; a 3-month return is multiplied by 4. For periods of more than 1 year, divide the return by the number of years.

Ask: what the customer pays a dealer to purchase a security; the dealer's "ASKing" price.

Asset: a "plus" to an individual's or business's account, e.g., cash, inventory, equipment.

Asset Allocation: an investment style that focuses on a mix of equity, bond, and money market exposure, i.e., 40% equity, 45% bonds, 5% money market.

Assignment (of contract): passing off, selling, or otherwise transferring a client's advisory account to another party. Not allowed without written consent of client.

B

Balance of Payments: money in versus money out of the national economy for both trade and investments. Surplus equals "net money in," while a deficit equals "net money out."

Balance of Trade: money in versus money out of the country for imports/exports only. Surplus equals more exports; deficit equals more imports.

Balance Sheet: a statement of financial condition prepared by both individuals and businesses showing assets and liabilities, where the difference between assets and liabilities equals "net worth," which is, hopefully, a positive number.

Bank Holding Company: a company whose assets hold banks. For example, BankOne, Citigroup, or JPMorgan-Chase. All three are public companies whose stock must be registered with the SEC. A "bank stock" does not have to be registered with the SEC because it is regulated by bank regulators (FDIC, FRB, state banking authorities).

Basis Point: measurement of a bond's yield. 100 basis points = 1%. 50 basis points = ½ of 1%.

Benchmark Portfolio: the index that a portfolio manager is trying to beat. For example, a large cap fund manager would be trying to beat the DJIA. A small cap manager would be trying to beat the benchmark of the Russell Small Cap Index (Russell 2000).

Beta: the volatility of an individual stock compared to the overall market (S&P 500). A beta of "1" means the stock moves in lock-step with the overall market. A beta of more than 1 means the stock is more volatile than the overall market; a beta of less than 1 means the stock is less volatile.

Bid: the amount a customer can receive from a dealer when selling a security.

Bond Point: $10. A quote of "96" means 96 bond points or $960.

Book Value: theoretically, what a share of stock would be worth if the corporation were sold at auction today, with the proceeds used to pay off the creditors and the excess paid out to shareholders. Value investors like to buy stocks near or below book value.

Broker-Dealer: a business entity effecting transactions in securities for the accounts of others (broker) or its own account (dealer).

Business Risk: the risk that a company will not be able to compete or operate effectively within its industry.

C

Call Risk: the risk that interest rates will drop, prompting issuers to call (buy back) their bonds or preferred stock.

Callable: a bond or preferred stock that the issuer can buy back after a certain date for a certain price.

Capital Gain: selling a security for more than you paid. Proceeds minus cost basis = capital gain/loss.

Common Stock: a basic form of equity/ownership in a business that provides voting rights to the owner and a claim on earnings/dividends.

Compensation: any form of economic benefit, including money, material goods, even soft dollar compensation (research services, software, clearing services, etc.).

Consent to Service of Process: a form filed by an issuer, agent, broker-dealer, IA, or IAR which gives the Administrator the authority to receive service of process (court papers) on behalf of the party filing the consent with the same force as if served on the suddenly-hard-to-locate party.

Constant Dollar Risk: the risk that inflation/rising prices will erode the value of a fixed-income payment. A 6% coupon payment on a bond won't provide much purchasing power if consumer prices are rising faster than 6%.

Convertible Securities: bonds and preferred stock that allow the holder to use the par value toward the purchase of the issuer's common stock at a set price.

Cost Basis: the money that has already been taxed and gone into an investment. The amount above this cost basis is usually taxable as a capital gain when realized.

Current Yield: annual interest compared to/divided by market price. An 8% coupon bond bought at $800 has a current yield of 10%. The nominal yield is 8%, but compared to the $800 paid for the bond, the bond is currently yielding 10%.

Custody: possession of securities and/or cash.

Cyclical: an industry highly dependent on the business cycle, susceptible to recession. For example, steel and auto manufacturing are highly cyclical industries that do well during expansions and get crushed during recessions/depressions.

D

Debenture: a corporate bond backed by the issuer's "full faith and credit" or ability to pay. No specific assets are pledged as collateral to secure the loan.

Default Risk: the risk of getting stiffed by the issuer of a bond.

Defensive: an industry that is not highly susceptible to economic downturns, e.g., food, alcohol, cigarettes and other important industries.

Deflation: falling prices.

Depression: 6 quarters/18 months of economic downturn.

Diluted Earnings: the earnings per share that would result after the conversion of all convertible preferred, convertible bonds, and warrants into common stock. Same earnings pie cut into more (smaller) equity slices.

Discount Rate: the rate of interest that the FRB charges member banks.

Discretion: choosing the asset/amount/activity on behalf of a customer. Time/price do NOT equal/involve discretion.

Dividend: a payment from a corporation's profits to an equity holder that must first be declared by the board of directors.

Donation: a tax-deductible gift to a charitable organization where the donor deducts the fair market value of the security from income for purposes of reducing taxes paid.

Duration: a measure of a bond's price volatility. A duration of "10" means that for every 1% change in interest rates the bond's price will go up or down 10%.

E

Earnings Per Share: net income minus preferred dividends divided by the number of outstanding common shares. Or, "earnings available to common divided by outstanding shares." The size of each slice of the company's "earnings pie."

Exclusion: excluded by definition. For example, a bank is excluded from the definition of "investment adviser."

Exemption: excused from registration hassles. A Treasury Bond is a security, but it is excused from having to register.

Expected Return: the return an investor expects. Mathematically, the investor takes the chance of receiving a certain return times that return. If an investment has a 10% chance of returning 40% and a 20% chance of returning 20%, the expected return is 10% of 40 (4%) plus 20% of 20 (4%)...8%.

F

Fed Funds Rate: overnight lending rate between/among banks.

Federal Covered: covered exclusively at the federal level, SEC-registered.

Fiduciary: party who makes investment decisions for another party, putting the other party's interests first and foremost.

Fiscal Policy: tax and spend policy enacted by Congress and the President.

Form ADV: registration form filed by Investment Advisers with the SEC. Has a Part 1 and a Part 2—Part 2 can be used as the IA's disclosure brochure to customers.

Fraud: willful, knowing, intentional deceit used for wrongful financial gain.

Frontrunning: buying securities just ahead of a large customer order, hoping the large customer order will push up the value of the stock you just acquired in your sneaky, and highly unethical, maneuver

Fundamental Analysis: analyzing financial statements in order to uncover investment opportunities.

Future Value: what an investment will be worth in the future, given a certain rate of return for a certain period of time. Measures compounding that, unfortunately, hasn't happened yet.

G

GDP: gross domestic product. Basically, it's the sum total of the economy's output, the total value of all goods and services being provided by the economy currently.

Gift: what it sounds like. Taxable to the giver if it exceeds $12,000 (a number set to be constantly increased).

Gross Margin: the first measure of a company's profitability. Revenues minus cost of goods sold equals gross revenue. Divide/compare that to the revenues to get "gross margin." No other costs/subtractions have been made from the income statement, so this measure of profit is not very deep.

Growth Investing: purchasing stocks in companies whose earnings are expected to grow faster than other companies' or faster than the overall market. Since much speculation is built into the stock's price, growth investors often pay high multiples, i.e., PE or price-to-book.

H

Holding Period Return: the return an investment provides irrespective of time frame. A 10% return over a 5-year holding period is simply a holding period return of 10%.

Hypothecation: using a security as collateral to secure a margin loan. Similar to pledging the house you haven't paid for as collateral to borrow money to buy the house. When you hypothecate a security, you use the value of the stock you haven't fully paid for yet as the collateral to secure the loan used to buy the security.
    Whatever.

I

Income Statement: sometimes called an "earnings statement" or "statement of earnings," since everything needs at least three names in this business. The company starts with revenues and then makes line-by-line subtractions to represent all the costs the business has to pay out of those revenues. Starts with "revenue," and ends up with "net income" to show a company's "bottom line." From this "bottom line" or "net income" the company may, or may not, distribute preferred dividends and common dividends.

Index: a grouping of securities used to track the overall market or segments of the market. The S&P 500 represents 500 of the most important stocks in the overall market, thereby standing as a proxy for the "overall market." The DJIA tracks the 30 largest companies' stocks. The Russell 2000 tracks small cap stocks, etc.

Inflation: rising prices, thought to be the result of a fast-expanding economy. Or, too much demand for, and not enough supply of, money.

Interest Rate: the "extra" you pay to borrow a certain amount of "principal." Or, "the cost of money."

Interest Rate Risk: the risk that interest rates will rise, having an adverse effect on the price of outstanding bonds. Greatest for longer-term bonds.

Issuer: a person/entity who issues or proposes to issue a security. The name of the company or the government on the security itself—GE is the "issuer" of GE stock.
   Go figure.

J

JTWROS: Joint Tenants With Rights of Survivorship, a type of investment account usually shared by a husband and wife, where the assets of the deceased pass directly to the survivor...thus the "rights of survivorship" part of the title.

JTIC: Joint Tenants in Common, a type of investment account shared by two or more persons where the assets of the deceased pass to the deceased's estate, not the surviving account owners.

K

Keogh: a qualified retirement plan available to sole proprietors with self-employment income. Not available to corporations.

L

(Charles) Laffer: the Laffer curve argues that a reduction in tax rates actually leads to more revenues collected by the IRS, because lower tax rates stimulate economic activity. Associated with "supply side economics."

Legislative Risk: the risk that legislators will screw things up even more than they already have. For example, if investors lose favorable tax treatment for municipal bond interest or cash dividends on stock, the market price of those investments might plummet.

Liability: a minus to your account, something you have to pay out, e.g., accounts payable. One of the three categories on a balance sheet: assets, liabilities, net worth.

Limit Order: an order to buy or sell a security at a set price or better.

M

Market Cap (capitalization): share price times the number of shares outstanding. The total market value of a company's outstanding common stock. At the time of this writing the "market cap" for Microsoft is approximately $270 billion.
   Which is a lot.

Market Order: an order to buy or sell a security that does not specify a particular price. Executed at the best possible price as quickly as possible.

Market Risk: the risk that the overall stock or bond market could crash.

Monetary Policy: fighting inflation and goosing the economy by manipulating short-term interest rates. Enacted by the FRB/FOMC, not Congress & President (fiscal).

Municipal Security: a security issued by a municipality borrowing money to construct roads, sewers, schools, stadiums, etc. Usually pays federally tax-free interest.

N

NASDAQ: National Association of Securities Dealers Automated Quotation System. Over-the-Counter stocks with enough interest among traders to make it worth quoting prices all throughout the day. 4-letter symbols such as MSFT, PSFT, ORCL, and INTC are NASDAQ stocks.

Net Margin: the percentage of money that's left after paying all the bills. A company with $100 million in sales and $10 million in net income has a 10% net margin.

Net Worth: assets minus liabilities. Hopefully, assets are bigger. If not, find another prospect.

Non-systematic Risk: the risk that any one stock price could really suck today. Especially if it's one of yours.

NSMIA: National Securities Markets Improvement Act, 1996. Legislation that created "federal covered" status for certain investment advisers and certain securities. Seeks to clarify confusion and eliminate red tape created by redundancies and discrepancies between federal and state securities laws.

NYSE: New York Stock Exchange. An "auction market" associated with screaming lunatics in funny-colored jackets making more money than most people will ever see in their lives so don't knock 'em.

O

Operating Margin: a company's "operating income" compared to/divided by revenues. EBIT (earnings before interest and taxes). Does not reflect the "bottom line," but does go further down the income statement than "gross margin."

Opportunity Cost: the return on the security you could have bought but didn't.

OTC Bulletin Board: the over-the-counter stocks not welcome on NASDAQ. Many thinly traded stocks with very wide "spreads," which is another way of saying "liquidity risk."

P

PE ratio: the price of the stock compared to/divided by the earnings each share represents. If the EPS (earnings per share) equals $1, and the stock costs $20, the PE is 20.

Passive Management: exclusive use of index funds rather than actively selecting securities. Linked heavily with "Random Walk Theory" and "Efficient Market Theory."

Pass-through Certificate: a funky debt security based on a pool of mortgages paying investors part of the interest and principal being returned by the homeowners every month. GNMA, for example. Like a bond, except it repays principal gradually, rather than at maturity-only.

Pink Sheets: thinly traded over-the-counter stocks associated with wide "spreads" or "liquidity risk."

Preferred Stock: a fixed-income equity security with a stated rate of return, which makes it very sensitive to interest rates.

Present Value: the amount of money an investor needs to invest in order to have a certain amount of money in the future, given a certain time frame and rate of return. For example, if you need $100,000 in five years and expect a 5% rate of return each year, the present value is the amount you need to invest in order to have that $100,000.

Primary Market: where issuers raise capital by selling/issuing securities to investors. As opposed to the secondary market, where securities are traded among investors.

Prime Rate: interest rate paid by creditworthy corporations for unsecured loans.

Principal: A) to have capital at risk in a transaction. B) the amount of money to be repaid on a bond at maturity. C) the supervisor at a broker-dealer responsible for sales activities, advertising, compliance, etc.

Progressive Tax: a tax where the rate increases as the amount of the thing being taxed increases, e.g., income, estate, and gift taxes.

Prospectus: disclosure document used to give prospects a fair chance of evaluating a security about to be issued.

Purchasing Power Risk: inflation or "constant dollar risk," also. The risk that a fixed income payment will lose value due to inflation.

Q

Qualified Plan: a plan offered by an employer that must follow the rules of ERISA. Contributions are made with pre-tax dollars, leaving participants with no cost basis; therefore, all distributions are taxable at the ordinary income rate.

R

Recession: two quarters/six months of economic decline. Not as serious as a depression.

Regressive Tax: any flat tax, such as sales, gasoline, or excise.

Reinvestment Risk: the risk that interest and/or principal payments from debt securities will not be reinvested at attractive rates. Eliminated with zero coupons, such as STRIPS.

REIT: Real Estate Investment Trust. An equity security that usually pays the owner high dividend yields and allows him/her to participate in real estate without the traditional problems of liquidity and prohibitively large, Donald Trump–sized capital commitments.

RIA: Registered Investment Adviser. Not a credential, just a statement of fact, which is why it can't be used on business cards as if it's another "CFP" or "MBA" type thing.

Riskless Rate of Return: the rate on 3-month (90-day) T-bills. Used as a comparison in the Sharpe ratio to show if an investment with real risk did significantly better than the worry-free return on short-term T-bills. If not, why take that risk?

S

Secondary Market: where securities are traded among investors, with none of the proceeds going to the issuer. NYSE or NASDAQ, for example.

Senior Securities: debt securities that give investors senior claims against corporate assets in a bankruptcy proceeding.

Sharpe Ratio: a measurement designed to show if an investor is being compensated for the risk taken. Return minus "riskless rate of return," divided by standard deviation. The higher the number, the better the investor is being compensated for risk.

Soft Dollar Compensation: compensation paid in the form of research or software or other services, rather than in dollars and cents.

Solicitor: one who solicits. Some IAs outsource the sales activities to "solicitors."

Spread: A) primary market = difference between POP and proceeds to issuer, what is kept by the syndicate in exchange for lining up the IPO. B) secondary market = the difference between a dealer or market maker's BID and ASK prices.

Standard Deviation: the amount that an investment could deviate from its expected return.

Stop Order: an order that won't be executed until the market price first hits or passes through the stop price, at which point it becomes a market order, executed immediately. Usually used to protect a long position (sell-stop) or a short position (buy-stop).

Stop-limit Order: starts out as a stop order. Once triggered, it's executed at the limit price or better.

Systematic Risk: the risk that the overall market could plummet.

T

Technical Analysis: following stock prices and volume levels, not companies. The use of charts.

Treasury Security: a debt security issued by the U.S. Treasury. For example: T-bill, T-note, T-bond, STRIP.

V

Value Investing: buying stocks that are priced below what you think they're really worth. Usually involves buying stocks that are currently being hammered by the markets and the media.

W

Working Capital: Current Assets minus Current Liabilities. A short-term measure of liquidity for a company.

Wrap Fee/program: charging an advisory client one fee for all services rendered—advice, execution, billing, etc.

Y

Yield Curve: plotting the different yields currently available on debt securities according to their term-to-maturity. A positive yield curve shows yields on long-term securities higher than short-term. An inverted yield curve would be inverted.

Yield to Maturity: factors in all the coupon payments received plus/minus what the investor in a debt security makes/loses at maturity.

Z

Zero Coupon Bond: a bond that does not distribute interest payments per se. Rather, the par value goes up over time, and the difference between the purchase price and the par value is treated as interest income. Eliminates "reinvestment risk."

INDEX

A

Accrued Interest 230, 441
Active Management 95, 108, 441
Alpha 87, 107, 108, 441
Annualized Return 85, 86, 107
Ask/Asked 3, 175, 235, 307, 308, 310, 311, 339, 449
Asset Allocation 13, 41, 97, 98, 108, 115, 117, 259, 441
Assignment 19, 20, 29, 33, 56, 441

B

Balance of Payments 64, 267, 441
Balance of Trade 64, 106, 441
Balance Sheet 39, 41, 66-68, 70, 73, 93, 95, 106, 113, 140, 179, 215, 237, 263, 442, 446
Bank Holding Company 44, 45, 47-49, 442
Basis Points 18, 61-63, 232, 442
Benchmark Portfolio 92, 442
Beta 75, 76, 86, 87, 97, 115, 442
Bid 3, 28, 62, 76, 175, 235, 306-308, 310-312, 442, 449
Bond Point 232, 442
Book Value 93, 94, 106, 442
Business Risk 75, 106, 442

C

Call Risk 77, 78, 442
Callable 78, 78, 218, 227, 229, 442
Capital Gains 16, 17, 19, 33, 56, 85, 95, 112, 118-123, 125-130, 220, 239, 252, 254, 255, 259, 263-265, 267, 270, 288, 442, 443
Common Stock 1, 3, 5, 22, 65, 67, 69, 71, 72, 77, 91, 93, 119, 121, 123, 156, 192, 201, 213-218, 230, 231, 234, 235, 244, 245, 294, 295, 442, 443, 446
Compensation 3, 6, 14-19, 21, 25, 26, 29, 31, 32, 41, 44, 45, 47, 50, 53-56, 59, 62, 145, 151, 176, 206, 283, 284, 443, 449
Consent to Service of Process 42, 151, 181, 197, 443
Constant Dollar Risk, see "purchasing power risk" or "inflation risk"
Convertible Securities 443
Cost Basis 123, 124, 127, 129-131, 216, 254, 255, 266, 267, 271, 280, 287, 442, 443, 448
Credit Risk 64, 77, 234, 227-229
Current Yield 83, 107, 226-229, 264, 439, 443
Custody 22-24, 29, 33, 41, 43, 56, 175, 182, 262, 443
Cyclical 44, 65, 104, 443

D

Debenture 44, 189, 225, 234, 235, 443
Default Risk 77, 87, 194, 235, 237, 443
Defensive 47, 65, 71, 104, 190, 443
Deflation 58, 59, 104, 443
Depression 58, 104, 443, 449
Diluted Earnings 443
Discount Rate 61, 62, 91, 105, 443
Discretion 22-24, 28-31, 33, 42, 43, 56
Donation 124, 130, 444

Duration 77, 88, 89, 107, 444

E

Earnings Per Share 71, 72, 92, 218, 439, 443, 444, 448
Exclusion/excluded 11, 32, 41, 42, 44-50, 139, 150, 158, 170, 180, 283, 444
Exemption 11, 41, 46-50, 130, 141-143, 150, 152, 154, 158, 158, 193, 196-198, 201-203, 206, 270, 271, 444
Expected Return 86, 87, 91, 97, 107, 108, 441, 444, 449

F

Fed Funds Rate 62, 105, 444
Federal Covered 15, 28, 30, 42, 48-50, 55, 150, 151, 155, 195, 196, 198, 444, 447
Fiduciary 21, 24, 28, 30, 31, 110, 115-117, 145, 146, 178, 202, 444
Fiscal Policy 60, 105, 444
Form ADV 38-41, 43, 49, 444
Fraud 15, 17, 22, 28, 29, 33, 49, 55, 116, 148, 149, 152, 153, 161, 162, 165, 170, 175, 190, 192, 193, 206, 207, 312, 444
Fundamental Analysis 65, 444
Future Value 89-91, 108, 125, 445

G

GDP 57-60, 65, 83, 104, 445
Gift 124, 130, 136, 138, 192, 440, 444, 445, 448
Gross Margin 20, 72, 445, 447
Growth Investing 92, 93, 108, 445

H

Holding Period Return 85, 107, 445
Hypothecation 180, 445

I

Income Statement 66, 70, 71, 95, 106, 111, 112, 128, 139, 140, 263, 445, 447

Index 17, 18, 57, 58, 60, 75, 91, 92, 94, 95, 104-106, 108, 110, 114, 115, 137, 245, 250, 261, 304, 439, 442, 445, 448
Inflation 57-60, 77, 78, 84, 85, 89, 104-107, 137, 236
Interest Rate 4, 59-63, 68, 77, 78, 83, 87-89, 91, 104-107, 116, 164, 194, 219, 220, 225-228, 230, 232, 233, 235, 237, 260, 263, 269, 439, 442, 444, 446-448
Interest Rate Risk 77, 78, 87, 116, 164, 259, 446
Issuer 2, 5, 11, 12, 62, 64, 83, 117, 140-142, 144, 148, 149, 151, 154-157, 170, 171, 175, 179-181, 190, 191, 193, 196, 197, 201,202, 206, 207, 217-219, 225, 227, 229, 230, 233, 234, 237, 239, 263, 264, 306, 441-444, 446, 448, 449

J

JTWROS 109, 439, 446
JTIC 109, 439, 446

K

Keogh 113, 126, 129, 131, 285, 446

L

Liabilities 2, 24, 66-69, 93, 106, 111, 113, 138, 141, 179, 182, 184, 210, 215, 221, 243, 442, 446, 447, 450
Limit Order 307-311, 446, 450

M

Market Cap (capitalization) 98, 99, 108, 260, 446
Market Order 308-310, 447, 449
Market Risk 75, 76, 447
Monetary Policy 60-62, 447
Municipal Bond 4, 62, 76, 84, 112, 122, 128-130, 136, 150, 194, 232, 238, 239, 259

N

NASDAQ 2, 21, 47, 49, 75, 92, 95, 147, 161, 195, 196, 198, 217, 307, 447, 449
Net Margin 71, 72, 447
Net Worth 4, 18, 19, 56, 66-69, 106, 113, 142, 182, 221, 442, 446, 447
Non-systematic Risk 76, 96, 107, 108, 447
NSMIA 15, 150, 195, 447
NYSE 2, 6, 75, 147, 195, 217, 306, 307, 310, 313, 447, 449

O

Operating Margin 72, 447
Opportunity Cost 76, 447
OTC Bulletin Board 21, 151, 447

P

PE Ratio 5, 72, 73, 87, 88, 92, 94, 107, 448, 449
Passive Management 95, 108, 448
Pass-Through, Pass-Through Certificate 226, 261, 449
Pink Sheets 21, 151, 196, 448
Preferred Stock 67, 69, 93, 139, 215, 216, 218-220, 235, 244, 245, 260, 442, 443
Present Value 89-91, 108, 448
Primary Market 2, 3, 6, 157, 165, 201, 202, 306, 448, 449
Prime Rate 61, 62, 105, 448
Principal 3, 5, 6, 20, 21, 38, 39, 42-44, 46, 62, 63, 67, 77, 89, 90, 114, 125, 129, 143, 146, 164, 174, 179, 209, 225, 228, 229, 232-234, 236, 237, 270, 278, 304, 308, 440, 446, 448, 449
Progressive Tax 124, 130, 448
Prospectus 1, 18, 140, 141, 174, 175, 178, 190, 192, 194, 196, 251, 258, 262, 264, 265, 271, 279, 448
Purchasing Power Risk 77, 78, 269, 448

Q

Qualified Plan 131, 266, 283-286, 448

R

Recession 58, 65, 104, 105, 443, 449
Regressive Tax 124, 130, 449
Registered Investment Adviser, RIA 12, 16, 449
Reinvestment Risk 77, 78, 106, 449, 450
REIT 113, 120, 128, 130, 139, 219, 220, 253, 288, 290, 440, 449
Risk-Adjusted Return 89
Riskless Rate of Return 87, 449

S

Secondary Market 2, 3, 6, 83, 143, 179, 194, 202, 306, 448, 449
Sharpe Ratio 87, 88, 107, 449
Soft Dollar Compensation 31, 54, 443, 449
Solicitor 25, 26, 43, 56, 449
Spread 2, 3, 6, 63, 64, 105, 110, 179, 233, 236, 288, 307, 447-449
Standard Deviation 87, 91, 107, 115, 449
Stop Order 73, 157, 206, 209, 308-312, 449, 450
Systematic Risk 76, 450

T

Technical Analysis 65, 73, 95, 450
Treasury Security 129, 182, 236, 238, 450

V

Value Investing 93, 94, 108, 450
W
Working Capital 67-69, 106, 450
Wrap Fee 13, 31, 41, 118, 450

Y

Yield Curve 44, 62, 63, 232, 233, 236, 450
Yield to Maturity 83, 84, 227, 229, 232, 440, 450

Z

Zero Coupon 77, 88, 106, 107, 236, 449, 450

First Books®
Order Form
RELOCATION AND BUSINESS RESOURCES

	# COPIES	TOTAL
Training Guides for the Securities Exams		
Pass the 6™ 2ND EDITION by Robert Walker	_____ x $49.95	$_____
Pass the 63™ 2ND EDITION by Robert Walker	_____ x $37.95	$_____
Pass the 65™ by Robert Walker	_____ x $89.95	$_____
Pass the 66™ by Robert Walker (forthcoming)	_____ x $	$_____
Pass the 7™ by Robert Walker	_____ x $89.95	$_____
Relocation Books—Invaluable guides for people moving to a new city		
Newcomer's Handbook® for Atlanta	_____ x $24.95	$_____
Newcomer's Handbook® for Boston	_____ x $23.95	$_____
Newcomer's Handbook® for Chicago	_____ x $21.95	$_____
Newcomer's Handbook® for London	_____ x $20.95	$_____
Newcomer's Handbook® for Los Angeles	_____ x $23.95	$_____
Newcomer's Handbook® for Minneapolis-St. Paul	_____ x $25.95	$_____
Newcomer's Handbook® for New York City	_____ x $22.95	$_____
Newcomer's Handbook® for San Francisco Bay Area	_____ x $24.95	$_____
Newcomer's Handbook® for Seattle	_____ x $21.95	$_____
Newcomer's Handbook® for the USA	_____ x $23.95	$_____
Newcomer's Handbook® for Washington D.C.	_____ x $24.95	$_____
Neighborhood Guide for Texas	_____ x $17.95	$_____
The Moving Book: A Kids' Survival Guide	_____ x $20.95	$_____
Max's Moving Adventure	_____ x $ 8.95	$_____
The Pet-Moving Handbook	_____ x $ 9.95	$_____
SUBTOTAL		$_____
POSTAGE & HANDLING ($8.00 first book, $1.50 each add'l.)		$_____
TOTAL		$_____

SHIP TO:

Name _____

Title _____

Company _____

Address _____

City _____ State _____ Zip _____

Phone Number (____) _____

E-mail _____

Send this order form and a check or money order payable to:
First Books®
6750 SW Franklin St., Suite A
Portland, OR 97223-2542
P: 503.968.6777   F: 503.968.6779
Allow 1-2 weeks for delivery
www.firstbooks.com